Living Water

Volume 1

D. MARTYN LLOYD-JONES

Contents

Note

These sermons, which were preached in 1967 and 1968, are the last Sunday morning sermons preached by Dr Lloyd-Jones as the Minister of Westminster Chapel, before illness caused him to retire.

They have been edited lightly – enough to avoid repetition but not so much that his 'voice' cannot be heard through the printed pages. Over the years many people have commented on how they can hear him speaking as they read.

We owe a particular debt of gratitude to Rhona Pipe of Watermark, who for many years has worked tirelessly on the final edit of our father's books.

Elizabeth Catherwood and Ann Beatt

1

The Possibilities of the Christian Life

Jesus answered and said unto her, Whosoever drinketh of this water shall thirst again: but whosoever drinketh of the water that I shall give him shall never thirst; but the water that I shall give him shall be in him a well of water springing up into everlasting life. (John 4:13–14)

I should like to consider with you the famous story of our Lord's meeting with the woman of Samaria, which is to be found in the fourth chapter of John's Gospel. It is very difficult to think of any particular text because I want to consider the story with you in general, but perhaps it is only right that we should isolate verses 13 and 14. I am not proposing to expound these verses now because they are the central point of the story. I want rather to introduce the subject.

For some time now we have been studying John's Gospel, and we have been doing this in a particular manner.[1] Our concern has

---

[1] For chapters 1 and 2, see D. Martyn Lloyd-Jones, *Joy Unspeakable (including Prove All Things)*, Kingsway Publications 1994.

not been so much to go through the Gospel verse by verse as to expound and illustrate its great central theme. And I have been suggesting that the theme, in many ways, is to be found in the sixteenth verse of the first chapter where we read, 'And of his fulness have all we received, and grace for grace [grace upon grace].' In other words, the theme of this Gospel is the fullness of the Lord Jesus Christ available for his people; or, to put it another way, the theme of this Gospel is eternal life.

In chapter 10 we read that our Lord said, 'I am come that they might have life, and that they might have it more abundantly' (John 10:10), and we see that same emphasis here in chapter 4. So we are picking out that theme because this is, after all, what Christianity means, this is the Christian offer, the Christian possibility. Our whole trouble, surely, is that we fail to realize this: we are ever reducing the gospel, making something small out of it, something that *we* do, our practice of religion. The tragedy is that we think of our own selves, and our busy-ness, and our own activity instead of realizing that there is the wonderful possibility of receiving of his fullness and more and more of it, 'grace upon grace', 'springing up into everlasting life'. And this failure, it seems to me, is the greatest tragedy of all.

In the church today the tendency is to look at the world all the time and to see the tragedy of the world. That is perfectly right, of course; the church is to be evangelistic. But the question is: How is the church to be evangelistic? And I contend that what the New Testament itself tells us, and what the history of the church tells us, is that the church is most successful evangelistically when she herself is as she ought to be. Why are the masses of the people outside the church? I do not hesitate to say that the reason is that they fail to see in us anything that attracts them, anything that creates within them a desire to receive what we have, or anything that rebukes them and condemns them for their way of living. Not that we should necessarily put that into words, but it should just be seen.

It was by the quality of its life that the church conquered the ancient world, and that is how she has always conquered during times of reformation and revival. It is revival that has been the greatest means of evangelism, and revival means Christian people, members of the Christian church, suddenly being awakened by the power and the enlightenment of the Spirit to the possibilities of the Christian life. And there is no doubt, I repeat, that the trouble at the present time is that we are living so far short of what is offered us here and of what is possible to us.

Have we received of our Lord's fullness? Are we receiving of it progressively? These are the all-important questions. If this well of water is not within us, we are not only robbing ourselves of the riches of his grace, but we also become unworthy representatives of the gospel, and the world outside remains in ignorance and in darkness. So the high road to revival and to evangelism is a church that realizes what she ought to be, what she can be. And when I say, 'church', I mean, of course, every one of us as individuals. The church consists of a number of believers. It is not something theoretical, on paper. It is you, it is I, it is all of us. And so we face this great theme together.

Now the fullness of life available to us is, I repeat, the theme of John's Gospel. Sometimes the message is explicit and direct, as we have it here, and sometimes the Gospel puts it in terms of an anecdote, a story, an illustration – how our Lord called certain men, or how he behaved at the marriage feast in Cana of Galilee or in the Temple in Jerusalem, or how he dealt with a man called Nicodemus (the great theme of the third chapter). So it is direct and indirect, explicit and implicit. But it is always there. The wonderful thing about the Gospels is that they present their teaching to us in such an interesting variety of ways. Further, the teaching is most instructive with regard to the hindrances that block our receiving of this fullness. The Gospels are of great value to us because humanity does not change, we are all still the same. So here, in these pictures, we see how people stumbled, and what it was that held them back from this blessing – and this remains true today. So we take up this theme of the fullness of life offered by our Lord, and we take it up in terms of this great old familiar story of our Lord's dealings with the woman of Samaria.

Now it is customary to take this incident, this story, in an evangelistic sense. The woman is an unbeliever and we are shown here how she is brought to belief. But though that is true, the message is as applicable to us as believers as it is to an unbeliever. For the astounding thing is that even when we have come into the Christian life, we tend to go on repeating the same old mistakes, and carry over with us certain characteristics and habits. The apostle Paul makes this very point in dealing with the members of the church at Corinth. They had believed the gospel, they were Christian people, and he writes to them as a church, but this is what he says to them: 'I have fed you with milk, and not with meat: for hitherto ye were not able to bear it' (1 Corinthians 3:2). 'And I still have to do that,' he says, in effect, 'because of your condition. Though you are now Christians, you are reverting to the old way of thinking and I must get you out of that. The principles of the gospel are still the same.' That was the essence of that first great problem at Corinth; they were tending to introduce their old worldly wisdom even into the message concerning the cross, so Paul had to go back to first principles, and he constantly has to repeat them all the way through the epistle.

And it is the simplest thing in the world for me to show you that the way in which our Lord handles this woman of Samaria is not only applicable to the handling of an unbeliever but also of believers who for some reason or another have not known much about this fullness and 'grace upon grace', who have known very little about this condition in which we 'never thirst'. So let us look at this story from this standpoint – it is put before us in a dramatic manner. For now, I just want to introduce it to you because there are many general lessons here that we neglect at our peril. Indeed, not only that, some of these general lessons are, I think we will agree, among the most encouraging and moving aspects of this whole doctrine.

There are just two people to consider – the woman of Samaria and our blessed Lord and Saviour Jesus Christ. Let us look at this woman for a moment. What do we learn from her as we consider her in general? The first thing, surely – and this is wonderful – is that the great and glorious blessing of the Christian gospel is offered to all types of people. This is what I have sometimes described as the romantic element in the gospel and in these Scriptures and you cannot help being struck by it. Take, for instance, the third chapter of John, which is mainly given over to that great man Nicodemus, a ruler of Israel, an erudite man, a big man in every respect. You cannot imagine a greater contrast than that between Nicodemus and the woman of Samaria, yet the same Lord deals with the two people, and he is concerned about precisely the same message.

Look at the contrast: man – woman; Jew – Samaritan. These are not just empty terms. In verse 9 we are told in passing that Jews had no dealings with Samaritans. We will have to come to the specific meaning of that later. But there was an old feud, an old trouble, between them, so that in the ancient world Nicodemus, a Jew, and the woman, a Samaritan, presented a remarkable contrast. There was also, of course, the contrast, between men and women.

Whatever else Christianity may have done, it has been the overriding power that has liberated woman and given her a standing that she had never had before. In the ancient world women were despised and it was felt that certain things were not possible to them at all; but one of the central themes of the gospel is that in Christ Jesus, 'There is neither Jew nor Greek, there is neither bond nor free, there is neither male nor female' (Galatians 3:28) – which means that from the standpoint of salvation, from the standpoint of obtaining these great and glorious blessings, the distinction between male and female has gone. This is a misunderstanding that should never have come in, in connection with the things of God. The difference between man and woman, however, is not abrogated and when you come to applications and positions in the church, and various other things, the essential distinction is still maintained in the teaching.

So in this story we are at once reminded that the blessings are open to all types of people: woman as well as man; Samaritan as well as Jew. But an *ignorant* woman! Not a learned man, not a teacher, not a Pharisee well versed in the Law, but a hardworking woman. But still more – a woman who is a flagrant sinner. That comes out in the course of the conversation.

'Go, call thy husband,' our Lord says, 'and come hither.'

And the woman says, 'I have no husband.'

'Quite true,' says our Lord, 'you have had five husbands, and the man you are now living with is not your husband' (verses 16–18).

That is a typical picture of life among such people: sin, open and unashamed. But there it is in contrast with that remarkable man Nicodemus, who is not only a great teacher, but also a good and highly moral man, a religious man. And the marvellous truth that this story teaches us here, at the very beginning, is that all that our Lord has to give, this 'fullness', is as open to people like the woman of Samaria as it is to the Nicodemuses of this world. Have you not often been struck by this – that the glorious statement recorded in verses 13 and 14 is made to this woman? That is why I say that it is a very grievous mistake only to apply this story evangelistically. There is nothing higher in the whole realm of Scripture for any Christian than this:

Whoever drinketh of this water shall thirst again: but whosoever drinketh of the water that I shall give him shall never thirst; but the water that I shall give him shall be in him a well of water springing up into everlasting life.

That is the topmost level of Christianity and it is spoken to the woman of Samaria! This is something that we must lay hold of. Furthermore, it is to this same woman that our Lord says, 'I that speak unto thee am he' (verse 26). It is to her that he says explicitly, in a way that he did not to others, that he is the Messiah.

Now why are we emphasizing this point? It is because if you go through the history of the church you will find that there has always been a tendency to think that what may be called 'the higher reaches' of the Christian life, the profound experiences of God and of the Lord Jesus Christ and of the Holy Spirit, are reserved for certain special people. You are familiar with what may be called the 'Catholic' type of teaching. It starts by dividing Christian people into two groups – the religious and the laity, special Christians and ordinary Christians – and then says that it is only those who go in for the cultivation of the soul in this special manner who can ever hope to arrive at the high and great and glorious experiences of the Christian life.

There are many books that trace this teaching. One of the best is the Bampton Lectures of 1928 by Kenneth Kirk, published under the title *The Vision of God*.[2] Kirk traces this idea in the experience of God's people throughout the centuries, bringing out this well-known fact very clearly. It is at the basis of the whole concept of monasticism. The teaching is that if you want to have high and exalted spiritual experiences, then you must go out of life, as it were; they are not for you if you are in business or engaged in the ordinary affairs of life. A housewife? It is impossible, she does not have the time. This is a full-time occupation. So you segregate yourself. You go off into a cell and there you spend your time cultivating the soul. This view, of course, is also at the very root of the whole idea of mysticism, which takes you painfully through various stages until you arrive at the ultimate stage of illumination, that knowledge that leads to such glorious experiences.

Now this is an attitude that we have tended to carry over with us into Protestantism, but it is quite wrong, it is untrue to the teaching of the Scriptures, and even if we had no other, this one case of the woman of Samaria would be more than sufficient in and of itself to put us right. Nothing is postulated in us – nothing at all. The woman of Samaria is the absolute proof of that. We must never say, 'I'm just an ordinary Christian, these realms are not for me.' They are for you. They are all for everybody. The woman of Samaria is here as a great pillar, as it were, announcing this fact, calling attention to it. We must not indulge in these artificial and unscriptural divisions and distinctions. Nor must we evade the challenge of our Lord's words by saying, 'Ah, well, of course, I wish … but I can't, I'm so involved in other things.' That is wrong.

---

2 Kenneth E. Kirk, *The Vision of God: The Christian Doctrine of the Summum Bonum*, Longmans, Green & Co., 1931. This was republished in 1991 by Morehouse Publishing, Harrisburg, Penn.

Let me elaborate. Let us look for a moment at the unexpectedness of this event and its surprising character. There it is, just an ordinary day in the life of the woman of Samaria. She has her house to look after, she has food and drink to provide, we do not know for how many. But we do know that it is essential that she should go to this particular well to draw water. We do not know exactly how far she has to walk, but it is not difficult to see that it must be a fair distance because she regards it as an arduous task. When our Lord makes his great statement, she says, 'Sir, give me this water, that I thirst not, neither come hither to draw.' She has to go back and forth, often, perhaps, in the blazing sun. Some suggest that it is because of her character that she has gone at the sixth hour (verse 6), that is, at midday, the hottest time of the day. If she were to go at the usual times for drawing water, the other women would look at her, and she knows everybody is talking about her because of her immoral life. So a kind of shame makes her choose the hottest time of the day. So there she is, she arrives at the well on an ordinary day, expecting nothing at all to happen – the humdrum character of a life of sin. Then suddenly there is this encounter, this amazing thing happens that changes the whole of her life. There is this complete revolution – from nothing to fullness.

Now here again, I suggest to you, is one of the most wonderful and glorious aspects of the Christian life. There is no life as romantic as this. In every other view of life you can more or less anticipate what is going to happen. Oh, I know there are surprises now and again, but there is nothing in any way comparable to this. This is what, to me, makes a meeting like this in the house of God, so amazing. It is the essence of the romance of preaching. I never know what is going to happen when I enter this pulpit. I do not control it. That is the wonder of it, the glory of it. A man who does control it is a poor preacher and a still poorer Christian.

No, no; the unexpectedness! You go, perhaps, out of routine, you do things because you are called to do them and because you are expected to do them and you may have got into a state in which you expect nothing to happen. But suddenly the Lord is there and you are amazed at the consequences. The hymn by William Cowper sums it up so well:

> Sometimes a light surprises
> The Christian while he sings;
> It is the Lord who rises
> With healing in his wings.

Let me emphasize this point. There are many Christian people today who have got into a kind of humdrum state of existence – not necessarily because of anything that is wrong in them. Maybe you are one of those people. You may be a busy housewife or a busy man earning money to keep your family. There is work to be done, there are mouths to be fed, there are clothes to be dealt with – all these tasks; and it is the simplest thing in the world to settle down, as it were, into a routine in which you expect nothing to happen. You just go on, 'The daily round, the common task', the drudgery of life.

Possibly one of the most devastating things that can happen to us as Christians is that we cease to expect anything to happen. I am not sure but that this is not one of our greatest troubles today. We come to our services and they are orderly, they are nice – we come, we go – and sometimes they are timed almost to the minute, and there it is. But that is not Christianity, my friend. Where is the Lord of glory? Where is the one sitting by the well? Are we expecting him? Do we anticipate this? Are we open to it? Are we aware that we are ever facing this glorious possibility of having the greatest surprise of our life?

Or let me put it like this. You may feel and say – as many do – 'I was converted and became a Christian. I've grown – yes, I've grown in knowledge, I've been reading books, I've been listening to sermons, but I've arrived now at a sort of peak and all I do is maintain that. For the rest of my life I will just go on like this.'

Now, my friend, you must get rid of that attitude; you must get rid of it once and for ever. That is 'religion', it is not Christianity. This is Christianity: the Lord appears! Suddenly, in the midst of the drudgery and the routine and the sameness and the dullness and the drabness, unexpectedly, surprisingly, he meets with you and he says something to you that changes the whole of your life and your outlook and lifts you to a level that you had never conceived could be possible for you. Oh, if we get nothing else from this story, I hope we will get this. Do not let the devil persuade you that you have got all you are going to get, still less that you received all you were ever going to receive when you were converted. That has been a popular teaching, even among evangelicals. You get everything at your conversion, it is said, including baptism with the Spirit, and nothing further, ever. Oh, do not believe it; it is not true. It is not true to the teaching of the Scriptures, it is not true in the experience of the saints running down the centuries. There is always this glorious possibility of meeting with him in a new and a dynamic way.

And I will emphasize that further by putting it like this: often this comes to us in the line of ordinary duty. The woman of Samaria was not in a religious service when she met our Lord. She was doing her daily work, her regular task. This is another great Protestant principle. Martin Luther rediscovered it, in a sense – at least, it was given to him to see it. And he put it in his own dramatic way. He said that you could be serving the Lord and knowing the Lord and realizing his presence just as much if you were a chambermaid brushing the floor, as if you were a monk in a cell counting your beads and fasting and sweating and praying. That is the basis of the whole Protestant notion of vocation, but I am now using it in the sense that at any moment there is a great and a grand and a glorious possibility of meeting our Lord.

A friend was only telling me his story the other day. He was a minister who was having a great trial. He and his wife were passing through an unusually difficult period in their lives – sickness was involved, as far as he was concerned – and everything was calculated to crush his wife. But he told me how one evening, at the very depths of this depression and trial and tribulation that had overtaken them as a little family, his wife, having put the children to bed, went to read her daily portion of Scripture.

Now there are people, of course, who say that if you do not read the Bible and pray the first thing in the morning, it is terrible, but she did not have the time in the mornings, she had a husband and children to see to. The time does not matter; do not become the slaves of systems, my dear friends, be open. It is not when you read the Bible that is important, it is how you read it. And the woman was right: she knew that having put the children to bed, she would have a little quiet. So she went, not expecting anything, just doing something that was routine. But suddenly she found that her Lord was there and she had the most marvellous experience of her life, an experience that enabled her not only to have an entirely new view of what was happening to them, but also to help her husband, and soon they entered into the position of release and of victory.

Now this is a great principle. The experience of meeting the Lord is not confined to certain places. Of course, we must come to certain places. Do not misunderstand me. I am not foolish enough to become a devotee of this latest vogue of talking about 'religionless Christianity', which says that churches are not needed. That is just nonsense, of course, apart from being unscriptural. But what I am saying is this: do not think that such experiences only happen in a place such as this, or in a cathedral, perhaps. They can happen to you anywhere. The Lord can come anywhere. That is one of the great messages of this story – and I will be elaborating that – 'neither in this mountain, nor yet at Jerusalem', but by the side of a well – anywhere in the line of ordinary duty.

And the other point I would like to stress – and, to me, this is an essential part of this message and is, I think, of very real significance – is that our Lord deals with this woman alone. This is not accidental. The disciples have gone into the neighbouring town to buy provisions, leaving our Lord there alone, and the woman, probably for the reason I have given you, is also alone. So at the side of the well they meet alone. I think that this is an important principle with regard to this whole question of truly 'receiving of his fullness'. What I mean is that in this incident there is an emphasis upon the personal element in our faith, in our religion; it is an emphasis that we must not forget. Our Lord, I am going to show you, has contrived the circumstances so that he can talk to this woman alone.

Now if we neglect the personal element in the Christian faith, we will go wrong all along the line. It is personal in the matter of our original salvation. You are not saved in crowds, you are saved individually. We come to a personal knowledge of God, we have personal dealings with God. It was a sad and sorry day in the history of the Christian church when the Emperor Constantine took the Roman Empire into the Christian church. She has never really recovered from that. You cannot be saved in families, you cannot be saved in countries, you cannot be saved in chapel-fulls. Conversion may happen to a number of people in the same service, but it is always intensely personal and individual. So conforming to a certain moral or ethical pattern does not make you a Christian. There must be a personal encounter with him, personal dealing, personal knowledge.

I could illustrate this from many places in the Scripture, but one of the tenderest and most beautiful examples is to be found in the book of the prophet Hosea. The prophet is dealing with the church in the Old Testament; his book is specifically a message to the church, which is depicted as a faithless wife. But here is the message in Hosea 2:14: 'Therefore' – having described her sinfulness and unfaithfulness – 'behold, I will allure her, and bring her into the wilderness, and speak comfortably unto her.' She will be taken out of the towns, out of the busy-ness of life, into a wilderness, a solitary place. There will be this isolation, this personal element. I will take her there, says God, and in the isolation and the emptiness of the wilderness I will 'speak comfortably unto her'.

Now this alone-ness is an essential principle in connection with the whole of this particular teaching about the fullness of God. In the records of people who have been led into some deep knowledge of God you will often find that they have first of all been led into a wilderness. There has been a kind of isolation, a solitary meeting by the well-side. The principle, it seems to me, is that it is possible for us all to go on living the rest of our Christian lives as ordinary Christians: 'I was saved on such-and-such a date, gave my testimony, was baptized [perhaps], and am a member of a church. There I am, and I will go on being like that.' There are many such people. They have never grown and they die almost exactly as they were at their conversion.

You, too, can go on being an ordinary Christian, but you can also know something about this 'well of water'. And if you are to become such a person, you will find that he will 'allure' you, he will separate you, he will speak to you alone. Nothing may be happening to anybody else – do not worry about that. He will draw you. Perhaps it will be to a wilderness. He may have to lead you through a period of tribulation. He may not. That is not the point at the moment. The point I am making is that it must be intensely personal.

There was once a philosopher who said a wise thing about these matters. He said: 'Religion is what a man does with his own solitude.' And that is true. However, I prefer it as it was put by Pascal, who was one of the great teachers on this subject. He was a man who had this meeting with the Lord by the side of the well, a man to whom this same great and glorious message was given in different words. And so he put it like this: 'All the ills of man stem from his inability to be still in his own room.' Now if that statement applied to men and women 300 years ago – as it certainly did – how much more so today?

One of the most difficult things in life is to be still. There is so much noise: the noises of the world, exaggerated now by these new agencies – television, radio and so on. Noise! But you have to be still, you must stop, you must be isolated, you must think. You cannot meet with the Lord in the midst of the noise and the bustle and the fury of life. You may be a very busy person but stillness is still possible. You must be quiet in your own room. It is only then that you are likely to meet with him. Stillness is one of the great prerequisites.

My dear friend, I am holding before you a glorious possibility. I do not care who you are or what you are or what your work is – I am not interested in any of these things. This one case gives me authority to say this: the fullness of the Lord is open to you, so do not evade it on any grounds or bring up any arguments. This woman demolishes all your arguments. If you have not received consciously of his fullness and are not rejoicing in it more and more, somewhere, the trouble is yours, and we shall be considering what these troubles are.

However, let us go on and take a brief glance at our blessed Lord himself. Another great lesson of this story is that this fullness is all in him and it is all of him. As I have shown you, there is nothing in the woman of Samaria. In that sense, virtually nothing is postulated of us at all. Oh, what amazes one in this story is the glory of his person and the wonder of what he does! Have you ever looked at it like this? Look at him, what do we read here? Well: 'He must needs go through Samaria. Then cometh he to a city of Samaria . . . Jacob's well was there' – then notice this – '*Jesus therefore, being wearied with his journey*, sat thus on the well' – which means, 'by the side of the well', the surroundings are included in the word 'well' – 'and it was about the sixth hour. There cometh a woman of Samaria to draw water: Jesus saith unto her, Give me to drink.'

Now what does this tell us? It tells us that our Lord is tired and sits down to rest. He is too weary to go with his disciples to the city to buy provisions. Moreover, he is thirsty, so he asks the woman for a drink of water after she has drawn it from the well.

'What of it?' you ask.

What of it! My dear friend, that is the essence of the Christian message: Who is this who is sitting at this well? Who is this who is thirsty?

> Who is this so meek and lowly,
> Child of lowly Hebrew maid?

Who is he? And that is the astounding thing:

> 'Tis the Lord of all creation
> Who this wondrous path hath trod.
> *William Walsham How*

Who is this who is weary? He is the Creator of the universe; it is by him all things have been made. Who is this who asks the Samaritan woman for a drink of water? He is the one for whom the whole cosmos has been created. He is the one who, according to the first chapter of the Epistle to the Hebrews, is 'upholding all things by the word of his power' (verse 3).

What does this mean? Have we become so accustomed to the Christian message that we are no longer thrilled and amazed and astounded by it? This is the glory of the message of the Christian salvation – the incarnation. He has humbled himself for our sakes. He is the Lord of glory still, though he is weary and sits down and is thirsty. What has happened? It is this: in order that you and I might have this well of water in us, he has laid aside the signs of his eternal glory, he has been born in the likeness of man, he has been born, indeed, in the likeness of sinful flesh (Romans 8:3). 'The Word was made flesh, and dwelt among us' (John 1:14) – and it is not an artificial body, it is as true a body as yours and mine. He is exhausted, and he is thirsty, and he has done all this and humbled himself in order that we might have this great gift, this great blessing of eternal life.

Now I am putting it like this because if we do not know this fullness of life, it means, in a sense, that we really have not understood the whole doctrine. What right have we to say, 'I only want forgiveness from him; I only want to avoid hell' – and stop at that? No, no; he came 'that they might have life, and that they might have it more abundantly' (John 10:10). Let us never forget this. So if the devil tempts you and says, 'This is not for you', then say, 'It is! I know he has done all this for me.'

So look at him. Not only did our Lord come from heaven to earth, he subjected himself to our frailties and our weaknesses, he was 'made of a woman, made under the law, to redeem them that were under the law' (Galatians 4:4–5). His was a true physical body; he was truly man. He knows something about our frailties.

But in this story he gives himself still further. Can you not see this further outstanding aspect: that though he is tired and thirsty, he keeps that on one side, pushes it back, because he is much more concerned about the woman's real thirst, her real need. He is not thinking about himself, he is thinking about her, and even when he asks for water, his ultimate objective is not so much that he may slake his thirst as that he may introduce the subject of salvation and this fullness. And our Lord is still like that:

> In every pang that rends the heart
> The Man of Sorrows bears a part.
> *Michael Bruce*

Does this not stand out about him throughout the pages of the four Gospels? Look at him there on the cross in the agony and the pain and the shame of it all, look at him crying out, 'I thirst.' We cannot imagine the agony that he was suffering, and yet you remember that even there he turned aside to help that dying thief who was aware of his desperate need, and administered to him the word of comfort and of salvation.

So let us draw blessed encouragement and consolation from all this. He is the Lord of glory. He has all knowledge. Look at him as he talks to this woman; look at his behaviour. He knows all about her. He knows all about her immoral life – she is amazed at that. And he knows all about each of us. He knows all about our needs, our troubles and cares. 'For we have not an high priest which cannot be touched with the feeling of our infirmities; but was in all points tempted like as we are, yet without sin' (Hebrews 4:15). What a sympathetic High Priest! He is your High Priest if you are a Christian. Go to him, venture on him, let nothing hinder you.

I must emphasize one other point, and it rises from this interesting phrase that we find in the fourth verse: '*And he must needs go through Samaria.*' Now what does this mean? Well, most of the best commentators are quite agreed on the meaning, and it seems to me to be beyond any doubt. Some translate these words, 'it behoved him to go'; others, 'it was necessary for him to go'. Does this mean that there was only one road between Jerusalem and Galilee? No! It does happen to have been the shortest, but it was not the only road; he could have gone at least two other ways. So these words do not indicate a physical necessity. What then? It is a spiritual necessity. This is not an accident but a part of the great plan. Again, here is one of the most astounding things about this whole gospel of salvation and what it offers us. The real force of these words is this: 'he was aware of a compulsion sending him through Samaria'. What is it? It is the meeting with the woman of Samaria.

This meeting serves many purposes, as we shall see. We have already seen that our Lord wanted to break down the division between Jews and Samaritans, between men and women. But the great thing is that it was not an accident. In this realm nothing is accidental. Is it not one of the great marks of the Christian salvation that God has planned it before the foundation of the world? Not only that, he knew us individually before the foundation of the world. Our names were written in the Lamb's Book of Life before we were ever born. This is glorious! This is wonderful! The whole doctrine of the call is involved in this phrase. He knows us one by one and all about us, and he meets us: 'he must needs'. He knows this compulsion. He knew it in the days of his flesh, and he singled out this woman, as he did others of whom we read at the end of the first chapter of John's Gospel.

How surprised Nathanael was when our Lord said to him, 'Before that Philip called thee, when thou wast under the fig tree,

I saw thee' (John 1:48). He constantly says, 'Mine hour is not yet come' (for example, John 2:4). There was always 'the hour'. Everything is a part of God's great plan and purpose of salvation. The Son of God comes to meet us in his own appointed time and way. As we have seen, from our standpoint, we never know when. We must always be expectant, always open, always, as it were, anticipating by faith. But he comes! 'And he must needs go through Samaria.'

These are subjects that ought to thrill us to the depth of our beings. It is what *he* does. We would not be here at all but for that. It is he who has already met you and spoken to you, and called you out of darkness into his light; and he will go on doing that. This is his principle of operation – never lose sight of his constant personal interest and concern. And it is this constraining love of his that leads him to do it. Who knows whether, in his glorious plan and eternal wisdom, the hour appointed when he will meet with you in some hitherto unknown and unexpected and unanticipated manner may not be at hand? Thank God we are his workmanship, and the work that he began is a work that he will continue. So Paul wrote, 'Work out your own salvation with fear and trembling. For it is God which worketh in you both to will and to do . . .' (Philippians 2:12–13).

There, then, are just some preliminary principles and lessons that we learn as we take a general glimpse at this amazing, unexpected meeting between the Lord of glory and the woman of Samaria. May God bless them and apply them to our individual souls.

2

Our Lord's Approach and Our Prejudice

Jesus answered and said unto her, Whosoever drinketh of this water shall thirst again: but whosoever drinketh of the water that I shall give him shall never thirst; but the water that I shall give him shall be in him a well of water springing up into everlasting life. (John 4:13–14)

We are looking at this great story of our Lord's encounter and dealing with the woman of Samaria from the standpoint of the light that it throws on our spiritual condition and because of the possibilities that it shows us of this spiritual, this Christian, life into which we are come. The story is, of course, primarily concerned with evangelism, but the principles that govern evangelism are exactly the same as the principles that continue to govern the whole of the Christian life, and, as I have indicated, there is here conceivably some of the richest teaching on the subject that we will ever find anywhere. The Son of God came into the world not merely to procure forgiveness of sins, but also

to give us the life that is life indeed, this fullness that never fails –
and that is the subject matter here.

But, of course, the story does not merely consist of this statement.
We are given very many details about what happened between our
Lord and this woman, and these show us how he dealt with the
whole situation. So we have begun by taking a general view of
the whole story. It is a great mistake simply to isolate certain verses
of Scripture. Nothing in Scripture is unimportant. Keep your eye
on everything, examine everything. There are amazing riches and
most encouraging teaching to be found here if we only take the
trouble to look. So we considered the woman of Samaria in general
and learned certain lessons from her. And then we ended by looking
at our Lord himself and at all the amazing things we are told here
about him.

But there is one further important aspect of our Lord himself
and his dealing with this situation that I am anxious to put to you
for your consideration, for here again I think you will find that we
will derive not only instruction but also great encouragement, and
that is the object of all that we are attempting to do.

Look at our Lord's method, it is most important. The way in
which he deals with this whole situation tells us a great deal about
ourselves. The wonderful thing is that he still works in the same
way with us. He is still the same in the glory. John, in the first
chapter of the book of Revelation, tells us about the vision, the
revelation, that he had of our Lord, and he writes, 'And when I saw
him, I fell at his feet as one dead.' But this same Lord, John says,
'laid his right hand upon me' (Revelation 1:17). That is what he
did while he was here in the days of his flesh. He is still doing it.
He is still 'the Lamb that was slain' (Revelation 5:12). He who
once was dead is 'alive for evermore' (Revelation 1:18). He works
now, of course, chiefly through the Holy Spirit. But it is his action.

You remember how Luke starts his second book, the book of the Acts of the Apostles: 'The former treatise have I made, O Theophilus, of all that Jesus began both to do and to teach' (Acts 1:1); and now Luke goes on to tell Theophilus of the continuing work of the Lord Jesus Christ that he does through the Holy Spirit. And the comfort to us of this story in John 4 is that the way our Lord handled the woman of Samaria is the way he handles us. And so we meet together here in church with the feeling uppermost in our minds that our being here at this moment is not accidental. 'He must needs go through Samaria' in order to meet the woman of Samaria; he meets with us in the same way. Let us realize that. We may have thought we had come here from custom or out of habit, but, believe me, if you are in his hands, there is more to it than that. He arranges these things for our good and for our eternal benefit.

Let us, then, look at our Lord's method. We notice first that he is always in control. That is what strikes us on the very surface of this story. The meeting appears to be accidental, but it is not. Watch how he handles the whole situation from beginning to end. Thank God for this. It is our comfort, our greatest consolation. If he were not in control, not a single one of us would ever be saved and arrive in the glory. The woman with her glibness and her cleverness talks a lot and wriggles, as I am going to show you, but he is in control. Be very careful what you are doing. If you are a Christian at all, he commands your situation, and he will bring you to the desired end.

The author of the Epistle to the Hebrews puts that like this: 'Whom the Lord loveth he chasteneth, and scourgeth every son whom he receiveth' (Hebrews 12:6). If you are one of his people, be careful, I say again. He has taken hold of you, you are in his hands, and if you do not come willingly in response to his appeal, he will still get you there. 'Whom the Lord loveth he chasteneth.' If you are in control of your religion, I doubt whether you are a Christian at all. If you are not conscious of being in his hands and of being dealt with, I think you had better examine your foundations again. Once he sets his heart and affection upon a person, he always takes charge and he does not let go. So at this moment a very searching question we must each ask ourselves is: Who is in charge of my life? If we know that we are in his hands, we have the greatest comfort and the greatest consolation that a human soul can ever have.

But then I immediately want to add to that our Lord's amazing gentleness. Look at his gentleness with this woman! Remember her character – she is living in adultery and has been for some time. Notice that he does not bludgeon her; he does not force the situation. He is in control but that does not mean bullying people; it does not mean doing violence to them or dragooning them. Our Lord never did that. We are told that in him was verified the prophecy from Isaiah, 'A bruised reed shall he not break, and the smoking flax shall he not quench' (Isaiah 42:3). I say once more: thank God for this, for what are all of us but bruised reeds or smoking flax?

With smoking flax there is a good deal of smoke – but is there any fire? It is almost impossible to tell, and our tendency is to stamp upon it. We say that it is only smouldering, that the fire has gone out, and we crush it. But our Lord does not do that, and I repeat, if he did, none of us would be here in church. In fact, our Lord does the exact opposite. One is amazed at his gentleness with this woman. And this is the experience of all the saints. Philip Doddridge, in his hymn, 'O happy day that fixed my choice', puts it like this:

> He drew me, and I followed on,
> Charmed to confess the voice divine.

'He drew me'! Doddridge is there thinking of that word in the prophet Hosea: 'I drew them with cords of a man, with bands of love' (Hosea 11:4). He draws. He never drives.

Now we are always in danger of forgetting this, are we not? We want to foist our opinions upon people and force them to accept what we say. But it cannot be done in this realm, and, in any case, we are unlike our Master when we attempt to do that. The gentleness! Or take it as the apostle Paul puts it in Romans 8:14: 'For as many as are led by the Spirit of God, they are the sons of God.' But you notice how Paul puts it? The sons of God are those who are 'led' by the Spirit, not driven, not carried, but led. The Spirit persuades, he puts the truth to us, he enlightens us, he leads us on. This is a most remarkable aspect of this great story.

As we consider our own spiritual lives and experiences, we must always remember our Lord's gentleness. Do not forget that the Holy Spirit is said to resemble a dove. He woos, he leads, he persuades, he suggests, he works in us 'both to will and to do of his good pleasure' (Philippians 2:13). He can be grieved, too, and he can be quenched. So here is a great lesson for us. We are in a realm that is very sensitive – the soul, the spirit. We are in a realm that is quite unlike the clash and the clamour of the world outside. We forget that at our peril and to our very great loss.

Another aspect of our Lord's approach is what I may call his indirect method. He goes to Samaria to meet this woman because he is concerned about her soul, but he does not immediately take hold of her and say, 'Are you saved?' That is how some of us tend to speak, is it not? No, no; our Lord has an indirect method. 'There cometh a woman of Samaria to draw water: Jesus saith unto her, Give me to drink', and as the conversation goes on, they seem to be talking at cross purposes. Our Lord is putting a riddle to her, as it were. When the woman says, 'How is it that thou, being a Jew, askest drink of me, which am a woman of Samaria?',

our Lord replies, 'If thou knewest the gift of God, and who it is
that saith to thee, Give me to drink; thou wouldest have asked of
him, and he would have given thee living water.' She does not
know who he is and he knows that, and he knows that he is
talking about a type of water that she does not understand and
know about; but still this is his method and thus, gradually
and indirectly, he brings her face to face with the vital truth.

What is the application to us? It is that our Lord still uses this
same method with us and we often miss him because we do
not realize it. We have an idea that our experiences of him must
happen directly, in dramatic, climactic moments. They do sometimes, but not always by any means. You never know where you
are going to find the Lord. You never know what kind of question
is going to bring you to him.

I am an advocate of this indirect method. I have been saying for
many years from this pulpit that the best method of evangelism is,
to me, always the indirect approach. I am saying this in passing, but
what an opportunity we have for evangelism as individuals at the
present time. I mean something like this. You do not always need to
start by talking to people about their souls – talk to them about the
state of the world, talk to them about the state of society. Start there,
a good way off, as it were, with a general question. And then, as you
handle that, you will be able to lead the conversation on to their
own personal condition and the state of their own soul. That is how
we are able to do with others as our Lord did with this woman.

You may well find that our Lord will teach you the most
wonderful spiritual lessons you have ever had in a way that you
would never have imagined. Certainly that is my experience, as it
has been the experience of God's people throughout the centuries.
He may speak to you through a physical illness, something as far
away from the spiritual context as you can imagine. But we are one

and it does not matter where he starts, he can use that to bring us to the centre. If you will not listen to the preaching of the gospel, then perhaps you will listen when you are put flat on your back in bed and cannot move and are cut off from all the things that keep you going. He does that kind of thing. The indirect method: questions that do not at first seem to be directly spiritual but lead you on until you come to the vital point. Be ready always to hear him, be ready to find him anywhere, or for him to find you at any given point. You must not stereotype God's methods. You must not work them out into steps or a technique or a rule. No, no; he does not work like that; he is the Lord of creation and he varies his methods just as much as he varies the colour of the flowers. So watch his methods and especially this indirect method.

The next thing we notice is how, by means of this indirect way, our Lord arouses the interest of this woman. He is puzzling her. She has never met anything like this before: what is he doing? Oh, he is leading on to this great central statement – that is what he is doing – but he does it by arousing interest and creating curiosity. And he still does this; he creates desires and longings within us. We cannot understand them, we do not know why we have them, but that is his way. He will lead you to read a book that you had never heard of. He will somehow put it before you in a most amazing manner. It seems to be accidental but it is not. He puts things in our way or he stops certain things or he suggests others. And all along he is arousing our curiosity – 'What is this?' We will read a biography of a saint and say, 'Is this Christianity? Well, if it is, I haven't got it, and if it is, then I ought to be concerned about it, I ought to be enjoying it and experiencing it.' In a thousand and one different ways he creates these longings and aspirations within us.

I simply ask a question at this point: Has he aroused a longing in you for this well of water? Is there a dissatisfaction, a spiritual dissatisfaction? Do you know anything about this, or are you perfectly at ease and content, feeling that you have got it, got everything, know it all? Oh, when he deals with you, he will go on arousing this curiosity, this desire, this longing for something you have never hitherto known. This dis-ease, this lack of satisfaction, perhaps at first some vague longing for something that up to now you have not known, is a sure sign that he is dealing with you.

And that brings me to my next point, which is that our Lord leads us on from step to step. This is always a great characteristic of his method. Watch it in this story. There is a kind of sequence. From the very beginning, he knows what he is doing; when he starts right over there, he knows he is going to end here, and he brings us step by step, from stage to stage. This is a principle that is described in the Epistle to the Hebrews: 'Let us go on unto perfection' (Hebrews 6:1). Go on! The Christian life is a life of growth, a life of development. You do not remain as you were when you were born as a babe in Christ, you grow 'in grace, and in the knowledge of our Lord and Saviour Jesus Christ' (2 Peter 3:18). It is an increasing life, a progressing life, a well of water that goes on springing up for ever and ever 'into everlasting life'.

The apostle Paul, at the height of his great experience as a Christian, gives an account in the third chapter of the Epistle to the Philippians of how he had been delivered from his old state and condition as a Jew. Then he says that he rejoices in this:

> *Not having mine own righteousness, which is of the law, but that which is through the faith of Christ, the righteousness which is of God by faith*

– but he is not satisfied. What does he want? What is his greatest longing and desire? It is this –

> *that I may know him*

– but he does know him! Yes. It is because he knows him that he wants to know more and more of him and to know him better –

and the power of his resurrection, and the fellowship of his sufferings, being made conformable unto his death; if by any means I might attain unto the resurrection of the dead.

I believe that is final spiritual perfection; then he adds, and this is the point –

Not as though I had already attained, either were already perfect

– he knows he is saved, he knows he is forgiven, he knows he is regenerate, but he has not fully attained yet unto perfection –

but I follow after

– 'follow after'! There is one leading him and he is following him –

if that I may apprehend that for which also I am [I have been] apprehended of [by] Christ Jesus. Brethren, I count not myself to have apprehended

– in all its fullness, of course not; who can get a full comprehension of this? –

but this one thing I do, forgetting those things which are behind, and reaching forth unto those things which are before, I press toward the mark for the prize of the high calling of God in Christ Jesus. (Philippians 3:9–14)

Paul presses towards the mark because he is being pressed. He has already said this in the second chapter, in these words:

Wherefore, my beloved, as ye have always obeyed, not as in my presence only, but now much more in my absence, work out your own salvation with fear and trembling. For it is God which worketh in you both to will and to do of his good pleasure. (Philippians 2:12–13)

This, then, is always true of our Lord's method. He leads us on. Are you progressing? Do you know more about him and about these things than you did a year ago? He is never static. There are always deeper depths; there are always richer glories. Oh, to me there is nothing more pathetic than an old Christian who is always talking about his conversion and who stops there, as if nothing happened after that. It violates this great, glorious principle – the growth, the development, the being 'led on' by the Son of God until we reach absolute perfection.

Then notice – and thank God for this – our Lord's wonderful patience. Is he not patient with this woman? Do we not all feel rebuked as we read the story? He puts up with her interjections, her clever remarks, her glibness, her debating points – he suffers it all. We might spend our whole time on that. None of us would be here were it not for the patience of God, and the patience of the Lord Jesus Christ. We read in the Old Testament of God's patience and longsuffering with his ancient people: 'suffered he their [evil] manners in the wilderness' (Acts 13:18). The foolish people! They insulted him, they spat upon his laws, they turned to the gods of the nations, but he did not blot them out of his book. They turned back to him when they were in trouble. Of course they did, the cowards! And we are all so like them. But his loving kindness and his longsuffering and his patience never fail.

And you see our Lord's longsuffering with this woman – his patience with her, his tolerance. It is based upon his knowledge and upon his power. He knows the end so he is patient with us. He knows our condition; that is why he came into the world. He knows what men and women in sin are like in a way that we will never know. We know something about it but we do not know it in its depths. He sees what utter victims we are of the devil and his powers and his influences. And so he knows that he must be patient with us. I repeat, he does not bludgeon or dragoon us, but he is so loving and patient with us in order that he may bring us to that desired end.

But the last point I would make concerning our Lord's method, and again it stands out here so prominently, is his perseverance. He is not only patient, but because he is in charge, his patience assumes the form of perseverance and leads to it. Indeed, the patience is based upon the perseverance, his knowledge of the end. Read the story again and watch how our Lord will not be sidetracked. The woman tries several times over, but he will not have it. He keeps on, he persists, until eventually he has brought her to face the vital question.

And it is still the same. As I said earlier, our Lord will not let us go. He does not let this woman go. She wriggles, she tries her best, but he perseveres. And this is our only hope. If it were not for his perseverance, there would be no such thing as the final perseverance of the saints. If it were left to us, we would all fail, every one of us. We have failed. How we know this! Paul says to the Ephesians, 'We are his workmanship, created in Christ Jesus . . .' (Ephesians 2:10). Some say that the original idea there is, 'We are his poem.' Or you can think of that verse in terms of a potter making some beautiful vase. The point in both cases is that God is the author, he is the artist, he is the maker. And he never leaves his work unfinished. We start things and then stop, leaving them in an imperfect condition, but our Lord cannot do that, he would deny himself if he did. He is God the Son; he is perfect.

He made the world perfect and the regeneration will be perfect. We see that all there in this story, in the way our Lord persists and perseveres with this woman until he brings her to that desired end.

And the apostle Paul makes the same point to the Philippians. He is an old man, in prison, and there are rumours that the Emperor Nero may put him to death at any moment. But he is thinking of the little church in Philippi where there were quarrels and disputes, and you would imagine that he would be in the depth of depression. But he is not; this is what he says: 'Being confident of this very thing, that he which hath begun a good work in you will perform it until the day of Jesus Christ' (Philippians 1:6). That is the rock on which we stand. Yes, says Jude, 'Unto him that is able to keep you from falling, and to present you faultless before the presence of his glory with exceeding joy' (Jude 24).

God says in his prophecy concerning this great salvation that was to come through his Son, 'Yea I have loved thee with an everlasting love' (Jeremiah 31:3). Not a temporary love:

> Mine is an unchanging love

says the poet so rightly.

> Higher than the heights above,
> Deeper than the depths beneath.
> *William Cowper*

It is changeless. It is absolute. It is eternal.

Paul refers elsewhere to this perseverance that is the perseverance of God, the perseverance of Christ. 'Moreover' – listen to this logic – 'whom he did predestinate, them he also called: and whom he called, them he also justified: and whom he justified, them he also glorified' (Romans 8:30).

'But,' you say, 'we're not yet glorified.'

I know we are not in actual practice, but in the mind and the purpose and the plan of God we are already glorified, and if you are a Christian at all you will be glorified. Why? Well, the end of that chapter in Romans tells us:

> *For I am persuaded [I am absolutely certain] that neither death, nor life, nor angels, nor principalities, nor powers, nor things present, nor things to come, nor height, nor depth, nor any other creature, shall be able to separate us from the love of God, which is in Christ Jesus our Lord. (Romans 8:38–39)*

Our Lord's perseverance! He will not let us go.

The work which his goodness began,
The arm of his strength will complete;
His promise is Yea and Amen
And never was forfeited yet.

Things future, nor things that are now
Nor all things below or above,
Can make him his purpose forgo
Or sever my soul from his love.

Augustus Toplady

I say once more, as I said at the beginning of this study of our Lord's method: be careful, my dear friend. If he has started a good work in you he will complete it. You may rebel – you will suffer if you do. You may fight against him – you are only bringing trouble upon yourself. You say, 'But I want a bit of pleasure in the world, I'm young.' All right, you go after it, but you will pay for it. If he has started a good work in you, he will finish it. If you try to remodel this mould, you will only be inviting the chisel and the hammer, and he will go on with his work until you are faultless and blameless and spotless in his presence in the glory everlasting.

Oh, let us learn these lessons as we thus just look in general at our Lord's dealing with the woman of Samaria. There is the foundation of all our hope. What hope would there be for the Christian church today if it were not the church of God? Look what men have done to her in the past centuries. Look what they are trying to do with her now. Look at what is happening. There would be no hope at all were it not that his purposes are for ever sure. Whatever the position may be today, I know the ultimate is guaranteed. And though everything seems to be going the other way at the moment, that way will end in destruction. And however small a company the faithful people of God may be, it is all right, they shall shine as the sun, they will reflect the glory of God, the Father, the Son, and the Holy Spirit.

The next step we come to is this one, the hindrances. Here is the goal: 'Whosoever drinketh of the water that I shall give him shall never thirst; but the water that I shall give him shall be in him a well of water springing up into everlasting life.' Have you got this water? Do you know about it? If not, why not? It is because of hindrances, and the hindrances are entirely of our own making. That is one of the great lessons of this story. Look at this poor woman; there is the great offer but look at the difficulties and the obstacles that she creates and raises, spiting herself, standing in her own light and robbing herself of this great gift. See all the hindrances – there are many here and we must deal with them because the things that hindered this woman are still hindering God's people.

We are at a vital part of this teaching. It is no use my just standing here and saying, 'Here is this well of water, have you got it?' Each of us must face the question: If I do not have it, why not? So I must deal with the hindrances as our Lord dealt with them in the case of this woman. He still does that – through preaching, through the Scripture and in many other ways.

What are these hindrances? Well, some are immediately obvious on the surface. They are the prejudices that we hold in general. Look at this woman with her prejudice about Jews and Samaritans, about male and female, and with regard to worship – which I shall deal with on its own.

You may be saying, 'You're wrong to deal with this chapter as you are. You should be taking it evangelistically. The moment we become Christians we are no longer troubled by those questions of Jews and Samaritans and so on.'

Is that so? Are you so much of a novice in the spiritual life that you have not yet realized that many of these old prejudices follow us into the Christian life?

'But,' you say, 'Paul wrote, "If any man be in Christ, he is a new creature: old things are passed away; behold, all things are become new" ' (2 Corinthians 5:17).

But does that mean that you are therefore an entirely different person? Of course not. That idea is just an abuse of Scripture. We must learn that we carry prejudices from the old life into the new life. This is not my opinion, let me prove it to you. Look at the church at Corinth. Look at those early chapters of the First Epistle to the Corinthians. Paul there has to deal with the question of human, worldly wisdom because the members of the church at Corinth were beginning to bring that in. They had been converted, they were truly Christians, born again, but they were now beginning to look at the cross in a philosophic manner and, Paul says, if you do that you are making it of none effect, and then he has that great argument. But here is the material question: Why were the Corinthians doing that? And there is only one answer: it was because they were Corinthians, because they were Greeks, because that was their background. Philosophy! Understanding! Reason! That was what they boasted of. Though they were in the Christian life, philosophy had trapped them and Paul had great difficulty with them.

Of course, it was equally true of the Jews; you see them, too, stumbling. Even the apostle Peter stumbled over the question of going down to preach in the house of Cornelius. It took a vision to open his eyes. Peter! He was not only born again, he had also passed through Pentecost, yet the old Jewish prejudice was still there. And, indeed, Paul tells us in Galatians chapter 2 how, later on at Antioch, Peter began to dissemble. You do not finish with the past, the old prejudices still tend to follow. The Epistle to the Hebrews would never have been written were it not that the people to whom it was written were Hebrews, and they, again, were tending to carry their old prejudices into the Christian life. You do not get rid of all your problems the moment you become a Christian. I know that evangelists sometimes give that impression in order to get results, but what they say is misleading, and that is why many people fall away or are disappointed. No, no; you must take the position as it is put in the Scriptures. You will find there that many prejudices tend to carry over into the Christian life and can stand between us and this great blessing.

What are they? Well, even nationality! We must all bear this in mind. What is the place of nationality in Christianity, in the spiritual life? What a problem, what a question that is! It is very interesting to read the history of the church and the theological debates and see this influence creeping in. There is, of course, an essential difference between, say, an Englishman and a Scotsman. It is said that the Scots have theology in their bones and in their blood. Their history seems to indicate that. They are very different from the English, who are empiricists by nature and do not like definitions or too much reason. That kind of national background and prejudice is part of our makeup and we do not finish with it when we become Christians. Then look at the Germans, their delight in words. It is characteristic of all German theology. The French outlook is very different and the outlook of the Latin races is different again.

Now this, of course, can be exaggerated and people have made too much of it. This was the whole thesis of a book I once read in which the writer said that you could explain whether people were Protestant Reformed Calvinistic or Catholic in their doctrine purely in terms of climate. The further south, the nearer you go to the equator, he said, the more likely you are to be Catholic; in the colder regions, the doctrine is harder – Calvinistic. And therefore, it was not surprising that Calvinism came from John Calvin, who lived in Geneva. He had quite forgotten that Calvin was a Frenchman! I am just showing you by illustration that these prejudices and predispositions tend to persist and to follow us. You cannot just say, 'Ah, that woman was unconverted, and of course while you are unconverted you are full of prejudices.' Examine yourself, my friend. We must all examine ourselves. To what extent are we allowing prejudices to influence us and to govern us, not only national prejudices but traditions and customs, the way in which we have been brought up, our background?

Have you not found in your spiritual experience that there is often a very great difference between two Christian people as a result of their backgrounds? One of them has been brought up in a church or a chapel, in a religious home, and has always been familiar with Christian teaching, but is now converted, born again, a true Christian. And here is another who comes from an entirely pagan background, with no Christian teaching at all, but again is now born again. Although they are both Christians, their problems are often very different – very different indeed. The first has much more to shed than the second.

The problems of people who have always regarded themselves as Christians are often much greater than those of people who had previously had nothing to do with the church. In a final sense, of course, there is no difference. All I am showing is that the devil makes use of these factors, and the prejudices will keep on creeping back – the reliance upon your works, upon your goodness, upon your attendance at the house of God or upon saying your prayers. The tendency of these people, always, is to fall back on works. Or there is an insistence upon worship, or on a particular religious habit or custom. There is a common prejudice in this country as to what Christianity is, and it is very difficult to shake yourself free from it. These prejudices are there, they keep on seeping in, and people have to fight against them. You do not shed them completely, they do not drop off altogether, the moment you come into the Christian life, and at times they constitute some of the greatest difficulties and problems faced by Christians.

People say, 'Why are you talking about this "well of water", I've always been a Christian?' Or, 'I've been a Christian for so long, ever since I was a child.' I received a letter only this week from some friends in the north of England whom I do not know and have never seen, as far as I know – a husband and wife writing to me together. They had had some bit of help from reading something that I have been privileged to write. But what was interesting in their letter was this: 'At first we did not like it, we were annoyed by it.' That is their term, not mine – they were 'annoyed'. Why were they annoyed by what I had written? Ah, because of this prejudice! They had been brought up in a certain way, the way I have been describing, and their first reaction was one of annoyance: 'What is this man saying? Is he suggesting we are not Christians? But we are Christians.' And so, you see, people put up a barrier. The Lord is speaking to you, he is offering you something that you have not got so that you will never thirst again – the 'well of water'. But you put up an obstacle, you say, 'What's this?'

Remember the Jews: it is all there in the eighth chapter of John's Gospel. Our Lord had been preaching and we are told that as a result, 'many believed on him'. And he looked at them and said, 'If ye continue in my word, then are ye my disciples indeed; and ye shall know the truth, and the truth shall make you free.' What a wonderful promise! But do you remember the reaction? 'They answered him, We be Abraham's seed, and were never in bondage to any man: how sayest thou, Ye shall be made free?' (John 8:30–33). You see the prejudice? There is nothing more terrible than allowing some old, general prejudice so to influence us that far from accepting this gracious, loving offer, we even resent it because it carries the implication that we are not everything that we ought to be. God have mercy upon us!

Let us learn the lessons that we find enshrined here in the whole story of our Lord's dealing with the woman of Samaria. We raise the obstacles – and I am only beginning on this. Thank God, he perseveres and is patient with us, and is determined to bring us to the desired end.

3

Spiritual Dullness and Evasive Tactics

Jesus answered and said unto her, Whosoever drinketh of this water shall thirst again: but whosoever drinketh of the water that I shall give him shall never thirst; but the water that I shall give him shall be in him a well of water springing up into everlasting life. (John 4:13–14)

We have been seeing that the essence of Christianity, ultimately what it really means to be a Christian, is that we have within us a well of water springing up into everlasting life. And we are taking this old story, this great incident in our Lord's life and ministry, because it shows us how this can be true for us. Have we got this 'well of water' that puts us into such a condition that we shall 'never thirst'? 'Never' is a very big word. It means everything, any conceivable condition. Need I indicate to you the importance of this great statement, and the importance of our examining ourselves in the light of it? How do we stand up to life? How do we stand up to what happens to us in life? What if we should have an experience such as hundreds of people have had since Friday? What would we be like now? How would we react?[1]

This is what Christianity is about. It is not about some theoretical consideration of life; it is the most practical thing in the world. The object of this great salvation is to enable us to live in this world and to look forward to the glory that is to come. We cannot truly do that unless we are Christians. Without this life that Christ came to give, life is mere existence, and you soon discover that when you are face to face with tragedy and calamity and find you have nothing at all. So this is the most important subject we can ever consider together. This is the possibility, this is what can be true of all of us, this is the great offer of the Christian gospel.

Now we have been taking a general look at our Lord's meeting with the woman of Samaria. We have looked at the person of our Lord himself and at the way he deals with us, and I trust this has given us great comfort and consolation. As our Lord persisted with this woman until she came to see the truth, so he persists with us. And we have now begun to consider the hindrances and obstacles that keep us from knowing much about 'the well of water springing up into everlasting life' – as they were true in the case of this woman, so they are, in principle, still true of all of us. We have dealt with some general prejudices that hindered this woman. She turned to our Lord in amazement when he asked her for a drink of water. She said, 'How is it that thou, being a Jew, askest drink of me, which am a woman of Samaria?' We face national prejudices, class prejudices, race prejudices, sex prejudices and so on. There is almost

---

[1] The reference here is to the terrible events on 21 October 1966 when 144 people, including 116 children, were killed after a coal tip engulfed a school, a cottage and a farm in the village of Aberfan in Wales.

no end to them. What harm they have done in the life of the individual Christian, what harm they have done in the life of the church throughout the centuries: the things we cling to so tenaciously simply because we have been born like that!

The second great hindrance is spiritual dullness or spiritual slowness. Here is an obstacle to growth that is shown very plainly by this woman of Samaria. She shows us that you can be intelligent, you can be quick and alert, you can be subtle at disputation, and yet the whole time be spiritually dull. Now this comes out in the way that this woman materializes everything our Lord says to her. He is speaking to her in a spiritual manner but she does not see it. Let me illustrate what I mean. Our Lord said to her, 'If thou knewest the gift of God, and who it is that saith to thee, Give me to drink; thou wouldest have asked of him, and he would have given thee living water.' It is a purely spiritual statement.

But in reply, the woman says, 'Sir, thou hast nothing to draw with, and the well is deep' – she completely misses the spiritual import of his statement. She thinks of the material well in front of her and is saying: 'You have no bucket, you have nothing to draw with and the well is deep: where are you getting that living water from?' And then on she goes: 'Art thou greater than our father Jacob, which gave us the well, and drank thereof himself, and his children, and his cattle?'

Then comes the great statement of our text, thoroughly spiritual, gloriously spiritual. But listen to the woman's words in verse 15: 'The woman saith unto him, Sir, give me this water, that I thirst not, neither come hither to draw.' She is saying: 'I have to keep on coming back and forth to this well to draw water. I would be very glad if you could do something to put an end to that – it would save me a lot of bother.' She has no spiritual perception, she does not understand, everything is brought down to her level.

Now here, again, is a most important principle. It is not the first time we meet it in this great Gospel. Nicodemus, of whom we read in the early part of the third chapter, materialized our Lord's spiritual statements in exactly the same way. You see, this is not a question of learning; spiritual understanding has nothing to do with natural ability, nothing at all. Thank God for that, otherwise salvation would be the prerogative of a certain small company of people! No, when our Lord interrupted Nicodemus and said, 'Except a man be born again, he cannot see the kingdom of God,' Nicodemus said to him, 'How can a man be born when he is old? can he enter the second time into his mother's womb, and be born?' (John 3:3–4). Poor Nicodemus! He did not see the spiritual, he could only think of the flesh, the material. And our Lord said to him, 'That which is born of the flesh is flesh: and that which is born of the Spirit is spirit. Marvel not that I said unto thee, Ye must be born again' (John 3:6–7). In both Nicodemus and the woman of Samaria we are shown the kind of attitude that is a hindrance to obtaining of this great fullness.

The apostle Paul says exactly the same thing about the Corinthians; and not only about them, but about the 'natural man' in particular. In 1 Corinthians 2 he puts forward certain propositions. He says:

But God hath revealed them [these things] unto us by his Spirit: for the Spirit searcheth all things, yea, the deep things of God. For what man knoweth the things of a man, save the spirit of man which is in him? even so the things of God knoweth no man, but the Spirit of God. Now we [Christians] have received, not the spirit of the world, but the spirit which is of God; that we might know the things that are freely given to us of God. Which things also we speak, not in the words which man's wisdom teacheth, but which the Holy Ghost teacheth, comparing spiritual things with spiritual. But the natural man receiveth not the things of the Spirit of God: for they are foolishness unto him: neither can he know them, because they are spiritually discerned. But he that is spiritual judgeth [understands] all things, yet he himself is judged [known] of no man. (1 Corinthians 2:10–15)

The cleverness, the ability, all these things that are all right in and of themselves, do not help us here, indeed, they can be a veritable hindrance. If we constantly hold on to them, desiring this understanding that we cannot have in and of ourselves, we are raising difficulties and obstacles to receiving the fullness.

Someone may say, 'But all Christians, surely, have the Spirit in them.' Perfectly right. 'Now if any man have not the Spirit of Christ, he is none of his' (Romans 8:9). A man or woman cannot be a Christian without having the Spirit, the Holy Spirit, in them. But then the fallacy comes in. It is assumed, therefore, that while this spiritual dullness is true of an unconverted person, like the woman of Samaria, it cannot be true of a Christian. But it can! The fact that we have become Christians, that we are born again, that the Spirit of God is in us, does not mean that we have solved all our problems; that is only a beginning. We now have to go through a great process of readjustment, and it is because so many people fail to realize that, and, still more, fail to act upon it, that they are constantly in trouble.

Listen to the apostle Paul putting this as an appeal to the church at Rome: 'I beseech you therefore, brethren, by the mercies of God, that ye present your bodies a living sacrifice' – we must do this now; we have become Christians but we still need to do this – 'holy acceptable unto God, which is your reasonable service. And be not conformed to this world' – Christian people have to be told that: Do not go on conforming to this world – 'but be ye transformed' – how? – 'by the renewing of your mind' – this is what I am talking about – 'that ye may prove what is that good, and acceptable, and perfect, will of God' (Romans 12:1–2).

Now all that is addressed to Christians. Spiritual understanding is not something that happens automatically. Not at all! You must work out your own salvation in this way. You must start thinking in a new way, and apply this new thinking all along the line. Another statement of the same truth is to be found in Paul's Epistle to the Ephesians. 'Do not go on living as the other Gentiles do,' says Paul, in effect. Then:

> *Ye have not so learned Christ; if so be that ye have heard him, and have been taught by him, as the truth is in Jesus: that ye put off concerning the former conversation the old man, which is corrupt according to the deceitful lusts; and be renewed in the spirit of your mind. (Ephesians 4:20–23)*

Now that is the whole problem. When men and women become Christians, they see a big truth, a broad distinction; but having seen this, they now, by renewal in the very spirit of their minds, have to go on working this out. This principle is constantly put before us in the New Testament Epistles. The apostle Paul repeats it in 1 Corinthians 3: 'And I, brethren, could not speak unto you as unto spiritual, but as unto carnal, even as unto babes' (verse 1). He is saying: I cannot give you the teaching I want to give you because your thinking is still wrong. You are thinking in the old way and not in the new.

We find the same teaching in the Epistle to the Hebrews. The writer has a great doctrine to unfold, the doctrine of our Lord as 'an high priest after the order of Melchisedec'. He goes on to say: 'Of whom we have many things to say, and hard to be uttered, seeing ye are dull of hearing' (Hebrews 5:10–11). He cannot give them the comfort and consolation and the teaching he wants to give them because, though they are Christians, they are still thinking in the old unspiritual, material way.

And, similarly, the apostle Peter says:

> *Ye are a chosen generation, a royal priesthood, an holy nation, a peculiar people; that ye should shew forth the praises of him who hath called you out of darkness into his marvellous light: which in time past were not a people, but are now the people of God: which had not obtained mercy, but now have obtained mercy.*

Then here is the appeal –

> *Dearly beloved, I beseech you as strangers and pilgrims, abstain from fleshly lusts, which war against the soul; having our conversation [our behaviour] honest among the Gentiles . . . (1 Peter 2:9–12)*

Now you see the appeal? All this is addressed to Christians, and it is because we fail to realize this that we are so frequently in trouble and raise these hindrances that prevent us receiving of this well of water that springs up into everlasting life.

But why do we do this? This to me is a most important matter. It is a great tragedy that though this offer is here before us – the very thing we stand in need of, the secret of all the saints and the noblest souls that this world has ever seen – that though it is all offered to us by our Lord, as he offered it to the woman of Samaria, yet so many of us are burdened, troubled, unhappy, conscious of failure and without consolation. What a tragedy it is that people who were meant to live as princes are living as paupers; that those who were meant to be receiving 'the unsearchable riches of Christ' (Ephesians 3:8), should be living in penury.

My friends, this ought not to be, and it is important not only from the standpoint of our own happiness and wellbeing as Christians, but still more in view of the state of the world outside.

People are unhappy, they do not know what to do or where to turn, and here are we claiming to be Christians. They look at us and think, 'Can these people help us?' But if they see that we react as they do, that we have no comfort and consolation, that we have nothing that differentiates us and lifts us above our circumstances, they will not listen to us. They will say, 'These people are all talk, there's nothing in it,' and they will not be interested. So from every standpoint it is vital that we should examine ourselves in the light of this kind of hindrance, this spiritual dullness and slowness that remains on the earth on a material level and fails to realize what is being offered us in Christ Jesus. Why, I ask again, are we like this?

Well, here are some of the answers. First of all, it is partly habit. We are all creatures of habit and custom and, I say again, the fact that you have become a Christian does not mean that all your old habits drop off; they do not. Our old habits are like old autumn leaves that you see on the trees in spring. These old leaves take a long time to drop off, they have to be pushed off slowly by the new buds. You are born again; essentially, you have become a new person; yes, but you are so constituted that the body in which you live in this world – and, remember, the New Testament regards the body as a sort of tent in which people live – is a part of you. Man is body, soul and spirit, and the body is a creature of habits and customs. And that applies to the mind, to the brain – the brain as distinct from the mind; the brain as an organ; the brain, if you like, as a kind of machine. It runs in grooves; it repeats things.

There is value in habit, but it can also be a great problem for we are often unaware of it. You have a mind that has been accustomed to thinking in a given way, along a given line and though you have changed, you will find that you will have to be renewed constantly 'in the spirit of your mind'. In order to get this mind – I should not call it a machine, but we do, language is inadequate here – this faculty that I have, to change, I must train it to think in the right, the Christian, way – it will not happen automatically.

Secondly, we allow spiritual dullness because of the feeling that we have had everything; we have had it all at conversion and there is nothing more to be had. This has been a very popular teaching, and it accounts, it seems to me, for a great deal that is true of the Christian church today. There are many Christian people who are exactly the same now as they were 50 years ago, and they are always looking back. This is a terrible attitude, and it is an obstacle to receiving this fullness about which we are reading together.

Another cause is laziness, a failure to exercise our senses, a failure to apply ourselves to the truth, and to apply the truth itself to us. This is a very serious matter, and I want to deal with it in a very serious way. Laziness, I believe, is one of the great enemies of the Christian, especially at the present time, though, of course, it is always wrong. The New Testament is always urging us to activity, and particularly to mental activity. Listen to the apostle Peter again: 'Wherefore gird up the loins of your mind' (1 Peter 1:13). Now that is an appeal to Christians, but we are lazy, we do not like doing that. Or take it again as it is put by the author of Hebrews:

> *For when for the time ye ought to be teachers, ye have need that one teach you again which be the first principles of the oracles of God; and are become such as have need of milk, and not of strong meat. For every one that useth milk is unskilful in the word of righteousness: for he is a babe. But strong meat belongeth to them that are of full age, even those who by reason of use have their senses exercised to discern both good and evil. (Hebrews 5:12–14)*

If ever a text were needed by the modern Christian, it is that! What laziness there is, what failure to study, to apply the mind!

We are living in an age that likes to be entertained; the element of entertainment has come increasingly into Christian activity and Christian worship – the element of singing and storytelling and talking about experiences, while there is this great truth waiting for us. We are meant to 'gird up the loins of our mind', not just to sit back and say, 'Wasn't it nice? Wasn't it enjoyable?' Oh, what a tragedy it is that with all of these riches people should be spending their time in sheer entertainment!

Fourthly, there is the magical view of faith taken by many people. I cannot call it anything else. These people seem to think that faith is a magic word that completely changes everything. In other words, there is the danger of putting the experiential and the subjective in too prominent a position. Now we must never forget these aspects of the Christian life – I started by emphasizing that. A mere theoretical Christianity is of no value, it is a contradiction in terms. But there is the opposite danger of so emphasizing the experiential and the subjective that we really know nothing about the truth as such. We have had one vital experience – thank God for it, it does make us Christians – but if you hold on to that alone you remain a 'babe in Christ', and it is terrible to see a child that never grows up. Have you not seen it sometimes? A person of 40 or 50 years of age still with the mentality of a babe? Some of the Christians to whom the Epistle to the Hebrews was written were like that, as we have seen, and Paul suggests that the Corinthians were like that, too. And that is very often because we have this magical or semi-magical view of faith.

A fifth reason is that in preaching and teaching we tend to put too much emphasis upon the will and upon surrender. This is mainly the responsibility of preachers. It has been a characteristic of evangelical Christianity since about the middle of the 1870s – a direct attack upon the will and an emphasis upon 'making a decision' and upon 'receiving the Lord'. The great truth, the body of doctrine, has not been unfolded because people have become impatient with that; they say they do not have the time, they can no longer sit and read. Yet your great-great-great-grandparents did have the time, and they did read, though they worked much harder than you will ever work and for much lower wages. They found the time and they went into the profundities. But this new teaching has come in that does not start with the mind and the understanding, nor even with the heart, but with the will. Surrender! Always surrender! In every type of preaching you are always being told to come forward to make some sort of a decision.

Now that is not the New Testament way. I defy you to find such teaching there. The New Testament, indeed, as I am trying to show you, does the exact opposite. So I will put my sixth point like this: all the previous suggestions that I have made to explain why Christians are being hindered in their spiritual growth are ultimately due to one basic cause, and that is a completely defective, totally inadequate, view of the Christian gospel. Here is the real trouble. We reduce this 'glorious gospel of the blessed God' into just one thing, and always the same thing, always this matter of deciding and receiving.

This last week I had the privilege and pleasure of talking to two ministers from another part of the world. One of them said something that I thought was most interesting because it is equally true of this country. He was talking about evangelical people and he said, 'I have a problem in my church. Ever since I have been more expository in my preaching, concentrating more on teaching them the truth, some of the people are beginning to complain that I am no longer preaching the gospel.' 'No longer preaching the gospel' – because he was expounding the Scriptures, unfolding these great truths!

What is the matter with these people? Well, they have reduced the gospel to just one act, and that alone must be preached, so that unless there is 'something happening', as they put it, unless somebody is making a decision in every single service, the gospel has not been presented. Is it not astonishing that Christians can speak like that with the New Testament and the teaching of the Epistles open before them? They do not know what the gospel is. That is a terrible thing to say, but it is true. At the most, they just know the first beginnings of the gospel, but no more. And they think that is all. They do not want to be taught, they are intolerant, and they become critical, as that good friend was telling me.

What do I mean? Well, take that great third chapter of the Epistle to the Ephesians. My dear friends, this is the gospel! As Paul puts it:

Unto me, who am less than the least of all saints, is this grace given, that I should preach among the Gentiles

– what? Just, 'Come to Jesus and be saved'? Of course, that is the first thing. But no –

the unsearchable riches of Christ. And to make all men see what is the fellowship of the mystery, which from the beginning of the world hath been hid in God, who created all things by Jesus Christ. (verses 8–9)

This great mystery about the church! The principalities and powers in the heavenly places are going to understand this, even they are going to be instructed, through the church, through us. And so Paul says:

For this cause I bow my knees unto the Father of our Lord Jesus Christ

– what is he praying for? –

that he would grant you, according to the riches of his glory, to be strengthened with might by his Spirit in the inner man; that Christ may dwell in your hearts by faith; that ye, being rooted and grounded in love, may be able to comprehend with all saints

– wherever they are, everywhere –

> *what is the breadth, and length, and depth, and height; and to know the love of Christ, which passeth knowledge, that ye might be filled with all the fullness of God. (verses 14, 15–19)*

Now that is the realm into which you and I have come, but so many people are not interested. They are interested in activities – it is all right to be active and interested in evangelism, it has its place – but to give the impression that this is the first priority, the biggest thing, the central thing, the thing that is needed most of all, is just to twist the Scriptures completely. That is only the beginning, and a church that remains at the beginning is infantile.

My dear friends, how much of your time do you spend in thinking about subjects such as this? Are you studying your Scriptures to find these riches, these depths and heights? Are you giving yourself to this? Do you really mean these words when you sing them:

> Just as I am, of that free love,
> The breadth, length, depth, and height to prove
> Here for a season, then above,
> O Lamb of God, I come.
>
> *Charlotte Elliott*

Have you heeded the exhortation of the author of the Epistle to the Hebrews there at the end of the fifth chapter? Have you, too, been chastened and reprimanded? This is what you need. The writer starts off in chapter 6 by saying, 'Therefore leaving the principles [the first beginnings, the mere introduction] of the doctrine of Christ' – you must not reduce the doctrine of Christ merely to the matter of conversion; that is being done, and the church has lost her balance, she has lost the real essence of her being – 'let us go on to perfection.' This is what we are to pursue: 'perfection'. Or think of it in terms of the majestic, glorious first chapter of Paul's Epistle to the Philippians where he suddenly seems to open the front door, as it were, into the heavens, and give us a glimpse of the glory of the Lord. That is what you and I are meant to enter into.

So, therefore, I would sum up this section by saying that perhaps the greatest cause of spiritual sloth is a superficial form of Bible study. We have been so concerned that people should read the Bible at all that we have fallen into the error of teaching them to read it in a superficial manner. We skim through the Scriptures, taking broad strides, chapters at a time, sometimes a book at a time, and we think we are studying the Scriptures! Then, having a general knowledge of their contents, and being able to classify and tabulate them, we think we know them. But that is not the way to get at 'the breadth and length and depth and height', that is not the way to investigate 'the unsearchable riches of Christ'.

No, no; you must take time, you must go down to a deeper level, you must investigate the teaching. There are gems and nuggets here – get down to them! Not just a little portion of Scripture, with some brief words of comment, often leaving out the context. No, no! That is better than nothing, I agree, but if you stop at that you are children and you know nothing about the unsearchable riches. The bane of our Christianity has been superficial Bible reading, superficial Bible study. It is stories as told to children, whereas we ought to be behaving as adult believers.

There, then, is a group of hindrances that I have put under the title of 'spiritual slowness'. Shall I put this very practically: Are you with me in all this, or are you saying, 'What's he talking about? What's all this about? I don't understand it. I wanted to have a nice feeling. I wanted to go out of church feeing happy, but here you are making me feel unhappy.' Is that it? If it is, examine yourself, examine your very foundation. A failure to enjoy these spiritual riches, a failure to desire more and more of them, is indicative of the fact that we are but children. And we have no right to remain as children. 'Gird up the loins of your mind.' Pull yourself together. Give time to this. It is a painful process, it needs discipline. You must harness all your senses, you must use them. You must study in a way you have never studied before, and then you will begin to have an increasing appreciation of these 'unsearchable riches of Christ'.

Let me give you one other big heading, which is evasiveness. This, again, is painfully clear in the case of the woman of Samaria. Her cleverness comes out, but unfortunately it is the evasiveness that strikes us most of all – how she shifts her ground and moves from one topic to another. I have already given you examples, but let me give you just one more. Our Lord now sees that he must be very personal with her, and press the matter and really pin her down. So we are told in verse 16: 'Jesus saith unto her, Go, call thy husband, and come hither.' When the woman answers, 'I have no husband,' Jesus says, 'Thou hast well said, I have no husband: for thou hast had five husbands; and he whom thou now hast is not thy husband: in that saidst thou truly.' But, you see, instead of concentrating on that, the woman says, 'Sir, I perceive that thou art a prophet' – she would have been very glad to have discussed him instead of herself – 'Our father worshipped in this mountain' – he is talking to her about her adultery, her immoral life, but she wants to talk about where you worship – 'and ye say, that in Jerusalem is the place where men ought to worship.'

Now that is what I mean by evasiveness. We are all experts at this; we are all like this woman of Samaria. How we evade the issue, how we parry the question! It is because we do not like being searched, we do not like being examined, we do not like being disturbed. This is the 'natural man', the old nature that is still with us. You do not get rid of your old nature when you are a Christian, when you are born again. The old man has gone but the old nature has not gone, and the old nature, the natural self, does not like being searched. That element remains in us. We resent it, we do not want to be made to feel that we are wrong; we even dislike the very process that disturbs us out of our sloth: 'Why, we are Christians! I was converted. There's the date, there was the test, that's how it happened.' Right! But here is a man saying, 'But look here, you've not got much, have you? You don't seem to know much about the real gospel and its riches.' And we resent this, we thought we had it all in one packet – everything; and we dislike this suggestion that there is anything wrong with us as we are. And, of course, we dislike the feeling of condemnation still more. We shuffle under it, we feel it is wrong. People in this world need condemnation, of course, but *we . . .?!*

And then you see what happens. The woman evades the question by taking up other questions. And we do the same thing. We shield ourselves as she does. She is saying, 'I can see that you are a prophet. Now this is interesting. I'm interested in prophets' – she knows something about the Old Testament, the five books of Moses, at any rate – 'I see you are a religious teacher.' Ah, then she would be very happy! She is not facing the question of her own life but wants to know about 'this mountain', worship, God and so on. And we take up these questions, we evade the issue in just the same way.

Now I have pointed out that when our Lord begins to deal with us, he does disturb us. There is no greater disturbing power in the universe than the power of the love of Christ, that 'kind but searching glance' of his, before which 'all things are naked and opened' (Hebrews 4:13). He searches us for our own good, but it is painful, so we evade it by taking up other issues. We have seen how the woman of Samaria did it, but what about us? Among the commonest of all questions at the present time are questions about apartheid in South Africa. It is honourable to talk about that, is it not? You see, in denouncing somebody else, you are shielding yourself. While you are denouncing these people, or friends in America, or somewhere else, over this colour problem, you are full of righteous indignation. Very clever; but you are just evading the problem of your own life, the running sore of your soul.

A second, and one of the commonest ways of evading the truth among those of us who are evangelical Christians, is to spend the whole of our time in attacking modernists and Roman Catholicism. That is all right, they need to be attacked and we must attack them, we are to defend the truth, but if you spend all your time doing this, you are probably evading the searching glance of the Son of God. We are all experts at this, but if your purpose is to shield yourself and to evade your Lord's words to you, you will still go on thirsting, and you will have no reserves in your life in the hour of trial and calamity.

And along the same lines, another tendency we have is to explain away our sins and faults and deficiencies. There is a technical term for this: we are experts at rationalizing our sins. We can explain them. Of course, if we see the same fault in somebody else, we denounce it, but in our case, somehow or another, there was a difference and extenuating circumstances. We can twist it. Oh, how clever we are! Why do we do all this? Because we always want to be on good terms with ourselves. We want to be happy. Happiness must be put first and we do not like the probing, we do not like that application to the wound that makes it smart and burn. It is for our good, it is for our healing, but we do not like it. We do not like even temporary pain, we want ease – we are like children. And so in clever ways we evade issues and explain away sin.

Or, finally, I will put it like this. There is no more subtle way of evading and hindering what the Son of God says to us for our good and for our happiness and our ultimate salvation than a process of balancing, a wrong kind of balance. There is a true balance, but there is a wrong kind as well, and that is the attempt to balance failure in practice by theoretical knowledge. This woman was doing that. We all know exactly what it is. We have failed in practice, we have done something wrong. So, then, against that we say, 'Ah, well, but we've been reading and we've gained a lot of knowledge, and we know so much more than we knew before.' We put the theoretical knowledge over against the practical failure and we feel we have squared the accounts. All right! If I did not have this knowledge, of course, it would be altogether bad, but I do have it. So on balance I am really quite a good Christian.

We are balancing knowledge of theology against life and living and experience. But all the theological knowledge in the world is of no value to us unless we have a living experience of the grace of God. Do not be a fool. The final audit will take place, the ultimate Accountant will appear, and all your clever balancing will be revealed for the mere artifice, the sham, the hypocrisy, that it is. God preserve us from the terrible danger of this false balance of putting one thing over against another. Christianity never does that. There is a true balance here. It is a wholeness, a completeness; it is all-inclusive.

This is what I mean. To me, the glory of the Christian gospel is that it takes in the whole person. It starts with my mind, my understanding. It is truth presented to the mind. But it does not stop with the understanding. What next? Experience. It is feeling, response, the knowledge that something is happening. And then practice. The mind, the heart, the will are all involved. I must never put these up one against another, they should all be equally engaged, they should all be actively, fully involved. You do not stop on the level of activity and decision and the will. Nor do you remain always in the realm of the emotions and just be sentimental and tell stories. I have several times been in religious conferences where teaching was supposed to take place and have heard men take a text and then immediately begin to tell a story. And they will go on telling stories for an hour, with no exposition. You must not stop at experience only.

The apostle Paul expressed once and for ever this truth that the whole personality is involved when he said, 'But God be thanked, that ye were the servants of sin, but ye have obeyed [will] from the heart [emotion]' – what? – 'that form of [sound] doctrine [teaching] which was delivered you' (Romans 6:17). The truth came, and the mind was given the ability to apprehend it by the Holy Spirit, but it did not remain there. It moved the heart, it melted the individual, who then put it into practice by the exercise of the will. That is Christianity, and any artificial division of these three, or, still more, any attempt to play one against two, or two against one, any division, any dichotomy, is wrong, and is dangerous to the soul.

4

Wrong Ideas of
Worship and of God

The woman saith unto him, Sir, I perceive that thou art a prophet. Our fathers worshipped in this mountain; and ye say, that in Jerusalem is the place where men ought to worship. Jesus saith unto her, Woman, believe me, the hour cometh, when ye shall neither in this mountain, nor yet at Jerusalem, worship the Father. Ye worship ye know not what: we know what we worship: for salvation is of the Jews. But the hour cometh, and now is, when the true worshippers shall worship the Father in spirit and in truth: for the Father seeketh such to worship him. God is a Spirit: and they that worship him must worship him in spirit and in truth. (John 4:19–24)

The fundamental statement with which we are dealing is to be found in John 4:13–14. But I would now like to call your attention to John 4:19–24 because we are dealing at the moment with the hindrances, the things that stand between us and the realization of what we are told in verses 13 and 14. It is in verses 13 and 14 that we are given the offer of the Christian faith, the Christian message. It is a message about life and how to live it, and here is the offer, the incomparable offer, made by the Son of God that he will give us new life that will be in us 'a well of water springing up into everlasting life', and that having this we shall 'never thirst'. This is a promise that our Lord constantly repeats and, as I have been trying to show, it is in particular the fundamental message of this Gospel according to St John. This is Christianity – nothing less than this.

The suggestion I am making is that the state of the church today, and the state of our own individual lives, is very largely to be explained by the fact that we have failed to realize that the true Christian position is this fullness – a fullness of experience of our Lord and his love and his grace. And I am calling attention to it not only that we may cease to rob ourselves of the riches of his grace, but also, still more, that we may be able to function truly as Christian people. The world, as we are aware, is in a terrible condition, it is going from bad to worse, and we know that there is nothing that is of any value, nothing that can avail at a time like this, save this gospel.

But people are not concerned about the gospel, they will not look at it, and I hold the view that this is because of what they see in us or, at any rate, what they fail to see in us. It is because we so often give the impression that we are essentially like everybody else, but with a bit of religion added on, that people are not interested in our faith and all our claims. But when they see Christians who are filled with this 'fullness', Christians who have this 'well of water' springing up within them, they always pay attention. That is the testimony of the great revivals in the history of the church.

To me, the most urgent need of the hour is not for evangelism but for revival of the church because it is a revived church that evangelizes in the most effective manner. That has been God's way of evangelism throughout the centuries. He has always started a work in his own people – formal, lifeless people have suddenly been transfigured and transformed and filled with life, and the moment the world has seen that, it has come crowding into the church to hear the message. For some reason or another, we modern Christians seem to have forgotten all that. And therefore, I say again, the most urgent thing for us is to make sure that we are people who correspond to this description and manifest in our daily lives what it means to be a Christian.

We have been looking at the hindrances that stand between us and the realization of this essential Christian experience. We considered first certain general prejudices and then went on to look at spiritual dullness and slowness and some of its aspects and causes. We considered also what I called 'evasiveness' and we saw the way in which this Samaritan woman wriggled and twisted and turned in her efforts to avoid conviction.

Let us now turn to some further hindrances. I want in particular to take the two that are suggested by the nineteenth verse to the twenty-fourth verse of this chapter: wrong ideas of worship and wrong ideas of God. These two are obviously intimately related and in one sense you cannot separate them. Worship is worship of God. So there is a unity between the two. And yet, as I think I can show you, because we do tend to divide them, it is important that we should consider them separately.

Now this is the most crucial matter of all. What is the end and object of Christian salvation? It is to bring us to God, to reconcile us to him. Many other blessings are given – thank God for them all – but the primary object of Christianity is not to make us happy, but to bring us to a knowledge of God, to enable us to worship God. We are made for that. 'The chief end of man is to glorify God and to enjoy him for ever' (*Westminster Shorter Catechism*). Man is meant to worship God. 'Thou shalt love the Lord thy God with all thy heart, and with all thy soul, and with all thy mind, and with all thy strength' (Mark 12:30). That is the ultimate object of it all. So, I repeat, there is nothing more important than this – the true worship of God. And it is quite clear that failure in our worship of God is one of the great hindrances that stand in the way of receiving this blessing. It is obtained from God, and it is only as we are in a right relationship to him that we have any hope whatsoever of receiving it.

Now you notice that this story, again, gives us very clear and plain teaching with regard to the worship of God. This woman makes most of the mistakes that we all have made, and she is particularly at fault over this matter of worship. The more she talks, the more she betrays herself and reveals the inadequacy and the wrongness of her ideas. She is a religious person, remember, in spite of her sin, and she is interested in worship. She makes this point: 'Our fathers worshipped in this mountain; and ye [you Jews] say that in Jerusalem is the place where men ought to worship.' She is interested in this subject and she has her point of view with regard to the God who is worshipped. But our Lord proceeds, as you see, to show her the hollowness of all her talk about worship and about God, and he makes it quite plain and clear to her that all that she has is valueless, and that she must think anew about these matters.

So let us try to look at these wrong ideas of worship. What is worship? What is it to worship God? What is it to pray? I wonder how often we have stopped to ask that question? I wonder how often we have said, as the disciples said to our Lord and Saviour: 'Lord, teach us to pray, as John also taught his disciples' (Luke 11:1)? They put that request to him as the result of observing him praying and they must have been convicted that he was doing something that they knew nothing about, and they therefore asked for this instruction.

So I simply ask: Have we ever expressed that desire? I am putting it in that way in order that I may introduce this thought: Must we not all plead guilty to worship that has been completely thoughtless? We have not even stopped to think what we are doing. We have not stopped to realize what we are engaged in. Surely the fundamental trouble with all of us is thoughtlessness. Is it not amazing to realize what a number of things we can do quite mechanically? Have you not often found yourself getting on your knees by the side of your bed and saying your prayers without realizing what you were doing? You were actually thinking about something else while you were uttering the words. We have all done that. It is terrible that it is possible for our worship to be quite thoughtless.

And add to thoughtlessness, ignorance. Our Lord says to this woman: 'Ye worship ye know not what: we know what we worship.' There is a great deal of ignorant worship. Again, we must ask ourselves: Do we know what we are doing? If we would know this Christian experience as it is set before us here and as we see it in the lives of the saints throughout the centuries, we must face these questions. Those men and women have always been people who have faced them, and as the result of that they have felt a profound dissatisfaction with themselves – and that is the first step, always, in the direction of this great experience.

We are all like this woman, governed by habit, custom, indeed, even by tradition, and, still worse, by prejudice. You see the way she puts it: 'Our fathers worshipped in this mountain; and ye say, that in Jerusalem is the place where men ought to worship.' Now that word translated 'ought' really means 'must'. Our Lord used the same word in the twenty-fourth verse: 'God is a Spirit: and they that worship him *must* worship him in spirit and in truth.' It means 'necessary'. In this woman's words you see the power that tradition and prejudice exercise upon us in the matter of worship.

I think this is true of many of us. We may have been worshipping, as we think, for years in a given way and manner. Why have we done that? There is only one answer: it is how we were brought up. We have never thought about it, we have never examined it, we have never asked any questions. It was the thing to do; it has always been done. We have inherited a custom, we have inherited a tradition, and, indeed, a prejudice. It is amazing to read the long history of the church and see the quarrels and the fighting that have taken place over the question of worship, and it has generally been entirely due to prejudice. People do not know why they belong to different sections of the church, they have never examined it. They were 'brought up to it' and therefore they not only assume it is right but prejudice comes in and they will fight for their tradition with bitterness and intensity. The history of the church is unfortunately full of such battles. And the result of our thoughtlessness, our ignorance and our prejudice is that a great deal of our worship is very hypocritical. But I am concerned to enter into the ways in which this entirely false approach to worship manifests itself in detail.

The devil, of course, is above all concerned to prevent our worshipping God. He does not mind our being happy as long as he can keep us from true worship. If the devil is likely to bring out all his reserves at one point more than another, it is when we are trying to worship God, either alone or as a company of people. And the only way to deal with him is to watch his every device, to be aware of everything that he has always done throughout the centuries, and is still doing, in his attempt to stand between us and the worship of God in spirit and in truth.

So what are these methods? Well one, of course, and it is before us very obviously here, is to make us think that worship is confined only to certain places. The Samaritans said that worship could only take place in the building they had on that mountain, while the Jews tended to say that you could only worship God in the Temple, in Jerusalem. Our Lord says that they were both wrong. He says, 'The hour cometh, when ye shall neither in this mountain, nor yet at Jerusalem, worship the Father . . . the hour cometh, and now is, when the true worshippers shall worship the Father in spirit and in truth.'

There are many people today who have imagined all their lives that they are Christians, and they only worship, as they think, when they enter a church or a chapel – nowhere else. For them, worship is confined to particular buildings, and they will go into those buildings when they want to worship God, as if they cannot get into contact with God out in the open air or anywhere else. I am not talking now about a public act of worship for exposition of Scripture, and for praise and so on, I mean prayer during a weekday, a lunch break – it must be in a particular place, as if God were confined to these places.

But not only is worship confined to certain places, still more pathetic, to me, is the way in which the worship of such people is determined and controlled by these different places. I mean something like this: when they are in a certain type of building, then they adopt a certain form of worship, but in another type of building, which they regard as not consecrated, they will behave in an entirely different manner. In one building they are serious and take on what they call 'a devotional air', and nothing must break into the ceremony and the form, but in a public building where there is also the reading of Scripture and prayer and so on, their behaviour is different.

Now these people claim to be worshipping God in both places. But they will do things, and admit things, and approve of things in the public building that they would look at with horror if allowed in a building that they regard as consecrated. And that just means that their worship is entirely governed by the type of building they are in. It is not worship 'in spirit', it is not controlled by the Spirit – it is controlled by the accident of place.

Another way in which this approach to worship shows itself is that such people only pray or worship at particular times. They may express amazement at Muslims, who pray at regular times, but really, in principle, they are no different. They may say their prayers morning and evening, and not pray at all during the rest of the day. God is worshipped at set times. Now that is not the biblical notion of worship, that is just a habit or custom that we have developed. There are certain things we do – we get up in the morning and we wash, and brush our teeth and so on, and we get on our knees and say our prayers – it is a part of the ritual, the routine of life. There it is, morning and evening, no more.

In other words, this whole conception of worship is mechanical, it is a matter of doing our duty, and, indeed, our very terms tend to show that. We talk about 'saying our prayers'. Saying our prayers! And that is what we so often do. 'Saying prayers' is not necessarily praying. It can be, but generally it is not. Or people talk about 'going to a building to say a prayer', while others say, 'Let us have a word of prayer', and the glibness with which they say it shows that they have no conception of, and have never stopped to think about, what they are doing. It is impersonal, it is just something extra that they do. It is cold, it is lifeless, there is no reality at all. Is it not true to say of so many of us that our supposed worship has been quite as mechanical as that?

And then another way in which this mechanical approach shows itself is this – and this is what our Lord explains so plainly to this woman – it is an external form of worship, it is all outside us. Consider the importance some people attach to posture – you must kneel, or you must stand. Again, they tend to vary the posture according to the building they are in. But is it not amazing to notice the extent to which the place we are in imposes itself upon us and determines what we do? Not that we have ever thought about it, we have just been brought up that way. Worship is therefore a matter of posture. When I am in a given posture, I am worshipping; if I am in a different posture, I am not worshipping. Is worship primarily a matter of posture?

Now these things must all be considered. Posture does come into worship but if it comes into it at all, it must always come in. If our posture is determined by our realization that we are in the presence of the living God and speaking to him, then that must always be the case. There must not be this variation, otherwise we are being inconsistent. But to so many of us worship is purely a matter of posture, it is nothing but form, ceremony, ritual. If you read the accounts of revivals, you will read of how 200 years ago, and still earlier, before the Protestant Reformation, there were a large number of priests in this country who literally could not pray. They could read prayers out of a book but they could not offer prayer themselves. And there are many people like that still. Such worship is entirely external, it is generally conducted by somebody else and we participate in the matter of posture, but do not enter into it any more than that.

Or let me put it to you like this to show that we must be balanced. There are other people to whom worship is a purely intellectual matter. To them, worship, if you analyse it, is really just an interest in a certain type of teaching. This has been, perhaps, the curse of nonconformity; it is the charge, at any rate, that has been brought against the Free Churches. It is said that we do not worship but only come to chapel to hear sermons. And that has been very true. That has been the danger of the Free Church type of service over and against the other, which is liturgical, external and elaborate. But, you see, it is assumed that the form and the ceremony comprise the worship and when people say, 'You nonconformists, you don't pay much attention to worship', all they really mean is that we do not read payers and that we do not have a set form and ritual.

But there is an element of truth in this criticism and we must face it. If we are only engaged intellectually and if we are only concerned about ideas of salvation, and if we are only interested in doctrine in and of itself, then we are not worshipping at all. The value and the purpose of all knowledge and all doctrine and all thought is to bring us into a living communion with God, and merely to come to listen to sermons is not worship. It ought to aid worship, it ought to end in worship, it ought to promote worship, but it is not worship in and of itself. And there is no question whatsoever but that the parlous state of the Christian church today, and therefore the state of the world, is due, on the one hand, to a mechanical, lifeless worship composed of forms and externals and, on the other hand, to an intellectualization that has turned the faith into a philosophy. People speak to one another and give one another their own ideas, and God is often not worshipped at all.

So these are some of the ways in which the devil, by insinuating wrong ideas of worship into our minds, would lead us astray. Let me come to another of the devil's methods, and this is very common at the present time – it is what I would call a purely psychological notion of worship. Here, again, is something that manifests itself in myriads of ways. For years I have known men who are only interested in what they call 'beautiful services'. And they are experts in these matters, liturgical experts. A service can be very beautiful: everything arranged perfectly, the right kind of music at the right point, and the beauty of the diction of the prayers.

Now the people who want this type of service are really interested in aesthetics and not in worship. For them, worship has to be beautiful and then they come out of a service and say they feel better. But if you ask them *why* they feel better, or in what way, all they can tell you is that somehow or another the atmosphere has given them a quiet or a happy feeling; they feel they have been in the presence of that which is beautiful. The Greeks worshipped goodness, beauty and truth, and so do these people, though they use the name of God. They approach worship in the intellectual way that I have been describing, and their only test is goodness, beauty and truth, sometimes applied quite unashamedly.

I remember once hearing a man preaching on the wireless on what he called 'prayer' and, as such people do, he had given his sermon a caption, which was this: 'Five minutes a day for health's sake'. And his point was that as you do your physical jerks for five minutes a day and your body feels better, so you just give five minutes a day to prayer and feel altogether better in your spirit. He told us to 'think beautiful thoughts' and he said that if we do, we will feel happier, and will be able to go through life with a lighter step. Then he went on to say that we could even do this with regard to other people. Is somebody ill? Well, now, concentrate your thoughts upon this ill person, think kindly of him, think beautifully of him, think of him in a healing manner, and somehow or another all this will be transmitted to him and he will feel better; he may not get well, but he will feel better. That was this preacher's idea of prayer and you can see that it is purely psychological.

Now you may be amused at that but examine your own prayer, examine your own notion of worship! The church today is full of this kind of talk. There are people who preach what they call 'positive thinking' and the idea is that you refuse negative thoughts, you cut them out. You must always be positive and always try to think beautifully as well as positively, and then you will feel better. And that is regarded as the worship of God – moral uplift.

Now these ideas are tremendously popular today and they are regarded as truly Christian. But the great question that arises is this: Are people who take them up doing anything other than giving themselves a psychological boost? Of course, psychological treatment can make you feel better and it is foolish to say that it cannot. But the vital question is: What are you concerned about – feeling better or coming into the presence of God? Psychological treatment masquerades as worship of the living God, it is not worship 'in spirit and in truth'.

Let me sum it all up by saying that the danger confronting us all is that of taking up religion and confusing it with true worship and the praise and adoration of God. There are many people – not so many in this country, perhaps, because it is not the thing to do – but there are countries where the percentage of the population that attends a service once a Sunday is very high indeed. But the question is: What are they doing? One is often given the impression that they have simply taken up religion. But why? It may be because they feel that religion will help them. There are many who are led by a sheer spirit of fear and go to a place of worship purely as a bit of insurance. They are afraid – afraid of Communism, afraid of bombs, afraid of another world war, afraid of what might happen – so they take up religion exactly like the poor old pagan whom they despise, the person who worships the moon, or the sun, or the stars, or anything else out of a spirit of fear. They do not know, but they feel that on the whole religion might help them, that it might be good for them. Yes, you can take up religion but if you do, you will not be worshipping God.

And then there are others who go to church and indulge in what they call 'worship' simply because they think that in this way they will acquire merit. They think God will be pleased with them and they will gain a good mark because they have done the right thing. They take up religion to placate God. They are like poor Saul, that first king of Israel. Saul was a man who fell into a terrible error. He had been given a commandment, God had told him what he was to do, but he did not do it. He thought he was improving on what God had said. He thought that by sacrificing the best of the animals instead of destroying them and offering them as a sacrifice to God, he would be pleasing God, but he was not. 'Behold', said the prophet to him, 'to obey is better than sacrifice, and to hearken than the fat of rams. For rebellion is as the sin of witchcraft' (1 Samuel 15:22–23). So often we have tried to buy merit, as it were, by externally worshipping God. We have balanced the wrong, the sin we have committed, by this good act of attendance at the house of God. We are supposed to attend the house of God but if you regard it as merit, you might as well have stayed at home. We come to worship God.

Well, now, those are some of the ways in which the devil deludes us and makes us think, like this poor woman of Samaria, that we are worshipping God when we are not the 'true worshippers' of whom our Lord speaks. This is what we must be concerned about. Are we true worshippers or not? So I ask you again in these terrible days in which we are living: Have you ever even thought about these things? Have you examined yourself? Do you know what you are doing? Why did you come to the house of God this morning? Is it true worship, or is it something else?

Then let me just say a word about the second of the two hindrances we are now considering. We have looked at wrong ideas of worship, and now we come to wrong ideas of God and, of course, this is the explanation of everything else. If our ideas of God are wrong, our ideas of worshipping him will be wrong. It is this that is at the root of all the hindrances to which I have referred, all the mistakes, all the defects in our worship and all the sin of which we are so guilty. Oh, that we might become true worshippers! You know, when we become true worshippers, the revival for which we pray and long will already have come. There is so much religion, so much form, so many services, so many meetings, but how much worship, how much contact with the living God?

What are our thoughts of God? Well, like the woman of Samaria, we think we know who we are worshipping, but our Lord is probably saying to us, too, 'Ye worship ye know not what.' Do we know? How often do we think about him? Is not this the tragedy with so many of us? We say, 'I've always believed in God.' And because we have always believed in him, we do not know what we believe about him.

'I was always brought up to believe so I always have.'

But have you? What is your God? Whom do you worship? What do we really know about God? The moment we examine ourselves, we discover that our ideas of him are very vague and often quite pagan. God, to so many, is nothing but some Force, some great Power. Others talk about him unhesitatingly as 'the ground of being' or as 'the Absolute' – some philosophical idea. And these self-same people who have such ideas of God are often ready to go through all the ceremonial and ritual and all the set forms, but there is a blank contradiction, there is no relationship. And that is why things are as they are. In our thinking about God, are we at all in advance of this woman, or in advance of the poor benighted, ignorant pagan?

Then we move on a bit: there are some who think of God as Creator only. It is this same idea of 'Force'. God as the great eternal Power that created everything – remote, unknown and unknowable, not concerned about us. That was the creed of so many before the Evangelical Awakening 200 years ago; it was called 'deism'. The deists believed in God, but they called him the great Watchmaker. He had made the universe and wound it up and then put it down and ceased to have anything further to do with it. Deists cut out all God's interventions in the world, all that is miraculous and supernatural; they excluded all that is really the essence of the Christian doctrine of salvation. God, the great Creator, was cold, distant and unconcerned. And there are many today who have no idea of God other than just that.

And then there are others whose main feeling is one of terror. I am thinking of the people who have said their prayers regularly and perhaps have gone to public worship, but the moment anything goes wrong, either with them or their loved ones, or some kind of calamity takes place, they turn against God; they blame him and have feelings of anger and hatred with respect to him.

Their idea of the God whom they think they have been worshipping is that he is against them, that he is some awful Power that delights in playing with helpless human beings and bringing suffering upon them, some fearful Being, towering over them, as it were, waiting to destroy them. Much of this has been said again this last week.[1] And many of the people who say this are church members who regard themselves as 'worshipping

---

[1] This, again, is a reference to the Aberfan disaster (see footnote on page 47).

people'. But in a time of crisis we reveal our true thoughts about God. We go on with our habits and customs and traditions, with our forms and ceremonials or our intellectualization. It is all right as long as everything is going well, but when we are in trouble, what are our thoughts of God then? What do we feel at that moment? That is always the test.

But then I must go right to the other extreme: there are people who are guilty of sheer presumption, of an easy familiarity with God. I have often referred to the people who say, 'Dear God', and talk to him easily, glibly and familiarly, and think that this is the hallmark of worship and of a truly evangelical position. But it is equally wrong. Why do I say this? Because the Scripture itself tells us that we must always approach God 'with reverence and godly fear' – not only in certain buildings but wherever we are. Whether we are in a so-called 'consecrated building' or in a public hall, God is the same, and we do not vary our approach to him according to the circumstances in which we find ourselves – 'for our God is a consuming fire' (Hebrews 12:28–29). There are people who seem to regard God as some indulgent father who is always ready to smile upon us, and the glory, the greatness and the majesty of God never seem to have entered into their comprehension at all.

And, finally, there are people who seem to think that God is just some kind of agency to help us; their whole notion of God is mechanical. 'Are you in need?' You go to the machine, you offer your prayer and then get out what you want. God is really nothing but some great reservoir on which we can draw. Their whole attitude to God comes out in the way they talk and in their actions.

And so the devil in his great concern to keep us from the true and living worship of God will drive us to one or other extreme.

He does not care where we are as long as we are deluding ourselves and not really worshipping God. Here is this poor woman of Samaria who can talk easily about the worship of God and yet knows nothing at all about it.

So I leave you with a great central question: When we get on our knees, what are we doing? When we come to public worship, who have we come to meet? Have we come to meet anybody except one another? If we have come to meet with God, what are our thoughts about him? Oh, my dear friends, this is the source of all our wrong thinking in the details; it is here we go wrong. If we only started with the living God and realized that everything we do is in relationship to him, it would control everything else. We take God for granted. Indeed, he is mentioned less and less. There are those who do not even pray to him but always pray, as they put it, to 'Jesus'. There are those who pray only to the Holy Spirit. God over all is forgotten or ignored.

The need of the hour, the personal need of every one of us, the need of the whole church of God at this time, is to know the living God. 'This is life eternal, that they might know thee the only true God, and Jesus Christ, whom thou hast sent' (John 17:3).

5

True Worshippers

Jesus answered and said unto her, Whosoever drinketh of this water shall thirst again: but whosoever drinketh of the water that I shall give him shall never thirst; but the water that I shall give him shall be in him a well of water springing up into everlasting life. (John 4:13–14)

I start with the question that I have already put to you: What is your religion? Is it something that you do or is it something that is happening within you? Have you got life? Have you got within you this 'well of water springing up into everlasting life'? To be content with anything short of that is so wrong, it is so sad. It is wrong and sad from our own personal standpoint. Why should we live as paupers when we are meant to be princes? Why should we be in a state of penury when we are meant to enjoy plenty? It is tragic to see Christian people who have remained children, still concerned about the first principles of the gospel of Christ, knowing nothing about 'the exceeding riches of his grace' (Ephesians 2:7), 'the unsearchable riches of Christ' (Ephesians 3:8). It is so sad that people should have all this offered them and still not know it, not possess it and not enjoy it.

Why is it that so many of us fall so far short of the fullness of life offered to us in Christ Jesus? And my suggestion is that in this story of our Lord's meeting with the woman of Samaria we are given in a remarkable manner an account of some of the main hindrances and obstacles to the receiving of this great gift that the Son of God came from heaven to this world to give us. So we have been looking at these issues – the prejudices, the spiritual dullness, the evasiveness and the wrong ideas about worship and about God.

But, come, let us look at this positively. Our Lord says: 'The hour cometh, and now is, when the true worshippers shall worship the Father in spirit and in truth.' So here is the great question: Are we true worshippers? Now what does this mean? First of all, 'true' means real, 'real worshippers'. We can think we are worshipping without being worshippers. But how do we become real, genuine worshippers?

Well, let us start with the question: What is worship? Here, surely, is a question that needs to be asked because we tend to use this word wrongly, indeed, we sometimes use it in such a vague way that it finally means nothing. The root meaning of the Hebrew word that is translated 'worship' in the Old Testament means 'to bow down'. And that is the essence of true worship; it means that we bow down in the presence of God.

I could illustrate this to you at great length. Take, for instance, the second of the Ten Commandments, which, after prohibiting us from making 'any graven image', goes on to say, 'Thou shalt not *bow down* thyself to them, nor serve them' (Exodus 20:4–5). And then there is a particularly clear illustration in connection with the temptations of our Lord in the wilderness:

Again, the devil taketh him up into an exceeding high mountain, and sheweth him all the kingdoms of the world, and the glory of them; and saith unto him, All these things will I give thee, if thou wilt fall

down and worship me. Then saith Jesus unto him, Get thee hence, Satan:
for it is written, Thou shalt worship the Lord thy God, and him only
shalt thou serve. (Matthew 4:8–10)

There is the basic idea in connection with this word 'worship' and it is very important that we should realize exactly what it means and its uniqueness.

Now the whole life of the Christian should be lived in the service of God but the whole life of the Christian is not worship. Worship is a very special act. Our whole life should be lived to the glory of God, but to say, therefore, that the whole of one's life is worship is just to confuse terms. Indeed, it is a very dangerous confusion. I am elaborating this point because there is a good deal of such teaching at the present time. There are people who say, 'If you have given your life to God and if you live the whole of your life to his glory, the whole of your life is an act of worship.' But that is just, I repeat, not only to confuse the meaning of the terms, it is to miss the special meaning of this word 'worship'.

Some people make the same error in connection with prayer. I know of very orthodox Christian people who do not have prayer meetings in their churches. Why not? It is because they have intellectualized the whole of the Christian faith. They spend their time in thinking about God and in trying to work that out in practice and in detail, and they say that the whole of one's life is prayer. But it is not. Prayer, again, is a special action. It is right that one's whole life should be lived for God. The demand of God is totalitarian and we should love him with all our heart and mind and soul and strength. Yes, that is all right – the whole of life is to be lived in the service of God – but these particular actions are special, and we are taught about them in a special way in the Bible itself. It is important, therefore, that we should realize this about prayer and about thanksgiving and the various aspects of worship.

So let me put it negatively to you like this. We often call a service like this 'public worship'; well, it should be, but it is not always. We can go through a whole service and, alas, there may have been no real worship at all. What we have done is all right but we have stopped short of true worship. To read the Bible is not, in and of itself, worship. I read the Bible and I meditate upon it and if I do this properly and clearly it should lead me to worship God, but I can read and meditate and not worship.

This is also true even of praying. Prayer is not of necessity worship. Again, prayer should always lead to worship, but you can pray and spend your time in prayer with petitions and even with thanksgiving without worshipping. And this, I think, is where so many of us tend to go astray; we forget the most important aspect of all. It is the same with singing. Singing should always lead to worship and if we are singing a hymn that is conducive to worship, and contains the vital element of worship, it may in itself be worship, but we must not assume that all hymn singing is worship.

Similarly, listening to sermons or lectures or addresses may stop well short of worship. A sermon worthy of the name should always lead to worship, and if it does not, it is a bad sermon. If it ends with the focus on the preacher or on some particular point he has made, it has missed the mark, missed the aim. No, the purpose of preaching is to lead us to worship God.

What, then, does worship mean? It means bowing down before God and adoring him for himself. That is why I am drawing a distinction between prayer and worship. Prayer, if it is just petition, is not worship; if it is just thanksgiving, it is not worship. You may be grateful, you may thank God for blessings that he has given you, but you can be so interested in and concerned about the blessing that you forget the one who has blessed you. The mark of worship is that it is this 'bowing down' before God himself, being concerned about God himself, apart from what he does and all the blessings we have had from him. Oh, it is just because he is God that we fall down before him, bow before him and adore him.

There are many examples of worship in the Bible. A perfect illustration of what I am trying to say is in the book of Exodus. When God gave a revelation of himself to Moses, Moses just fell to the ground and worshipped (Exodus 34:8). In exactly the same way, Joshua, after a revelation was given to him, 'bowed down before him' and simply worshipped God. This is what we read:

And it came to pass, when Joshua was by Jericho, that he lifted up his eyes and looked, and, behold, there stood a man over against him with his sword drawn in his hand: and Joshua went unto him, and said unto him, Art thou for us, or for our adversaries? And he said, Nay; but as captain of the host of the LORD am I now come. And Joshua fell on his face to the earth, and did worship. (Joshua 5:13–14).

That is worship; Joshua realized the Presence. He had not understood, he had been putting his question, concerned about this fight and this victory that he was desiring, as we do in so much of our praying. But when he realized the presence of God, he 'fell on his face to the earth, and did worship'.

I could give many other examples. There is a perfect description of worship in the fourth chapter of the book of Revelation where the 24 elders fall down before God (Revelation 4:10). That is worship. We must not forget this. Worship is very special; it is unique. It is the high watermark of the whole of our relationship with God. And our Lord is speaking about worship to the woman of Samaria. She has her mechanical notions – 'in this mountain' – similar to so many today, who can only worship in a given type of building with ceremony and ritual, as we have seen. All right, if these aids to worship help you, use them, but all I ask is this: Have they led you to worship? Do you know what it is to fall down in the presence of God and adore him because he is who and what he is?

Let me give you an example from the history of the church, just to show that genuine worship is not confined to biblical times, neither the Old Testament nor the New. Worship happens in every time of revival and reawakening, and you also find it in the individual experiences of people who have had some signal manifestation of the glory of God, who have been filled with the Spirit and have been greatly used of God. Let me give you this one illustration; you will find it in the journal of John Wesley for 1 January 1739. I often think that this was a more important and vital experience in the life of John Wesley even than that which happened to him at Aldersgate Street on 24 May 1738. He and his brother Charles, George Whitefield, Joseph Ingham and some others were in the room in Fetter Lane where they used to meet. They were having what they called a 'love feast', and had been together for hours. This is what Wesley writes:

> About 3 o'clock in the morning, as we were continuing instant in prayer, the power of God came mightily upon us inasmuch that any cried out for exceeding joy, and many fell to the ground. As soon as we were recovered a little from the awe and the amazement at the Presence of his majesty we broke out with one voice, 'We praise thee, O God, we acknowledge thee to be the Lord.'

They began to sing the *Te Deum*, which is often sung today. But you see the difference? They did not sing it because it was announced at a given point in the service. No: they 'broke out with one voice'. They knew they were in the presence of God – as

John Wesley put it: 'as we were continuing instant in prayer, the power of God came mightily upon us'.

Now there are people who not only know nothing about that, they even argue against it. They say, 'As long as you are a Christian, and have given your whole life to God, you do not look for anything further. You just go on serving God and do not worry about any experience.' Oh, what a tragedy! This is the object of all knowledge; if your theology does not bring you to something like this, it is of very little value to you. Nor is anything else you may have – all your diligence, all your assiduity in these matters, all your concern, are of no value. This is what we are meant to come to, this is worship. You bow down, you are humbled, you are silent, you are filled with awe at the presence of the majesty of God, and you can do nothing but adore him. Now that is true worship.

Now do not misunderstand me. I am not here to say, 'Stop praying, therefore, if you do not experience this.' No, no; that would be quite wrong. We must go on praying, we must do everything else. But all I am saying is that the real danger confronting us all is to stop at what we do, to stop at the means of grace, to stop at our own Bible reading, our own prayer, our own diligence. Oh, what a tragedy it is to stop at the means and to fail to see that God has provided them for us in order to lead us on to this act of worship, the high watermark! Go through your Bible, go through the biographies of the saints, and you will find that this is the highest point that any man or woman can ever reach. This is a foretaste of heaven. This is a glimpse of the glory. This is a touch of the everlasting. And this is the essence of true worship.

Oh, do not merge this into something general, do not miss this, do not lose it. The first thing we must realize is the essential character of worship, and we must be content with nothing less than this. It is right, it is our duty, to pray, but if we go through our lives just saying our prayers, without knowing anything of what it is to fall down before God – well, I am not saying it is not Christian, but it is Christianity at its very lowest. We are only just in the kingdom. But here are the riches, here are the glorious possibilities. Our Lord died on the cross not merely that our sins might be forgiven, but, as Peter puts it, he died, he gave himself for us, 'that he might bring us to God' (1 Peter 3:18). Or as Hebrews 10:19 puts it: 'Having therefore, brethren, boldness to enter into the holiest of all by the blood of Jesus . . .' What is your thinking about 'the blood of Jesus'? Do you stop at forgiveness or do you realize that this blood brings you into the Presence, into the holiest of all? There you realize the Presence and you worship him, you bow down before him.

So, as we have seen in the case of John Wesley, we find true worship of God in individual experiences and in the great revivals, which are but wonderful records of this very thing. You read about people who have been Christians for years and are good people, but suddenly the revival comes, the Spirit of God is poured out, and they are overwhelmed, as Wesley was. If ever there was a man who was non-emotional it was John Wesley. He was hard-headed, as it were, intellectual, the scholar – as far from emotionalism as you can imagine a man to be. But remember what he had to say about himself on 1 January 1739 – this is what happens in revival. There are these people praying, and suddenly the power of God, the glory of God, is manifest and the result, as in Wesley's description, is that sometimes they literally fall to the floor, overwhelmed. They feel they are nobody; they feel they are nothing; they feel doubtful as to whether they have ever been Christians at all; they doubt whether they have ever really prayed; they have never really worshipped. They have been taking things from God. They have been using Christ just to soothe their consciences. They have been interested only in the first principles of the gospel of Christ. But now they know – and that is revival. They have a sense of the glory of God, and there is nothing to do but to fall before him and to adore him in wondering worship and praise.

There, then, is something of a definition of what is meant by worship. I am concerned to show the uniqueness of this act, and to emphasize that we must be content with nothing less. Do not listen to people who say to you, 'You're a Christian, you've given your life to God, just go on serving, don't worry . . .' Oh, my dear friend, this other is what you are offered and if you are not anxious to obtain it, if you are not thirsting for it, if you are not longing for it, then all your understanding has missed the point, you are misinterpreting the Scriptures and the great Christian tradition.

So, then, how are we to come to the point at which we worship God? Well, the second principle that I find here is this – that we must submit ourselves entirely to the teaching of the Bible concerning this matter. Our Lord puts it like this: 'Ye worship ye know not what: we know what we worship: for salvation is of the Jews.' That is a most important statement from every standpoint. These Samaritans, as we have seen, only had the Pentateuch, that is, the five books of Moses – that is all they had of the Old Testament. They did not have the prophets and their teaching or the book of Psalms.

Now our Lord is including the Pentateuch in his statement here. But the Samaritans even narrowed the five books of Moses down to the mechanics – 'this mountain', and the particular ritual that they believed in. So there was this dispute as to whether you should worship here or there – you know the interest that is so common today in postures, in whether you should stand or kneel, and in ceremony and ritual, the mere externals of religion. Oh, the tragedy of it all! No, no, says our Lord, you do not know, you do not understand: 'We know what we worship: for salvation is of the Jews.'

In essence, that statement by our Lord means that we do not start with our ideas of worship. That is the danger. We do not take human ideas of worship, for the history of the church shows us so plainly that as the centuries pass, people always try to add to worship and to make up a system. That is why, when you look at a Church such as the Roman Catholic Church of today, and compare it with the Christian church as it is here in the New Testament, you feel you are in two entirely different realms. From where did they get all their practices? Well, they borrowed. They borrowed from Old Testament practices that, even according to the teaching of Scripture, should have been left behind, and they also borrowed from the mystery religions. And whenever the Roman Catholic Church went to a country that a Western nation had taken over, they believed it was right to incorporate into the act of Christian worship and praise various rituals from the pagan religions. So you have a kind of syncretism and you elaborate and elaborate and elaborate, and all the attention is paid to the externals and the trappings. But the vital and real aspects are never known and are never experienced at all.

So we must turn away from that. You can have textbooks that will teach you, it is claimed, how to worship, and there are people who are 'experts' in liturgies and litanies and so on. They say they can teach you, and it is all very beautiful and wonderful. Ah, but the question is: Does it lead to worship? Are you being moved by the stained glass windows? Are you being moved by the beauty of the diction or by the exact precision of the arrangement of the service? You can be moved aesthetically and we often fool ourselves and think that is a spiritual experience. But it is not. We must, I repeat, go back and receive our instructions from the Bible itself. Here and here alone do we find true worship.

Let me put it to you like this. Look at the trouble God took (if I may so put it) in instructing Moses with regard to worship.

I know that it was chiefly external there in the wilderness, but it was symbolic – it was all meant to convey to us the real, essential spirit. That is why our Lord says, 'The hour cometh when ye shall neither in this mountain nor yet at Jerusalem, worship the Father' (John 4:21). Not even in Jerusalem, because worship is something that is done 'in spirit and in truth'. But there in the Old Testament is this instruction, given simply to convey to us the idea that our own thoughts concerning worship are quite inadequate, and we must be instructed by God himself.

There is an incident in the Old Testament that surely ought to fix this in our minds once and for ever. It concerns an event that is called 'the rebellion of Korah'. There were three men in the camp of Israel – Korah, Dathan and Abiram. They were prominent princes and were very able men. But they became jealous of Moses and Aaron. They said, 'Who are these two men who arrogate unto themselves the right to dictate to us as to how we should worship? We know as well as they do how God is to be worshipped.' So they set themselves up and called a public meeting. Then they addressed the crowd and the people were very ready to listen to them and to agree with them. People are always ready to listen to new ideas, they are always after some novelty. And these men persuaded the people. They said, 'This is how we should worship, not the way that these others tell you.' And you remember what happened: God punished Korah, Dathan and Abiram and their households in a most terrible manner. The ground opened, and they were swallowed up and disappeared (Numbers 16).

But God did not leave it at that. He called Moses and said, in effect, 'I want this to be fixed and established in the minds and the hearts of these people and all their descendants after them.' And so he told Moses to bring together the twelve princes of the twelve tribes of Israel. Each prince was to bring a rod with him, and each man was to write his name upon the rod. Aaron was to bring a rod with his name on it for the house of Levi. They handed their rods to Moses, who put them in the tabernacle. Then God told Moses to leave the rods there overnight and look at them the following morning. God said, 'The man's rod, whom I shall choose, shall blossom' (Numbers 17:5) – he would be the man who was teaching the truth as God had given it.

So they did this, and when Moses went into the tabernacle in the morning, he saw that 'the rod of Aaron for the house of Levi was budded' (Numbers 17:8). And God told Moses to put 'Aaron's rod that budded' (Hebrews 9:4) in the ark of the covenant as a permanent 'token' or memorial. What was it to be a token of? Well, just this very question of worship. It is God who teaches us how to worship. It is he, and not men, who appoints the high priest. They may be very able and clever men such as Korah, Dathan and Abiram, it does not matter. It is God who is to be worshipped and he tells us how, and we must not deviate from the teaching.

So we must not be deluded by these appeals to beauty, order and arrangement. No, no; worship is a matter of 'spirit and of truth', and God has instructed us and his Son has instructed us. You see him here, you see him worshipping God. Of course, his whole life was lived for God, but you find that he would rise 'a great while before day' and go out to a solitary place to pray, or he would pray all night on a mountain (see, for example, Mark 1:35; Luke 6:12). He would go apart from the people in order that he might have quiet and silence, and pray and adore and worship God. Our Lord constantly did this and he teaches us to do the same. So we need the instruction that our Lord gave to the woman of Samaria at this point: 'Ye worship ye know not what: we know what we worship: for salvation is of the Jews.' We must look to him and listen to him, and be led by him, and by him alone. The moment we deviate from that, we have already gone astray.

Now those are the main matters with regard to worship that are taught here – I am confining myself to this record only. What about the true ideas of God? You cannot separate the two, they go together. As we think of God, so we will worship. So our Lord also gives this woman instruction with regard to God. He says, in effect, 'You do not know; you think you are worshipping God, but you are not, you are worshipping something created by your forefathers.' And, oh, how terrible it is to realize how often we have been guilty of the same self-deception.

Do we know whom we worship? Who is our God? What is our God? Have you faced these questions? You can go through life dropping down on your knees, saying your prayers, without having thought about who you are praying to. This is vital, for our ideas of God, as we have seen, can be so wrong, so false. We confine our worship to buildings. We think of God as mere Force, mere Power, 'the ground of our being', and all that the modern philosophers are teaching about him, even from Christian pulpits. It is such an utter travesty of the truth. That is why the church is as she is. No, no; we must take our teaching from the Lord himself, and here it is.

The translation of the Authorized Version in verse 24 is, 'God is a Spirit', but a better translation is, 'God is Spirit'. What a contrast this is with the localizing of God – 'this mountain', 'Jerusalem', particular buildings. No, no, says our Lord, get rid of that. 'God is Spirit: and they that worship him must worship him in spirit and in truth.' Now this is a subject that the early Christians, the apostles and other teachers, had a great fight about, even with the Jews; the Jews had gone astray on this matter. Take, for instance, the martyr Stephen; this is how he puts it in his great address to the Sanhedrin:

But Solomon built him an house. Howbeit the most High dwelleth not in temples made with hands; as saith the prophet, heaven is my throne,

*and earth is my footstool: what house will ye build me? saith the Lord:
or what is the place of my rest? Hath not my hand made all these things?
(Acts 7:47–50)*

And Paul has to make exactly the same point when he arrives in
Athens. Here are the Athenians with their temples all over the
place, and Paul says: 'I perceive that in all things ye are too
superstitious' – that means, 'too religious', worshipping these
various gods; and so the apostle puts it to them in these words –
'For as I passed by, and beheld your devotions, I found an altar
with this inscription, TO THE UNKNOWN GOD' – then
exactly like our Lord to the woman of Samaria, Paul says –
'Whom therefore ye ignorantly worship, him declare I unto you'
(Acts 17:22–23). He is the apostle; he is sent. He has been given
the revelation, the message and he does not argue, he does not
philosophize, he *declares*, and he has had experience of this
'living God' through the Lord Jesus Christ. 'Whom therefore
ye ignorantly worship . . .'

And, oh, beloved people, let us examine ourselves. Are we
worshipping 'ignorantly', or do we know the God whom
we worship? 'Him declare I unto you.' And then Paul says:

*God that made the world and all things therein, seeing that he is Lord
of heaven and earth, dwelleth not in temples made with hands;
neither is worshipped with men's hands, as though he needed
any thing, seeing he giveth to all life, and breath, and all things.
(Acts 17:24–25)*

There, then, is the great principle: God is Spirit. God is the
living God. He is completely unlike the pagan gods, which
were made out of gold and silver and wood. The people had to
carry their gods and put them on pedestals before they bowed
down and worshipped them. The people themselves were doing

everything; their gods were dead. The psalmist ridicules this in various places:

> *Their idols . . . have mouths, but they speak not: eyes have they, but they see not: they have ears, but they hear not: noses have they, but they smell not: they have hands, but they handle not: feet have they, but they walk not: neither speak they through their throat. (Psalm 115:4–7)*

But that is not God, the living God! God is Spirit. You cannot confine God to 'this mountain', or 'Jerusalem'. Why not? Because God is everywhere, he is omnipresent.

Listen again to the psalmist putting this in the glorious way that the psalmists do:

> *Whither shall I go from thy spirit? or whither shall I flee from thy presence? If I ascend up into heaven, thou art there: if I make my bed in hell, behold, thou art there. If I take the wings of the morning, and dwell in the uttermost parts of the sea; even there shall thy hand lead me, and thy right hand shall hold me. If I say, Surely the darkness shall cover me; even the night shall be light about me. Yea, the darkness hideth not from thee; but the night shineth as the day: the darkness and the light are both alike to thee. (Psalm 139:7–12)*

And that is what our Lord is teaching here: God is Spirit, and he is everywhere. Nothing is hidden from his sight: 'But all things are naked and opened unto the eyes of him with whom we have to do' (Hebrews 4:13). Oh, my language is inadequate! Even the Bible is inadequate! It can only give us glimpses and pictures. The glory of God, filling the universe: the universe he made. He is over all, reigning and ruling over all. 'For our God is a consuming fire' (Hebrews 12:29). 'God is light, and in him is no darkness at all' (1 John 1:5). God is Spirit, and his might and his power are illimitable. He is the living God, the Father of all spirits. God is.

And everything else has come into existence only as the result of his great and holy will, and the work of his power.

But we must not stop at that. If we did, we would all be filled with terror and alarm. 'God is a Spirit [God is Spirit]: and they that worship him must worship him in spirit and in truth.' You cannot conceive of it, but, thank God, our Lord went on to say something further to this woman. Do not forget that he also said this: 'The hour cometh, and now is, when the true worshippers shall worship the Father in spirit and in truth: for *the Father seeketh such to worship him.*' And this, of course, is the special revelation that has come through our blessed Lord and Saviour. In the Old Testament, we find the prophets almost grasping this truth – 'Like as a father pitieth his children' (Psalm 103:14), but they do not get any further. It is the Son who shows us the tender loving care of the Father. He is '*Abba,* Father'.

Then there is that beautiful phrase of the apostle Paul, which ought to thrill our hearts to the depths. He talks about 'the God and Father of our Lord Jesus Christ' (2 Corinthians 11:31). That is the idea of Fatherhood. The Father and Son are like one another. So we have the glimpses of Jesus – and, ah, that is the Father: 'He that hath seen me hath seen the Father' (John 14:9).

What does this mean? This is the wonderful truth – this is a part of this great offer of life that is life indeed – eternal life. We must ever remember that this great God, the Father of all spirits, God who is Spirit, the everlasting Creator, the God of glory, is one who, according to the counsel of his own will – and it baffles us and amazes us – has set his heart and his love upon us. Before the very foundation and creation of the world he knew you and he chose you; he has 'called you out of darkness into his marvellous light' (1 Peter 2:9). Why? So that you might 'receive the adoption of sons' (Galatians 4:5). You are not merely forgiven, you are adopted into the family of heaven, you are a child, you are a son of God. He is concerned about you, and he knows all about you.

There is a hymn that puts it so well:

Centre and soul of every sphere,
Yet to each loving heart how near.
                    Oliver Wendell Holmes

Do you realize that when you pray or when you worship? Before you begin to utter a sound, realize who God is. Remember the principle of recollection. You must stop, you must think what you are doing. And then you remember who God is – 'Centre and soul of every sphere', and you feel, 'I cannot do anything.' Then you remember, 'Yet to each loving heart how near.' 'The very hairs of your head are all numbered' (Matthew 10:30).

We should never go into the presence of God without remembering all this rich teaching that is given to us. Let me give you one more example before I close. It is in the sixth chapter of the Second Epistle to the Corinthians, where again this same matter is being dealt with:

What agreement hath the temple of God with idols? for ye are the temple of the living God; as God hath said, I will dwell in them, and walk in them; and I will be their God, and they shall be my people. Wherefore come out from among them, and be ye separate, saith the Lord

– it does not matter how small the number is –

and touch not the unclean thing; and I will receive you, and will be a Father unto you, and ye shall be my sons and daughters, saith the Lord Almighty. (2 Corinthians 6:16–18)

And the author of the Epistle to the Hebrews caps it all: 'Wherefore God is not ashamed to be called their God' (Hebrews 11:16). The Father! The one who 'loves you with an everlasting love', the one who is interested in you.

And Peter ends it all by saying: 'Casting all your care upon him' (1 Peter 5:7) – who? The Spirit! The eternal Spirit! 'The Father of lights, with whom is no variableness, neither shadow of turning' (James 1:17). Yes, all that is true of him. But as for you, you cannot 'cast your cares'. You have come into this service overwhelmed with grief, or sorrow, or shame, or disappointment. Life has been harsh and cold, the devil has tempted you and you are full of cares and anxiety, you have come burdened: 'Casting all your care upon him; for he careth for you.' God is Spirit, yes, but God is my Father in and through my blessed Lord and Saviour.

These are the preliminaries to worship, and until we are right about them, we shall know very little about 'the well of water springing up into everlasting life'. God grant that the particular hindrances – wrong ideas about worship, wrong ideas about God – may, in the light of the teaching we have seen, have been removed and that we now may realize the presence of God and know something about that experience that Wesley and the others had in Fetter Lane: 'We praise, we worship thee, O God.'

6

In Spirit and in Truth

The woman saith unto him, Sir, I perceive that thou art a prophet. Our fathers worshipped in this mountain; and ye say, that in Jerusalem is the place where men ought to worship. Jesus saith unto her, Woman, believe me, the hour cometh, when ye shall neither in this mountain, nor yet at Jerusalem, worship the Father. Ye worship ye know not what: we know what we worship: for salvation is of the Jews. But the hour cometh, and now is, when the true worshippers shall worship the Father in spirit and in truth: for the Father seeketh such to worship him. God is a Spirit: and they that worship him must worship him in spirit and in truth. (John 4:19–24)

We are considering the great offer of the Christian gospel in John 4:13–14. This passage shows us the condition in which we should all be as Christian people. Our Lord's promise is that whoever drinks of the water he shall give shall never thirst – *never thirst*! This is an all-inclusive word. It does not matter what the state of the world: whether we be at peace or in the midst of war, the Christian should never thirst. Christians are rendered immune to 'the slings and arrows of outrageous fortune', they are rendered immune to any trial or tribulation that may come across their path.

But the great question is: Do we know this? Have we this well of water springing up within us? Are we in a condition in which we never thirst? And we are considering some of the hindrances to obtaining this fullness of the Lord Jesus Christ, which gives perfect, enduring satisfaction. And at the moment we are dealing with the hindrance that arises from the fact that our ideas of worship and our ideas of God, the God whom we worship, tend to be so wrong.

We are looking, therefore, at verses 19 to 24 in this chapter, and we have seen that when we worship God, we reach the highest point that any human being can ever reach. But the great question is: Do we know what it means to worship? Do we know whom we worship? How tragic it is that people should be fooling themselves by imagining that they are worshipping God when they are doing something which, according to our Lord's own teaching, is quite valueless!

Now this subject is rather appropriate on this particular morning – Remembrance Sunday.[1] Various meetings are being held throughout the country – but what is their meaning? What is their value? This is an important question. If we believe that the only hope for the human race is knowledge of God and to be blessed by God, then nothing is more important than worship and prayer. Therefore we are dealing with the very essence of our modern problem and condition. Everything else is failing – there is no need to waste time in illustrating that. In spite of all the efforts of humanity throughout the centuries, the long history of what is called civilization is a record of failure, and the world is

---

[1] Held in Britain on the Sunday nearest to 11 November.

in as desperate a condition today as it has ever been, if not, indeed, worse; our only hope is in God.

And now today, Remembrance Sunday, people in large numbers are adopting at any rate the attitude and the posture of prayer and of worship; but have we not a right to ask whether they know what they are doing, whether it has any meaning for them? Is it real worship? The Samaritans thought they were worshipping God, and we ourselves know from our own experiences that we have often imagined that we have been worshipping God when we have been doing nothing of the kind from the standpoint of this teaching in John 4. I would be wasting your time and mine if I were to speak this morning on the state of the world, giving my opinion on the international problems and trying to tell statesmen how to solve them. That is not only folly, it is also sheer impertinence. I am in no position to do that. And when the Christian church spends a morning like this in that way, she is displaying her ignorance of her own truth. No, no; we are here to teach people how to worship, how to know 'the only true and living God', and nothing matters but this. Rulers and monarchs, potentates and powers, they are all mortal and are all going to die, but the soul remains face to face with God.

So to look at the meaning of worship is not only the right thing to do, it is the only relevant thing to do at a time such as this. This is the instruction that the world needs above all else, and it is only obtainable from the Bible. Our Lord says, 'We know what we worship: for salvation is of the Jews', and by 'Jews' he means all the teaching of the Old Testament. God had manifested himself to the Jews in a special manner, he had given his truth through them, they were to be the teachers of the whole world. It was to them and to them alone, that he had given his living oracles – 'the lively oracles' (Acts 7:38) – and there is no knowledge in connection with worship apart from that revealed to us in the Scriptures.

So we are tied entirely to this book, and we have already been seeing what worship really means. It means 'bowing down in the presence of God'. All that we do in a service such as this is meant to lead to that, and to the extent that it does not, the service has failed. We started with the true idea of worship and the true idea of God. 'God is Spirit' – and God, blessed be his holy name, is also 'the Father'. Our Lord teaches this woman that she must be clear and right in her ideas as to what worship is, and as to who and what God is. We must start with that.

The assumption is that we all know who God is and can go into his presence whenever we like. Some people only attempt this, or even think they are attempting it, once a year – Remembrance Sunday, and perhaps Easter Sunday in addition. But, my dear friends, that can be nothing but sheer blasphemy. If God is God, and if we know who God is and what God is, we should be constantly seeking his presence and bowing ourselves down before him. Not occasionally, but constantly. 'Thou shalt love the Lord thy God with all thy heart, and with all thy soul, and with all thy mind, and with all thy strength' (Mark 12:30). Everything we have and are, always, should be directed towards him and his eternal glory.

That is our starting point, but we do not end there. You notice that our Lord also teaches the woman what is necessary on our side, as it were. We start with a true notion of worship and a true idea of God, but still we must learn, we must all learn, how exactly we are to worship God, this 'only true and living God'. And our Lord's answer is that we must worship him 'in spirit and in truth' and this is what I now want to direct your attention to, but I take it in the reverse order. We must worship God in truth, and we must worship God in spirit. I take them in this order because we start with ourselves and we work up to what is ultimately most important of all.

What does our Lord mean by saying that we must worship God in truth? This is most important. Our Lord is contrasting true worship with that false idea of worship that characterized the life of the Samaritans. So he says worship must be 'in truth'. But what does this mean in practice? First of all, it means, of course, that worship must never be thoughtless. You cannot worship God in truth if you do not stop to consider what you are doing. I need not stay with this; we know what it means because we have all been guilty at this point. We can come to this house of God Sunday by Sunday and never realize what we are doing. We may come to meet one another, to have happy fellowship together. All right. But is that the purpose of this service? Do we stop to think? Do we ask ourselves why we are here? Thoughtlessness is the opposite of truth. Mechanical worship is the opposite of worshipping in truth.

When I say 'mechanical', I mean that we just come to church out of habit or custom or obligation. That is where you must be careful on a day like Remembrance Sunday. If your thoughts are governed by something other than God – by history, by events, by the past, by the future – if the occasion itself is more important than the act of worship, then no worship is taking place. To put anything before God is to cease to worship him; indeed, it is to insult him. But we are all subject to this; we are all prone to it. We do not stop, we do not think, it is the thing to do, everybody does it and so, like sheep, we do, too. There is national hypocrisy as well as personal hypocrisy.

All this, to me, is so important for this reason: today the masses of the people in this country, especially the so-called 'working classes', are outside the Christian church. Why is this? Here is our great problem. Our great question today is: Why is it that people will not even stop to consider Christianity? And you will find, if you talk to them, that their answer, in some shape or form, is that they have reacted against hypocrisy. 'A lot of nonsense,' they say. The church, unfortunately, has given the impression that she is on the side of power and of might; and, of course, this has been the stance of the church in every country. So we see the different countries praying for their success in war, both sides praying at the same time As a result, the average person thinks of the church as an adjunct of the state, a sort of court chaplain to whom authorities turn for prayer when they are in need or in trouble.

It is for us to tell people that worship must be true, it must be 'in truth'. It must not be thoughtless, it must not be mechanical, it must not be governed by anything other than our realization of whom it is we are approaching, what he is, and why we should always approach him 'with reverence and godly fear' (Hebrews 12:28). This should be obvious, should it not? And yet we are all guilty – is this not amazing? I am as guilty as any of you. How often have I got on my knees and said my prayers while my thoughts have been elsewhere; I have not stopped for a second to realize what I am doing. I have rushed through my prayers, as it were, so that I could go on to something else. But that is not worshipping God in truth. My dear friends, we had better start by – and let me put it in this way in order that you may remember it – we must start by stopping. You do not start speaking at once, you stop, you think, you recollect, you realize what you are doing; you ask questions, you prepare yourself. Worship is impossible apart from that. Never must it be thoughtless; it must always be 'in truth'.

And that leads me to the second point – and it follows, of course, from the first – worship must never be hypocritical, it must never be dishonest. Now there is always an element of thought in hypocrisy. That is why hypocrisy is actually worse than thoughtlessness. Up to a point, the hypocrite does know what he is doing, there is a deliberate element, and to the extent that it is deliberate, it is dishonest. There is an idea that somehow or another we can fool God, we can use him. We imagine that he is satisfied if we turn to him now and again when we need him and then carry on without him when everything is going well.

Again, we have all been guilty of this. We imagine we can use God. Individuals have thought this; nations think it. This is an expression of the national hypocrisy to which I have been referring. But, oh, how utterly foolish such an idea is! The biggest fool in the world is the hypocrite. He is in a much worse state and condition than the person who does not think at all, because though that person is saying, 'I'm going to turn to God, I'm going to worship him', for his own reasons, he has not stopped to realize what he is doing.

Now the Bible goes out of its way to give us teaching on hypocrisy and, quite apart from anything else, on its utter folly. It gives us instruction like this: 'Who shall ascend into the hill of the LORD? or who shall stand in his holy place? He that hath clean hands, and a pure heart' (Psalm 24:3–4). Or take David. David was an expert on this matter. Of course, he was a man of God, but he often played the hypocrite; his lusts, his passions, got the better of him. He had not finished with God, but he thought he was managing his sinfulness. Even in his greatest crime of all, his adultery and murder, David was happy; he thought all was well. Why? Because he had become a hypocrite. But David was brought to his senses and he passed through a hell, an agony of repentance, when God through his servant Nathan the prophet showed him the truth.

When David saw his sin, he said, 'Behold, thou desirest truth in the inward parts' (Psalm 51:6). God wants inward truth. He is never satisfied with an external appearance – which is, of course, the essence of hypocrisy. Hypocrisy is putting on a mask; it is putting on an appearance. It is satisfaction in the external and the outward and covering over that which is within. 'Thou desirest truth in the inward [innermost] parts', and nothing else will satisfy God. He knows all, he sees all, nothing is or can be hidden from his holy sight.

Or take it again in Psalm 66, where the psalmist says, 'If I regard iniquity in my heart' – if I regard it fondly; if I keep it there; if I shield it; if I go to God and my conscience accuses me but I cover over this thing and say, 'It's all right, I want this; I want God but I want this also', and make sure it goes on, then – 'the Lord will not hear me' (Psalm 66:18). I can fall on my face to the ground, it will not help me. I can take all the postures and the attitudes, all the appearances of worship, but it is no good: 'the Lord will not hear me'. So in a later psalm, we find the psalmist saying, 'Search me, O God, and know my heart; try me, and know my thoughts: and see if there be any wicked way in me, and lead me in the way everlasting' (Psalm 139:23–24).

Now that is it. Now this man is getting it right. He cannot trust himself, he cannot trust his own self-examination. He has been doing that, but he has realized that he is a hypocrite, so he does stop and think and question and examine himself. But he sees that even this is not enough; we are so subtle, and sin is so subtle with us, that we manipulate things to suit our own case. So he turns to God and says, 'Search me, O God' – you do it!

> I dare not trust the sweetest frame.
> *Edward Mote*

I cannot trust myself. God must examine me. This teaching runs right through the book of Psalms, and the prophets have exactly the same message: 'Who among us shall dwell with the devouring fire?' (Isaiah 33:14). These are the questions that the people of God have always asked.

Exactly the same teaching is found in the New Testament. In 1 Timothy 2:8, Paul says, 'I will therefore that men pray everywhere, lifting up holy hands, without wrath and doubting' – 'holy hands, without wrath'! Clean hands! Without pride, without a bitter national spirit, and without wrath against an individual. And 'without doubting'. And the author of the Epistle to the Hebrews has precisely the same teaching:

> *Having therefore, brethren, boldness to enter into the holiest by the blood of Jesus, by a new and living way, which he hath consecrated for us, through the veil, that is to say, his flesh; and having an high priest over the house of God; let us draw near*

– how? –

> *with a true heart*

– that is the first thing he emphasizes –

> *in full assurance of faith. (Hebrews 10:19–22)*

Notice the words, 'true heart'. This means, 'with honesty'. There must not be any dishonesty in our hearts; there must be 'truth in the inward parts'. The heart must be honest; it must be open. And without this, whatever we may do, individually or nationally, prayer and worship are a mockery, a sham, and God will not hear us. A 'true heart' is part of worshipping God in truth.

But we must go beyond that: the heart must also be a united heart, it must not be divided. The psalmist prays: 'Teach me thy way, O LORD; I will walk in thy truth: unite my heart to fear thy name' (Psalm 86:11). Now, again, we all know something about this 'divided heart'. The psalmist knew himself. He knew that there were parts of him that were right, parts that were wrong, parts that desired God, parts that desired evil. Oh, the apostle Paul has put it once and for ever for us when he says, in effect, in Romans 7: 'With my mind I acknowledge the truth of God's Law and its rightness, and desire to live it and to practise it, but I find another law in my members' (see verses 22–23) – here is the division.

The great problem in life is how to have a united heart, how to be whole, how to be unanimous, how to bring the whole of our being and personality to this great place in which we realize that nothing is higher or greater or more wonderful than worshipping God and praying to him. James puts this in terms of the 'double minded man' (James 1:8). It is the same teaching in the sense that it shows the division again. There can be a division, an uncertainty, in the mind as well as in the desire. Is this not one of the things that curses all of us, this difficulty of uniting ourselves, bringing ourselves into oneness, into unanimity? But only then will we be in the position of truth.

There must be no lies, nothing hidden, nothing unworthy: 'Unite my heart to fear thy name' – the whole being is involved. That is a part of worshipping God in truth. It is with 'all thy heart, and soul, and mind, and strength'. Nothing is left out. It is a total allegiance to God, a total seeking of God, a total prostration of one's self in 'the presence of his Majesty', as John Wesley put it in the quotation I have already given you. All this is absolutely essential.

And then this is what it all leads to: when we have realized something of what we are doing, and when we have realized what is true inside us, we come to a point in which we are humbled and contrite. Now look at the eloquent teaching that you find in the Bible itself – thank God for it. It is the paradox of the godly Christian life that this brokenness is what brings us immediately into the presence of God. This is directly opposite to the world's ideas. The world teaches us self-confidence, self-assurance; it gets us to take pride in ourselves, individually and nationally; in various ways it is always boosting our ego. And the more it does, of course, the farther it moves from God. God is 'the high and lofty One that inhabiteth eternity, whose name is Holy' who dwells 'in the high and holy place, with him also that is of a contrite and humble spirit' (Isaiah 57:15). Or take David. David was farthest from God when he was relying upon himself, his powers and prerogatives as a king, his right to get anything he wanted, even another man's wife. But he got back into the presence of God when his heart was broken and he said, 'A broken and a contrite heart, O God, thou wilt not despise' (Psalm 51:17).

We are not worshipping God unless we are humble, unless we are broken: this is an essential part of worshipping God in truth. And, surely, is not this the very element that is most lacking in us at the present time? The trouble with us as a generation of Christian people is that we are all so healthy, we are all so happy, as it were, so glib, so easy. How many 'broken' Christians do you know? How many humbled Christians? There is a type of Christian today who has never repented, who does not know what that means, who has never been humbled in the presence of Almighty God. There is nothing more terrible than to go into the presence of God in a self-confident manner.

Now you need not take my word for this, it is the clear teaching of the Scriptures. This pride was the whole trouble with the Jews at the time of our Lord; it was the whole trouble, too, with the apostle Paul. This is what he says:

> For we are the circumcision, which worship God in the spirit, and rejoice in Christ Jesus, and have no confidence in the flesh. Though I might also have confidence in the flesh. If any other man thinketh that he hath whereof he might trust in the flesh, I more: circumcised the eighth day, of the stock of Israel, of the tribe of Benjamin, an Hebrew of the Hebrews; as touching the law, a Pharisee; concerning

zeal, persecuting the church; touching the righteousness which is in the law, blameless. (Philippians 3:3–6)

And Paul used to go to God like that, thanking God that he was such a man. But then he realized that he had never worshipped, that that was a mockery, a sham, it was a form of blasphemy. That was the very essence of his conversion.

Our Lord gave us exactly the same teaching in his parable about the Pharisee and the tax collector who went up to the Temple to pray. The Pharisee marched right up to the front and said, 'God, I thank thee, that I am not as other men are . . . or even as this publican. I fast twice in the week, I give tithes of all that I possess' (Luke 18:11). He thinks that he is worshipping, that he is pleasing God; he feels all is well. What is the matter with the man? He has never been humbled! He is congratulating himself in the presence of God, he is thanking God that he is what he is and for the contrast of the tax collector.

But that is the opposite of worshipping in truth. That is a lie! No one can stand like that in the presence of God. It is the other man in the story who is worshipping, the poor tax collector who just gets inside the door and who is ashamed even to lift up his face to look to heaven, but beats his breast and says, 'God be merciful' – be propitiated – 'to me a sinner' (verse 13). That is the man who goes home justified, says our Lord. Why? Because here is a man who is humble, a man who realizes that he is nothing. To approach God with any kind of pride or self-satisfaction, whether it be personal or national, is a mockery of worship; in the sight of God, it comes near, I repeat, to blasphemy. Yet that is something of which we are all guilty. If we realize who God is, if we realize the truth about ourselves, we shall be humbled and broken.

Have you ever felt that you have no right to go to God? I do not think we have ever really been to God unless we have known that we have no right to turn to him, no right to pray. 'Who am I?' says David, in effect, at the height of his glory. 'Who am I, and who are my people that we should be building a house for your name and for your glory and for your worship? Who am I? I am unworthy and so are my people' (see 2 Samuel 7:18). That is worshipping in truth. It is realizing your utter nothingness and your entire dependence upon the love and the grace, the mercy and the compassion of God. He is to be approached 'with reverence and godly fear'. How much reverence and godly fear do you see today, with your bright and breezy services and everything going with a swing? My dear friends, let us come back to the Scriptures, God is to be worshipped in *truth*. You can never worship God self-confidently, though you are a Christian. Our Lord prayed like this: 'Our Father, which art in heaven, Hallowed be thy name' (Matthew 6:9). 'Holy Father,' he said when he prayed himself (John 17:11).

We come, then, confessing our sins, acknowledging our unworthiness, admitting that we are not worthy of the very least of God's mercies. That is the way to pray! That is worshipping in truth.

But then our Lord also says that we must worship 'in spirit': 'They that worship him must worship him in spirit and in truth.' There are those who say that this should be translated 'by the spirit' and there is really no difference between the two. This is the most important point of all. The other is preliminary; it is really dictated to us by common sense. But this is not, and we need the instruction of the Scripture. God's word comes to us and knocks us down, and if we have not been knocked down by the Scripture, then we do not know it.

But to go on to the positive teaching: worshipping in or by the spirit is emphasized everywhere in the New Testament when worship is being referred to. You get it in the Old Testament to a degree, but really, the Old Testament is prophesying this. Joel, you remember, in his great prophecy quoted by the apostle Peter on the Day of Pentecost saw this – this is what the prophets were given to see:

And it shall come to pass in the last days, saith God, I will pour out of my Spirit upon all flesh: and your sons and your daughters shall prophesy, and your young men shall see visions, and your old men shall dream dreams: and on my servants and on my handmaidens I will pour out in those days of my Spirit; and they shall prophesy. (Acts 2:17–18)

After the coming of the Saviour and the pouring out of the Spirit, the whole of worship will be revolutionized. That does not mean that the Old Testament worship was not right. It was, but it mainly comprised externals – the Temple, the tabernacle, the forms, the ceremonies, the ritual and so on. Now all that has come to an end. Zechariah has the same idea when he says that in those days God will shed forth 'the spirit of grace and of supplications' (Zechariah 12:10). The whole of the Old Testament points forward to this element of worshipping in the spirit, which is the great characteristic of the age after the coming of the Saviour.

There is a great statement of this by the apostle Paul in his letter to the Romans: 'I beseech you therefore, brethren, by the mercies of God, that ye present your bodies a living sacrifice, holy, acceptable unto God, which is your reasonable service' (Romans 12:1). Now a better translation there is, 'present your bodies a living sacrifice, holy, acceptable unto God, which is your spiritual worship' – 'spiritual worship'! A worship with the mind, a worship with the understanding, a worship in which the spirit is involved. It is not mechanical. Paul has a picture there. In the Old Testament the people presented the bodies of bulls and of goats and lambs, but now you present your own body as a living sacrifice. You present yourself. This is spiritual worship in contrast to the external, more mechanical and localized worship of the Old Testament.

But come back again to Philippians 3:1–3; here is a most important statement. The apostle Paul had to spend much of his time and energy in arguing against the so-called Judaizers, those Jews who were trying to add on something to the gospel of Christ. Yes, they had believed the gospel, they said, but they were adding circumcision, they were trying to bring in bits of the Law. Paul was always fighting this. He says to the Philippians:

> *Finally, my brethren, rejoice in the Lord. To write the same things to you, to me indeed is not grievous, but for you it is safe. Beware of dogs, beware of evil workers, beware of the concision.*

Then here it is –

> *For we are the circumcision*

– these people want you to be circumcised, but 'we are the circumcision'. Who is the circumcision? You are Gentiles, Paul says, but you are the circumcision. Why? This is the reason –

> *which worship God in the spirit [or by the spirit]*

– you see the contrast? It is the contrast between worshipping God in the spirit and worshipping him as the Jews wanted, in the Temple and by means of circumcision and so on –

> *and rejoice*

– not in the fact that we are Jews, not in the fact that we belong to a particular nation, not because of our history and our superiority to everybody else. No, no –

> *in Christ Jesus.*

And to make it doubly certain, Paul adds –

and have no confidence in the flesh. (Philippians 3:1–3)

None at all. Paul tells us that if any man has a right to that, he has. That is how he once was, but he has been delivered from all that: 'But what things were loss to me, those I counted gain for Christ' (verse 7). 'No confidence in the flesh': this is an essential part of this spiritual worship.

Or take what Paul says at the end of the Epistle to the Ephesians. Having told the Christians in Ephesus to put on the different parts of the whole armour of God, he says, 'Praying always with all prayer and supplication *in the Spirit*' (Ephesians 6:18). And nowhere is this put before us more clearly than in the little Epistle of Jude, where such wonderful things are crammed into a short space: 'But ye, beloved,' Jude says, 'building up yourselves on your most holy faith, *praying in the Holy Ghost*, keep yourselves in the love of God' (Jude 12). What could be clearer than that?

Or take it put differently but meaning exactly the same in Romans 8:

> *Likewise the Spirit also helpeth our infirmities: for we know not what we should pray for as we ought: but the Spirit itself maketh intercession for us with groanings which cannot be uttered. And he that searcheth the hearts knoweth what is the mind of the Spirit, because he maketh intercession for the saints according to the will of God. (Romans 8:26–27)*

Is not that true today? 'We know not what we should pray for as we ought.' What can you pray for in a world like this? What does this world deserve from God? Look at the way it has behaved; look at the way it is behaving. Look at the way in which, for over a century, it has asserted its intelligence, its understanding, its philosophy, its science, and ridiculed God. And look at the state of the world – two world wars, everything we are thinking of on this Remembrance Sunday and all that is happening at the present time. What should we pray for? Have we a right to pray for peace? Do we deserve peace? Does the world deserve peace? These are the questions we ought to be asking, and not in a spirit of self-congratulation, thanking God for this or that. No, no; we ought to be examining ourselves. Have we even a right to turn to him? 'We know not what we should pray for as we ought.' And when we really stop to think, we realize that we do not know. But here is this wonderful message: 'The Spirit himself maketh intercession for us with groanings which cannot be uttered.'

Thank God for this. This is what saves us, this is what enables us to pray at all. And you and I as Christians should be 'praying in [by] the Spirit'. And surely this is the greatest lack of all among us. Do we know what it means to pray in the Spirit? What is praying? I ask again: Is it just saying our prayers? Is it just turning into a building and 'saying a prayer', 'offering a prayer'? Or, as people put it, and we think sometimes that it is the hallmark of evangelicalism, is it saying, 'Let's have a word of prayer'? Think of the way in which that is said – as if to say, 'Let's telephone so-and-so, let's have a word with old so-and-so'!

Beloved people, is it not about time we began to think? Praying in the Spirit – what does it mean? Well, it means, initially, realizing our utter inability and our need of the Spirit. We cannot pray without him. It is impossible. And he has been sent and has been given in order to put us right on this matter. Again, in his letter to the Ephesians, Paul describes praying in this way: 'Through him we both have access by one Spirit unto the Father' (Ephesians 2:18). The three Persons in the blessed Holy Trinity are involved in this matter. The Spirit alone can get us into the right frame and condition for worship.

Would you dream of going to see the Queen at Buckingham Palace without preparing yourself? But how infinitely more important is it for us to prepare ourselves when we go to have an audience with the King of kings and the Lord of lords! You need instruction and advice from the courtiers if you are to be fit to go into the presence of the Queen. There is only one who can put us into the right frame to pray to God, and that is the Holy Spirit; and we must start by asking him to do this for us, to deal with our spirits. We need the understanding that he alone can give us so that we will 'know what to pray for as we ought'. We need his aid for such things as the ordering of our thoughts and the use of words. This is the beginning of praying in the Spirit – the realization that I cannot pray, that perhaps I have never prayed at all, and that it is only as the Spirit leads me, guides me, instructs me, shows me the way and prepares me that I can pray at all. So I begin to worship and to pray, relying utterly and absolutely upon the power of the Holy Spirit. That is the beginning of 'praying in the Spirit'.

7

Praying in the Spirit

Ye worship ye know not what: we know what we worship: for salvation is of the Jews. But the hour cometh, and now is, when the true worshippers shall worship the Father in spirit and in truth: for the Father seeketh such to worship him. God is a Spirit: and they that worship him must worship him in spirit and in truth. (John 4:22–24)

The question we are dealing with at the moment is: Are we true worshippers? Are we worshipping God in spirit and in truth? We have seen already that that implies a true idea as to what worship is and a true idea also of God. We know nothing of God apart from this revelation in the Bible. It is in that sense that it is true to say that 'salvation is of the Jews' – not of the Samaritans, nor of anybody else. Philosophers do not help us, they know no more than anybody else. We are entirely shut up to this revelation that God has been pleased to give of himself, first of all through the Jews, but more fully and more gloriously in and through his Son, our blessed Lord and Saviour, then through the church and through the New Testament Scriptures.

So we have been considering all that and now we come to this very practical aspect of the matter: we must worship 'in truth' and 'in spirit'. We have seen that to worship God 'in truth' means that we must come with honest, open, true hearts and allow ourselves to be searched and examined by him. But then we moved to this second aspect of worship, which is the most important of all – we must worship him 'in spirit'.

We have seen that our greatest lack at the present time is our inability to pray 'in the Spirit' (Ephesians 6:18). There is nothing that is more inadequate about us all than our prayer life, both private and public, and above everything else we need the ability to 'pray in [or by] the Spirit'. We said in the last study that to pray in the Spirit means, first of all, a consciousness of our utter inability. We realize that by nature 'we know not what we should pray for as we ought' but that 'the Spirit itself maketh intercession for us' (Romans 8:26), and he will help us to order our thoughts and our words. That is the beginning of praying in the Spirit. But that is not all. It also includes this: that we should be sensitive to the presence and to the leading and to the promptings of the Spirit.

Now the Christian life is represented in many places in the Scriptures as a life in the Spirit. That is particularly the favourite contrast drawn by the apostle Paul. You find it to perfection in the eighth chapter of the Epistle to the Romans where Paul talks of the difference between being 'in the flesh' and 'in the Spirit': 'For the law of the Spirit of life in Christ Jesus hath made me free from the law of sin and death' (Romans 8:2). The Christian life is prompted and determined by the Spirit, and this is particularly true of our praying. There is no area in which it is more important that we should realize the influences of the Spirit than in this very matter of prayer. One of the great functions of the Holy Spirit is to lead us, to instruct us, to guide us, and, indeed, to prompt us in prayer, and it is vital that we should realize this.

Our Lord in talking to the woman of Samaria is drawing a contrast between a mechanical, formal, external type of worship and that which is 'in spirit'. The Spirit alone can produce this, and he does so by working upon us, working in our minds and in our desires, working in the whole of our being. Here is something that is basic to our worship. Are we aware of the working of the Spirit within us, in particular in this matter of prayer? Are we aware of the Spirit calling us to pray, indicating to us what we should pray for and how we should pray? It is very clear, surely, in the teaching of the Scriptures that the Holy Spirit does this, and that this is what makes real worship and real prayer.

Let me put it in terms of that expression used in the fifth chapter of the Epistle of James where James says that 'the prayer of faith shall save the sick' (James 5:15). I am concerned here not with the question of healing, but with the character of the prayer. What exactly does James mean? People often get into trouble over this: that is why I am calling attention to it. A similar statement, which has often perplexed people and caused a good deal of misunderstanding is found in Mark chapter 11. We read here:

And in the morning, as they passed by, they saw a fig tree dried up from the roots.

– this is a barren tree that on the previous day our Lord had cursed –

And Peter calling to remembrance saith unto him, Master, behold, the fig tee which thou cursedst is withered away. And Jesus answering saith unto them, Have faith in God. For verily I say unto you, that whosoever shall say unto this mountain, Be thou removed, and be thou cast into the sea; and shall not doubt in his heart, but shall believe that those things which he saith shall come to pass; he shall have whatsoever he saith. Therefore I say unto you, What things soever ye desire, when ye pray, believe that ye receive them, and ye shall have them. (Mark 11:20–24)

Now here is a statement that is parallel to that made by James:

Is any sick among you? let him call for the elders of the church; and let them pray over him, anointing him with oil in the name of the Lord: and the prayer of faith shall save the sick, and the Lord shall raise him up; and if he have committed sins, they shall be forgiven him.

And James ends by saying:

The effectual fervent prayer of a righteous man availeth much. (James 5:14–16)

People have often taken those texts and have tried to work themselves up into a kind of certainty – 'When you pray, believe you have already received it . . .', and have tried to persuade themselves that this is true. But then the prayer is not answered, or, at any rate, not answered in the way that they asked or expected, and they are cast down and begin to doubt God and his promises. But all that is due to a misunderstanding of the meaning of this 'prayer of faith'. It seems to me that the only adequate explanation of these passages is that they are a typical example and illustration of praying in the Spirit. Praying in the Spirit is a prayer that is given to us by the Holy Spirit himself, created within us by him, and as he does this he gives us an absolute certainty with respect to it.

There is a very interesting statement that throws light on this back in Psalm 10: 'LORD, thou hast heard the desire of the humble: thou wilt prepare their heart, thou wilt cause thine ear to hear' (verse 17). Now you notice the sequence – 'LORD, thou hast heard the desire of the humble.' On what grounds does God hear? Well, here are the two steps: 'Thou wilt prepare their heart' and, 'Thou wilt cause thine ear to hear.' In other words, God prepares our hearts to pray, gives us the petition, if you like, and then he hears the petition that he himself has placed in our hearts. But the first move is to prepare our hearts.

There are many examples in the Scriptures of God answering Spirit-led prayer and to me they are both important and fascinating. Take, for instance, that great story to which James refers in his fifth chapter, the story of how Elijah prayed that there should be no rain, and there was none for three years and six months. Then he prayed that there should be rain, and the rain came. How did this happen?

Now there is something here that we, I am sure, tend to ignore completely. In 1 Kings 18, we read the dramatic story of Elijah on Mount Carmel, and how he stood alone against 850 false prophets, how God answered him, and how the rain eventually came. But we tend to miss or fail to notice as we should the first verse of that great chapter:

> *And it came to pass after many days, that the word of the Lord came to Elijah in the third year, saying, Go, shew thyself unto Ahab; and I will send rain upon the earth. (1 Kings 18:1)*

By now it is, you notice, the third year of the drought. But God starts the whole movement by telling Elijah that the rain is going to come. You find a similar statement in verse 41 of that same chapter, 'And Elijah said unto Ahab, Get thee up, eat and drink; for there is a sound of abundance of rain.' And that really means that before he began to pray for the rain, Elijah had already heard the 'sound of abundance of rain'. If you like, it was raining in his spirit while the drought was at its highest in the surrounding countryside.

So one of the actions of the Spirit in this whole matter of prayer is to give us the prayer. He leads; he directs. This, therefore, is the prayer of faith. It is not people whistling in the dark to keep up their courage, and trying to persuade themselves: 'I do believe, I am believing', while knowing the whole time that they do not believe. It is not that. There is an absolute certainty. There is calm; there is peace; there is confidence; there is great assurance. You can never work up the prayer of faith it is impossible. It is always given.

Let me show you this from another angle. Take the book of Acts and the accounts that are given us there of the miracles that were worked by the apostles. Now you notice that there were no failures – the apostles were always successful. They were not making experiments, they were men under commission, and on each occasion they were given a commission. Take the first one: Peter and John were going up to the Temple at the hour of prayer – they were going there to pray. Suddenly they were confronted by a lame man sitting at the Beautiful Gate of the Temple, and he was asking for alms. He was not asking for healing, but for a bit of help to eke out his miserable existence.

Then we are told, 'Peter, fastening his eyes upon him with John, said, Look on us.' What made them do that? There is only one explanation: they were given a commission, a command, to heal this man. All they had to do was to speak the word: 'In the name of Jesus Christ of Nazareth rise up and walk', and they knew that he would rise (Acts 3:1–11). It was not that they decided in cold blood, as it were, that they would heal this man and then worked up the appropriate faith. It was the other way round. The commission came, the Spirit guided and directed them, they spoke, and the miracle happened. And it is exactly the same with all the other examples that we are given in Acts of the wonderful works that were done by the apostles.

You and I cannot generate the prayer of faith. It is given. So one of the first things we must learn is that it is always a possibility; we are now in the realm of the Spirit and not in the flesh, the Spirit is in us and one of his functions is to deal with us in this matter and to guide and direct us.

Let me give you an example from history. If you read the accounts of the great revivals that have taken place in the history of the church, you will generally find that long before the revival broke out, one man, or a group of people, one woman, two women – I am thinking of specific instances – suddenly felt a call to prayer. In 1858, in Northern Ireland, it was just one man, a labourer, who suddenly felt a pressure on his spirit, a call to pray for the Spirit of God to come powerfully upon the churches in his area that men and women might be converted. Now this man did not suddenly decide that he would do this. There are so many people who read these stories and read about 'the prayer of faith', and then decide that they are going to do something similar. This always seems to me to be very pathetic. No, no; this prayer is given, people are moved and led by the Spirit.

Again, in America in 1857, one man began praying in the city of New York; or we read about the two women who prayed for D. L. Moody. In the Welsh Revival of 1904/5, a young man called Evan Roberts began to feel a pressure to pray. People could not understand it. He had always been a good man, like many others, always religious, always zealous, but the pressure came upon him and he could do nothing about it. It was the leading of the Spirit.

Now this precursor, this prayer before all the great revivals, is one of the most amazing factors in the whole economy of God and his dealings with men and women. Why does he work in this way? I do not know; nobody knows. But it is wonderful that he should bring us in, and, as it were, give us a part. God seems to be answering the prayers of his people, and, of course, in a real sense, he is doing that. But let us always remember that he has initiated the movement.

Elijah could hear 'a sound of abundance of rain' before he began to pray for the coming of the rain. So we must keep ourselves sensitive to the leadings and the promptings of the Spirit.

But we must not misunderstand this by coming to the conclusion that we just sit down until we are moved. That, of course, is the error of the people called Quakers. They do nothing; they might go through a whole meeting with nothing at all being said. They are waiting for the moving, the promptings, of the Spirit. That is to misunderstand the work of the Spirit because we are commanded to pray. It seems to me that we put ourselves on the direct road to being sensitive to the influences of the Spirit when we begin to pray. But we pray realizing our inability; we begin, if you like, by even asking the Spirit to move us, to guide us and to direct us. We must start praying by asking God to help us to pray, acknowledging our lifelessness and our dullness and our slowness.

We place ourselves at his disposal, telling him how unworthy we are and how dead we are, and asking him to enliven us, to quicken us and to move us. That is the best way; not to sit down passively and wait and do nothing until the moving comes. No, no; do all you can while realizing its uselessness; wait for him expectantly; ask him to come and keep on asking, yielding yourselves utterly to him. Then you will become increasingly conscious that he is moving you and leading and directing you. He will call you to pray – you will not understand it, you will not know why it is happening – but he will call you to pray for particular things, particular persons, and he will make you pray in a particular manner.

This is all important. Here is the entire contrast between true prayer and the mere formal, mechanical reading or reciting of prayers, a mere external worship. There is nothing more vital for us than that we should grasp this great contrast that our Lord is drawing here in the story of the woman of Samaria. So we do not think so much in terms of beautiful services as of spiritual services, the presence, the leading, the power, the promptings of the Spirit. We are aware that we are in the realm of the Spirit and that he is leading and directing us. Read your Scriptures bearing that in mind and you will see more and more clearly all I am trying to say.

Another part of the Spirit's work is this: it is he alone who can make us clear as to our only way of access into the presence of God. Do we realize the difficulty of praying and of entering into God's presence? That is why this phrase, 'saying your prayers', is so appalling. Do we realize what it means to go into the presence of God, into the holiest of all? We are all ignorant about this. People talk glibly about prayer and say, 'I don't believe in God any longer. I prayed and nothing happened.' That just betrays a complete ignorance of God. They do not realize who God is and what he is. They regard him as just some sort of slot machine out of which they can get what they want when they want it. No, no! When we considered what worship is, we also considered who God is, and this is an equally important question in connection with prayer. How can one pray to God at all? Well, apart from the instruction of the Holy Spirit, we will never know anything at all about this. How can we go into the presence of God?

> Eternal Light! Eternal Light!
> How pure the soul must be,
> When, placed within thy searching sight,
> It shrinks not, but with calm delight
> Can live and look on thee.
>
> Oh, how shall I, whose native sphere
> Is dark, whose mind is dim,
> Before the ineffable appear

And on my naked spirit bear
The uncreated beam?

Thomas Binney

Have you ever felt like that? Have you ever felt you have no right to pray? I do not think that we know much about praying if we have not had some kind of consciousness of our total unworthiness and inability. 'How should a man be just with God?' (Job 9:22). 'Who shall ascend into the hill of the LORD? or who shall stand in his holy place?' (Psalm 24:3). These are the all-important questions. How can it be done? Of course, we all go astray by nature. We think we can go in to God's presence: we have done a lot of good, we have not committed certain sins. Oh, how useless it all is! No, no; there is only one who can instruct us and that is the Holy Spirit. Paul puts it like this: 'Therefore being justified by faith, we have peace with God through our Lord Jesus Christ: by whom also we have access by faith into this grace wherein we stand' (Romans 5:1–2). Nobody apart from the Spirit of God can ever show us what it means to be justified by faith. He enlightens us so that when we go on our knees and feel cold and a stranger; or when our conscience condemns us and the law of God is thundering at us and we see our utter unworthiness so that we feel, 'I cannot pray, I have no right to pray, I have forfeited every claim upon God and his love', then the Spirit will come and say, 'You are justified by faith. You have peace with God. Your sins have been dealt with.'

Again, in the Epistle to the Ephesians, the apostle Paul reminds those people that at one time they were afar off:

For he is our peace, who hath made both one . . . that he might reconcile both unto God in one body by the cross [Jews and Gentiles], having slain the enmity thereby: and came and preached peace to you which were afar off, and to them that were nigh. For through him [the Lord

Jesus Christ] we both have access by one Spirit unto the Father. (Ephesians 2:14, 16–18)

The Spirit has enlightened us. He gives us the assurance that we can approach God, and we need this assurance every time we attempt to pray. You have to answer an accusing conscience before you can pray with any boldness and with any assurance. The author of the Epistle to the Hebrews expresses this aspect of the Spirit's work in his own striking manner:

Having therefore, brethren, boldness to enter into the holiest

– how? –

by the blood of Jesus, by a new and living way, which he hath consecrated for us, through the veil, that is to say, his flesh; and having an high priest over the house of God; let us draw near with a true heart in full assurance of faith, having our hearts sprinkled from an evil conscience, and our bodies washed with pure water. (Hebrews 10:19–22)

Now it is only the Holy Spirit who can do that for us. He answers the accusations of conscience and of the devil. He applies the truth to us. He makes it living, he makes it real, and so we are able to pray to God with this assurance. This is a very special part of the work of the Holy Spirit – he enlightens the mind. The apostle Paul draws this contrast in the First Epistle to the Corinthians: 'But the natural man receiveth not the things of the Spirit of God: for they are foolishness unto him' (1 Corinthians 2:14). How, then, do we know them?

Eye hath not seen, nor ear heard, neither have entered into the heart of man, the things which God hath prepared for them that love him. But God hath revealed them unto us by his Spirit: for the Spirit searcheth all things, yea, the deep things of God. (verses 9–10)

Furthermore, the Holy Spirit reveals God's truth to us by creating within us what the apostle Paul calls 'the Spirit of adoption': 'Ye have not received the spirit of bondage again to fear; but ye have received the Spirit of adoption, whereby we cry, Abba, Father' (Romans 8:15). Now that is real prayer. You do not bow down before 'whatever gods may be'; you do not bow down before some God who is distant; nor do you bow down in easy familiarity with a God whom you think is much nearer than he really is. No, no; we know what we are doing because the Spirit has created within us the Spirit of adoption. He has revealed to us God, the Father. This is exactly what our Lord is telling this woman of Samaria: 'the true worshippers shall worship the Father in spirit and in truth'.

My dear friends, when we get on our knees to pray, do we always know that God is our Father? We say, 'Our Father, which art in heaven' – do we realize its content? Do we feel that the Spirit of adoption is in us? This is praying 'in the Spirit'; it is a cry that comes up within us. Again, you cannot create this awareness: it is either there or it is not. You can utter the words, you can try hard to convince yourself, but you know perfectly well that you are failing, the doubt remains. It is the Spirit who puts within us a Spirit of adoption that cries out, 'Abba, Father'.

But now let us approach this matter from the practical side. We have considered the principles governing this whole matter of praying in or by the Spirit. But someone may say, 'But how may I know that I am praying in the Spirit?' And that is a very good question. I would divide the answer into two main headings. First, there are certain regular ways in which we may know this. I must not use the word 'ordinary' because there is nothing ordinary when the Spirit is acting in power, but I am trying to distinguish between his regular, and, under the second heading, his exceptional work – the ordinary and the extra-ordinary – because there is a real and definite distinction. You find it in the Scriptures, you find it in the lives of the saints and you see it also in the history of the church, in the distinction between the regular life of the church and the exceptional periods of revival and of re-awakening. It is important that we should draw this broad distinction because if we set out simply to test ourselves by the exceptional or the unusual, we will depress ourselves, and that is very wrong. So we start with the regular, the usual, the customary – or, at least, what should be the customary in the lives of all people who are living in the realm of the Spirit.

How, then, may I know that I am praying in the Spirit and not just saying my prayers or taking part in a public act in which prayers are read or recited ritualistically, or somebody offers a mechanical sort of extempore prayer – you can be as unthinking in extempore prayer as you can in read prayers.

First, for me, is the realization of God's presence. If you realize God's presence, you need not have any doubt, indeed, you will not have any doubt, that you are praying in the Spirit. This is absolute. To realize the presence of God is an absolute proof that you are praying in the Spirit, because it is the Spirit who gives us this blessed assurance. There is not only the assurance within us that cries out in a filial manner, 'Abba, Father', but there is also the assurance that he is present and he is listening. This is possible to all of us in the realm of the Spirit.

Let me give you some examples. In the Free Church of Scotland, about a hundred or so years ago, there was a saintly young minister by the name of Hewitson. He actually said this: 'I am better acquainted with Jesus than with any friend I have on earth.' A sober statement. He meant it: it was true. Or listen to another, a Methodist minister, John Brash, who lived into the present century. You do not always start in the way described by John Brash, and yet, with the Spirit, you can start in this way – there are many others who have been very young and yet have been able to say similar, and even greater, things. You will find many examples in the journals of Whitefield and others, but this is what John Brash wrote at the end of his life:

> I have a singular experience in prayer; no sooner do I open my lips to God and in particular business, than a voice more distinct than I can describe says, 'Your prayer is answered.'

He wrote that it did not always happen, but it happened with increasing frequency. Then let us go back three centuries to old Thomas Manton, one of the Puritans. On the subject of knowing that you are in the presence of God and that your prayer is heard, this is what he says:

> Sometimes the Spirit witnesseth it more explicitly by expression, as if it were said when you go to prayer, 'Be of good cheer, thy sins are pardoned, God is thy God.' At other times by impressions or more secret instincts.

What he means is this – and it is so true, of course – that there are degrees of this awareness of the presence of God. It can be vivid, dramatic, as it were, absolutely certain, and there are lesser degrees, but they are equally certain. There are some who say they are almost hearing a voice. Not that they hear an audible voice, but it is as if a voice were saying, beyond any question, 'God is your God; your sins are forgiven, your prayer is already heard.' Now nothing but the Holy Spirit can do that. That is something that cannot be counterfeited. This is the particular operation of the Spirit upon us, and the moment you ever have any realization of the presence of God, you can be certain that you are praying in the Spirit.

And that, of course, leads to the second aspect of praying in the Spirit, which is this – a sense of privilege! Being in the holiest of all. Being in the presence of God! Christian friends, how much do we know about this? There are people who use strange expressions with regard to prayer. They talk glibly of having their QT. They mean 'quiet time', but they refer to going into the presence of God as 'had my QT'! Do we realize what we are saying? Is not this the explanation of the poverty of our lives and the poverty of the whole condition and state of the church – why she is so ineffective and why things are as they are? It is no use saying, 'I pray; I've had my QT', or, 'I've had my DPM' – daily prayer meeting! How can these things be? What is the matter with us? Where do we get our ideas of worship and of prayer from? Certainly not from the New Testament. The New Testament writers describe praying as entering into the 'holiest of all' (see Hebrews 9:8).

I have often noticed the contrast between people who are punctilious about their outward behaviour at garden parties and similar occasions, and their behaviour when they are in the presence of God. They are more careful when they meet with one another than in their meeting with God. They watch the niceties at social events but assume that you can rush into God's presence. You go in and you go out; you have done it and off you go.

My dear friends, what do we know about worship? What do we really know about prayer? You are in the holiest of all and it is the highest, and to be admitted there, to have an audience, to have access, is the greatest privilege that can ever fall to the lot of a human being. These are the terms – 'Lord of lords, and King of kings' (Revelation 17:14; 19:16). It is not surprising, therefore, that the author of the Epistle to the Hebrews tells us always to serve God 'with reverence and godly fear: for our God is a consuming fire' (Hebrews 12:28–29).

Last week I said that the trouble with us is that we are all much too healthy. I say it again in a different form this morning. What is lacking among us is the fear of God. We are not humbled, we are not broken, we do not realize our unworthiness, we do not realize the greatness, the glory, of the privilege of even being allowed into the presence of God, leave alone to speak to him. But this realization is inevitable when the Spirit is leading us and preparing us and directing us. Prayer in the Spirit always realizes the presence of God, and there is an awe, there is a humility, there is a humbling – 'reverence and godly fear'.

'But,' you say, 'that's Old Testament.'

It is not. I am quoting the New Testament to you. That is exactly where people misunderstand these distinctions. God is still the same God. The Spirit gives me assurance of my acceptance, but that does not change my idea of God. It should deepen it, it should enhance it, and it has always done so in the case of God's true people.

Then, thirdly, any prayer in the Spirit is always a living act. We all know what it is to feel deadness in prayer, difficulty in prayer, to be tongue-tied, with nothing to say, as it were, having to force ourselves to try. Well, to the extent that that is true of us we are not praying in the Spirit. The Spirit is a Spirit of life as well as of truth, and the first thing that he always does is to make everything living and vital. And, of course, there is all the difference in the world between the life and the liveliness that is produced by the Spirit and the kind of artefact, the bright and breezy imitation, produced by people. I was once just a listener and a looker-on at a prayer meeting presided over by a lady who sat at a table with a ruler in her hand, and she was tapping the table, telling people when to stop and others when to start. She was controlling the meeting absolutely, and this was regarded as being highly spiritual!

And there are others whom I have known – God knows, we are all guilty in these matters – who have tried to work up something. I have known men in prayer meetings who, feeling that there was a dryness and a hardness and a coldness – and they were right in feeling that – wanted to take charge, and started singing choruses, singing hymns, trying to work it up. That is not life. The Spirit alone can give life. You and I can produce excitement. It is simple to produce excitement by speech, by singing, by many other methods, and this is constantly being done. So we have a bright and breezy prayer meeting and we think there is great vigour and power. But it is all mechanical, it is all human and carnal. The Spirit – he makes it real.

In chapter 2 of his first letter to the Corinthians, Paul asks: 'What man knoweth the things of a man, save the spirit of man which is in him?' (1 Corinthians 2:11). This is a vital chapter on this whole matter. How does one person communicate with another? Ah, Paul says, it is by a correspondence of spirit. You meet a man and you take to him and he takes to you and you are one. There is a freedom of communion, you can speak openly, you are making contact, as it were. It is the difference between polite formality at the great receptions when you all put on an appearance of affability and friendliness but may be thinking exactly opposite thoughts, and an immediate accord and unity.

That is it in the natural realm; now apply all this to the spiritual realm: this is what the Spirit always does. He makes our relationship with God living; he makes it vital; you know you are in the presence of God and you are speaking to God and listening to him. You are aware of a communion, a sharing, a give and take, if I may use such an expression. You are not dragging yourself along, you are not forcing, you are not trying to make conversation with somebody whom you do not know. No, no! The Spirit of adoption in you brings you right into the presence of God, and it is a living act of fellowship and of communion, vibrant with life.

So what do we know about praying in the Spirit? Is not this the need of the hour? Look at the state of the church, look at the state of the world. We have tried everything: we have exhausted our ingenuity, our methods, our endeavours, our organizations without even touching the problem. Nothing but a great outpouring of the Spirit of God will ever touch this situation. How does that come? It comes, as I have been showing you, in answer to our prayers. Yes, but the prayer is initiated by the Spirit of God. Do we know anything about this depth of prayer, this desire for such prayer, this realization of the presence of God, this living communion, this living prayer and worship and adoration? 'They that worship him must worship him in spirit and in truth.'

8

Characteristics of Praying in the Spirit

But the hour cometh, and now is, when the true worshippers shall worship the Father in spirit and in truth: for the Father seeketh such to worship him. God is a Spirit: and they that worship him must worship him in spirit and in truth. (John 4:23–24)

We have been considering the regular manifestations of worshipping or praying in the Spirit. The first is the realization of God's presence, and the second, which is invariable, is a great sense of privilege that we are admitted into the presence of God. There is nothing comparable to this. My third point is that when we are praying in the Spirit, the prayer is always a living act, the mechanical aspect has gone and it is living, it is instinct with life.

But now I want to add the next characteristic, which is always boldness and assurance. This is a most important matter. There is a kind of paradox here and yet it is something that is taught us right through the Bible. It is that God must be approached 'with reverence and godly fear' because he is 'a consuming fire'

(Hebrews 13:28–29) and because he is who and what he is – yet, at the same time, we are encouraged by the Scriptures to come into the presence of God with boldness and assurance.

Now this is a remarkable fact and it is in many ways the secret of true prayer, prevailing prayer, prayer that you can be sure that God will answer. Now there is a very notable example of this in the Old Testament, again in the case of Elijah on Mount Carmel. We have seen how Elijah is referred to more than once in the New Testament as a great example of what it is to pray, and there is a remarkable illustration here. He was opposed by some 850 false prophets, the King and Queen were against him, and he seemed to be standing almost alone. And here comes this great trial when Elijah challenged these false prophets to pray to Baal to see if he could answer them. Elijah said that the test should be this: he and they should each offer a bullock as a sacrifice. They should prepare their offerings, and put them on wood on their respective altars, but without lighting a fire under the wood. Then Elijah said: You pray to your gods and ask them to send down fire from heaven, and I will do the same, 'and the God that answereth by fire, let him be God' (1 Kings 18:24).

And the story goes on to tell us how these false prophets did all this and prayed to their god, Baal, from morning until noon, but nothing whatsoever happened, there was a dead silence. Then Elijah called all the people to come near to him, and he repaired the altar of the Lord 'that was broken down' and put everything in position for the sacrifice. And then we read:

And it came to pass at the time of the offering of the evening sacrifice

– now this is praying –

that Elijah the prophet came near, and said, LORD God of Abraham, Isaac, and of Israel, let it be known this day that thou art God in Israel,

> *and that I am thy servant, and that I have done all these things at thy word. Hear me, O LORD, hear me, that this people may know that thou art the LORD God, and that thou hast turned their heart back again. Then the fire of the LORD fell, and consumed the burnt sacrifice, and the wood, and the stones, and the dust, and licked up the water that was in the trench. (1 Kings 18:36–38)*

Now that is a great and a wonderful illustration of boldness and confidence in prayer in the presence of God. And the New Testament exhorts us to approach God with the same assurance. The author of the Epistle to the Hebrews, for instance, deals with this. He is writing to these Hebrew Christians, who were being persecuted and tried. They had been robbed of their possessions, they were passing through a very hard time and had become uncertain. Here again were people who were thinking of going back to the Jewish Temple, reverting to the old ways and customs. You see the relevance of all this for today? We are living in an age when everybody is telling us to go back to Rome, to something that was shed 400 years ago; the whole tendency is to go in that direction.

Now the difficulty with people who are subject to that kind of appeal is that they really do not know how to pray. To the extent that you need these artificial, external aids, you are defective in your spiritual experience of worship. Anything that drives us back to priests or forms or ceremonies or ritual – all that is indicative of the fact that we are reverting to an Old Testament rather than a New Testament view of worship. So here is the New Testament teaching as expressed by the author of Hebrews:

> *Seeing then that we have a great high priest, that is passed into the heavens, Jesus the Son of God, let us hold fast to our profession. For we have not an high priest which cannot be touched with the feeling of our*

infirmities; but was in all points tempted like as we are, yet without sin. Let us therefore

– watch that 'therefore' –

come boldly unto the throne of grace, that we may obtain mercy and find grace to help in time of need. (Hebrews 4:14–16)

Now you see the exhortation? Be certain, be sure, come boldly in the light of this truth unto the throne of grace. The writer says it again in the tenth chapter – the repetition is necessary because we are so slow to learn these lessons!

Having therefore, brethren, boldness to enter into the holiest by the blood of Jesus, by a new and living way, which he hath consecrated for us, through the veil, that is to say, his flesh; and having an high priest over the house of God; let us draw near with a true heart in full assurance of faith, having our hearts sprinkled from an evil conscience, and our bodies washed with pure water. (Hebrews 10:19–22)

The great thing there is the confidence in Christ and by his blood.

Now these are exhortations to boldness, to assurance, to confidence and we must examine ourselves in the light of this teaching. Do we pray like that? Remember, this is not a contradiction of the teaching about approaching him 'with reverence and godly fear', which the writer of Hebrews goes on to emphasize at the end of the twelfth chapter – no contradiction at all. A line is drawn here between a carnal confidence and a spiritual confidence. There are people who try to work up a carnal confidence and affect an easy familiarity with God. That is abominable and verges on the blasphemous. No, no; this is a spiritual confidence and it is based upon what God has already done for us in Christ. You will find that all these exhortations to boldness in prayer are always the result of this argument. I have given you two examples from the Epistle to the Hebrews: 'Having therefore' in the tenth chapter, and 'Let us therefore' in the fourth chapter. You do not just try to work yourself up or to persuade yourself; you take the doctrine, you accept it and work it out, and then you find that it leads to this confidence.

Let me give you another example of the same argument. It is in the glorious statement in the eighth chapter of the Epistle to the Romans, where the apostle Paul is dealing with the same truth. Like the Hebrews, the Christians in Rome were passing through a time of trouble. So the apostle starts by saying, 'I reckon that the sufferings of this present time are not worthy to be compared with the glory which shall be revealed in us.' All right; there is the ultimate, but the problem is, how am I to live in the present time? Here is the difficulty, and we have seen that Paul has told us that part of the answer is that though 'we know not what we should pray for as we ought: the Spirit itself maketh intercession for us with groanings which cannot be uttered'. Then he goes on to say, 'And we know that all things work together for good to them that love God' (Romans 8:18, 26, 28). It is this that gives us confidence.

But here is the best and most glorious statement of all: 'He that spared not his own Son, but delivered him up for us all, how shall he not with him also freely give us all things?' (verse 32). Now that is the basis of confidence and of assurance. It is an argument that you cannot turn back. If God has done this greatest thing of all for us in giving up his only begotten Son even to the death and the shame and the agony of the cross, 'how shall he not with him also freely give us all things?'

So you put all these arguments together. Are you conscious of sin and failure? Do you have a sense of shame? You need mercy!

So how do you get it? You go with boldness unto the throne of grace. If you are a Christian, you know it is a 'throne of grace'; you are going 'by the blood of Jesus'; there is the proof of God's grace. Or are you passing through a time of testing and of trial and feel the need of strength and of grace in order to keep going? Well, you will 'find mercy, and obtain grace to help in time of need'.

Now this boldness is always a manifestation of a true enlightenment of the Spirit. The Spirit is leading you and controlling you in all your praying. So, again, this is an infallible test of whether or not we are worshipping in the Spirit. There is no hesitation, no uncertainty, but with 'full assurance of faith' you go right into the presence of God; it is purely spiritual.

But that in turn leads me to another element that is vitally important – warmth. Warmth and ardour! Is not this something on which we should concentrate? Is there warmth in our praying – warmth in our personal praying, warmth in our collective praying together? You can have a very beautiful service but it can be cold, as cold and clean as an iceberg. You cannot help admiring it, but it does not move you or touch you. It has its own steel-like perfection, but that is not praying in the Spirit. Everything the Spirit does is perfect, it is full of light, it is full of knowledge, it is full of understanding. But, oh, there is something still more precious and valuable, and that is the warmth, the ardour.

When the Holy Spirit is dealing with us, he deals with the whole person. The Spirit does not merely deal with our minds, he deals with our hearts as well, and he deals with our wills. So often the tragedy in our Christian lives is that we divide ourselves up in a thoroughly wrong way. Some people are all intellect in their religion; others are all heart and no understanding, and so their spiritual lives become a riot and excess and ecstasy and false enthusiasm; yet others are only interested in the realm of activities.

But the Holy Spirit deals with the whole personality. Now, once more, this warmth is not something that you and I can work up. Many people have often tried to do that, many are still trying. There are people who even clap their hands or sing particular hymns and choruses in prayer meetings to try to work up some enthusiasm. But that is a direct assault upon the emotions, which should never be done; it is always bad. No, I am talking about something that the Holy Spirit does, and does invariably.

Let me take you back again to that incident on Mount Carmel: you remember that fire fell upon the altar. There is an element of fire in connection with Old Testament worship – the permanent fire upon the altar in the Temple is characteristic of what we are told about worship throughout the Old Testament. And this is equally true of worship in the New Testament. When the Holy Spirit came, 'cloven tongues like as of fire' settled upon the heads of the people who were assembled together in that upper room (Acts 2:3). Indeed, John the Baptist said in his prophecy: 'I indeed baptize you with water; but one mightier than I cometh, the latchet of whose shoes I am not worthy to unloose: he shall baptize you with the Holy Ghost and with fire' (Luke 3:16). Or take that incident in the fourth chapter of Acts when, after the release of the apostles, there was this falling of the power of the Holy Spirit, and the warmth and the ecstasy (Acts 4:31).

Let me put it to you in the words of Thomas Manton, one of the Puritans. He says: 'Fire from heaven to consume the sacrifice was the solemn token of acceptance heretofore [in the Old Testament]. Fire from heaven is the token still, even a holy ardour wrought in us by the Spirit.' And this is beyond dispute. You cannot read the book of Acts without being conscious of that warmth, that fire of the Spirit. The idea that the true Christian is someone who just has a cold intellectual understanding of theology is a complete denial of the whole of the New Testament. Nothing, in a sense, is further removed from the work of the Holy Spirit than a coldness, a lifelessness, a mechanical perfection. The Spirit always melts, he warms. He is a fire, a burning fire. You will find, in the history of many branches of the Methodist Church, both Armenian and Calvinist, that 'fire' was always a term that they were fond of using. They would say of a certain minister, 'Yes, it was at that point that he got his baptism of fire.' There were others who talked about 'a spirit of burning'. These were just terms that they used to describe this element of warmth that had come into their worship, this great characteristic of the operation of the Holy Spirit. An unintelligent emotionalism, however, is equally a denial of the whole of the New Testament. We must be careful, my friends, to observe this on both sides.

But let me give you another characteristic of the Spirit, and that is the element of freedom in prayer, the element of liberty, which, again, is a most thorough test. How much do we know about this? Do you know the difference between forcing yourself to pray, struggling to find words and thoughts, desires and expressions, and, on the other hand, being carried along, as it were, on the crest of a wave, while you are more or less a spectator?

Again, I could elaborate on this at great length. It is an important point. The Spirit is the Spirit of liberty and freedom as well as the Spirit of truth and love. Any man who has ever preached in a pulpit will know exactly the distinction that I am drawing. It is a most remarkable aspect of preaching. There is all the difference in the world between a preacher himself preaching, and a preacher preaching in the liberty and freedom of the Spirit. Yet any man who has ever experienced this will not only know exactly what it is but he will also know that, in a sense, it is impossible to describe it; it is just one of those things that you know.

And it is precisely the same with regard to prayer. So much of our praying is halting, lacking in any warmth and inspiration. We, as it were, are having to pray, and, of course, it is right that we should. I would again issue a warning that I am not teaching a passivity, I am not saying that you do nothing until you feel moved, until you feel like it. I say, pray that you may be moved, pray until you are moved. In 1738, when they were travelling somewhere between London and Oxford, John Wesley said to Peter Boehler, 'Yes, I see now this doctrine of justification by faith quite clearly, I have got it in my mind; but, you know, I don't feel it. Had I better stop preaching until I feel it?'

'No,' said Peter Boehler, 'go on preaching until you do feel it.'

And, of course, Wesley soon afterwards did feel it, in Aldersgate Street – and that is another illustration for you about this warmth and this fire that I have been talking about. There was John Wesley, in every respect, a cultured, able man, an honest man, a religious man, a man who had now come to see the meaning of justification by faith only; and yet he was cold; he was unmoved; he had not got a message; he could not preach; he was not an evangelist. But there, you remember, in Aldersgate Street, as a man was reading from the Introduction to Luther's commentary on the Epistle to Romans, suddenly he felt his heart 'strangely warmed', and it was the warming of his heart that turned the erudite, pedantic, scholarly John Wesley into a flaming evangelist. That is the Spirit.

But the Spirit not only gave John Wesley the warmth, he also gave him freedom. He had not been able to preach without reading his sermon, and when Whitefield suggested that he should preach in the open air, he not only thought it was wrong, he felt he could not do it. But he very soon found he could – at least, he was enabled to by the Spirit. The Spirit gives liberty; he gives freedom. 'Where the Spirit of the Lord is, there is liberty,' says

Paul (2 Corinthians 3:17) – not only moral liberty, but liberty in speech, liberty in prayer, liberty in every conceivable respect.

There is also a statement that Peter makes, in a slightly different connection, but he is really dealing with exactly the same experience. What is prophecy? Did the prophets give their messages as the result of their study and their observation and their thinking – is that it? No, no, says Peter, here is the truth: 'Knowing this first, that no prophecy of the scripture is of any private interpretation' – now that is often misunderstood. People think that Peter means that you cannot understand the prophecies unless you are inspired. But he is not talking about that, he is talking about the prophets and what they did. He means that prophecy is not a man's theory. Well, what is it? 'For the prophecy came not in old time by the will of man' – a prophet could not prophesy whenever he liked; a man could not get up and say, 'Now I'm going to prophesy' – 'but holy men of God spake as they were moved' – carried along, borne along – 'by the Holy Ghost' (2 Peter 1:20–21).

Those holy men of God were not only given understanding, they were also given liberty, they were given freedom – freedom of expression, the words came to them. And this happens in preaching, and it also happens in prayer. All I am saying is that when you do find this liberty and freedom, you can be sure that you are praying in the Spirit. Again, I add that you can pray without this, but this is the ideal, this is how we should always be praying.

There is an incident within my own experience that demonstrates this to perfection. I remember being in a prayer meeting that I used to attend regularly every week. On this occasion it was a hot summer's evening, as I remember well, towards the end of June or the beginning of July. We started at 7.15 and I asked somebody to open the meeting by reading the Scriptures and praying. He did so and one or two others took part in prayer. Everything was just as usual – it was always a good prayer meeting, it was always a benediction to one's soul – but then an older man stood up to pray, a man who was well known to all of us as a man who normally stumbled in his praying. He was a man who knew his duty and he took part in prayer, but – we draw these distinctions, do we not? – there was nothing very inspiring about the way he normally prayed. But this night, before he had spoken two or three sentences, I and everybody else present became conscious of the fact that something was happening. He was an entirely different man. His voice deepened and he was speaking with freedom and liberty, and an eloquence such as I had not only never heard from him, but perhaps had never heard from anybody else in prayer. He was a transformed man, entirely transformed, and the words were pouring from his mouth in perfect order, and with warmth and freedom and power and liberty.

The effect of that was that all the others felt the same power and the same freedom, and they went on praying non stop, one after another, without anybody being called and without any intermission until about ten minutes to ten. We were all conscious that we were out of time, in the realm of the eternal and the spiritual. What was that? That was praying in the Spirit. It was the liberty and freedom of the Holy Spirit. And that is what I am referring to. It can happen in a prayer meeting, or it can happen to you individually, in private, when you are 'led out', as it were. The Spirit takes hold of you and you are praying in the Spirit with glorious freedom and liberty.

Closely associated with this freedom, is the element of fervency. Here, again, is something that we need to recapture – this is why I am taking time over this subject. I am one of those who holds the view that nothing is going to save the church, and save the whole

of civilization, as it were, but a mighty spiritual revival, and it has generally been the case, as we have seen, that God has led people to pray before revival comes. So we must learn how to pray and what it means to pray in the Spirit. Mechanical prayers, lifeless prayers, in the end avail very little, but this kind of prayer really does achieve something.

I am not saying that without reason. I am talking here about 'fervency', and I get my authority from statements such as these: 'Epaphras, who is one of you, a servant of Christ, saluteth you, always labouring fervently for you in prayers, that ye may stand perfect and complete in all the will of God' (Colossians 4:12); and a verse we were looking at last week: 'The effectual fervent prayer of a righteous man availeth much' (James 5:16).

What do I mean by 'fervency'? It is, if you like, the element that is represented by the word 'Oh' – the exclamation 'Oh' coming out in our prayers. You find this constantly in the prayers of the psalmists and you will find it in many of our hymns.

> Oh for a heart to praise my God,
> A heart from sin set free.
> *Charles Wesley*

> O Spirit of the living God,
> In all thy plenitude of grace,
> Where'er the foot of man hath trod,
> Descend on our apostate race.
> *James Montgomery*

This 'Oh' expresses the longing that leads to fervent desire in praying. This fervency always happens when the Holy Spirit is leading our prayer, and when we are truly praying 'in the Spirit'. Can you not see the complete contrast between this and cold, mechanical, so-called beautiful prayers? That is the great contrast that our Lord is drawing here in his conversation with this woman of Samaria, the contrast between the kind of worship that he offers and the kind of worship that is not only true of Mount Gerizim but also of so much of the Temple, with its formality and ritual. No, no, he says: The time is coming and now is, when men shall worship neither here nor there, not even in the Temple.

Where, then?

Well, wherever there is a soul filled with the Spirit. That is what our Lord is saying. And when the soul is filled with the Spirit, the prayer is entirely transformed; it becomes moving and it becomes fervent.

Another great essential, and characteristic, of prayer in the Spirit is invariably the element of gratitude and thanksgiving, of praise and love. Paul puts this for us so plainly in Philippians chapter 4: 'Be careful for nothing' – whatever has happened to you, it does not matter what it is, do not be consumed with anxious care, do not let anything get you down, in nothing be anxious; but what, then? – 'but in every thing by prayer supplication with thanksgiving let your requests be made known unto God' – and then – 'And the peace of God, which passeth all understanding, shall keep your hearts and minds through Christ Jesus' (Philippians 4:6–7).

When the Spirit is leading our worship, the element of gratitude and of praise and of thanksgiving is quite inevitable because the Spirit has been sent to glorify the Lord Jesus Christ, and the Lord Jesus Christ says that he has come to glorify the Father. And when the Spirit enlightens us and moves us, he shows us what God has done for us, and all the privileges and excellencies of this Christian life.

So I would simply ask you a question: In your praying daily at home is there thanksgiving? Is there praise, adoration and worship? Oh, here is the characteristic of worship in the Spirit.

So much of our praying is nothing but petitions and perhaps grumblings. Let me put it in a phrase, and here is perhaps the best test of all by which you can tell whether or not you are worshipping the Spirit: Which are you more concerned about – the glory of God or your own wellbeing? If your prayers are self-centred and about yourself, there is not much of the Spirit. Now I am not saying that you should not pray for yourself: you should; you must let your requests be made known unto God, it is all right. All I am questioning is the relative proportion, the relative position, of your prayers for yourself and your praise of God. If there is no praise and thanksgiving at all, then is it praying at all? If the prayer is in the Spirit, then whatever your circumstances and mine, the element of praise and of thanksgiving will predominate.

There is a classic example of this prayer of praise in the book of Acts. Paul and his companion Silas arrived at Philippi, and in a very unjust manner they were scourged – their backs lashed with whips – and then they were thrown into prison, into the innermost prison, and their feet were put fast in the stocks. It was not only painful, it was a most undignified procedure. What was their reaction? 'And at midnight Paul and Silas prayed, and sang praises unto God' (Acts 16:25). Now only the Holy Spirit can enable one to do that, and he always does. Whatever your circumstances, he renders you immune to them and he gives you this knowledge of God. The saints have always testified to this, particularly in times of difficulty and trial. The Spirit has given them such understanding and such enlargement of heart that this is what they do.

Then there is that glorious example that we have already looked at in Acts 4. Here is the early church. Peter and John have only just escaped with their lives – they might very well have been put to death by the Sanhedrin. But the council has set them free on condition that they stop teaching and preaching in the name of Jesus. So the apostles go back to the church and tell them about these threats and all that has happened. And what is the result? It is this: 'They lifted up their voice to God with one accord' – they begin to pray.

And what do they pray about? Do they start with themselves and the fact that they are being threatened, and that Peter and John have just escaped by the skin of their teeth; do they start with their own predicament? Of course not. 'Lord,' they say, 'thou art God, which hast made heaven, and earth, and the sea, and all that in them is' (Acts 4:24). Worship! Adoration! Praise unto God! That is praying in the Spirit. And it was because they prayed like that, that the Spirit came upon them again in a great baptism of assurance, and of power, and of praise, and of thanksgiving, so that we read, 'and great grace was upon them all'. That is the characteristic of praying in the Spirit.

Now it is only the Holy Spirit who can do that. The devil can counterfeit many things: he can make you happy, he has often made us happy, all of us, has he not? He can counterfeit happiness all right, that is how he uses the cults. And drink can make people happy; whisky can make people happy. Yes, the devil can delude us, but there is one thing he not only cannot do, he never will do, and that is to make us praise God – never! He hates God too much to do that. So whenever you find you are praising God and thanking him and adoring him, and worshipping him with the whole of your being, you can be quite certain that this is no counterfeit.

The last characteristic I mention is that of persistence. Persistence! 'Labouring fervently', says the apostle Paul about Epaphras (Colossians 4:12). This is another characteristic of the New Testament Christian. It characterized the early church even before the Day of Pentecost. They met together, and they were praying together. These are the very words: 'These all continued with one accord in prayer and supplication, with the women, and Mary the mother of Jesus, and with his brethren' (Acts 1:14). The apostle Paul himself tells us many times how much of his life he spent in prayer: 'Now I beseech you, brethren, for the Lord Jesus Christ's sake, and for the love of the Spirit, that ye strive together with me in your prayers to God for me' (Romans 15:30). Strive! Labour! Agonize! Where has this gone to in our day? You find it in the Old Testament and in the New and if you read the history of the church, and of individual saints in the church, you will read about their agonizing in prayer. But we all think that the high watermark of spirituality is a brief prayer; there it is and it is left.

Take Paul again in Ephesians 3 – I am just giving you illustrations:

Wherefore I desire that ye faint not at my tribulations for you, which is your glory. For this cause I bow my knees unto the Father of our Lord Jesus Christ, of whom the whole family in heaven and earth is named, that he would grant you, according to the riches of his glory, to be strengthened with might by his Spirit in the inner man. (Ephesians 3:13–16)

Paul was always striving in prayer. He tells us, 'Pray without ceasing' (1 Thessalonians 5:17) – never stop, never quit praying. Our Lord had already said it all: 'Men ought always to pray, and not faint' (Luke 18:1). The alternative to fainting is praying, and we must keep going. Paul puts it again in Ephesians 6. Having described the elements of the whole armour of God, he ends by saying:

Praying always with all prayer and supplication in the Spirit, and watching thereunto with all perseverance and supplication for all saints; and for me, that utterance may be given unto me, that I may open my mouth boldly, to make known the mystery of the gospel. (Ephesians 6:18–19)

All I am saying to you, my dear friends, is that when the Spirit is leading us in worship and in prayer we keep on, we persist. So it comes as a practical test. Look at the state of the church today, look at the things that are happening, look at the state of the world. We know, not only from the Scriptures, but also from the past history of the Christian church, that when God intervenes in mighty revival, these things are dealt with. The church is arrested from sleepiness or going back to Rome, or whatever it is, and she is revived and renewed with power, and then the world outside is influenced – this can happen in no other way.

But how are we to get this revival of the church? Are we praying fervently? Are we praying persistently? Are we praying always? Are we crying out unto God to have mercy and to have pity and to come among us? We are all always called to prayer in this way: 'persevering thereunto', without intermission.

There, then, are some of the regular characteristics of praying and worshipping in the Spirit. The exceptional ones, I can give you very briefly, then you can work them out for yourselves. The apostle John, this same man whose Gospel we are considering, says of himself:

> *I John, who also am your brother, and companion in tribulation, and in the kingdom and patience of Jesus Christ, was in the isle that is called Patmos, for the word of God, and for the testimony of Jesus Christ. I was in the Spirit on the Lord's day. (Revelation 1:9–10)*

What is John talking about? Not something ordinary, but something quite exceptional. He was taken up by the Spirit, he was lifted up out of the realm of the ordinary, the human, the natural, and he was given the vision of spiritual things.

Similarly, in 1 Corinthians 14:14–15, the apostle Paul draws a distinction between praying with the understanding, and praying with the spirit. Now there is no doubt that he meant praying in tongues, but that is not essential. You can be lifted up into the realm of the Spirit and you do not quite know what you are doing. That is praying in the Spirit in an exceptional way. And this has so often been seen in times of revival: you have read it. People are gathered together in a church, in a building, and suddenly the Spirit comes and they begin to pray and they go on praying for hours, perhaps into the early hours of the next morning; but nobody is conscious of boredom, nobody is conscious of time; they are out of time. The Spirit has come down.

The incident I talked about earlier when I was in a prayer meeting, I would describe as a touch of revival – just a touch, enough to know what it is. And anyone who has ever known that will never be satisfied with anything less: a touch of revival in which you go on for hours and hours night after night. This has happened frequently, and I would regard such experiences as exceptional instances of worshipping and praying in the Spirit.

God grants us these exceptional experiences periodically. What for? Well, just to let us know what is possible. This humdrum, mechanical worshipping of God – oh, it is all right, my friends, I am not despising the day of small things, but I am saying that we are living in such terrible times of confusion and of danger to everything we hold dear and valuable that we ought to be praying without ceasing in the Spirit, fervently, warmly ardently. Surely this is the need of the hour. But we start, of course, by realizing that this is true worship. Oh, may God give us understanding in these things, may he give us honesty as we examine ourselves, but above all may he so fill us with his Spirit that we shall be 'true worshippers', worshipping the Father 'in spirit and in truth'.

9

Who Is He?

Jesus answered and said unto her, Whosoever drinketh of this water shall thirst again: but whosoever drinketh of the water that I shall give him shall never thirst; but that water that I shall give him shall be in him a well of water springing up into everlasting life. (John 4:13–14)

In those wonderful words in John 4:13–14, our Lord, let me remind you, gives us the essence of the Christian message. He had come into the world in order to give this 'well of water springing up into everlasting life'. This is put in many different ways in this Gospel. In chapter 1:16, the apostle John says, 'And of his fulness have all we received, and grace for [upon] grace.' It is the same thought. Our Lord also says later, 'I am come that they might have life, and that they might have it more abundantly' (John 10:10).

So the question we are examining is this: Have we received this fullness, this well of water, this life more abundant, this life that is life indeed? And in studying the story of this woman of Samaria, and especially our Lord's dealing with her, we have seen many of the mistakes into which we are all so liable to fall. It should be the supreme object of our desire and of our endeavour to get into the position in which we shall 'never thirst' and we have therefore been looking at those various hindrances to our receiving this life.

But now, having done that, and without forgetting these very important negatives, we turn to the positive aspect, and I ask: What is the one great essential in this whole matter of receiving this life, this fullness?

There can be no difficulty about answering that question. The one absolute essential is submission to the Lord Jesus Christ and, as I tried to show in introducing this whole subject, we have here a wonderful account of how our Lord brought this woman to that position. From her original self-confidence and glibness in her talk about worshipping here and there and so on, he brings her to the place of final and complete submission. There is no hope of obtaining this fullness, this life, unless we believe in him, unless we listen to him.

But here arises the great question: Who is he? Who is it who speaks in this way? There is no hope for us until we are clear about who our Lord is. Without doubt, the main cause of trouble at the present time is ignorance with regard to the person of Jesus of Nazareth, this person of whom we read in these Gospels and who occupies the central position in the whole of the Bible.

Now the answer to this question is, of course, the message of this very season, this season of Advent.[1] It is his advent. It is all about him. So what better can we do during this season – for the next three Sundays, including Christmas Day itself – than consider who he is, why we should listen to him and why we should submit ourselves to him? It is only as we discover the answers to these questions that we shall be ready to submit ourselves to him and

---

[1] This sermon was preached on 4 December 1966.

thereby obtain this great and glorious blessing, which, after all, he came to give, and which is the central and essential message of the Christian faith. And here again, in this story of the conversation between our Lord and the woman of Samaria, we are given great light and instruction on who our Lord is. This is a most comprehensive story: I say again that the great central elements of the Christian faith are all here in a most wonderful manner.

Now you notice how this woman feels after the truth, moving from step to step. At first she imagines she is just meeting a stranger. He is obviously a Jew and she is rather amazed that he, a Jew, should have anything to do with her, a Samaritan and a woman. We have seen all that. But as our Lord leads her on, she begins to feel after the truth with respect to him, so let us look again at these verses. After our Lord has shown the woman that he knows all about the immoral state in which she is living – 'Thou hast had five husbands; and he whom thou now hast is not thy husband: in that saidst thou truly' – she says to him, 'Sir, I perceive that thou art a prophet.' Now she is advancing, she sees he is a prophet. And then in verses 20 to 26, we see how our Lord leads her on from stage to stage until the final statement, 'I that speak unto thee am he.'

Now at this point we can only introduce this subject. But let me say a hurried word in passing. Is it not amazing and extraordinary that it was to this Samaritan woman, a sinful woman, that our Lord should have made this great revelation with respect to himself? Thank God, there is no hope for any of us but for this. He himself said so often: 'I came not to call [save] the righteous, but sinners to repentance' (Luke 5:32), and that is the glorious hope of the gospel. It is to this woman, of all people, that he makes this tremendous disclosure.

But before we come to this final conclusion, we must consider the steps that lead to it because it is very important, if we are in any trouble about all this, that we should realize the error of the partial positions, however good they may seem to be. Now, as I said, here I can only make some introductory and preliminary remarks, but let us see some of the general principles that are taught here in this whole matter of our approach to the person of our Lord Jesus Christ.

The first principle is this: the exclusiveness of the Christian message. Indeed, I will use a stronger term – its intolerance, its claim for an absolute uniqueness. Now that comes out in these words: 'Ye worship ye know not what: we know what we worship: for salvation is of the Jews.' There it is, the statement of our Lord himself – 'salvation is of the Jews'. This is, of course, a crucial statement, and a principle that is asserted constantly in the New Testament. We find it repeatedly in this Gospel of John. Later on our Lord says, 'I am the way, the truth, and the life: no man cometh unto the Father, but by me' (John 14:6). Exclusiveness! Uniqueness! He says in chapter 8 of this Gospel: 'I am the light of the world' – that is an absolute statement, an absolute claim – 'he that followeth me shall not walk in darkness, but shall have the light of life' (John 8:12). And elsewhere he contrasts himself with other people who had offered themselves as shepherds: 'All that ever came before me are thieves and robbers . . . I am the door' (John 10:8–9).

And when we go on to the book of Acts, and come to our Lord's first preachers, the people he had set apart and called, to whom he gave the message, we find that they make exactly the same claim. Peter, for instance, preaching in Jerusalem and addressing the Jewish authorities, the members of the great Sanhedrin, says:

This is the stone which was set at nought of you builders, which is become the head of the corner. Neither is there salvation in any other: for there is none other name under heaven given among men, whereby we must be saved. (Acts 4:11–12)

It is an absolute statement.

There is another example in Acts 17, where the apostle Paul does not hesitate to say, 'Whom therefore ye ignorantly worship, him declare I unto you' (Acts 17:23). Again, this is an absolute claim, and the apostle repeats it in his epistle to the Corinthians: 'For other foundation can no man lay than that is laid, which is Jesus Christ' (1 Corinthians 3:11).

Why am I giving you all these quotations? Because this is the essence of the modern difficulty. People today resent this kind of statement, and I believe that the church is as she is because of the confusion that is so obvious at this very point – the uncertainty with regard to this person and his uniqueness, and to the exclusive claim of the Christian faith. We pride ourselves on living in what we like to call an age of tolerance. 'Hah!' we say. 'People in the past used to be so narrow-minded, so dogmatic, but we, with our enlightened ideas, have come to see that there is a little bit of good in everything. We must not say that Christianity alone is right; we must not say that the other great world religions are wrong; we must not make a claim for exclusiveness.' In fact, there are some who go so far as to say that if you do, you are denying the Christian message. The whole idea of Christianity is that it is an easy tolerance, a spirit of give and take, a readiness to agree with everybody, as long as people are out for that which is good and helpful and so on.

So we are living in an age that talks about a World Congress of Faiths, and says we are all one, and it does not matter whether people even deny the whole of the Bible – it is still all right because there is some truth in everything. That, it is said, is the Christian spirit. And so Christianity becomes nothing but a kind of moral uplift, and the season of Christmas and of Advent is nothing but a time when we talk about goodwill and brotherliness and trying to get together and to understand one another.

But I am here to remind you that that is nothing but a complete contradiction of everything we find in the New Testament, and especially from the lips of the Lord Jesus Christ himself. Now I am emphasizing this, not because it gives me pleasure to do so, in one sense, but for this reason – that there is no hope of salvation apart from this gospel. Our Lord here says, 'salvation is of the Jews', and that is the claim that is made right through the Old Testament. This is most important and it is why we must keep on reading the Old Testament. There what we find is this: there was this nation, the Jews, among a number of other nations. Well, now, who were they? This is the vital point. Their great claim, the claim of all their teachers, patriarchs, psalmists and prophets, was always that they were the people of God, that they were not like other nations, that they were different. And their whole story, of course, demonstrates that fact. God made a nation for himself. He took a man called Abraham, called him out of paganism when he lived in Mesopotamia, in Ur of the Chaldees, and turned him into a nation in a miraculous manner. That is the story, that is the history.

So God was making a new nation, a people for himself. And that is why he gave them the Ten Commandments. He said that they must not live like everybody else, they were his people: 'Ye shall be holy: for I the LORD your God am holy' (Leviticus 19:2). The other people burnt their children as offerings to their gods, they ate all sorts of food and so on, but the people of Israel were told to live as a separate people, a people for God's particular possession, a part of his great purpose. And it was to these people alone that God was pleased to reveal himself, and give the Scriptures.

Now the apostle Paul, in writing to the Romans, makes use of that argument. In what way is the Jew different from everybody else? That is the question that was being put to him. He was preaching now to Jews and Gentiles alike, and so he was exposing himself to the charge: 'What advantage then hath the Jew? or what profit is there of circumcision?' And he replies: 'Much every way: chiefly, because that unto them were committed the oracles of God' (Romans 3:1–2) – by which Paul means the Old Testament Scriptures. The other nations did not have this revelation from God. They did not have the Ten Commandments and the Law or this great succession of prophets and psalmists and so on. No, this was unique to the Jews. And that is what our Lord means by saying, 'Salvation is of the Jews.' The Samaritans had the first five books of the Bible, the five books of Moses, but they had nothing else; and our Lord is saying, in effect, 'You are defective, you have not got the full truth, you do not have the real understanding, and you have misinterpreted even what you have got because you lack the teaching of the prophets.' 'Salvation is of the Jews': it is exclusive to them.

Now this is crucial; either this modern thought is correct or the Bible is correct. You cannot accept both because they are in blank contradiction to one another. The essence of the Christian message is this: 'Neither is there salvation in any other' (Acts 4:12). 'Salvation is of the Jews' – and this one who came out of the Jews, Jesus of Nazareth.

Notice how the apostle Paul puts this in Athens, of all places. Athens! The Mecca of all the philosophers, the cultural centre of the then civilized world, the great city, proud of its wonderful succession of teachers. All honour to them! I am not here to detract in any way from the greatness of Greece and especially of her great thinkers. But let us not forget this: it was to them that the apostle Paul said, 'Whom therefore ye ignorantly worship, him declare I unto you' (Acts 17:3). You remember why he said that? He found their city crowded with temples and altars – the god of war, the god of peace, the god of love and so on. And then there was this extraordinary altar with this inscription on it: 'TO THE UNKNOWN GOD'.

You see, the Greeks had got as far as to discover that there was a God behind the gods whom they thought they knew, that there was a mysterious power at the back of them all; they were seeking after him but they could not find him. They were worshipping him, as they thought, but in ignorance. Why? Because they were not Jews; they were relying upon their own thoughts, upon their own reason, their own understanding. So the apostle Paul did not hesitate to say to them, 'Whom ye ignorantly worship, him declare I unto you.'

And of course Paul makes exactly the same point to the Corinthians: 'For after that in the wisdom of God the world by wisdom knew not God, it pleased God by the foolishness of preaching to save them that believe' (1 Corinthians 1:21). That is a categorical statement: 'The world by wisdom' – by philosophy, human understanding, human thought and endeavour – 'knew not God.' I find it astounding that the modern world can be talking as it does, and, alas, that so much of the modern church can speak as it does, in the light of all this. Here are our Lord himself and his chosen apostles who founded the Christian church, standing on this one position that no one by seeking can ever find God (see Job 11:7); that the world with all its wisdom and all that it has, can never arrive at a knowledge of the truth.

Now the world has failed to do this; and it is most important that we should realize that. This is not a matter for argument, nor even for discussion: we are facing facts. The ancient world with its master philosophers failed to arrive at a knowledge of God, and all the philosophers who have lived ever since have not advanced at all upon the thinking of Plato, Socrates, Aristotle and the rest.

And what is it we know today? What is the purpose of falling back upon human thought and ideas? Religions such as Confucianism, or Buddhism, or Hinduism, or Islam are all man-made religions. What is the point of turning to them and saying that there is a little bit of truth in them, that they can all help us with their insights and we must all pool our ideas? It is a denial of this gospel. It was because the world in its wisdom had completely failed to find God that God manifested himself and the truth concerning himself, first through the Jews, his people, and then supremely in this one who came from the Jews according to the flesh, Jesus of Nazareth, the Son of God.

I have to start with this because, I say again, it is absolutely crucial. If you do not confine yourself entirely to this book and its revelation, you will go astray in this question of God, and of worshipping God, and of obtaining this well of water springing up into everlasting life. If you are in any doubt with regard to Jesus of Nazareth, you will never get this blessing. I put it as categorically as that.

And, again, the history of the world substantiates the contention to the very hilt. Look at all the great people who have lived throughout the centuries, able, good men and women, endowed with amazing propensities, many of them, the great people of history; but read their biographies, or their autobiographies, and you will find that however towering and shining their genius may have been, however wonderful and glittering their achievements, if they did not know this person, if they did not submit themselves to him, their lives were unhappy and disappointing. They went out into darkness, they had nothing to comfort them. Even at their greatest moments, they were the victims of circumstance and chance, and from the height of their achievements, they could be cast down to the depths of despair and despondency.

I would almost make it compulsory for all people, especially Christian people, to read the biographies, autobiographies and memoirs of people of this century who have mixed with some of the greatest men and women history has ever known – read them! And you will discover that no one will ever have this well of water, this peace, this satisfaction, this rest of soul and of mind and of spirit, except they get it from Jesus of Nazareth.

The Christian faith makes an exclusive claim, and that the church should be doubtful or hesitant about it, is astonishing: that is to deny the very foundation of the whole of the faith. 'Ye worship ye know not what: we know what we worship: for salvation is of the Jews.' There is no hope in the world apart from the message of this book; there is no knowledge of God apart from the revelation that we are given here. I say we must stand on it. Not that we should be dogmatic and arrogant, but if we have any concern about the souls of men and women, if we are sorry for those who are unhappy, why, it is our duty to tell them not to look anywhere else; this, and this alone, holds out any hope, and this is full of hope. The exclusiveness of this message!

But I want to go on to show you why this message is exclusive and why it must be exclusive. My second principle, adduced from this teaching, is that the message that we have here is a message of God acting, God doing things, and that is what explains the uniqueness. This is the essence of this great message. Peter preaching at Jerusalem on the Day of Pentecost made this point, and, indeed, even the people, all the strangers who were at Jerusalem on that occasion, in listening to the apostles speaking in these strange languages, made the same point: 'We do hear them speak in our tongues the wonderful works of God' (Acts 2:11). And that is what Christianity is about – the wonderful works of God!

Go back to your Old Testament – what is it about? The tragedy is that people think of the Bible as if it were a book of philosophy, or a book of religion, a book just for the purpose of teaching us certain religious ideas. Of course, that is included, but before that, this is a book of the actions of God. 'In the beginning God created . . .' (Genesis 1:1). That is how it starts. Read the Old Testament and you will find this: God doing things! Of course, people do things, too, but all they do is generally wrong and they get themselves into misery. We would not be here if we had only the actions of men and women.

Adam and Eve were perfect. God put them into Paradise and all was well. So how has the world become as it is? It is because of their rebellion and disobedience. They brought down misery on themselves and on their world. And ever since they have been making a mess of things, thinking they were going to put everything right but never succeeding, buoying themselves up on a false optimism, always crashing down in the next century.

That has been the story of civilization from the very beginning, and there would be no hope for us were it not that God has acted. There are the man and woman in misery in the Garden, hiding behind the trees, and God comes down. They hear the voice of the Lord God in the cool of the evening, and he tells them what he is going to do – and here is our only hope. This is the preparation for the coming of the Son of God, this is the anticipation of the gospel: the seed of the woman shall bruise the serpent's head (Genesis 3:15). God is going to do it.

And that is what you find in the whole of the Old Testament, as I have been reminding you. God creating a nation, God giving the Law, giving his people the knowledge and the information. It is all the activity of God. And look at the story of these chosen people, these particular people whom God makes his own. Constantly they went astray; they were fools enough to envy the other nations! 'Give us a king,' they said. 'Other nations have kings; give us a king.' So God gave them a king, and kings led them into endless trouble.

The people were always lusting to live as the surrounding nations lived; they wanted the same kind of immoral life. They did not want to keep to God's laws. So they always got themselves into misery and into trouble. Other nations came and conquered them and they would very soon have been finished altogether as a nation and as a people had God not delivered them time and time again. He did it when they were in Egypt; he did it when they were in Babylon. This is the whole story: God acting, God teaching them – the mighty acts of God.

And what was it that happened at Bethlehem so long ago? The answer is this: 'God so loved the world, that he gave his only begotten Son' (John 3:16). 'When the fulness of the time was come, God sent forth his Son, made of a woman, made under the law' (Galatians 4:4). It is God! And that is what makes this message unique. All the so-called great world religions are the result of human efforts and endeavour, as we have seen, and so are the philosophies, the art, all the thinking, every endeavour. And not one is exclusive; not one is unique. For anyone to claim uniqueness and exclusiveness and finality is sheer arrogance.

But here we are not dealing with what people have done; the whole point of this message is that God has done this. That is why it is absolutely exclusive. You do not put God into competition with human beings. So why do you want to put the Christian religion into a World Congress of Faiths? Or why do you turn to philosophy for help? You are bringing God down to a human level and putting the Son of God into competition with men. It is blasphemy! We must be intolerant about this.

Look at what the apostle Paul says to the Galatians. He had been preaching in Galatia and churches had been established as the result of his mission there. But other teachers had come and had said, 'Oh, yes, Paul was all right, but of course he doesn't understand it all. He didn't tell you that you must be circumcised. But you must, you know! It's not enough just to believe the gospel, you must be circumcised as well.' And the Galatians thought this teaching was an advance, and they were turning to it. But this is how Paul deals with these ideas: 'Though we, or an angel from heaven, preach any other gospel unto you than that which we have preached unto you, let him be accursed' (Galatians 1:8). Now that is a very strong statement. If a man comes to preach to you, he says, I do not care if he is an angel from heaven, if he preaches a gospel that does not tally with mine, let the curse of God be upon him; he is a liar!

If you are concerned, therefore, about receiving of our Lord's fullness, you must come to the position in which you accept this exclusiveness – and you must do so because it is God acting, God offering. The gospel must be the only way because it is the action of God himself. There, then, is our second principle.

But that, in turn, of course, leads on to the third point: the historicity of this message. We must emphasize that this is a message that is based solidly upon, and comes solely from, historical events. People sometimes put this question: Could anyone still be a Christian if it could be proved that Jesus of Nazareth had never lived at all? Now if you are ever presented with that question and hesitate for a moment, then you are denying the faith. There is no hesitation about this. This faith depends entirely, completely, solely upon the historical fact of Jesus of Nazareth and the truth concerning him.

This, again, is crucial. We are not dealing here with a teaching. 'Believe me,' says this Jesus of Nazareth. 'I am he.' The gospel is all about a person. If we do not understand that during the season of Advent we have missed the whole point. Christianity, I say again, is not a system of ideas, it is not just a school of thought that you put by the side of other teachings, religions – call them what you like – it is not that at all. Of course, there is teaching, but it is teaching that is derived from a person. Much more important than what he taught and said, is the truth about the person, what that person did, what happened to him. We are not saved by ideas. To think that we are is a complete denial of all of the Christian faith.

There are so many people today who seem to think that Christianity is just a collection of beautiful thoughts. I am not surprised that the vast majority of the people of this country are outside the church. I am not a bit surprised. They have been told by the church herself that Christianity is nothing but beautiful thoughts, that even if Jesus of Nazareth had never existed, and all the facts about him were wrong, you would still have Christianity! But the man in the street has a certain native logic, and he says, 'Well, I can read books and get beautiful and uplifting thoughts at home. If Christianity is just being kind and pleasant and brotherly, with vague talk about goodwill and fellowship, especially at Christmastime, then I don't need to go to church and I don't need a Bible. This is something that everyone, unless they are really beyond the pale, believes in and likes to do.'

Yet that is what is passing as Christianity today. All of us are already Christians; we do not know it, but we really are, and the business of preaching is just to tell us that we are all right, that God loves us all and all is well. So you do not need this special person, Jesus of Nazareth – his birth in a stable is unnecessary. We are told that it does not matter whether it is true or not. It does not matter whether or not he died on the cross. This meeting at a Communion table is all rubbish, a bit of folklore.

But that is to deny completely the very essence of the Christian faith. This *is* all about a person. The Communion table tells us that this person was nailed to a tree, his body was broken, his blood was shed. That is history; that is fact. It is as much fact as Julius Caesar conquering this country in 55 or 54 BC, whichever date the latest historian has decided on. Our Lord's life and death and resurrection are absolutely basic and central. If these events did not take place, then I have no message, and there is no salvation. But our Lord says, 'Salvation is of the Jews.' 'I am he.' The Christian faith is historical, and centres round this person.

I am only giving you general principles, but you must be clear about them. They control the very approach to our Lord. It is no use saying, 'I'm interested in Jesus' – I want to know what your approach to Jesus is. Are you just regarding him as a great human teacher, philosopher, moral aesthete? Ah, if you are, you might as well stop being interested in him. You must take him as he is revealed in the Scriptures.

So I come to my last point for now. I have been emphasizing the historicity of Christianity, so I end by saying this: this person is the dividing point of history, he is the dividing point of all time. You see, Christianity is as historical as that. It not only belongs to time, it divides time. Listen to the way our Lord puts it: 'Woman, believe me, the hour cometh' – what is this hour? Listen – 'and now is' – it has come. What is this 'hour' that he is talking about? Ah, that is one of the most wonderful things we can ever understand.

There is the past: past history. I have been reminding you of the history of the Jews and the Old Testament. We can sum it up like this: the whole of the Old Testament is looking forward to the coming of a person.

This message is stated in Isaiah 40:1–5, in one of the most glorious passages in the whole of the Old Testament: 'Comfort ye, comfort ye my people, saith your God.' Why? What is the source of the comfort? Oh, it is this one who is going to come. 'Prepare ye the way of the LORD' – a messenger will come, he will arrive in a wilderness and say, 'Prepare ye the way of the LORD, make straight in the desert a highway for our God. Every valley shall be exalted; and every mountain and hill shall be made low.' Take away the rough places, make everything smooth. It is the coming of the Lord, and all eyes shall see him. He is coming! All flesh shall see the salvation of God.

Now in his first letter, the apostle Peter makes a statement that is germane to the whole matter we are dealing with and is wonderful in and of itself. Peter, after reminding these people about the salvation of their souls, goes on to say this:

Of which salvation the prophets have enquired and searched diligently, who prophesied of the grace that should come unto you: searching what, or what manner of time the Spirit of Christ which was in them did signify, when it testified beforehand the sufferings of Christ, and the glory that should follow. Unto whom it was revealed, that not unto themselves, but unto us they did minister the things, which are now reported unto you by them that have preached the gospel unto you with the Holy Ghost sent down from heaven; which things the angels desire to look into. (1 Peter 1:10–12)

What a statement! But you see it is a perfect summary of the whole of the Old Testament. What is the meaning of the 'paschal lamb' killed when the Children of Israel left Egypt? It was a prophecy of the Lamb of God who was going to come, who would take away the sins of the whole world. And the lamb that was sacrificed morning and evening in the tabernacle and then the Temple was also a prophecy. All the great events of the Old Testament are types and shadows – they are all pointing forward. He is to come. The seed of the woman who will bruise the serpent's head (Genesis 3:15). The whole of your Old Testament! It is past but it is looking forward to a new age, the coming of a new time, a glorious time, when the Messiah, the Deliverer, will come.

But now he says, 'Woman, believe me, the hour cometh, *and now is*.' So I ask again: What hour? It is the hour that the whole of the Old Testament is anticipating. Our Lord said to the Jews: 'Your father Abraham rejoiced to see my day: and he saw it, and was glad' (John 8:56). The hour! The hour when God's Son, the Deliverer, is going to come. So he says, 'The hour cometh, and now is.' The past is ended, we are in the new age, here is a new beginning.

This is stated repeatedly in a glorious manner in the New Testament. I have already quoted from Galatians 4: 'When the fulness of the time was come' – when all the time of the Old Testament had come to an end, had been fulfilled, when God's hour had arrived, the hour that God had in his mind from all eternity. He has an hour, a fixed point. He knows the end from the beginning – 'God sent forth his Son, made of a woman, made under the law, to redeem them that were under the law' (Galatians 4:4–5). Or again, 'For all the promises of God in him are yea, and in him Amen, unto the glory of God by us' (2 Corinthians 1:20).

Then listen to this – what a word for a flabby, sentimental, loose-thinking age such as this: 'But as God is true, our word toward you was not yea and nay' (2 Corinthians 1:18). I do not make a Christian assertion at one point, then when I am given another question take it back. That is 'yea and nay'. You cannot at the same time say that this gospel is historical and yet be doubtful whether or not it is historical. That is 'yea and nay'. And the people of this country are outside the church today because the church is so anxious to please people, to try to attract them to a failing church, that she is saying 'yea and nay'. And the people will not listen, and I do not blame them, for that is not the Christian message.

As God is true, our word toward you was not yea and nay. For the Son of God, Jesus Christ, who was preached among you by us, even by me and Silvanus and Timotheus, was not yea and nay, but in him was yea. For all the promises of God in him are yea . . . (2 Corinthians 1:18–20)

The great 'Yes' of God.

He has ended an era; he has started a new one. The whole of history revolves round this blessed person who was talking to the woman of Samaria by the side of the well. He not only belongs to history, he divides history. BC – Before Christ, preparing for him; AD – *Anno Domini* – the year of our Lord. He is indeed not only Saviour, but the Lord of history. The hour has struck; the hour has arrived. The focal point of all history is in this one person. Who is he? That is the question. And there is only one answer – he gives it himself. 'I am he'! The Saviour of the world.

10

Our Need for Salvation

The woman saith unto him, Sir, I perceive that thou art a prophet. Our fathers worshipped in this mountain; and ye say, that in Jerusalem is the place where men ought to worship. Jesus saith unto her, Woman, believe me, the hour cometh, when ye shall neither in this mountain, nor yet at Jerusalem, worship the Father. Ye worship ye know not what: we know what we worship: for salvation is of the Jews. But the hour cometh, and now is, when the true worshippers shall worship the Father in spirit and in truth: for the Father seeketh such to worship him. God is a Spirit: and they that worship him must worship him in spirit and in truth. The woman saith unto him, I know that Messiah cometh, which is called Christ: when he is come, he will tell us all things. Jesus saith unto her, I that speak unto thee am he. (John 4:19–25)

Christians (let me remind you) are those who have received the 'well of water springing up into everlasting life'; they are people who, as we read in the sixteenth verse of the first chapter of John's Gospel, have received 'of his fulness' and 'grace for [upon] grace'. This is essential Christianity, this is what we are meant to be like. We are to be a rejoicing people. When our

Lord first came into this world, his coming was accompanied by a heavenly choir singing, praising, and that is the great note of the New Testament – as it must inevitably be in the light of our Lord's word here telling us what we are offered. So the great question is: Do we rejoice like this? Do we rejoice in Christ Jesus?

Now that is what we are considering together, and having looked at the difficulties, we have come now to the positive approach. So I put this question: What is it that is absolutely essential to the receiving of this great blessing that will fill us with a joy unspeakable and full of glory? And the answer is that it is an understanding of and a realization of the truth as it is in Christ Jesus; it is utter submission to him. He dealt with this woman in such a way that he brought her to that point, and it is the point to which we all have to come. Ultimately, the cause of our trouble is uncertainty about him, failure to realize as we should who he is, why he came and what he has to give to us.

So we are looking at our Lord as he was pleased to manifest himself to this woman of Samaria, and to help us to understand who he was, we are using her stumbling efforts because they so truly represent the position of many of us at the present time. This is, of course, the great message of Advent. Why should Christian people be thrilled and rejoice as they contemplate, at this season of the year, what happened when the Son of God was born as the babe of Bethlehem? That is the question that is before us and we are given great instruction here concerning it.

Having considered together certain general characteristics of this message, we must now go on. I ask, therefore, in the light of all that we have seen: Why are people so blind to him? Why are they so slow to realize the truth of this message of Advent? Why are we all ourselves so little moved by it? Why is it that we do not rejoice in it as we should and as the first Christians so clearly did and as Christian people have always done in every great period of reformation and of revival?

Well, I think that another of the answers to those questions is our failure to realize our true need, or, to put it another way round, our failure to realize what is to be found in him and what is possible to us and for us in him. It is only the people who have realized their need who truly rejoice in him. So let us see how this story of our Lord's handling of the woman of Samaria helps us to realize this aspect of the truth. Last time we considered our Lord's words to the woman of Samaria: 'Salvation is of the Jews', looking mainly at the words 'of the Jews'. Today we return to this statement, but I want now to emphasize this word 'salvation'.

A strictly accurate translation here should be this: 'We know what we worship: for *the* salvation is of the Jews.' It is the salvation that has been talked about, that the Jews were waiting for. That is the term that our Lord uses. Then look at the terms that are used by the woman: 'Sir, I perceive that thou art a prophet.' A prophet! Then she goes on and says, 'I know that Messias [Messiah] cometh, which is called Christ: when he is come, he will tell us all things' – 'prophet', 'Messiah', 'all things'! What does she mean by these terms? What is her connotation? And what does our Lord mean when he talks about 'salvation'? This is of the very essence of this matter.

Now the terms 'prophet', 'Messiah', and 'salvation' obviously refer to the Old Testament and its teaching. That is a part of the meaning of this phrase of our Lord: 'Salvation is of the Jews.' I am not now concerned to emphasize the exclusiveness – we have done that – but do hold it in your mind; it is essential to the understanding of this teaching. Our Lord says that the salvation comes 'out of' the Jews, and there he is not only referring to the fact that he himself actually did come of the Jews according to the flesh, but he is referring also to the fact that the whole teaching, the whole concept, the whole purpose of salvation is something that God has provided and worked out through this particular nation, the Jews.

In other words, all these terms tell us that the Old Testament is the preparation for the New Testament, and there is a sense in which we simply cannot understand the New Testament truly apart from the Old Testament. We have to approach the New Testament in the light of the teaching of the Old. That is why the Holy Spirit guided the church in the early centuries to include the Old Testament with the New, and that is why it is fatal for Christian people to think they do not need the Old Testament. The two belong together and each casts its light upon the other.

Now the main function of the Old Testament is to show us the need of the salvation that our Lord talks about; and, of course, that is the whole function of the prophets. Indeed, the term 'Messiah' suggests the one who is coming to provide this deliverance, this salvation, the satisfaction of the need that exists. The Old Testament shows us this plainly and clearly and it does so in many different ways: in particular statements, in its explicit teaching.

If you want to know the beginning of this gospel, if you want to understand the connotation of this word 'salvation', and the real meaning of the word 'Messiah', you must go back to the beginning, to Genesis 3:15, where we are told that the seed of the woman will bruise the serpent's head. That verse is the first statement, the first teaching, concerning this salvation. Man has sinned, he is in a position of hopelessness and despair. There will be enmity between him and the seed of the serpent; life has become chaotic. Is there no hope? Here is the answer – salvation is coming, salvation will come – the seed of the woman shall bruise the serpent's head. That is the beginning of the whole message of salvation. Why does it not move us? It is because we have never realized our need of salvation as we should, we have never realized the truth about ourselves.

Then the Old Testament story continues: in promises, in covenants; God keeps on repeating what he is going to do. The story of Abraham and the creation of the nation, the repetition of the promises to Abraham and the renewal of the covenant, all cast their great light upon this person who has come.

And then the Law, with its underlining and pinpointing of sins and transgressions, of disobedience, is clearly designed to show us our need, to prepare us for the great salvation that was to come. We also see it enacted in the ceremonial and the ritual in connection with the tabernacle and the Temple. What is the meaning of all the details about the furnishing of these buildings? What is the point about burnt offerings and sacrifices and meal offerings and peace offerings? Is this just some ancient history of no importance and of no interest to us? Is this just a part of the folklore of primitive people? No, no; this is God's ordinance; it is God preparing the way. These are but types and shadows pointing forward to something that was going to come.

And then, of course, we find the promise of salvation in the great prophetic teaching. It is the great note of the prophets. There is a sample in chapter 40 of Isaiah's prophecy: 'Comfort ye, comfort ye my people, saith your God' (verse 1), and again in Isaiah 55: 'Ho, every one that thirsteth, come ye to the waters' (verse 1). These verses are all a part of the preparation for the coming of the Messiah.

Now the point I am establishing is that we only ever appreciate God's offer of salvation if we understand our need. There is no point in a promise of deliverance if we are not aware that we are captives. The Jews constantly failed at that point. There is a wonderful illustration in the eighth chapter of this Gospel of John, when our Lord says to some people one afternoon: 'If ye continue in my word, then are ye my disciples indeed; and ye shall know the truth, and the truth shall make you free' (John 8:31–32). Instead of standing up and praising God and thanking him, they stand on their dignity and say, 'We be Abraham's seed, and were never in bondage to any man: how sayest thou, Ye shall be made free?' (verse 33). They are saying: We do not need your talk about freedom.

What was the matter with these Jews? They did not realize their condition of serfdom and slavery. And if your heart is not moved and thrilled by the whole conception of the coming of the Son of God into this world and this great salvation, there is only one explanation: you do not know the truth about yourself, you have never seen your need, you have never learned the great lesson of the Old Testament.

So this is the background to these great statements – 'Salvation is of the Jews', and, 'When he [the Messiah] is come, he will tell us all things' – and I repeat that we can only understand them as we realize the need. So there are two things for us to consider. The first is the need itself; the second is the salvation that our Lord came to bring.

Look, then, at this need – what is it? It is man's condition. Men and women are vaguely aware that they have a need. The most thoughtless person is aware that there is something wrong. The giddiest person in London last night must have known in his or her heart that there is some lack somewhere. The woman of Samaria, living as she is in pleasure and in sin, knows there is a need. She is interested in prophets and she talks about the coming Messiah. Ah, yes, but the fact that the world and its individuals are aware of a need is not enough; it is of no value really. That can often lead to our just trying to forget it in another round of pleasure, or it can result in despair, cynicism and hopelessness. The important thing for us is to discover exactly what our need is – this is a part of the preaching of the gospel. It is only those who know their exact need, who will ever really rejoice in the Saviour and his salvation.

Now we must note, therefore, for a moment, certain false ideas with regard to the meaning of this word 'salvation'. Our Lord puts it like this deliberately: '[The] salvation is of the Jews.' The Samaritans had their idea of salvation but they had nothing but the five books of Moses so they did not understand. Because they lacked the further prophetic teaching, their whole notion of salvation was hopelessly incomplete. Not only that, we know that the Jews themselves at the time of our Lord had an equally inadequate view of salvation and of what the Messiah would do when he came. They were so consumed by political and military notions, they thought so much in terms of the greatness of the Jews, of Israel, that they did not realize their need and therefore were blinded to the real meaning of the term 'salvation'. This was the tragedy of the Pharisees, who were self-satisfied and pleased with themselves; and, indeed, we see even the disciples themselves stumbling and fumbling at this point. Even after the resurrection, they turned to our Lord and said, 'Wilt thou at this time restore again the kingdom to Israel?' (Acts 1:6). That is what they were after – political, military greatness, greatness in some human sense, this nation towering over all the other nations. But that is a complete misunderstanding of the meaning of salvation. The fact that the Pharisees and Sadducees and doctors of the law were interested in salvation was not enough, it had to be precise, they had to know the character of the salvation of which they stood in need.

And as this was the case away back at the time of our Lord's coming into this world nearly two thousand years ago, so it is equally true today, perhaps even more so. Today there is grievous misunderstanding of the meaning of this word 'salvation'. It has been the curse of the last hundred years that men whose duty it has been to teach and to preach the Bible and the message of the gospel have gone on using the terms but have evacuated them of their meaning. That is where the dishonesty comes in. They still talk about 'the Saviour', they still talk about 'salvation', but when they use those terms they no longer mean by them what the New Testament means or what our Lord himself so plainly taught.

So the fact that people say they believe that Jesus is the Saviour does not of necessity tell me anything at all. You have to ask them exactly what they understand by 'Saviour' and 'salvation'. And if you do, you will find that very often their idea of salvation is that we need help in order to save ourselves. That is the essence of the modern teaching and outlook. We are not basically wrong, we can save ourselves, but we do need some assistance. The whole notion of sin is no longer accepted: there is no such thing. There are inadequacies, there is a lack of development, but men and women are essentially all right and have it within them to put themselves right. There is no magic, they say, it is not done for you, you have got to do it yourself.

So, according to this modern view, what do people need? Well, they need ethical and moral teaching; they need instruction on how to live. Not only that, they need especially to be taught about love. This is the great, popular teaching of today: if only we could all grasp Jesus' teaching about love – that is how they put it – and put it into practice, all would be well. So we must listen to his teaching and we must, above all, look at him, see this love in him, see how he reacted to cruel and spiteful people, malign people, and see how he responded to persecution. Here he is – he is enacting the great principle of love. He teaches it, he lives it. He encourages us by his example and thereby he helps us, but we must rise up and deliver ourselves.

Now I want to show you once more that that teaching is all wrong; it is a denial of the whole of the teaching in the Old Testament; it is an utter contradiction of the teaching of our Lord himself and of all the apostles. What is the true view? 'Salvation is of the Jews.' Salvation is only understood in the light of this Jewish teaching, the Old Testament teaching, the background, the preparation.

What, then, is the teaching? At this point, I am only going to give you some headings, just a broad picture of the connotation of this word 'salvation', this glorious word. Well, the first thing we are told is that men and women are spiritually dead, they are ignorant of God: 'The fool hath said in his heart, There is no God' (Psalm 14:1). Our Lord in his great high priestly prayer says, 'O righteous Father, the world hath not known thee' (John 17:25). That is the trouble – it is the whole trouble with the world this morning. And this is still our trouble; it is our ignorance of God that explains why we are what we are. This ignorance is one of the manifestations of spiritual death.

People are not only ignorant of God, they are ignorant of the whole of the spiritual realm and they are ignorant of their own true nature. They do not know the truth about themselves. Modern man, so boastful about his achievements, is insulting himself and his own true nature; he does not realize his uniqueness but glories in the fact that he has evolved from an animal! Because he is spiritually ignorant, he does not see this and does not realize the true purpose of life.

But still more serious – and this is what I want to emphasize – men and women are incapable of appreciating the truth when it is put before them. They are blinded. Because they are spiritually dead, they lack a spiritual faculty, so much so that when they are confronted by the truth, they not only do not see it, they resent it and reject it. This is the answer to this notion that people are inherently good and can save themselves if they are given a little help and instruction. They cannot.

Now this is a teaching that is laid down by our Lord himself. 'How can ye believe,' he said to the Jews, 'which receive honour one of another, and seek not the honour that cometh from God only?' (John 5:44). And listen to the apostle Paul putting it explicitly and plainly to the Corinthians. He talks about the wonderful preparation that God made 'before the world unto our glory', and then goes on to say, 'which none of the princes of this world knew: for had they known it, they would not have crucified the Lord of glory' (1 Corinthians 2:7–8). The Lord of glory stood before them and they rejected him; they saw nothing in him. 'Who is this fellow, this carpenter?' They dismissed him, they denounced him, they called him a blasphemer. That is blindness, spiritual blindness, spiritual death. The truth incarnate was before them and they could not see him.

Paul goes on to put that quite explicitly: 'But the natural man receiveth not the things of the Spirit of God: for they are foolishness unto him: neither can he know them, because they are spiritually discerned' (1 Corinthians 2:14). That is our trouble. It is no use saying that all that people need is light and instruction. 'And this is the condemnation,' says John, 'that light is come into the world, and men loved darkness rather than light, because their deeds were evil' (John 3:19). Men and women are confronted by the light and they dismiss it, they joke about it, they laugh at it. They cannot see it because, 'The carnal mind is enmity against God: for it is not subject to the law of God, neither indeed can be' (Romans 8:7). It is impossible. The message of the whole of the Old Testament as it prepares the way for salvation, is, first, that man, when he rebelled against God, died a spiritual death.

Secondly, the Old Testament teaches that man is under the wrath and condemnation of God and his holy Law. The whole of the Old Testament deals with this. Why was the Law ever given? The Jews in their blindness misunderstood and thought that the Law was given in order that they might save themselves through it, but what a misunderstanding! The Law was never given to the Jews in order that they might put it into practice and thereby save themselves; they could not, because of their condition. No, Paul gives the answer: 'Moreover the law entered, that the offence might abound' – that is the purpose of the Law. 'But where sin abounded, grace did much more abound' (Romans 5:20). The object of the giving of the Law was 'that the offence might abound' – that it might be seen, brought out, displayed.

In Romans 7, Paul says this still more clearly:

Was then that which is good made death unto me? God forbid. But sin, that it might appear sin, working death in me by that which is good; that sin by the commandment might become exceeding sinful. (Romans 7:13)

The object of the Law is to bring out the true nature and character of sin. In Galatians 3:24, Paul sums it up in this way: 'The law was our schoolmaster to bring us unto Christ.' How does the Law do that? Paul writes to the Romans:

Now we know that what things soever the law saith, it saith to them who are under the law

– what for? –

that every mouth may be stopped, and all the world may become guilty before God.

That is the purpose of the Law.

Therefore by the deeds of the law there shall no flesh be justified in his sight: for by the law is the knowledge of sin. But now the righteousness of God without [apart from] the law is manifested, being witnessed by the law and the prophets; even the righteousness of God which is by faith of Jesus Christ unto all and upon all them that believe: for there is no difference: for all have sinned, and come short of the glory of God. (Romans 3:19–23)

That is it! That is a summary of the teaching of the whole of the Old Testament: man is not only dead spiritually, he is also under condemnation, he is under the wrath of God. Indeed, Paul, again, puts this so perfectly when he says:

I am not ashamed of the gospel of Christ

– that is litotes; he means, 'I am tremendously proud of it, I am thrilled by it, I boast in it, I want to tell everybody about it.' Why? He goes on to say –

for it is the power of God unto salvation to every one that believeth; to the Jew first, and also to the Greek. For therein is the righteousness of God revealed from faith to faith: as it is written, The just shall live by faith. For

– here is the reason why Paul glories in the great salvation, this is why he exults in it –

the wrath of God is revealed from heaven against all ungodliness and unrighteousness of men, who hold [down] the truth in unrighteousness. (Romans 1:16–18)

That is why this salvation is so wonderful. 'The wrath of God is revealed from heaven.' The whole of the Old Testament reveals God's wrath; the Law does that. Man is not only dead, he is facing eternal punishment, a continuation in this state of spiritual death and torment and unhappiness for ever and for ever.

Not only that; man is living a life that is 'in the flesh and after the flesh', he is under the dominion of sin and of Satan. Our Lord once said to certain people, 'Ye are of your father the devil' (John 8:44), and all men and women who are not in Christ are in the devil, as it were, and are his children. Without Christ, we are in the kingdom of darkness, the kingdom of Satan. When Paul was called on the road to Damascus, the commission our Lord gave him was this: I am going to send you to the people and to the Gentiles, 'to open their eyes, and to turn them from darkness to light, and from the power of Satan unto God' (Acts 26:17–18). Yes, says John, 'the whole world lieth in wickedness [the evil one]' (1 John 5:19). That is the position of the world that does not believe in Christ – under the dominion of sin and Satan, slaves of evil and of the devil, and not only that, but with a nature that is polluted, with 'an evil heart of unbelief', loving the darkness rather than the light. Or, again, as Paul puts it,

> *This I say therefore, and testify in the Lord, that ye henceforth walk not as other Gentiles walk*

– how? –

> *in the vanity of their mind, having the understanding darkened, being alienated from the life of God through the ignorance that is in them, because of the blindness of their heart: who being past feeling have given themselves over unto lasciviousness, to work all uncleanness with greediness. (Ephesians 4:17–19)*

That is it! The pollution of sin.

And, finally, man is under the power of death. There it faces him: 'the last enemy', and all his lifetime he is subject to bondage because of this fear of death.

My friends, this is the need of man; it is the teaching of the Jews, the teaching of the Old Testament, the revelation of God, given before the Advent. If you do not believe that, you will see nothing in what I am going to say about the great salvation. It is only those who have realized that this is the truth about themselves who ever rejoice in this salvation. 'Salvation is of the Jews.' So listen to our Lord, what is this salvation that he is talking about?

Let me give you some further headings to think about, and if they do not make you sing and rejoice, all I have said so far has meant nothing to you; you have never been convicted of sin, you just want to be religious, you just want a little bit of help. What does our Lord tell us?

He tells us, first, that he alone can give salvation, he alone can provide it. That is why he has ever come into the world. Salvation is of the Jews, and he is one of them, he comes out from them. God brought them into being in order that his Son might come. It is a salvation that is 'to the Jew first, and also to the Gentile' (Romans 2:10); it is a salvation that is to be preached, said our Lord, first in Jerusalem, then in Samaria, then in the uttermost parts of the earth (see Acts 1:8). It is the only salvation.

Our Lord came specifically to deliver us out of the predicament that has been outlined in the Old Testament. He says, 'The Son of man is come' – what for? To provide ethical, moral teaching? To give us an example of a life of love lived out before us? Of course, it is all that but that damns me more than anything else. I cannot face the Ten Commandments, leave alone the life of Christ. That shrivels me into hopelessness. No, no; 'the Son of man is come to seek and to save that which was lost' (Luke 19:10). This is the object, this great and glorious salvation.

Secondly, our Lord gives this salvation fully, he gives it entirely, he gives it completely. It needs no supplement, it brooks no addition, you must never add anything to it, whether circumcision, or Mary, the mother of Christ, or the church, or a priesthood. If you add anything, you are derogating, I say again, from his glory. Read your Scriptures, my dear friends, and pray for the Holy Spirit to open your understanding before you read them, and then you will see this glory being unfolded before you. Listen to our Lord himself putting it:

And he came to Nazareth, where he had been brought up: and, as his custom was, he went into the synagogue on the sabbath day, and stood up for to read. And there was delivered unto him the book of the prophet Esaias. And when he had opened the book, he found the place where it was written, The Spirit of the Lord is upon me, because he hath anointed me to preach the gospel to the poor; he hath sent me to heal the brokenhearted, to preach deliverance to the captives, and recovering of sight to the blind, to set at liberty them that are bruised, to preach the acceptable year of the Lord. And he closed the book, and he gave it again to the minister, and sat down . . . And he began to say unto them, This day is this scripture fulfilled [filled to the full] in your ears. (Luke 4:16–21)

There it is. It is a complete, it is a full, it is a perfect salvation. He is the fulfilment of all those glorious, thrilling, moving, triumphant prophecies that are to be found in the Old Testament.

Not only that: here he is at the end of his life, he has finished his teaching, he is under the very shadow of the cross, what does he say?

These words spake Jesus, and lifted up his eyes to heaven, and said, Father, the hour is come; glorify thy Son, that thy Son also may glorify thee: as thou hast given him power over all flesh, that he should give eternal life to as many as thou hast given him. And this is life eternal, that they might know thee the only true God, and Jesus Christ, whom thou hast sent. I have glorified thee on the earth: I have finished the work which thou gavest me to do. (John 17:1–4)

'It is finished' (John 19:30). Finished completely. 'When he had by himself purged our sins, sat down on the right hand of the Majesty on high' (Hebrews 1:3). He did everything that he came to do. That is what he means by this word 'salvation' – the fullness of it, the sufficiency of it. The apostle Paul, of course, is constantly trying to give expression to this. He says: Do not go back to philosophies or to vague teachings about angels and hierarchies, 'for in him dwelleth all the fulness of the Godhead bodily. And ye are complete in him' (Colossians 2:9–10). Listen to him bursting out at the very beginning of the Epistle to the Ephesians, listen to how moved he is, how thrilled: 'Blessed be the God and Father of our Lord Jesus Christ, who hath blessed us with all spiritual blessings in heavenly places in Christ' (Ephesians 1:3). That is the meaning of the word 'salvation', nothing less.

Peter is not to be outdone. His description is not as eloquent and as moving as that of Paul, but listen to him as he puts it like this:

Simon Peter, a servant and an apostle of Jesus Christ, to them that have obtained like precious faith with us through the righteousness of God and our Saviour Jesus Christ: Grace and peace be multiplied unto you through the knowledge of God, and of Jesus our Lord. According as his divine power hath given unto us all things

– the very term used by the woman of Samaria –

that pertain unto life and godliness, through the knowledge of him that hath called us to glory and virtue. (2 Peter 1:1–3)

And Peter goes on in verse 4 to talk about 'exceeding great and precious promises'. Oh, this is the meaning of salvation! Take Paul again, in his letter to the Ephesians:

That I should preach among the Gentiles the unsearchable riches of Christ . . . the breadth, and length and depth and height; and to know

the love of Christ, which passeth knowledge, that ye might be filled
with all the fulness of God. (Ephesians 3: 8, 18–19)

What is Paul describing? It is the salvation that is in our Lord
himself. And to the Corinthians he says, 'But of him are ye in
Christ Jesus, who of God is made unto us wisdom, and righteousness, and sanctification, and redemption' (1 Corinthians 1:30).
When Paul talks about wisdom, he means light, teaching. As John
says, 'No man hath seen God at any time; the only begotten Son,
which is in the bosom of the Father, he hath declared him'
(John 1:18) – he has taught, he has instructed, he has manifested
light and wisdom – wisdom from God. 'For after that in the
wisdom of God the world by wisdom knew not God, it pleased
God through the foolishness of preaching to save them that believe'
(1 Corinthians 1:21), and that wisdom gives us understanding. Oh,
that great hymn of Philip Doddridge expresses it all so perfectly:

> He comes, from thickest films of vice
> To clear the mental ray,
> And on the eyeballs of the blind
> To pour celestial day.

Have you got this life? This wisdom from God is a part of this
great fullness of salvation.

Then righteousness. 'There is none that doeth good, no, not
one' (Psalm 14:3). We are all condemned; we are guilty before
God; we can do nothing about it. You cannot erase your past, you
can never live properly in the future, what can you do? There is
only one hope for you, this salvation that he has come to give –
forgiveness of sins, to be clothed with the robe of his spotless,
perfect righteousness, reconciliation to God.

What else do you need? Sanctification! I need to be delivered
from the power of sin, from the pollution of sin within my life and

nature. Can our Lord do it? Yes, he can; it is a part of this salvation that he talks about – 'Salvation is of the Jews.' 'I am he,' says our Lord: salvation is in me.

What is sanctification? It is a new birth, a new nature, a new life, a new beginning, adoption into the family of heaven as a child of God, a progressive work of the Holy Spirit within me getting rid of sin, undoing the work of the devil and increasingly preparing me for the glory that awaits me. Oh, let Philip Doddridge put it again for us:

He comes, the prisoners to release
In Satan's bondage held:
The gates of brass before him burst,
The iron fetters yield.

He is the one who can cleanse us in this way and set us free 'in the liberty wherewith Christ hath made us free' (Galatians 5:1). Wisdom, righteousness, sanctification, and, at the end of it all, final glorification; deliverance from death. He has destroyed the last enemy and opened the gate of Paradise and of heaven. He has such power that he can change the body of my humiliation and fashion it like unto the body of his glorification. There is final, complete deliverance from sin in every shape and form.

'Tis thine to cleanse the heart,
To sanctify the soul,
To pour fresh life in every part
And new create the whole.
                              Isaac Watts

Everything will be perfect.

So what can we do as we contemplate this great salvation of his? We can do nothing better than remember the words of Jude:

Now unto him that is able to keep you from falling, and to present you faultless before the presence of his glory with exceeding joy, to the only wise God our Saviour, be glory and majesty, dominion and power, both now and ever. Amen. (verses 24–25)

Are you ready to ascribe salvation to him? Have you seen the fullness of the salvation that he came to provide? Beloved people, give yourselves no rest until you really are filled with a desire to praise him, until you rejoice in him with a joy that is 'unspeakable and full of glory'.

11

The Greatest Mystery of All

Jesus saith unto her, Woman, believe me, the hour cometh, when ye shall neither in this mountain, nor yet at Jerusalem worship the Father. Ye worship ye know not what: we know what we worship: for salvation is of the Jews. (John 4:21–22)

We have been looking together at our Lord's words, 'Salvation is of the Jews', and have been considering the importance of realizing our need for salvation. We have looked at the biblical teaching on salvation, and our Lord's teaching that full and complete salvation is found in him alone.

But that, of course, now brings us still more directly to this question: Who is this person who can speak like this? Who is this one who makes such a claim? Here we come to the very heart and centre of the whole Christian message. It is all about this person. It is not a philosophy, it is not just a teaching. It is not just a message about peace and goodwill, friendship and fellowship. Christianity is Christ, the person, and unless we are perfectly clear with respect to him and the truth concerning him, we will obviously go astray with regard to the whole message.

Again, this story of the woman of Samaria gives us most valuable instruction with regard to this subject. Indeed, it is the very point of the passage we are studying. The conversation ends in that dramatic statement, 'Jesus saith unto her, I that speak unto thee am he.' The woman has already said, 'Sir, I perceive that thou art a prophet.' She is an able woman, though a terrible sinner, and this much is clear to her from what our Lord has been saying. He has been able to tell her about her own personal life and the immoral state in which she is living. He has broken through all her talk about worship here and in Jerusalem. Knowing how utterly valueless so much of our talk about religion so often is, he has cut through it all and she recognizes that he is a prophet. Nicodemus had reached the same conclusion. John says: '[Nicodemus] came to Jesus by night, and said unto him, Rabbi, we know that thou art a teacher come from God: for no man can do these miracles that thou doest, except God be with him' (John 3:2). But this is not enough.

Now the New Testament often shows the failure to understand our Lord. It shows us how people were attracted and interested, could see so much, but could not really see who he was. He was a problem. 'Who is he?' That was the great question when he was here on earth. As he entered Jerusalem towards the end, there was a great stir in the whole city and everybody was asking, 'Who is this?' (Matthew 21:10). On another occasion it was put in a different form. People had heard him speaking about the Son of man and they said, 'Who is this Son of man?' (John 12:34).

This was a question, indeed, that our Lord himself encouraged people to face. He himself asked it in many different forms. Once he said, 'What think ye of Christ? Whose son is he?' (Matthew 22:42). On another occasion, he put the question directly to his own disciples: 'Whom do men say that I the Son of man am?'

And they gave him the various answers: 'Some say that thou art John the Baptist [risen from the dead]; some, Elias [Elijah]; and others, Jeremias, or one of the prophets' (Matthew 16:13–14). Even John the Baptist himself got into a state of confusion. There he was, lying in the prison, hearing how our Lord was spending his time up in Galilee preaching to poor people instead of going down to Jerusalem to be crowned King and to gather a great army and to rid them of the tyranny of the Roman occupation. So John sent his two messengers to ask: 'Art thou he that should come, or do we look for another?' (Matthew 11:3).

All these were the fumbling efforts of people to come to a conclusion with respect to this wonderful person. And it is all typified in this statement of the woman of Samaria: 'Sir, I perceive that thou art a prophet.' It was clear to them all that our Lord was unusual. They saw that there was a problem here. He had great learning and yet he had never been to the schools. 'How knoweth this man learning, having never learned?' (John 7:15, margin). He was able to do extraordinary deeds of power and yet he was a carpenter. Here was the enigma.

But I want to try to show that it is not surprising that they were in difficulty and that they stumbled in this way, for our Lord is a mystery, the greatest mystery of all. The apostle Paul put this once and for ever in his first letter to Timothy: 'Great is the mystery of godliness: God was manifest in the flesh' (1 Timothy 3:16). And this is where we should ever start: the mystery of this person who is to be found by the side of the well talking to this Samaritan woman, this sinner.

I also want to show you how, in this conversation, and especially in the passage recorded in verses 19 to 26, this mystery is put before us in a very striking manner. There is a contrast here. On the one hand, our Lord turns to this woman and says,

'Woman, believe me.' Now that is one statement – 'Believe me.' And at the end, he says to her, 'I am he.' These statements belong together: 'me', 'I'. On the other hand, and contrasted with this, is our Lord's statement, '*We* know what we worship': 'we'! Let us look at these statements and the contrast between them, because they hold before us the whole paradox and mystery and marvel concerning this blessed person.

First, our Lord said, 'Believe me . . . I am he' – I am the one who is going to tell you everything. I am the one who possesses all the knowledge that is necessary. He was constantly making this point. For instance he said, 'Ye have heard that it was said by them of old time . . . but I say unto you' (Matthew 5:27). Nothing is more characteristic of him than the way in which he separated himself from everybody else and put himself into a category entirely on his own. 'All that ever came before me are thieves and robbers,' he said (John 10:8). This Gospel of John is full of these great statements: 'I am the bread of life' (John 6:35); 'I am the door' (John 10:7); 'I am the light of the world' (John 8:12). And he is saying all that here when he states, 'Believe me . . . I am he.' He is claiming uniqueness, absolute authority as a teacher. Indeed, he is making what can only be described as a totalitarian demand for submission.

Now in our Lord's handling of people, we see many illustrations of his unique authority. For instance, we read that one day John the Baptist was standing with two of his disciples when our Lord passed by, and John said, 'Behold the Lamb of God!' When they heard this, the two disciples followed Jesus, and then we read: 'Then Jesus turned, and saw them following . . . They said unto him, Rabbi . . . where dwellest thou? He saith unto them, Come and see' (John 1:36–39), and he took them and instructed them.

Then we read that Andrew immediately brought Simon Peter to him: 'And when Jesus beheld him, he said, Thou art Simon the son of Jona: thou shalt be called Cephas, which is by interpretation, A stone' (John 1:42). He was speaking with the same authority. And the chapter continues, 'The day following Jesus would go forth into Galilee, and findeth Philip, and saith unto him' – this is the typical expression – 'Follow me' (John 1:43). Philip is to leave everything – 'Follow me.' There is the same great totalitarian claim and demand.

It is the same with Nathanael; our Lord sees him coming and says: 'Behold an Israelite indeed, in whom is no guile!' And then he goes on to say to him, 'Because I said unto thee, I saw thee under the fig tree, believest thou? thou shalt see greater things than these. And he saith unto him, Verily, verily [Amen, amen] I say unto you' – in this Gospel particularly watch this authoritative statement – 'Hereafter ye shall see heaven open, and the angels of God ascending and descending upon the Son of man' (John 1:47, 50–51).

We see the same authority very clearly in the second chapter in the way he speaks to his mother. Mary has come to him at the marriage feast of Cana of Galilee and says, 'They have no wine', and she suggests that he should do something about it, but he rebukes her: 'Woman, what have I to do with thee? mine hour is not yet come.' So he separates himself from his mother in this authoritative manner (John 2:3–4).

And then later on his authority is seen still more clearly when he goes into the Temple. John writes: 'And when he had made a scourge of small cords, he drove them all out of the temple, and the sheep, and the oxen; and poured out the changers' money, and overthrew the tables.' He clears them out and makes the unique claim: 'My Father's house' (John 2:15–16).

It is the same with Nicodemus. Nicodemus comes to him as a teacher and is more or less putting himself on the same level – he regards our Lord as a teacher who just has a little bit extra beyond what he himself has. Our Lord interrupts him and says, 'Verily, verily, I say unto thee, Except a man be born again, he cannot see the kingdom of God' (John 3:3). But, still more specifically, he puts it like this:

> *Verily, verily, I say unto thee, We speak that we do know, and testify that we have seen; and ye receive not our witness. If I have told you earthly things, and ye believe not, how shall ye believe, if I tell you of heavenly things? And no man hath ascended up to heaven, but he that came down from heaven, even the Son of man which is in heaven. (John 3:11–13)*

Now all these are but illustrations of our Lord's exclusive claim, and here he says to the woman that the water he will give will be 'a well of water springing up into everlasting life'. This is so characteristic of him. He puts himself into a special category: 'But believe me.' He had said it as a boy, 12 years of age, when he was found, you remember, by Joseph and Mary, in the Temple instead of being with them on the homeward journey. They had gone back to Jerusalem, and there they had found him arguing with the doctors of the law, confuting these men, and they rebuked him for not having gone with them. But he replied, 'Wist ye not that I must be about my Father's business [the things of my Father]?' (Luke 2:49). Even at the age of 12 he made this unique and exceptional claim. And it is all summed up in this phrase, 'Verily, verily', which means, 'Believe me', 'Listen to what I am saying.'

Indeed, later on in John's Gospel, we find that our Lord makes claims such as: 'I and my Father are one' (John 10:30); 'Before Abraham was, I am' (John 8:58). There is only one explanation of such statements. He is claiming to be God, and his enemies see that. 'Who is this fellow?' they said. 'This is blasphemy; he is claiming to be equal with God' (see John 5:18). Clearly, then, we are looking at one who is God!

But then the moment we come to that conclusion, we are taken by surprise. 'Woman, believe me,' our Lord says, 'the hour cometh, when ye shall neither in this mountain, nor yet at Jerusalem, worship the Father. Ye worship ye know not what: *we* know' – the one who has been saying 'I' now says 'we'. The one who has been separating himself from the rest of the human race, and later on says, 'I ascend unto my Father, and your Father; and to my God, and your God (John 20:17), the one who says, 'Ye are from beneath; I am from above' (John 8:23), suddenly says, 'we'. And this is, of course, where the problem arises, where the mystery comes in, and the enigma that has always puzzled humanity. The wise and the prudent came to him and they have been looking at him ever since but they do not know what to make of him because they are confronted by this 'I' and 'we', the separateness and yet the fact that he clearly belongs. He is one of the Jews, he belongs to this race of people. And that is why, at the beginning of the Gospels of Matthew and Luke we are given those genealogies tracing his ancestry. He does belong; he is 'of the seed of David', he goes back to Abraham; here is the line, you can see it.

And then he goes on and says, 'we worship'. We have seen that he is God but yet he says that he is one who worships as the Jews worship. And we read about him praying. So we can only come to the conclusion that he is a man; he is a man among men. He is saying, 'I am one of the Jews, and I am speaking to you as a Jew. You are a Samaritan; I am a Jew' – 'we' in contradistinction to the 'I'.

So here, in this one incident and in just these few verses, we are led into the very heart and centre of the great problem of the person of Jesus of Nazareth, and this is what baffled his contemporaries. This is something that can only be understood by those who are enlightened by the Holy Spirit. I referred you earlier to the scene at Caesarea Philippi when our Lord puts the question to the disciples: 'Whom do men say that I the Son of man am?' and they give him the various answers. Then he turns to them and says, 'But whom say ye that I am?' And Peter steps forward and says, 'Thou art the Christ, the Son of the living God.' And our Lord replies, 'Blessed art thou Simon Bar-jona: for flesh and blood hath not revealed it unto thee, but my Father which is in heaven' (Matthew 26:15–17).

Now there is the only way whereby we can ever understand this problem. What is the explanation of this mystery – 'Believe me' and yet 'we'? What is the meaning of the incarnation? The answer is put before us so frequently in these Scriptures. We have already seen it in this Gospel according to John:

> *In the beginning was the Word, and the Word was with God, and the Word was God. The same was in the beginning with God. All things were made by him; and without him was not any thing made that was made. In him was life; and the life was the light of men. (John 1:1–4)*

God eternal! Son of God, co-equal, co-eternal with the Father! Very God of very God! But, 'The Word was made flesh, and dwelt among us' (John 1:14). That is how this is put before us in the Prologue of John's Gospel but it is put in other places in an equally interesting manner.

In introducing his great Epistle to the Romans, the apostle Paul puts it like this:

> *Paul, a servant of Jesus Christ, called to be an apostle, separated unto the gospel of God, (which he had promised afore by his prophets in the holy scriptures), concerning his Son Jesus Christ our Lord, which was made of the seed of David according to the flesh; and declared to be the Son of God with power, according to the spirit of holiness, by the resurrection from the dead. (Romans 1:1–4)*

Here we have the two aspects brought together, and here the human is put first: 'made of the seed of David according to the flesh'. The apostle gives the same teaching in the eighth chapter:

For what the law could not do, in that it was weak through the flesh, God sending his own Son in the likeness of sinful flesh, and for sin, condemned sin in the flesh. (Romans 8:3)

'God sending his own Son' – 'me', 'I'; 'in the likeness of sinful flesh' – 'we', a Jew among Jews. But in the ninth chapter of Romans, the apostle puts it still more strikingly and specifically. He is troubled about the fact that the Jews have rejected the gospel concerning the Lord Jesus Christ, and this is why he says he is surprised:

Who are Israelites; to whom pertaineth the adoption, and the glory, and the covenants, and the giving of the law, and the service of God, and the promises; whose are the fathers, and of whom as concerning the flesh Christ came, who is over all, God blessed for ever. (Romans 9:4–5)

Now there Paul is emphasizing the words: 'of whom [the Jews] as concerning the flesh Christ came, who is over all, God blessed for ever'. 'God blessed for ever', yes, but a Jew, an Israelite! There is the same combination. This is the great truth on which we must concentrate. There is no question about this. 'Salvation', he says, 'is of [us] the Jews', not you. Samaritans are not from the Jews.

What, then, is the explanation of all this? I suppose in many ways the grandest statement of this truth that has ever been made is in the Epistle to the Philippians:

Let this mind be in you, which was also in Christ Jesus: who, being in the form of God, thought it not robbery to be equal with God: but made himself of no reputation, and took upon him the form of a servant, and was made in the likeness of men: and being found in fashion as a man, he humbled himself, and became obedient unto death, even the death of the cross. (Philippians 2:5–8)

It is all there again: 'believe me' – 'we'; 'being in the form of God' – and the explanation, 'he humbled himself' and 'made himself of no reputation'.

What does this mean? It means that he laid aside the signs and the externals, as it were, of his eternal glory and his Godhead. The translation 'emptied himself' is wrong because it is too all-inclusive. He did not empty himself of his Godhead, that is something that even he could not do. It is impossible for God to cease to be God. No, no; this old translation, the Authorized Version, is so much better here – he 'made himself of no reputation'. He still remains the one he is, he is still eternal God, but he no longer appears in the 'form' of God. He now takes the 'form' of a servant and is made 'in the likeness of men', and is 'found in fashion as a man'. He is still God. This is what we must hold on to; he is still God in all the fullness. That is why he can say, 'Believe me'; that is why he can say, 'I am he'; that is why he makes these exclusive, exceptional claims – he is God!

But – and this is the whole mystery and marvel of this message that we consider at this time of Advent – he became *truly* man. He did not merely appear in a kind of phantom body. You must not misunderstand these words 'fashion' and 'likeness' as meaning merely some kind of pretence, or some casing; that is wrong. He had a human soul – he said 'we'. He was truly a Jew, born of the Virgin Mary. He came, according to the flesh, from the Jews, the Israelites. He was 'of the seed of David' (Romans 1:3). He was as much of the seed of David as any other descendant of David. This substance, 'the flesh', has come down from David and before that from Abraham and all the others who appear in the genealogical tables.

So here is the only answer to the problem of 'I' and 'we': he is still God and yet he has become man. 'The Word was made flesh, and dwelt among us' (John 1:14). He had a real human soul and yet he was still God, the eternal Son. And the explanation of this is all there, in Philippians 2:6–8, as we have just seen. What happened was that though he was still God, he came into the world and was born as a man, and though he was still God, he lived as a man.

In Galatians 4:4 Paul puts it in this way: He was 'made of a woman'. He was as truly born of the Virgin Mary as any one of us was born of our mother. He did not have a human father, but nevertheless, his actual birth, as regards the flesh, was like every other birth. But not only that, he was 'made under the law'. Now this is the remarkable and amazing fact. As God he is the Lawgiver, he is above the Law. But he was 'made of a woman, made under the law', and that is the ultimate proof of the fact that he was truly a Jew. That is why he says to the woman of Samaria, 'We know what we worship: for salvation is of [us] the Jews.'

As a Jew, he was subject to the Law. Let us not forget these facts. This is where we see the glory of the incarnation. He was circumcised, as every Jewish male child was circumcised. He was still, remember, the eternal God, yes, but as regards the flesh, the human part of him, he was a Jew and submitted to circumcision. Not only that, we read that he was obedient to his parents, as we see plainly in the pages of the Gospel (Luke 2:52).

But, then, still more striking is the fact that when, at the age of 30, he set out on his public ministry, he submitted to baptism. John the Baptist's baptism was a baptism of repentance for the remission of sins and our Lord had never committed a sin, so John remonstrated with him. But he said, 'Suffer it to be so now: for thus it becometh us to fulfil all righteousness' (Matthew 3:15). He was identifying himself with us, he was one of us.

Not only that; we read that as he was baptized by John the Baptist, there in the Jordan, the Spirit descended on him in the form of a dove. The apostle John tells us that 'God giveth not the Spirit by measure unto him' (John 3:34); and that means that God gave him the Spirit and that he needed the Spirit. Indeed, he himself said later on, 'Him hath God the Father sealed' (John 6:27) – with the Spirit at Jordan and with the voice that came from heaven saying, 'This is my beloved Son, in whom I am well pleased' (Matthew 3:17).

Now all these things are manifestations of his humanity, of the fact that he was truly a man. Though he was Son of God, to do his work here on earth he needed the Spirit, and the Spirit came upon him and gave him power, anointed him. So when he went back to Nazareth and entered the synagogue and was given the scroll of Isaiah, he read, 'The Spirit of the Lord is upon me' (Luke 4:18; Isaiah 61:1). The Spirit had come upon him there at the baptism, enabling him to speak and to preach and to do his mighty works and to engage in his ministry.

But, as he says here to the woman of Samaria, he also worshipped, and we find accounts of him spending whole nights in prayer, rising up a great while before dawn in order to pray. This is what confuses people, on the one hand, this exclusive claim, yet on the other hand, we see him praying. 'If he is eternal God,' people say, 'why did he have to pray?' But he did have to pray, and he always prayed at great length before crucial events took place in connection with his ministry.

Now there is only one answer, and it is, as I say, that though he was still God, he was living as a man, he was living a life of utter dependence upon God, he was living a life of obedience. He said, 'I do nothing of myself' (John 8:28). The eternal God, the one by whom all things were made, and without whom nothing was made that was made (John 1:3), said, 'I can of mine own self do nothing' (John 5:30). The only explanation is that he had not lost his powers, but had decided not to use them. This is the essence of the incarnation. All the rest was still there but he laid it aside in the respect that he was not using it. Indeed, it could not even be seen. Those who were given the insight could say, 'We beheld his glory' (John 1:14) – yes, but they could not see without the Holy Spirit. Others looked at him and said, 'Who is this fellow? Who is this carpenter? Away with him. Crucify him.'

This leads me, of course, to the final question: Why did all this happen? Why did he do this? Why was the eternal Son of God born as a babe in the stable at Bethlehem? Why this story of the human person, Jesus of Nazareth? It took place because it was the only way whereby he could bring and give us this great salvation. 'Salvation', he says, 'is of the Jews', by which he is really saying: I am one who is bringing the salvation and I am a Jew, I have come out of the Jews. The nation was created, in a sense, in order that it might produce me.

But why is this essential? This is the most important question that one can ever ask. Why did the Son of God have to be born as the babe of Bethlehem, born of a woman, to become a Jew among Jews – why was this necessary? And the answer is that apart from this we cannot be saved. Why not? Because 'All have sinned, and come short of the glory of God' (Romans 3:23). We have all transgressed God's holy Law, we are all under the wrath of God. So how can we be saved? We can only be saved by a representative – someone must come and represent us before God. And because we are human beings, our representative must be a human being. One hesitates to say this, and yet one must say it – even God could not have saved a single soul without the incarnation, that is, without the life and death, burial and resurrection of the Lord Jesus Christ. God cannot just say from heaven, 'I forgive you.'

Why not? Because God is just, because God is holy, because God is righteous. God made a man, called him Adam; there was the representative of the whole of humanity. But Adam rebelled, he sinned, he fell; punishment must be given and the punishment was death, separation from God, even physical death. There is the problem. And as Adam was a man and as we are all human beings, the only one who can represent us and save us must also become a human being. The author of Hebrews puts it like this:

For it became him, for whom are all things, and by whom are all things [this is God the Father, it 'becomes' him] in bringing many sons unto glory, to make the captain [leader] of their salvation perfect through sufferings. For both he that sanctifieth and they who are sanctified are all of one [one nature]: for which cause he is not ashamed to call them brethren . . . Forasmuch then as the children [that is to say, us] are partakers of flesh and blood, he also himself likewise took part of the same; that through death he might destroy him that had the power of death, that is, the devil; and deliver them who through fear of death were all their lifetime subject to bondage. For verily he took not on him the nature of angels; but he took on him the seed of Abraham.

He does not partake of the nature of angels, he has not come to save angels. He has come to save men and women so he must take human nature: 'the seed of Abraham'.

Wherefore in all things it behoved him to be made like unto his brethren, that he might be a merciful and faithful high priest in things pertaining to God, to make reconciliation for the sins of the people. For in that he himself hath suffered being tempted, he is able to succour them that are tempted. (Hebrews 2:10–11, 14–18)

Now that passage means that we need someone to represent us. We are all sinners: what about our guilt? We cannot do anything about it and God cannot just say, 'I forgive it', as we have seen.

But here is one who says, in effect, 'I am the one who is going to bear your sins.' He has a right to do so because he is a man among men, he is not an angel. Here is a human representative, one of us – 'we'. 'We, the Jews.' 'We' members of humanity. But he has got to bear the punishment of our sins and that means death. He has got to deliver us from the Law of God that condemns us; he has got to deliver us from death itself and from the grave; he has got, at the same time, to be one who can sympathize with us and help us, for we need not only forgiveness of sins, we need help, we need strength. How can we pray? We go glibly into the presence of God and think there is no problem; but we are going into the presence of one who is 'a consuming fire'. He is the Judge of the universe, who can approach him? We need a representative, we need a high priest, we need a mediator: these are our needs. So he must be a man for all these reasons.

Then read the Epistle to the Hebrews again and concentrate on the Lord Jesus Christ as our High Priest. Listen:

> *Seeing then that we have a great high priest, that is passed into the heavens, Jesus the Son of God, let us hold fast our profession. For we have not an high priest which cannot be touched with the feeling of our infirmities; but was in all points tempted like as we are, yet without sin. Let us therefore come boldly unto the throne of grace. (Hebrews 4:14–16)*

And then in the next chapter:

> *For every high priest taken from among men is ordained for men in things pertaining to God, that he may offer both gifts and sacrifices for sins: who can have compassion on the ignorant, and on them that are out of the way. (Hebrews 5:1–2)*

How can he have compassion on the ignorant if he is not a man? How can he bear with our frailties if he does not know something about them himself? And here he is sitting at the side of the well in Samaria, tired and weary with the journey, suffering from thirst, asking for a drink. He is man; he must be man. He cannot sympathize, he cannot understand, he cannot help unless he is man.

And yet he must bear the punishment of my sins, he must conquer death and the grave; no man can do it. Adam was a perfect man, sinless, and yet he failed. And if God had merely created another perfect man like Adam, he would have failed in exactly the same way. No, there is only one way whereby this salvation can ever come to any of us, and it is this: that there must be a new humanity. And so the babe of Bethlehem was born, and the archangel in telling Mary of his coming birth said, 'That holy thing which shall be born of thee' (Luke 1:35). 'Holy thing'! The baby was not an ordinary child. 'The Holy Ghost shall come upon thee, and the power of the highest shall overshadow thee.' He is the Father, as it were. There was no human father. 'That holy thing shall be born of thee.'

In other words, he is God and he took on to himself human nature, becoming man – the Word: 'The Word was made flesh, and dwelt among us' (John 1:14). He must be both God and man. If he is not man, he cannot represent us, he cannot finally help us. But if he is only man, he cannot save us, he is not big enough, he is not great enough, he is not strong enough. So he is both God *and* man. He is God living as man, therefore able to take upon him my sins. He has obeyed the Law on my behalf, he has borne the punishment of my sins in his own body on the tree. He has conquered death and the grave. He has conquered all our enemies, and he has risen triumphant, and has taken his seat at the right hand of God in the glory everlasting. He is the only one who could not fail, he is the only one who has not failed, and therefore he is the only Saviour.

There it is: 'Believe me'; 'We know what we worship.' Very God of very God! And yet a man worshipping God and entirely dependent upon God. This is God's way. It was God's purpose that his only begotten, eternal Son should be born as a Jewish babe and live as a man and die as a man, and rise again, because the whole time he is still the eternal and everlasting God. He said he was the Son of God who had come from heaven but who was still at the same time in heaven (John 3:13). He was speaking to Nicodemus on earth but he was still in heaven. 'I'! 'We'! 'God'! 'Man'! 'The Word'! 'Flesh'! And thereby, and thereby alone, are you and I saved, and in him, and in him alone, is salvation possible.

12

'I am he'

Jesus saith unto her, I that speak unto thee am he. (John 4:26)

We are met together on this Christmas morning[1] to commemorate an event. It is always vital that we should remind ourselves of that and that is why I, as one who is a thoroughgoing Protestant and even a Puritan, believe in the observance of Christmas Day. We are always so much in danger of forgetting that we are dealing with facts, dealing with history. There is no greater danger than to regard the Christian faith, the Christian message, as just a philosophy, just a teaching. So it is very good that we should constantly remind ourselves that all we have and all we hope and all we hold on to is based solidly upon facts. And so we meet together today to remember what is, to all Christian people, the most important and, at the same time, the most amazing event that has ever happened in the whole long course of human history.

---

[1] Christmas Day 1966.

Indeed, I could go beyond that and easily show you that for the whole of humanity, even those people who do not believe this message, and who do not call themselves Christians, this is nevertheless the most momentous occurrence that has ever taken place. We have already reminded ourselves that this is an event that has changed the whole course of history. After all, why do we call this year 1966? It is because of the birth of that babe of Bethlehem: he has changed our calendars. He is the turning point of all history, and this is recognized by secular historians.

But, since Christmas Day this year happens to be on a Sunday, we are reminded in passing that he has also even changed our observance of the days of the week. Before his coming, the Jews observed the Sabbath, the seventh day, as the day that was given particularly to the worship of God. But our Sunday is the first day of the week and that is the day that all Christian people give to the worship of God and to the contemplation of our souls and eternal things. Why is this? Again, it is all due to this person – this person who came into the world as the babe of Bethlehem. He has changed everything. He towers 'o'er the wrecks of time'. He, and his cross, and the great message concerning him, have been the greatest factors in all human history. The question, therefore, that comes to us all is this: Do we realize the significance of this great, this extraordinary and momentous event that we are meeting together to commemorate and that, in a sense, we meet together to commemorate every Sunday?

Now it is quite clear, alas, that to many people in the world the significance of this day is not realized at all. We must all plead guilty that none of us realizes its full significance, and it does not influence the lives of any of us as it should. But it is clear that there are large masses of people in this and in other lands to whom Christmas Day really does mean nothing at all. I am not talking, obviously, about Christmas as a holiday, as it is normally regarded, but to the event that gives its name to all this – Christ's Mass, if you like – and therefore it is this that we must consider together.

Now the world remains very much as it was when this babe was born into it. Why was our Lord born in a stable? We are given the reason. It is 'because there was no room for them in the inn' (Luke 2:7). Here is a woman who arrives on the verge of giving birth to her first-born child and yet she cannot find a room in any of the hostelries of Bethlehem. I know it was an important occasion, it was the occasion of the taxing and people had to go to Bethlehem from various parts of the country – they had to go wherever their household and their lineage belonged – so Mary arrived with Joseph, the man to whom she was engaged. But they found there was no room for them in the inn, nobody would go out, nobody would vacate their room – sheer selfishness. I do not want to stay with this, but you see that it was because people did not realize what was happening. Nobody knew about the visitation of the Archangel to Mary. People did not know that the baby that was to be born had been described by the Archangel as 'that holy thing that shall be born of thee'. To them, Mary was just a pregnant woman and they were not concerned; they cared only about their own happiness.

And that is still a picture of the state of the world. It was a troubled world then – Palestine had been conquered by the Romans; they had to pay these taxes; there were troubles and problems and difficulties. A kind of 'credit squeeze' obtained even then, and there was much dissatisfaction, much unhappiness. The world then, as now, was a world of war, of suffering and of pain and sorrow, and it did not realize that someone was at that moment entering into the world who alone could really deal with all these problems. And the tragedy is that the world still does not realize it. A general lip service is paid to this time of the year but the whole significance of this momentous event is not realized, is not grasped.

What I now want to consider with you is the cause of all this trouble, and I will do so in the light of this statement made here in connection with the meeting of our Lord and the woman of Samaria. Here they meet by the side of a well. He is tired, so he has not gone with his disciples into the town to buy provisions. As he sits there in his weariness, this woman comes to draw water, as she regularly does, and he asks her for a drink. We have been considering their conversation, and have now reached the dramatic point where our Lord tells the woman that 'God is a Spirit: and they that worship him must worship him in spirit and in truth', to which she replies, 'I know that Messias cometh, which is called Christ: when he is come, he will tell us all things.' And our Lord says, 'I that speak unto thee am he.'

Now it seems to me that there are great lessons here for all of us on this Christmas morning. The first is this: the inexcusableness of our failure to recognize him. What do I mean by that? Well, this woman illustrates it so well. She says that the Messiah is coming and will tell them 'all things'. She means, of course, that though the Samaritans only had the first five books of the Bible, the five books of Moses, and did not have the books of the Prophets and the Psalms and so on, nevertheless, even among the Samaritans there was this glimmering of a knowledge of the Deliverer, the Messiah, the Saviour who was to come. So they were looking forward to him as the one who would solve all their problems. In the case of the Jews, this was, of course, still more clear because of the additional knowledge that they had from the prophets and others. The whole Jewish nation was looking forward to the coming of this great Messiah – and that is what makes their treatment of him utterly inexcusable. It is astounding that though he had been foretold, and foretold in detail right through the Old Testament – the very literature in which they gloried – when he actually came, the Pharisees and scribes, the religious leaders, the politicians, the Herodians and others, did not recognize him.

One of the most astonishing things that has ever happened in the whole course of human history is that the Jews failed to recognize their own expected Messiah. John has summed it up for us in the Prologue of this Gospel where he says, 'He came unto his own, and his own received him not (John 1:11). So here is the question that confronts us: Why did his own people fail to recognize him in spite of the knowledge that they had, and in spite of the fact that they were looking forward to the Messiah's coming? And unfortunately the answer is not difficult to discover. The real explanation was their false understanding with respect to the Messiah. It is not enough that we should expect a deliverer, what is most important is that our ideas concerning him should be accurate.

Now the trouble with the Jews was that their notion of the Messiah was of a political or military leader. They were expecting a great king, so they were assuming that he would be born in some grand palace. They were looking for something extraordinary and unusual to announce his coming – but it had to be their idea of what was unusual – and they were expecting his actions to be primarily political and military in character. So when a baby was born in a stable, they did not understand; they had not anticipated this poverty, this lowliness. It did not fit in with their whole idea of greatness and bigness and national glory.

The Jews' trouble was that they were nationalistic in their outlook, as the nations of the world still are. This is one cause of all our troubles. They were consumed with national pride, and so they had a picture of the Messiah that was completely different from the reality. Of course, this idea of a Messiah being born in a stable and placed in a manger was monstrous; it was just rubbish and folly. So they dismissed it.

And then when this baby grew up and began to preach at the age of 30, they were still offended. Why? Because he had not been trained as a Pharisee, or as a doctor of the law. He had been working as a carpenter. He was an artisan, one who worked with his hands. They said: Who is this fellow? 'How knoweth this man letters, having never learned?' (John 7:15). It was quite ridiculous that a peasant carpenter should stand up and claim to be an authoritative teacher. I am just showing you that it is no use saying, 'I know that Messias cometh', if your whole idea of what he is going to be like when he comes is completely wrong. But that was the trouble then and it is still the trouble today.

But we must take this a step further. Why did the Jews have this false idea of the Messiah? The answer to this is interesting and most important. They would have had no idea of a Messiah at all, and they would not have been expecting a Messiah, but for their Scriptures, but for their tradition. That is where the idea came from. And yet though they had the Scriptures, they were entirely wrong in their view of the Messiah. And the reason was that they had not studied their Scriptures as they should have done, and did not believe their Scriptures. If they had only done that, they could not have gone wrong, for the astounding fact about these Old Testament Scriptures is that they not only said that a Messiah was going to come, they gave explicit details about his coming and about him. For instance, the prophecy of Micah actually says that he would be born in Bethlehem – the exact place is named. Now the Jews thought that the Messiah would be born in Jerusalem, the capital city. All great things had to happen in the capital, not in a little place like Bethlehem. But if they had only read and understood their Scriptures, they would not have gone so wrong.

Then in the book of the prophet Daniel, the exact time of the Messiah's birth is prophesied; the fact that he was to be born of a virgin was prophesied by Isaiah; his poverty was prophesied. But these Jews were not aware of the facts. They took the idea of a Messiah, then they thought about it in their own terms instead of working it out and accepting it in detail as it had been expounded and unfolded in their Scriptures. Now this is a most important principle because this is still the explanation of why people do not believe in him and do not realize who he is and the significance of his coming. This, in a sense, is the tragedy of the whole of the human race. The tragedy is that we will not face the facts. We take out ideas and then we manipulate them according to our own concepts and our own philosophies. There is a lot of talk about Christianity, a lot of talk about Christian principles, but so much of it has nothing to do with what we read in the Bible. People have taken what they regard as a Christian idea and clothed it in their own language, in their own thought forms, and in the end it has no contact whatsoever with the details, the facts, that we are given here in the Bible.

Many people think they know what Christianity is, but they often say, 'Of course, I don't believe the facts'! They do not believe in the virgin birth, they do not believe in our Lord's miraculous powers, they do not believe in his atoning death or in his literal, physical resurrection and the ascension and so on. You often hear that on the television and the wireless, you often read it in the papers. They say they like the Christian idea, the Christian teaching about love and so on. But that is to repeat the very error of the Jews and the Samaritans. He must be taken as he is, and the tragedy is that people do not look at him as he is. They do not read their Scriptures, the whole story about this person from his very birth right on until his death and after that his resurrection and ascension. If only the world faced these facts!

Who is this person who has even changed our calendars, changed our observance of weeks coming one after another? Who is this person who has left an impress on the whole of human history in a way that nobody else has done? How do you explain him? I suggest that there is only one adequate explanation and that is the facts as they are given us in this book. That is why it is right and good for us to remember his birth in the stable, and everything else that follows. If only the world faced this and faced the whole course of the history of the Christian church! You cannot explain it away. Read the whole story of the last nearly two thousand years. You cannot explain the church herself except in supernatural terms.

The world is always expecting to get better. Humanity still foolishly believes that it can put itself in order. It has always believed that. That is what is meant by civilization. And yet we see our world in utter trouble today. If only the world would pay attention to his teaching and his prophecies! They think that he taught that war was going to be banished and that the world was going to get better and better. But he said the exact opposite. He said there would always be 'wars and rumours of wars' (Matthew 24:6). He said, 'As it was in the days of Noe, so shall it be also in the days of the Son of man' (Luke 17:26). He said that at the end of the world life would be very similar to life before the Flood and before Sodom and Gomorrah – 'they did eat, they drank, they bought, they sold, they planted, they builded . . .' (Luke 17:28). This person, the babe of Bethlehem grown to be a man and a preacher and a teacher, prophesied that the world would not remain as it was then, but would get worse, and towards the end it would be terrible, and nothing but his coming back again into it could deal with the situation, solve the problems and restore peace and order to the entire cosmos. But the world, instead of taking him as he is, instead of believing the facts, repeats the error of the Jews and the Samaritans, taking out one idea and then manipulating it to suit its own fancy.

So the story of this woman of Samaria has a great deal to tell us today. 'I know that Messias cometh.' Yes, but the question is: What do you really know? Have you accepted the statements in detail concerning this Messiah who is to come?

But that leads me to another principle, and this, of course, follows directly. There must therefore be something wrong with humanity, and the Bible tells us that there is: it is that we are all blind, spiritually blind. And so my next principle is that he can only be known as he reveals himself to us. Here is this woman of Samaria, obviously an able woman, though she lives, poor woman, such an immoral life – five husbands and is now living with a man who is not her husband. But she is interested and she is concerned, and our Lord speaks to her, reasons with her, leads her on and brings her to the point when she says, 'I know that Messias cometh.' She says that to him! She does not recognize him. And our Lord looks at her and says, 'I that speak unto thee am he.' I am the very one you are talking about. You say you are expecting the Messiah and that when he comes he will teach all things. Don't you realize that? 'Look at me again,' he seems to say. 'I am he!' He manifests himself to her.

So I take this up as a principle and it is undoubtedly true. We cannot recognize him except it be revealed to us. The apostle Paul puts this clearly to the Corinthians. He says:

> But we speak the wisdom of God in a mystery, even the hidden wisdom, which God ordained before the world unto our glory. Which none of the princes of this world knew: for had they known it, they would not have crucified the Lord of glory. But as it is written, Eye hath not seen, nor ear heard, neither have entered into the heart of man, the

things which God hath prepared for them that love him. But God hath revealed them unto us by his Spirit: for the Spirit searcheth all things, yea, the deep things of God. (1 Corinthians 2:7–10)

But our Lord himself had said this still more plainly:

At that time Jesus answered and said, I thank thee, O Father, Lord of heaven and earth, because thou hast hid these things from the wise and prudent, and hast revealed them unto babes. Even so, Father: for so it seemed good in thy sight. All things are delivered unto me of my Father: and no man knoweth the Son, but the Father; neither knoweth any man the Father, save the Son, and he to whomsoever the Son will reveal him. (Matthew 11:25–27)

Now what could be plainer or clearer than this? In other words, the principle is that as the result of the Fall and of sin, we have become such that we cannot recognize the Messiah, we cannot recognize our Saviour. As the princes of this world did not know him and crucified him as an imposter and a blasphemer, so the world still does not know him, and the teaching is that the world cannot know him, he has to be revealed to us. And the wonderful thing is that he reveals himself to the woman of Samaria. She sees it at once and she leaves her water pot and runs back to the city to say, 'Come, see a man, which told me all things that ever I did: is not this the Christ?'

As you read the story about his birth, you will find that right from the very beginning a revelation was needed. Even Mary, his own mother, did not understand. Read the first chapter of Luke's Gospel and you will see that Mary fumbled and stumbled though an Archangel was revealing the truth to her. Even after his birth she did not fully understand. The Scriptures record all this. She kept on stumbling because of the things he did and the things he would not do.

And in that wonderful second chapter of Luke's Gospel, we see how this selfsame point comes out. Look at the shepherds: why did they go to Bethlehem, and why did they become believers? The answer is that they were given a revelation. An angel had said to them, 'Fear not: for, behold, I bring you good tidings of great joy, which shall be to all people. For unto you is born this day in the city of David a Saviour, which is Christ the Lord' (Luke 2:10–11). A revelation! So they said, 'Let us now go even unto Bethlehem, and see this thing which is come to pass, which the Lord hath made known unto us' (Luke 2:15). And they hurried to Bethlehem where they saw everything exactly as the angel had reported it to them. The shepherds would never have recognized him but for the fact that they were given this revelation, this understanding.

The same is true of ancient Simeon, who holds the baby in his arms and says, 'Lord, now lettest thou thy servant depart in peace' (Luke 2:29), and of Anna, the prophetess. Then later on, when this babe has grown up and is in his public ministry, he puts the question to the disciples at Caesarea Philippi: 'Whom do men say that I the Son of man am?' They give the various answers. Then he says, 'But whom say ye that I am?' Peter says, 'Thou art the Christ, the Son of the living God.' Then notice what our Lord says to him: 'Blessed art thou, Simon Bar-jona: for flesh and blood hath not revealed this unto thee, but my Father which is in heaven' (Matthew 16:13–17). Flesh and blood! Human ability! Human intellect! Philosophies! They do not recognize him! They did not when he was here, they have never done so since. We reject him; we are blinded by sin.

God sometimes gives this revelation directly, in the way I have shown you, and as our Lord himself did here with this woman. Our Lord revealed who he was in his teaching, in the things he claimed for himself. 'Ye have heard that it was said by them of old time . . . but I say unto you' (Matthew 5:27–28). 'Before Abraham was, I am' (John 8:58). All this great teaching that we were considering last time – 'I am the light of the world'; 'I am the bread of life'; 'I am the way, the truth, and the life: no man cometh unto the Father but by me' – it was all revelation!

But perhaps one of the most interesting examples of all happened even after his death and resurrection. I am referring to the famous story of the two men going down from Jerusalem to Emmaus. There they are, their leader has been killed and laid in a tomb and they are utterly disconsolate. A stranger suddenly joins them and says, 'What are you talking about?'

They say, 'Haven't you heard? Jesus of Nazareth . . .'

'What about him?' he asks.

And they tell him – they do not recognize him. This is the risen Christ, the risen Lord, and he is talking to the two men. He goes on to give them instruction from the Old Testament; still they cannot recognize him. And then they get a bit tired, and they say, 'Come into the house with us and have something to eat.' And he goes in and takes bread and he breaks it, and as he does, their eyes are opened. He does that deliberately. He is manifesting himself, telling them in this acted parable, 'I am he. Don't you realize who I am?' Their eyes are opened. Their hearts were warmed by him even when they did not know him, but now he gives this positive revelation.

And since then our Lord has been revealing himself by the Holy Spirit to all who have become Christians. If you are a Christian, do not take any credit to yourself, you have had the revelation given you; the scales have been taken from your eyes; your eyes have been opened. Notice how Paul puts it there in 1 Corinthians 2:10. The princes of this world did not know him, 'But God hath revealed them [these things] unto us by his Spirit: for the Spirit searcheth all things, yea, the deep things of God.' No man or woman can be a Christian unless the Spirit opens their eyes and gives them the revelation and the understanding. The Holy Spirit has been sent in order to do this. Our Lord said, 'He shall glorify me' (John 16:14).

When our Lord was here in the flesh, he could say, as he said to the woman, 'I am he.' But he has gone, he is out of sight, and yet he has sent the Spirit, this 'other Comforter'. And the Spirit deals with us, he opens our eyes, he gives us understanding, he shows us our own need and the fullness that is in him, and we hear him whispering, 'Here he is; this is he.' As God during the days of his flesh spoke in a voice from heaven, saying, 'This is my beloved Son, in whom I am well pleased; hear ye him' (Matthew 17:5), so the Spirit speaks within, whispers, tells us, 'This Jesus is the Christ, the Saviour, the Messiah you are looking for.' And he can only be known as the result of this revelation. So I am not surprised that the world in general is rejecting him today. It is because of the blindness of sin. It is terrible that men and women do not recognize God's Son! He must reveal himself.

What does he reveal? Well, it is all here in this passage. He reveals the fact that he is the Messiah, the Saviour: 'Christ is all, and in all' (Colossians 3:11). The woman has said to him, 'Sir, I perceive that thou art a prophet.' She now says, 'We are looking for the Messiah,' and he says, 'I am he.' So what is he?

In the Old Testament history some people were prophets, some were priests, some were kings – always three different groups of people. But here is one who is himself Prophet, Priest and King. No one person is big enough to represent him, so you have to divide up his offices. But here he is, the 'all, and in all'. He is everything. Why, he is even the offering that the priest offers! He is 'The Lamb of God, which taketh away the sin of the world' (John 1:29). That is what he reveals. He is the fulfilment of all God's promises; he has the satisfaction that we all need; he is everything, 'the beginning and the ending', the first, the last (see Revelation 1:8). He is 'wisdom, and righteousness, and sanctification, and redemption' (1 Corinthians 1:30). That is what he reveals.

But he also reveals something else – he reveals the love of God. Why was he in this world at all? Why was that babe ever born? There is only one answer: 'God so loved the world, that he gave his only begotten Son, that whosoever believeth in him should not perish, but have everlasting life' (John 3:16). He reveals the love of God in spite of our unworthiness. He says: I am the one who God has promised to send to deliver you.

So shall we remind ourselves of this on this Christmas morning: the birth of this babe of Bethlehem is the proof of the fact that all God's promises are sure and will be honoured; yes, he is the guarantee of the prophecies and the promises running through the whole of the Old Testament. 'I am he.' Whatever God promises he always performs.

> For his mercies ay endure;
> Ever faithful, ever sure.
> *John Milton*

Read the Bible, get hold of the promises of God. Believe them! They are sure.

But let me end on this note: what always moves me so deeply as I read this particular story of our Lord's meeting with the woman of Samaria is his readiness to reveal himself. Look at this amazing story. Here he is, the Son of God, the Saviour of the world, the long-promised Messiah. The Pharisees, the scribes, the Herodians, the philosophers, do not recognize him, but he reveals himself – to whom? To the woman of Samaria, a woman living in adultery, a woman living in sin; to the shepherds by the angels and the heavenly choir.

What is the lesson? It is this: that again today he brings into this world hope for all. Not merely for intellectuals, for great people and for learned people. It is the exact opposite. He has not come merely for the sake of good people, religious people, moral people, Pharisees and scribes. No, no! He says himself: 'I am not come to call the righteous, but sinners to repentance' (Matthew 9:13). There is hope for the woman of Samaria living in sin, in squalor, in evil – it is to her he gives this blessed word of hope! He is the opposite of Pharisaism; he is the opposite of self-righteousness: 'They that be whole', he says, 'need not a physician, but they that are sick' (Matthew 9:12).

And so the apostle Paul reminds the Corinthians:

Ye see your calling, brethren, how that not many wise men after the flesh, not many mighty, not many noble, are called: but God hath chosen the foolish things of the world to confound the wise; and God hath chosen the weak things of the world to confound the things which are mighty; and base things of the world, and things which are despised, hath God chosen, yea, and things which are not, to bring to nought things that are. (1 Corinthians 1:26–28)

What a blessed thought! What a hope he has brought into the world! There is no one too bad to be saved and redeemed; he has hope for all. Indeed, all he requires of us is what he required of the woman of Samaria. What is that? Honesty! When he challenges her about her life, she does not deny it, she admits it. Honesty! He always asks for readiness to admit the truth about ourselves, however unpleasant it may be. And then readiness to listen to him, and readiness to believe what he says.

So the one question for every one of us is this: Has he revealed himself to you? Has he in some manner, some shape or form, said to you, 'I am he'? I am the one you need, I am the one you have been expecting. You have some dim, vague, uncertain notions: look at me again, I am he. I have come into the world for you, that you might be forgiven, that you might be born again, have a new nature, a new heart, start living a new life. I am the one who has come to do for you what you could not do for yourself, what the whole world could not do for you. I am the one whom God in his love has sent that you might have life, which is life indeed.

All that he demands is that we recognize our need, that we stop defending ourselves and explaining, that in honesty we admit our failure, our need, then listen to him and all he tells us. When we believe and give ourselves to him, he will give us life, life more abundant, life that is life indeed. He came into the world that we might have life. Here, again, is the question: Has he revealed himself to you? Have you heard him whispering: 'I am he'?

13

The Gift of God

Jesus answered and said unto her, If thou knewest the gift of God, and who it is that saith to thee, Give me to drink; thou wouldest have asked of him, and he would have given thee living water . . . Whosoever drinketh of this water shall thirst again: but whosoever drinketh of the water that I shall give him shall never thirst; but the water that I shall give him shall be in him a well of water springing up into everlasting life. (John 4:10, 13–14)

Here in John chapter 4, we are confronted, let me remind you, by the great and amazing offer that the gospel makes to all people, an offer of a new life beyond everything that we could ever have thought of or even imagined. So once again I ask: Do we know this new life? Have we experienced it? Indeed, I want to lead you into a further consideration of that very subject. We have been looking at many of the hindrances that stand between people and the realization of that life. And we have seen that the essential need, above everything else, is to understand who our Lord is. This is the most profound question we can ever face. 'Jesus saith unto her, I that speak unto thee am he.' Without the realization of who he is, there is no hope whatsoever; any uncertainty about the person of our blessed Lord and Saviour makes it quite impossible for us to receive this life, this blessing that he has come to give.

But we have still not finished with the subject; these, in a sense, are but the essential preliminaries. There is so much that has to be cleared away. We think we are Christians, we think we have 'got religion', we think we know how to worship, we think we know about God, and we have to be put right about all these ideas. And that can happen – we can be put right intellectually, and yet still not know and experience this great salvation as it is put before us here in the words of our blessed Lord himself. So we must come still more directly face to face with this great statement, and that is what I am anxious to do now.

It may be that at the beginning of a new year like this,[1] it is very good and appropriate for us to consider this very subject. The new year is a time for us to take stock, to examine ourselves. We are encouraged to do that in the Scriptures. The apostle Paul says to the Corinthians, 'Examine yourselves [prove yourselves], whether ye be in the faith' (2 Corinthians 13:5), and there is no better way of doing that than by looking at a great statement such as the one we are now studying, and again asking ourselves the question: Are we possessors of this life about which our Lord speaks in the glowing words found in John 4:10–14? Do we possess this living water? If not, why not? Now here we stand directly facing this most crucial question, and all I want to do now is to show you again some of the absolute essentials with respect to this whole matter.

Here is the first. We must realize our true need. I emphasize the word 'true' because we are all conscious of many needs, we all have

---

[1] January 1967.

many desires. There is nobody who is perfectly satisfied, there is always something that is lacking.

> Since every man who lives is born to die,
> And none can boast sincere felicity.
>   *John Dryden*

That is it; the poet Dryden puts it quite clearly. Nobody has known 'sincere felicity', by which he means unmixed joy. There is no complete satisfaction. Everybody in the world is aware of some need or other, and that, in a sense, is the greatest danger of all because these other needs very often hide from us the true need, the basic need. I suppose that in many senses this is one of the great problems confronting the preaching of the gospel. Humanity is aware of many, many needs, and yet the whole time is not aware of the true, the fundamental need, the real need at the centre. A very real danger, therefore, that confronts us all is the danger of just going on living day by day, year after year, taking life as it comes with its ups and its downs, coming to the conclusion that life always will and must be like that and that therefore we can do nothing better than just put up with it, reconcile ourselves to it and make the best of it, extracting out of it as much happiness and joy and satisfaction as we can as we go along.

Now that is, I say, a great danger confronting every human being in this world, and it is also a danger that confronts those of us who have become Christians. So that is why it is essential that we should stop and think and examine ourselves. And the kind of way in which we can prepare ourselves for this great offer, the way in which we can discover our true and basic need, is to ask questions such as this: On what are we actually living? By what are we living? On what do we really depend?

Now it is extraordinary that one has to put questions such as those, and yet I think you will all agree that these are the questions that really matter, because unconsciously we can be depending on quite a number of things, instead of upon our Lord and Saviour. Many dangers confront us, we all must examine ourselves at this point. I wonder whether we are kept going by our own activities, by the various things that we have to do? It is a question that every one of us should face. I must face it as I stand here in this pulpit. Am I living on my own activities? Am I living on my own preaching? I ask this question because it has been my lot in life more than once to visit men who have spent a lifetime in the ministry, preaching and teaching others, but who, because of ill health or old age, can do so no longer. I have often found such men in a state of depression, and there has been only one explanation for this. Unconsciously, they had been living on their own activities instead of living on the Lord. You can live on your preaching about the Lord instead of on the Lord himself.

Now this applies, I repeat, to all of us. The very routine of life sustains many people; they go on because they have to. There are certain things that must be done and if they are not done, everything will end in chaos. So they are kept going by the demands, the needs, the necessities of life. And very often when, for various reasons, such as illness or accident, they have to stop, they suddenly find that they have nothing to rest upon. Others are kept going by things that happen to them, by events and by circumstances, and so, centrally, they have nothing on which they can depend and on which they live, nothing that ultimately sustains them. So I repeat that question: What keeps you going? On what are you living? On what do you depend? What is the mainspring of your life?

Or, to put this question in a slightly different form: Have you a central rest in your life, a place of quiet, a place into which you can always retreat? Amid all the multifarious activities of life and of business, is there a place at the centre where you can always go, where you know that you will have peace and quiet, where you delight to go because it gives you ultimate rest of your soul?

Now I suppose this is the question of questions for a busy, bustling age such as this present one, that is kept going so much by its own works and entertainment. The trouble today is that people lack tranquillity, they lack a quiet soul, a quiet heart, a peaceful, restful heart. And we, as Christians, must ask ourselves this very question because the mere fact that we are Christians does not in itself guarantee that we automatically have this place of rest within us.

Let me ask another question, therefore, that I think will help to make it still more plain and clear: What is the exact difference between us as Christians and the best type of unbeliever? There are people in the world today who are not believers, they deny this Christian faith, but they are good, moral people. They are men and women of ability and of understanding; they are thinkers; they realize the futility of depending upon drink and drugs and pleasure; they are people who have faced life, who have come to certain conclusions and have a working philosophy, and they keep going on that. What is the exact different between you and such a person? Is there a vital, essential difference?

Or, to put it still more directly: What does the Lord Jesus Christ himself really mean to us? That is, ultimately, the only question that matters. We say we believe in him, we have accepted his statement, 'I that speak unto thee am he.' Very well, we have correct intellectual views concerning who he is. But that still leaves the vital question that we must face: Where exactly does he come in our lives, in our whole thinking and in our whole being? We shall never know him truly, and we shall never know this experience that he himself here describes to the woman of Samaria, until we realize our deepest need, which is this ultimate rest of the soul, the final peace and quiet and confidence and assurance, the ability to stand in the midst of life with all that is happening and all that may happen and know exactly where we are because of our relationship to him.

So this is our fundamental need. Our Lord presses it upon this woman in these words: 'If thou knewest the gift of God, and who it is that speaketh to thee . . .' That was her trouble. She was aware of many problems and many difficulties – that follows of necessity from the kind of life that she was leading, as we have been seeing – but she still did not know her real need. And that is the whole trouble with the world today. It does not know its central need. It says, 'If only we could have this or that. If this stopped, if that did not take place . . .' but that is not the answer. There is this ultimate, central need of the soul, and until we are aware of that, we shall never come to a true understanding of this great offer that is made by the gospel.

That, then, is the first principle, and now we move on to the second, which is this: We must realize also that this is a need that, even at its best and highest, the world can never satisfy. These are the steps through which the saints of the centuries have always passed in coming to this ultimate blessing of the Christian life, this place of peace and of quiet that nothing can disturb. Our Lord says, 'Whosoever drinketh of this water shall thirst again.' Now this is a specific statement and it is very important. He is referring, of course, primarily to that actual physical well. He is speaking in parables to the woman, leading her to the spiritual truth and significance of what he is saying and we must do the same.

Now we need to be reminded of this second principle because the devil is always tempting us, even as Christians, to find our satisfactions outside the Lord and apart from him. Our Lord himself often warns us against this very danger. It is the kind of warning that he gives to his own followers, to his own people, not to those who are outside. He says:

Take heed to yourselves, lest at any time your hearts be overcharged with surfeiting, and drunkenness, and cares of this life, and so that day come upon you unawares. For as a snare shall it come on all them that dwell on the face of the whole earth. Watch ye therefore, and pray always, that ye may be accounted worthy to escape all these things that shall come to pass, and to stand before the Son of man. (Luke 21:34–36).

Our Lord is saying that the cares of this life, and even things that are worse, can so keep us from considering him and the state of our souls that when the crisis arrives, we suddenly find that we have nothing. The New Testament is full of warnings such as this. There is the parable of the Ten Virgins, the five wise and the five foolish. The foolish virgins think that they are all right, they think that all is well, they are not aware that there is any difference between them and the other virgins, and yet when the crisis comes, they suddenly find that they have nothing at all (Matthew 25:1–13). It is this kind of negligence, this tendency to find satisfaction elsewhere, that stands between us and the receiving of this great blessing that our Lord offers.

Then we read, too, what the apostle Paul has to say about Demas. Demas was a Christian, one of the apostle Paul's helpers, but Paul wrote to Timothy: 'Demas hath forsaken me, having loved this present world' (2 Timothy 4:10).

Now the danger that I am trying to indicate is that of having our Christian faith as just a compartment in our lives. Oh, yes, we believe in the Lord Jesus Christ as the Son of God, we believe that we need salvation, forgiveness and reconciliation to God, and we are Christians. So we give it a place. We have settled that, we say; there we are, we have become Christians. But we go on living the remainder of our lives and, perhaps, the bulk of our lives in terms of the things that the world has to offer us. Our faith is merely something to which we return periodically. But that is a complete misunderstanding of the Christian faith. It is not merely meant to have a place in our lives, it is meant to have the central place. Now I am not talking about evil things but about the danger of living on the world even at its best. We have this little compartment that is Christian, but the rest is taken up with philosophy, politics, art and culture. And so often we are really living on these instead of on our Christian faith.

This is a very basic point, which our Lord makes quite plain: 'Whosoever drinketh of this water shall thirst again.' There is no final satisfaction there. And, of course, it applies not only to the activities and interests that I have mentioned, it applies even to our family and certain relationships in life. It is possible for you to be a Christian and yet really to be living on your family, relying on the love of your family, on the relationships in the family, the life of the family. I think this danger must be plain to all of us. It is of all these things, even at their very best, that our Lord said, 'Whosoever drinketh of this water shall thirst again.'

Now why does he say that? On what grounds is that true? We will never know this 'well of water springing up into everlasting life' until we are perfectly clear about the insufficiency of everything else in the world even at its highest. Why is this of necessity true? Well, the answers that our Lord is obviously suggesting are these. First, all these only give us temporary relief. 'Whosoever drinketh of this water shall thirst again.' You take a drink of this water and it satisfies your thirst, so you say, 'This is fine, this is good! I'm satisfied.' But our Lord says: No, you are not, because this is only a temporary slaking of your thirst, it is only a temporary satisfaction.

And this is true of everything that the world has to offer. The world's pleasures give immediate satisfaction, but they are not able to do anything beyond that. They will for the time being help you, perhaps, to forget your troubles, and your problems. The world knows this. It is the secret of pleasure – pleasure as a business. It succeeds because the people who run such businesses know perfectly well that we are going to get temporary relief. While you are looking at that film, you forget your troubles, your mind is directed away from them and you are happy. But then the film ends and you are left alone – back comes your problem. All the very best that the world can give us can only give us temporary relief.

But, beyond that, the world can never give us real satisfaction for the whole of our being. It is not merely that the relief is temporary, it is that it is never fully satisfying. There are many things in the world that give us intellectual satisfaction. There are people who find peace and quiet and rest by their study of philosophy and systems of thought. And while they are engaged in these questions, of course, they are all right. Some people turn to crossword puzzles or other word and number games – these are all escape mechanisms that take your mind off the problem, off the matter that is difficult and harassing. But they only deal with one part of you, they only deal with your mind; they do not touch your heart, they do not give you satisfaction down in the depths where your feelings are engaged and involved.

But there are other interests that deal with the heart only and have nothing to give to the mind. They can move us emotionally, sentimentally and so on, and, again, they give us a temporary sense of satisfaction. Now I am not here to denounce these, all I am saying is that the mistake, the tragedy, is that men and women tend to live on these things. Music can be wonderful! 'Music hath charms to soothe the savage breast' and it soothes many other breasts as well, thank God for it. We should thank God for cultural pursuits and interests that are produced by human ability. There is nothing wrong in them. Yes, but if you depend upon them, if you are living on them, if these are what keep you going, you are missing the great solution itself, and that is the whole tragedy. These never give complete satisfaction. They are only partial, even at their best. They never deal with the whole problem because they never deal with the whole of the self.

And here is the central message. The real problem is the problem of self. A human being is merely an intellect or a heart or an acting machine. There is a wholeness about life. It is very difficult to put this into words and yet we all know it. 'I am' – and the totality of my personality is the problem. Unless these interests and pleasures can satisfy me as a whole, then finally they are like this well of water to which our Lord pointed and said that when we drink its water we shall thirst again. We are individuals, we are entities, and inevitably we come face to face with our self at various points – when we have exhausted what the world can give us, or when, because of our physical condition, perhaps, we are no longer able to pursue these interests and to live on them. And there we are left alone.

And here is the whole problem of life; it is depicted in many, many pictures in the Bible itself. One of the greatest, one of the most moving of all, is the case of Jacob on that famous night when he knew he had got to meet his brother Esau the next morning. He had done well, he had prospered, he had his wives and his children, he had his cattle, his herds and his sheep. He had gone out as a fugitive, as an isolated individual, but here he was, coming back to his homeland a very wealthy man. And yet the problem remained: he had to meet Esau whom he had wronged. And then we read the tremendous story of what happened to him that night. There he was. He had sent all his cattle and his sheep and his goods on ahead. And then finally he had sent on his wives and his children. Then there is this tremendous statement in the Scripture – 'And Jacob was left alone' (Genesis 32:24).

And there was the problem. It was the greatest crisis of his life, and it led to the greatest blessing. But he had to be brought to that point. His danger was that of living on the goods, the possessions, the animals, the wives, the children, the family life, but he suddenly realized that he was alone, Jacob the individual, the entity. Though he owned all this, now he was back where he was when he had run away from the anger of his brother on that old occasion. 'Jacob was left alone.' And every one of us is left alone. There is that about every one of us that makes us alone, as Jacob was on that occasion, and we experience this from time to time. Then we know that all that we have and all that the world has given us, or can ever give us, can never deal with this problem of the self; I myself, my whole life, my future. Here I am, I stand alone. 'Jacob was left alone.' And it is because of this that these other things even at their best can never give us a true and a real satisfaction. 'Whosoever drinketh of this water shall thirst again.'

Now why is this the case? Well, this is the great message of the whole of the Bible. This is so because of the nature of man, because we are what we are. There is something tremendous about who we are, something that makes us all thank God for the fact that the world cannot satisfy us. Even if it gave us everything, if it gave us itself, it could not satisfy us. 'For what shall it profit a man, if he shall gain the whole world, and lose his own soul?' (Mark 8:36). Yes, that is it. Man is bigger than the universe. He is bigger than mountains, he is bigger than seas, he is bigger than everything that creation can produce. He is made in the image and likeness of God, he is made for God, so he is too big for the world, and the world cannot satisfy him. He has a soul within him, and that soul can be satisfied by nothing less than God himself and communion with God. It is in our realization of this need that we come to a true understanding of ourselves, our nature, our true being. This is painful at first, but once you see it correctly, you will realize that it is the greatest fact about you. You are so big that all the world has to offer can never give you final satisfaction. The very nature of men and women made in the image and likeness of God makes this inevitable.

But on top of this, there is the whole fact of sin – sin in our nature, sin in our acts – and this aggravates the problem. The prophet Isaiah says, 'The wicked are like the troubled sea, when it cannot rest' (Isaiah 57:20), and that is why the world is restless. The world does not know the truth about itself and it is trying to find its satisfaction where it can never find it, so it is restless, left to itself, unhappy, rushing from activity to activity to solace itself, and only ever finding temporary satisfaction. There is this motion, this constant trouble, this seeking for something it cannot find. This is the whole story of the human race.

And then, of course, there is the sense of guilt and the sense of shame and the sense of failure. There is no rest while these remain; there is no philosophy that can satisfy a troubled conscience. That is why the world at its best cannot ultimately satisfy me. My mind can be interested, my heart may be moved, but again I am left with the problem of myself; I forgot it while I was enjoying that symphony, or whatever it was, but it has ended and I am alone again. I lie on my bed, I am alone, and back it comes – myself. And I am aware within me of this struggle – the flesh: 'For the flesh lusteth against the Spirit, and the Spirit against the flesh' (Galatians 5:17). That is why human beings are restless and that is why it is true to say that the world, with all that it has to offer, can never satisfy our need.

'Whosoever drinketh of this water shall thirst again', and it is at this point, my dear Christian friends, that we see the real failure of humanism and the so-called 'good pagan'. Humanism is popular today; people are rejecting this gospel in terms of humanism. Of course, the humanist is an intellectual and he is interested in intellectual gymnastics, in thought, but the day will come when he will be incapable of doing that, and he will be left to himself. He has to turn to other things, to stimulants, to drink and to drugs. It is just here at the centre of his life that he fails most of all. You cannot live on your interests, you cannot live on your abilities, because they are all bound to come to an end and, in any case, they never give you complete satisfaction, as we have seen.

So we have come to an absolute, essential principle in connection with this whole great teaching. Not only must I realize my need, I must realize that it is a need that the universe cannot satisfy. If I could possess the whole world, it would not satisfy me. There is that within me that cries out for the living God himself. That is my way of saying what Augustine said perfectly: 'Thou hast made us for thyself and our hearts are restless until they find their rest in thee.' And this is true of every one of us. You all know this. If you could find rest and peace, you would have found it, but you cannot in and of yourself. Augustine has given us the reason.

Are you clear about this? Are you clear that the world in its entirety cannot satisfy you, that this need of yours is a need beyond the scope and the ambit and the ability of human beings at their very highest?

And that leads me to my third and last principle. Our Lord points out that we must realize the possibilities of the Christian life, and, God willing, we shall be considering this. The mere fact that you are a Christian does not mean that you know these possibilities. It is because Christians do not know them that the Epistles in the New Testament were all written, that is why they became necessary. If the moment people became Christians they suddenly understood and possessed all the teaching, they would not have needed these Epistles with their great instruction. No, no; we need to be instructed and our Lord instructs this woman of Samaria at this point. He puts it in these words: 'If thou knewest the gift of God' – if only you knew! But she did not know, and I feel that that is his word to us at the beginning of this new year. Christian people, at the present time we are in danger of limiting this gospel, in danger of reducing these glorious statements to the level of our own little experience. My dear people, we are only at the beginning of these things, we are but as children paddling at the edge of an ocean. Launch out into the deep! 'If thou knewest' the depth of what is offered in the glorious gospel!

'If thou knewest the gift of God.' What does our Lord mean by that? Some expositors say that he is referring to himself there. 'God so loved the world, that he gave his only begotten Son' (John 3:16). I reject that explanation because he immediately goes on to refer to himself – 'If thou knewest the gift of God, and who it is that saith to thee . . .'. So what is the gift of God?

God's gift is everything that God has made possible for us in and through the Lord Jesus Christ. God has treasured and stored up in him all the riches of his wisdom and his grace and his knowledge. It is all the blessings that come to us through Christ the Son of God.

This is not merely a matter of being forgiven or of taking a decision and becoming a Christian and a member of the church. It includes that, but that is the mere beginning, that is merely entering into the life, and the danger is that so many people stop at that. They are always looking back to something they once did, to a decision once taken. They say, 'I became a Christian', and from there on they have never grown, they have never developed, they know nothing about all that our Lord is referring to here. They have reduced Christian grace and the gospel to just this matter of having our sins forgiven and becoming Christians, to not doing certain things while going on living the humdrum, inadequate kind of life that I have been describing.

That is not it. This is the biggest thing in the universe, this is the most glorious life, and our Lord says to the woman, 'If thou knewest the gift of God'! It is a gift from God, it is all of God, it is of God from the beginning to the end. 'The wages of sin is death; but the gift of God is eternal life through Jesus Christ our Lord' (Romans 6:23). Christianity does not just mean that you live on your own activities, even on your own goodness, or your own striving. Of course, we must seek goodness, we must strive, but the essence is that God *gives* this. 'If thou knewest the gift of God.'

The apostle Paul puts it in this way: 'the exceeding riches of his grace' (Ephesians 2:7). And he says that he is privileged 'to preach among the Gentiles the unsearchable riches of Christ' (Ephesians 3:8). Do you know them? Are you possessing them? Are you rejoicing in them? Are you thrilled by them? This is what we need to face. 'If only you knew,' says our Lord to this woman. So I say this to myself and I say it to you – do you know 'the unsearchable riches of Christ?' Or are you a pauper? Are you living a life of stress and strain and unhappiness? If you are, your life is not compatible with what you believe. If there is no rest, no peace or joy, it is because you do not know the gift of God, you have reduced the Christian gospel, the offer of salvation in its fullness, just to some little level that is compatible with your thinking.

No, no; here is the word: 'If thou knewest' the things that are possible to you, what a transformation it would produce! This, it seems to me, is what the Christian church needs to concentrate on at the present time. All right, we have been forgiven, so now let us go on to perfection; let us know about 'the breadth, and length, and depth, and height' and 'the love of Christ, which passeth knowledge', that we might be 'filled with all the fulness of God' (Ephesians 3:18–19). That is Christianity. That is what our Lord is talking about here.

But let me close by just noting these two words that our Lord uses: 'living water'. This is what we must know about. What does he mean when he calls this gift 'living water'? He means that it is life-giving, it is enlivening, it is stimulating, it is invigorating. Have you got this life in you? Or do you have to drag yourself to worship God? Do you have to force yourself to live the Christian life? Are you a bit ashamed of it when you meet your clever friends in the world? If so, there is something radically wrong. It is 'living water'. It is not some cold, detached, theoretical, intellectual understanding of a number of doctrines. Yes, it is an understanding, but if it does not give life to you, if it does not enliven you, if it does not move you, if it does not invigorate you, you have not got the 'living water'.

What else? Well, it is always fresh. It is not water stored in a cistern; it is not static water. It comes out of a well opened on Calvary's hill, opened in the heart of God; it is flowing, and it constantly comes with its new stream, always fresh, always living.

So much Christianity seems to be stale, does it not? It is old, it is
ineffective, it is dull, it is lifeless, it is insipid, you feel it needs to
be purified. And the world is not interested in it because it looks
at it and sees the scum on the surface, and the things that should
not be there. It does not see the sparkle, it does not see the
light, the living quality. Oh, what a travesty all this is of the true
Christian life and the true Christian message!

And, finally, this water lasts. 'Whosoever drinketh of this water
shall thirst again' – but not those who drink the living water. Whatever may happen in the world, in the whole cosmos, nothing can
stop it, it springs up into everlasting life, it goes on. There will
never be a shortage, there will never be a drought, there will never
be a lack of supply. So not merely is your thirst satisfied, but you
have lasting life and power, and are ready to meet the world, the
flesh and the devil and anything that may come against you in this
year and in all the years that may be left to you.

I just want to end by asking you a question in the form of a
quotation from a hymn. I am not asking about your beliefs at the
moment, I am assuming them. Here is the question: can you say
something like this?

> O Christ, in thee my soul hath found,
> And found in thee alone,
> The peace, the joy I sought so long,
> The bliss till now unknown.
>
> Now none but Christ can satisfy,
> None other name for me . . .
> There's love, and life, and lasting joy,
> Lord Jesus, found in thee.
>
> I sighed for rest and happiness,
> I yearned for them not thee.

That is what I have been trying to say: do not seek the wells of the world, seek him!

But while I passed my Saviour by,
His love laid hold on me.

'He must needs go through Samaria.' 'God seeketh such to worship him.'

I tried the broken cisterns, Lord,
But ah! The waters failed!
E'en as I stooped to drink they'd fled,
And mocked me as I wailed.
Author unknown

And that is what the world ultimately does to us. In your need, in your failure, it will mock you, it will laugh at you, it will jeer at you. It has no use for failures, it will pass you by. But, thank God, our Saviour is the one who 'must needs go through Samaria', who meets the woman as she is, and gives her 'living water'.

'If thou knewest the gift of God . . .' Do you know it? Have you asked for it? Have you received it?

14

Christianity or Religion?

Jesus answered and said unto her, If thou knewest the gift of God, and who it is that saith to thee, Give me to drink; thou wouldest have asked of him, and he would have given thee living water . . . Whosoever drinketh of this water shall thirst again: but whosoever drinketh of the water that I shall give him shall never thirst; but the water that I shall give him shall be in him a well of water springing up into everlasting life. (John 4:10, 13–14)

We have been looking at this passage for some time because it is such a crucial statement. We see here what our Lord offers to give to all who come to him, even as he offered it to the woman of Samaria. This is essential Christianity, this is what Christianity really means, and that is why we are considering these words so carefully. To me, the only hope of true revival, the only hope of the church having any influence upon the world that is outside, is that you and I should show this kind of life in our daily living. Undoubtedly, the people who are outside Christianity – and they are in the great majority in this country – are in that position because they have no concept of what Christianity really is. They get their ideas from those of us who claim to be Christian, and they have come to the conclusion that we lead a miserable, poor sort of life. They are sorry for us because they feel that they have gained so much by being emancipated from the shackles of religion.

So the real explanation of the present state and condition of people today is that you and I are failing to show the real meaning of the Christian life. We are apologetic, we seem to be living it with a grudge. We will allow almost anything, the slightest excuse, to prevent our coming together to worship God. The man of the world would not dream of using such pretexts. But we do, we are half-hearted, and it is all because we ourselves do not realize as we should the nature of this life that is being offered us.

Now is not this, I say, true of all of us in a measure at the present time? I do not hesitate to say that the greatest sin of the modern Christian is the sin of reducing Christianity to the level of our own experiences and our own understanding. We limit 'the Holy One of Israel'. Now this is a most serious matter. It not only robs us of the blessings of the Christian life, it makes the church weak and ineffective and therefore, as I say, in a sense, it accounts for the condition of the world outside.

We must all be concerned about the mounting moral problem; we are aware of a declension. There were times when things were better, but why were they better? And the invariable answer is that the best periods in the life of this country, as in every other country, have always followed an evangelical revival, a true awakening produced by the Spirit of God. This does not mean that everyone has become a Christian, but when you have a powerful church, a powerful witness and testimony, it affects even those who are not Christians. The whole level of moral living is raised. You had it in the Elizabethan period, you had it at the time of the Commonwealth, you had it especially after the great

Evangelical Awakening of the eighteenth century, the effects of which were so clearly seen during the following century.

Now every true revival of religion is really a rediscovery of this great message that we are now considering. If you take the trouble to read the history of the church, you will find that its story can be represented in a kind of graph. It starts on the Day of Pentecost in that mighty outpouring of the Spirit, when the people were lifted up to the level described in the book of Acts and in the New Testament Epistles. But after that the church went down into a trough. Then there was a revival. That has been the story of the church. There has been a series of rises and falls. But there is always a fatal tendency in the church to settle down on a lower level and to be content with that. This level is characterized by an emphasis upon forms and externals, upon duties and human activities. Great emphasis is always placed upon dignity and ceremony and order and, corres-pondingly, there is a loss of life and vigour and power. Religion tends always to become respectable and people are content with that.

But then one individual, or a number of individuals, become convicted about the loss of life in the church. While they are reading the Scriptures that they have read so many times before, suddenly a word is illuminated by the Spirit and they are given to realize that their level of life is altogether too low. These people realize that they are no different from the Pharisees of old, who reduced the Law of Moses to the level of their own little rules and regulations and missed the whole spirit. They see that they have turned this great and glorious gospel into some neat little package and they have been satisfied with that. But now they are disturbed and condemned. They begin to think that they have never been Christians at all, and they proceed to pray and to read the Scriptures, and God hears them and answers them, and they are given this living water.

This happened before the Protestant Reformation, among little groups of people in various parts of Europe. So, for instance, we get the Waldensian Church in northern Italy, and the Brethren of the Common Life.[1] These small groups of people were awakened to see that the church – the Roman Catholic Church, of course, at that time – was a travesty of New Testament Christianity and of the New Testament church. And they began to understand that Christianity is living and life-giving.

But of course, we see this new life still more clearly in the Protestant Reformation itself. But we must be fair. The Protestant Reformation of the sixteenth century did not solve all the problems once and for ever. In the seventeenth century, the early part particularly, the great truth that had been rediscovered by people such as Luther and Calvin now hardened into a dead orthodoxy, a kind of scholasticism. It happened in this country and on the continent of Europe perhaps still more strikingly. The Lutheran Church became dead, solidified, very orthodox. Theologians would be arguing about minutiae, and Christianity was a matter of the intellect. Then certain men arose who began to say that although all this was all right for people who had an interest in intellectual disputes, it was not the Christianity that is found in the New Testament. That was the beginning of the movement known as Pietism. In Germany, certain men, Johann Arndt, Spener and others, began to teach this message, and it led to great results on the continent of Europe.

In Britain, the Puritans, up to a point, were doing exactly the same thing. But we see this still more clearly in the eighteenth

---

[1] The Brethren of the Common Life started in Holland in the late fourteenth century and spread into southern and western Germany and into Poland.

century. If you read the account of the Christian church in this country in the early part of that century, you will see how deplorable it was, and how dead. Not only the state Anglican Church, but the Nonconformist Churches also, had again become intellectualized and barren, splitting hairs about doctrines; and the moral condition of the nation was, if anything, even worse than it is today.

But then there was a great revival. How did it come about? Well, this is the interesting thing: it again came through people being brought back to the kind of statement that we find in our passage. George Whitefield and the Wesley brothers were pro-foundly influenced by two books. The first, *The Life of God in the Soul of Man*, had been written at the end of the previous century by a Scotsman called Henry Scougal. The other was by William Law – William Law's famous *Serious Call to a Devout and Holy Life*. But it was the book by Scougal that was especially influen-tial. When we read the journals of Whitefield and the Wesleys, we find that all three say that they read this book and saw that what they had regarded as Christianity was not Christianity at all. So they began to doubt whether they had ever been Christians, in fact, they were convinced that they had not. They did not have the 'life of God' in their souls; but they were quite convinced by the argumentation of the book that that was a true representation of the New Testament teaching. And it was this realization of the truth about the Christian life that really led to the Evangelical Awakening and revival.

Now it seems to me that this is the message that is needed today more than ever. Are we satisfied with the Christian life that we have and that we are living? Is it not our danger, too, that it all becomes hardened, that we are content with a little life, which is a good life, a moral life? Up to a point, even that is now beginning to be shaken, is it not? This is always so when you lose the true life.

Increasing concessions are being made by evangelical people over drink and various other issues. There is a general slackening all along the line. Christian people are also contented with a kind of decisionism. You make your decision, you take up Christianity, you attend a place of worship, and you indulge in certain activities – and there it is. You feel you have got it all and you now propose to go on living the rest of your life in this way.

But that is not New Testament Christianity, it is not the 'living water' that our Lord speaks about, and that is why it is having such little effect; it is lacking at this most vital point. So that is why we must look at this statement here most carefully and prayerfully. Over and against that neat, glib, self-satisfied kind of Christian life, we must look at this description. I am once more going to show you the difference between Christianity and religion. This is a very subtle danger, this tendency to persuade ourselves that because we have taken up religion, we have become Christians. Are we aware of the distinction?

There are many people who decide to become religious. But the question is: Are they Christian? Do we become Christians in that way? I have given you something of the testimony of history, and you will find that some of the most notable saints, people such as Whitefield and the Wesleys, had thought that because of their good works and activities, their moral efforts, their philanthropy, they were exceptionally good Christians. But they were not Christians at all. Why not? Because they knew nothing about this: 'Whosoever drinketh of this water shall thirst again: but whosoever drinketh of the water that I shall give him shall never thirst; but the water that I shall give shall be in him a well of water springing up into everlasting life.'

So let us look at this wonderful life that the Son of God has come to give us, and God grant that we may so see it that we shall

all be ashamed of ourselves and our self-satisfaction, and shall give ourselves no rest nor peace until we know for certain that we have within us this 'well of water springing up into everlasting life'. Oh, if this but happened, the revival we long for would have come, and the world and the church would soon begin to be different.

What, then, are the characteristics of this great life? Well, here are some that we can note. I would divide the characteristics into general and particular. And the first general characteristic is that it is experiential. It happens to us and we know it has happened. This cannot happen without our knowing it. The water was offered to us, we received it, we drank of it. There is a vital, inescapable difference in our lives. You find this, not only in these words of our Lord to the Samaritan woman, and in comparable statements elsewhere in the Scriptures, but also in the biographies of the saints and the history of the church. It is always the case.

So this is one of the ways in which we can see the difference between being religious and being Christian. You can be religious as the result of tradition: by being born and brought up in a certain country, in a certain family; by being taught to do certain things and always doing them. In this way, you are being religious, as the Jews and Muslims and members of other faiths are religious. And it is true of many people in the Christian church. These people adhere to the traditions and practices of the church. They have no idea what they are really doing or why they are doing it. All they know is that this is what they have always been taught and they imagine that it is what makes them truly Christian. This is their idea, their notion of Christianity. But this cannot be fitted into what our Lord said to the woman of Samaria. There is nothing experiential about it. These people are not what they are because of something that has happened to them in a vital sense. We can put it in the words of the hymn by Joseph Hart: 'True religion's more than notion.'

These words are the title of a recently published book, *More than Notion*.[2] Read it and you will see the very point I am making. You will read there of a family that was considered to be a very godly and noble Christian family, but one by one the members of that family began to realize that they had never been Christians at all. They were religious, yes – very good, very moral, very active – but they had not got anything within them, there was nothing vital, there was nothing living; they had not had the kind of experience that our Lord is speaking of. This, by its very nature, is experiential.

Now a further, very subtle danger comes in at this point. There are those who seem to think that experience of the power of the gospel is only possible to those who have been violent or profligate, as I know some of you here have been. I know something of this fallacy as I look back on my own early life and experience. You say, 'Ah, yes, of course, if a man had been a drunkard or something terrible like that, and then suddenly saw the truth, there would be a great change and of course he would be well aware of it. It is something big, it is dramatic. But if we have always been good and religious and moral, and have always lived a clean life, well, of course, we cannot expect anything like that.'

Now have you harboured that kind of argument? I remember someone once saying to me that she almost wished she had been a drunkard so that she could have had this great experience. Now you see the fallacy? It is to imagine that you can only have this great experience if you are coming from a position of violent negativity, as it were, to positivity. The answer to that way of thinking is found in Jesus' words to the woman of Samaria. There is as much, if not a

---

2 J. H. Alexander, *More than Notion*, Fauconberg Press 1964.

greater, difference between being religious and then receiving this life, as there is between violently evil conduct and good, respectable conduct. Why? Because this is life from God, and if you imagine that the difference between life from God and the good, respectable religious life is only slight, then you have misunderstood the whole case. And that is what is so wonderful about some of the experiences that I have already reminded you of. People such as Whitefield and the Wesleys were always exceptionally good, yet they were the people who had this profound experience. So you must not only think of coming up from the gutter to the level of the road. No, no; you must think of being moved from the level of the road to the skies, from man to God.

The second characteristic is that the Christian experience is received directly from the Lord Jesus Christ himself: 'If thou knewest the gift of God, and who it is that saith to thee . . .' And again, in the fourteenth verse, 'But whosoever drinketh of the water that I shall give him shall never thirst.' Again, this is a most important point, and I must emphasize it because it is the one thing that differentiates the Christian experience from what is commonly called mysticism, which can be one of the greatest dangers to true faith. Mysticism works like this. The moment you begin to feel dissatisfied with the neat, glib, 'package' kind of Christianity in which you think you have it all, and all you have to do is to go on like that for the rest of your life, the moment you see through that and begin to feel dissatisfied, you will probably start to read books, and there are many to choose from. And perhaps you will start reading about the mystics and their experience of God, their being raised to a new level of life. And you will say to yourself, 'Ah, yes, that life I've always been living is all right as far as it went but it doesn't seem to be true Christianity, I am in control of the whole thing. There is another order of life that is altogether different.'

But the difficulty is that those mystics, most of them, will tell you that this life is to be attained by following certain rules or practices that they will prescribe for you. And they say that as you go on and do this, you will pass through different stages and ultimately you will come to that stage of contemplation where you have your great experience. But the fallacy is that, generally speaking, the Lord Jesus Christ does not come into it at all. They will tell you to look into yourself; they will tell you to find God who is within you.

Quakerism, of course, has fallen into this error. Having started more or less in the right way, it went astray and the result is that the Lord Jesus Christ has come to mean less and less. What you do is sit in silence and wait; the life is within you and as you wait in silence, you discover this life and so develop it and foster it. Now that is the essence of the mystical notion. But the Lord Jesus Christ is not vital to it, he is not central, he is not essential. This life does not come from him directly, but from the contemplation of God as the result of travelling along this mystic way. It is not the Lord Jesus Christ offering you this living water and then you drinking it. It is not directly and immediately related to him.

Our Lord's words to the woman of Samaria not only differentiate the true Christian experience from mysticism, they also, of course, show the complete difference between it and the teaching of all the cults. I am not surprised that the cults are flourishing. When Christianity is moribund, when it is just orthodox and glib and self-satisfied and self-contained, then people in trouble will turn to something else and these other things can give some sort of an experience. We need not go into that, I have often mentioned it. But it is no use denying that the cults can help you; if they did not, they would not flourish, they would have long since ceased to be. They flourish because they can give some kind of relief, some kind of experience.

So how do you tell the difference between the cults and the fullness of life that our Lord is offering here? Well, here he is absolutely central and essential. This experience is based upon him. There must be no uncertainty about this. We see it from his words, 'If thou knewest the gift of God, and who it is that saith to thee . . .', leading on to the great statement in verse 26: 'Jesus saith unto her, I that speak unto thee am he.' It is all based upon the fact that he is the Son of God, the one who says, 'I am come that they might have life, and that they might have it more abundantly' (John 10:10). Christianity is Christ himself, and his teaching.

But still more, Christianity is based upon what our Lord does, what he did when he died on the cross and rose again in the resurrection, and sent the Holy Spirit down upon the church on the Day of Pentecost. He says here, 'The water that I shall give him . . .' and he is referring, of course, to the giving of the Holy Spirit. This is his great gift. Later in John's Gospel, we find parallels to our Lord's words here. In John chapter 7, for instance, we read:

> *In the last day, that great day of the feast, Jesus stood and cried, saying, If any man thirst, let him come unto me, and drink . . . out of his belly shall flow rivers of living water.*

And John explains:

> *This spake he of the Spirit, which they that believe on him should receive: for the Holy Ghost was not yet given; because that Jesus was not yet glorified. (John 7:37–39)*

This is all a reference to the life of the Spirit, the Spirit that he was going to give. And there are many other examples and illustrations of this teaching. So it is obviously an essential and central point that the Spirit is given because the Son of God has come from heaven and has become incarnate. He has come that we might have life, and the life he gives us is his own life. We are made 'partakers of the divine nature' (2 Peter 1:4). I shall elaborate on these words later – all I am emphasizing now is that there are, on the very surface, those two general characteristics about this life. It is an experience, and it is a direct experience of contact with the Lord Jesus Christ, and you are aware that it comes from him and from him alone.

But now let us look at the particular characteristics of this life, and they are put quite plainly before us in this passage in John 4. 'Whosoever drinketh of this water shall thirst again: but whosoever drinketh of the water that I shall give him shall never thirst' – why not? Well, because – 'the water that I shall give him shall be in him [within him] . . .' Now the particular characteristics are vital, and none more so than this. One of the greatest differentiating points between religion and Christianity is that Christianity is always something within, whereas religion is always external.

I remember reading a book on the Victorians, a book entitled *Poetry and Morals*, and in it there was one most illuminating sentence that I constantly return to because it is so true. In a sense, says the author, 'Religion overshadowed the Victorians, instead of penetrating them.' In other words, religion never got inside them. I am often tempted to put it like this: the first thing we must do, in a sense, is to forget the Victorians – I am speaking in a religious sense, primarily. The nineteenth century was a devastating century from the standpoint of true Christianity. As we have seen, there has always been a curious alternation in people's responses to God. It almost happens from century to century: a century of revival followed by a century of hardening, and then a revival again. And the Victorian period was an age of respectability, an age that prided itself on its intellect and its understanding, its scientific discoveries, its discovery of unknown parts of the world. You know the whole mentality and outlook that goes under the name of Victoria.

And this outlook influenced the Christian church, it even influenced the architecture of Nonconformist chapels so that from the square places of meeting – meeting houses, buildings in which you could meet and worship God and preach the gospel, square, unadorned, but excellent for preaching because of their fine acoustics – from that they went to mock Gothic and sham and pretence, with everything big and ornate. They had lost the spirit, they had become respectable, they had turned their Christian faith into religion. Their argument was, of course, that people had now become educated and you could no longer have the ignorant preachers of former times, Methodist or Strict Baptist or whatever you used to have. You must now have a cultured ministry. And they had it, and the more they had it, the more the Spirit went out, and the church became dead and fossilized and respectable.

That was what happened. And that was true of the so-called great Victorians, Matthew Arnold, John Ruskin and others. They could not leave religion alone, they were always playing with it, but they knew nothing about Christianity, nothing at all. Religion was, as that author says, something that 'overshadowed' them; it was there as a kind of cloud. It spoiled life for them, it made them unhappy, it made many of them morbid, but they never knew the release, the life, the power, the 'living water'. Tennyson, Browning, all these men, they came so near, so many of them, but they never experienced it, it never 'penetrated' into them.

But the first particular characteristic of the true Christian life and experience is that it 'shall be in him'! You see the contrast with the well? That is outside and the woman has to come back and forth to it. And our Lord says that religion is like that, it is always outside you. So let us examine ourselves in the light of this. Is what you regard as your Christianity something that is in you or outside you? Is it a part of you or is it apart from you?

Now there is no difficulty about answering this question, we all know this for certain one way or the other. Is what you regard as your Christianity a mere addition to your life, something that you add on to your life, or is it really central and within? This is a most terrible danger. I take it that many of us have known exactly what I am talking about. Here is your life, and the only difference between you and other people is that you have an appendix to the book of your life and in this appendix you are religious. You happen to go to a place of worship once on a Sunday, whereas other people never go at all. They are as moral as you are and their outlook on life is more or less yours, you just do this odd thing that they do not do – you tack on something extra. Religion is something that you add on, as you put on a coat and take it off again.

But by definition, that is not Christianity. Or we can put it another way: Is what you regard as your Christianity something that you take up occasionally, and then put down again, something that you indulge in spasmodically? Is it something that only applies to Sunday? Now that is very true of religion. Or let me put it like this: Is what you regard as your Christianity something that you have to be reminded of or something, perhaps, of which you have to remind yourself – 'I am a Christian, after all' – is that it? Now that again, I say, is religion.

Oh, this has been true of so many. They have assumed that they are Christians but Christianity does not mean anything to them. They have not thought about it for a long time. But then they are taken ill and it all comes back to them. They had to be taken ill before they were reminded that they were Christians. I have seen so much of this. Any man who has been any length of time in the ministry has seen it. He has seen people who, when things are going well, fall slack and say, 'Ah, there will be time for that later, but first there are interesting and wonderful things to do.' Then they are taken ill and suddenly they are most anxious to have some help and they come back to Christianity and they are zealous and they are praying and they remember their Bibles again. But that is not Christianity. That is something outside you, something that you can forget all about and have to be reminded of by illness or accident or bereavement or sorrow, or something unusual.

But so much that passes as Christianity falls into that kind of category and that is why the masses of the people are outside the church. They say, 'Those people don't believe in it themselves. They can forget all about it. It's not part of them. It's something that they have to be reminded of or remind themselves of when they are in trouble or at the beginning of a year or on festival days. Then they take it up and afterwards they put it down and forget all about it again.'

Or, lastly, is your Christianity just some vague general influence that affects only the surface of your life, only the outward part of your life and living? These are the questions we must ask ourselves. And the extraordinary thing about this is that we all know exactly what the answer is. We can try and argue with ourselves, but we know what we are doing.

There, then, is a description of religion which is outside. But here is something entirely different. 'The water that I shall give him shall be in him a well of water springing up into everlasting life.' This means even more than I have been saying so far. I have said that religion is outside your life while Christianity is a part of it, but I must go beyond that. It is not merely a part of your life – it is the centre of your life. Now there is no need to argue this, again, it must be true, by definition. This is the Son of God speaking, remember. It is the second Person in the blessed Holy Trinity. It is he who is giving this gift and, if you believe in him at all, you must believe that what he gives is central.

Now we know all of this, do we not, from natural analogies. We tend to evaluate the things we possess and the gifts we have in terms of the people who have given them to us. That is what puts value upon particular objects – and this is perfectly right. Very often, it is not its inherent value that makes us treasure a gift so much as the person who gave it to us. Now apply all that here. He gives this gift; and if we believe that, well, then, it is not peripheral, it is the most central thing in our lives. It is in us and it must control the whole of life; it becomes the spring of all our activities.

Christianity has often been called 'heart religion' and that is quite a good term, except that it is open to a little bit of misunderstanding. When it is called 'heart religion', the term 'heart' is used, as it is in Scripture, to mean the centre of the personality. It means that Christianity is not merely a matter of the head, not merely something intellectual, but that it really is there at the very centre and that it makes us what we are and controls everything that we do. Now that is the essence of this whole teaching. In other words, what our Lord is saying here is the answer to certain cries that come out in the Old Testament. Let me give you one or two as I close.

You remember David in Psalm 51? He has been guilty of terrible sins and he is well aware of the dreadful character of his sins; but that is not what really troubles him. What really troubles him is this: 'Behold, thou desirest truth in the inward parts' (Psalm 51:6). David had gone on being religious, conforming to the externals of religion, not only before he had committed his terrible sins but even during that time and afterwards, and he was not aware that anything was wrong. But when he is brought to himself, and brought to the place of repentance, he sees it all: 'Thou desirest truth in the inward parts.' And the moment we become aware of that, we begin to seek for this living water, and we are open to this message that is given here by the Lord to the woman of Samaria. We are no longer content with the externals and the surface and the superficial.

'Truth in the inward parts'! That is what I need; here it is offered me: '. . . shall be within you a well of water springing up into everlasting life'. Or look at David's corresponding prayer: 'Create in me a clean heart, O God; and renew a right spirit within me' (Psalm 51:10). He can see that his trouble is in his heart, and unless his heart is put right, nothing will be right. No appearances are adequate; while there is a single iniquity within, while a polluted fountain controls all my activities, all that comes out will never 'create within me a clean heart', or 'renew a right spirit within me'. No, here it is: 'a well of water springing up' from the centre of the personality. No longer outside or peripheral, but central.

Or take the way in which it is put in the book of Ezekiel. God has promised this, you see, he is preparing his people for it. And he is always contrasting the old with the new. He says, 'Then will I sprinkle clean water upon you, and ye shall be clean' (Ezekiel 36:25). But that is not all. 'A new heart also will I give you, and a new spirit will I put within you: and I will take away the stony heart out of your flesh, and I will give you an heart of flesh' (Ezekiel 36:26). I will be going on to elaborate this verse, God willing, but now I am simply making the general point that this living water takes out the stony heart and gives us a heart of flesh. It is experiential, as I have been saying. It is within, it is living and it is vital.

Or take it in the way in which Jeremiah puts it as quoted in the eighth chapter of the Epistle to the Hebrews: 'I will put my laws into their mind, and write them in their hearts' (Hebrews 8:10). Morality, religion outside you, laws written on tablets of stone to which you are trying to conform. But here is something 'within you', a spring, a 'well of water springing up into everlasting life'.

Have you got 'heart' religion or only 'head' religion or 'will' religion? Is it inside you at the very spring and source and centre of the whole of your personality? This is what our Lord gives; this is what he offers. 'The water that I shall give him shall be in him [within him] a well of water springing up into everlasting life.' God give us grace to be honest with ourselves. He does require 'truth in the inward parts' and he knows all about us. Let us examine ourselves honestly in the light of his word.

15

Power

Jesus answered and said unto her, If thou knewest the gift of God, and who it is that saith to thee, Give me to drink; thou wouldest have asked of him, and he would have given thee living water . . . Whosoever drinketh of this water shall thirst again: but whosoever drinketh of the water that I shall give him shall never thirst; but the water that I shall give him shall be in him a well of water springing up into everlasting life. (John 4:10, 13–14)

We are considering this great and glorious statement of the Christian gospel as it was made by our Lord and Saviour Jesus Christ himself to the woman of Samaria. This is essential Christianity and there is nothing more important than that we should be certain that we not only know that but should have experienced something of it. We are asking why it is that we know so little about this well of water springing up into everlasting life. We have considered the many hindrances and we are now looking at this matter positively.

I have suggested that first we must realize our need and we must be aware of the quality of the life we have and how it measures up to the standard that we see here. For instance, you can look at a liquid in a glass and it appears to be milk, but if an analyst comes to test it, he may find it is very deficient in fats and has a good deal of adulteration with water, so much so that it is not milk at all. And that is true of so much Christianity. It looks as if it is the right thing, but when you analyse it, you find that it is seriously defective. So we must really be aware of our need and we must see that nothing else in the world can satisfy it but this living water, and we must realize that this is indeed '*living* water'.

We are now considering the characteristics of this great life that our Lord has come to give us. I have suggested that they can be divided into general and particular characteristics. We have considered the two general characteristics: first, it is experiential, not theoretical; second, it is always intimately connected with the Lord Jesus Christ himself. It comes directly from him and thereby we differentiate it from all mystical experiences and all the cults.

Then we have started on the particular characteristics of this life, and the first is, of course, that it is within us, it is a 'well of water springing up into everlasting life'. The next point I want to note is that this life is a power. It is a power within us, a power that acts within us – 'shall be in him a well of water springing up'. Now if you know anything about a well, you know that that is its characteristic – it is living. What a difference there is between a well and a trough or a cistern with water in it; there is no life there. But here there is an activity springing up, a power, dynamism; there is a force. And this, our Lord tells us, is one of the outstanding characteristics of this life that he has to give us.

How do we know, then, whether or not we have this life? Well, let us test ourselves by this second particular characteristic, this manifestation of power within us. It means that the Christian life is not primarily a life of our activity. Of course, we have things to do, but that is not the essential factor. We are bearing in our minds, I trust, the contrast between religion – any kind of religion – and true Christianity, and this is one of the chief differences. In religion, it is our activity that counts the whole time. But here we are in a different realm altogether. Here is a power that is acting within us – 'a well of water springing up'. Whatever we may or may not be doing, it has life and vigour and power, and acts in us. And so the relationship between Christians and their activities is this – and this is where there is such a striking contrast with religion – Christians act because they are made to act; their action, their activity, is the result of this other, prior, activity.

In other words, we are dealing with what may be called the dynamic of the Holy Spirit. Our Lord says that he has this to give, he gives us life; he gives us the Spirit. There is a phrase in a hymn that says:

> O Jesus, light of all below!
> Thou fount of life and fire.
> > *Bernard of Clairvaux*
> > *E. Caswall (trans)*

You may criticize that – how can you have fire in a fountain? It does not matter. He is the fount. He is the source 'of life and fire'. Now I want to emphasize the aspect of fire. Life, yes, but fire! There is power in a fire and this is within us – a fountain within us – the dynamic of the Holy Spirit. The apostle Paul puts this in his own particular way in these well-known words:

> *Wherefore, my beloved, as ye have always obeyed, not as in my presence only, but now much more in my absence, work out your own salvation with fear and trembling. For it is God which worketh in you both to will and to do of his good pleasure. (Philippians 2:12–13).*

That is a perfect statement of this very point. We work out our own salvation 'with fear and trembling', but why do we? And the answer is that 'it is God which worketh in you both to will and to do'. We work out our salvation because he has first of all been working in us both the willing, the desiring, and everything else.

This power, this fire, is an essential characteristic of the Christian life (again, I am constrained to put it like this). But while it is very difficult to put these things in words, in the realm of experience there is no difficulty at all. It is the difference between life and a machine. The machine you have to wind up, and you wind it up and it will go for a certain length of time, but it stops and then you have to wind it up again. But this is life, and it is life within, a power that is operating within. In other words, the impulse does not come from ourselves. I have already pointed out that when religion is external, before practising it, you need a stimulus from outside – 'Ah! Sunday morning! Yes – different from other days.' So you do this and that. Or there is an illness, or an accident, or a death, or a funeral – something pulls you up. You have to be reminded. But it is not like that here; there is an impulse within, there is a call, an urging, that comes from within. A longing, is created. At this stage, it is not something you have done at all, it just happens to you. You find yourself the subject of an activity that is not your own, you are aware of a working within you.

I have often quoted or applied to this the words of Wordsworth. He meant something quite different but we can appreciate his words:

> And I have felt
> A presence that disturbs me with the joy
> Of elevated thoughts.
> *'Lines composed a few miles above Tintern Abbey'*

That is it: a disturbing. When, perhaps, you desire to go in a given direction, you are aware of an activity within you, some impulse, some call, some urging, some longing that has not come from you. Or you may be reading something secular, your thoughts may be otherwise engaged, but suddenly you are aware that there is something, someone, within you moving you, leading you in a particular direction. It is 'God which worketh in you'.

There it is; that is a very vital part of this whole Christian position. If we are not aware of the working of God in us, then I fail to see how we have any right to call ourselves Christians at all – we are merely religious. You can be religious in your use of Christian terminology; you can be religious inside a Christian church. But one of the vital aspects of Christianity is that our activities are always the result of his activity. It is the 'well of water', it is the life within that stimulates. 'God worketh in you both to will and to do' before you have ever done anything. Why did you desire it? Why did you will it? That is the question. We move because we are moved, we act because of the stimulus that has come apart from ourselves.

Now this, I believe, is a most important point for us at the present time. We are living in an age of activism and of activities; we are living in an age when people are so confused that they become children and like to have everything set out before them by rule and regulation, by numbers. To live according to a system, to live by rote, to live by obeying commands, is a very real snare. It is a snare that saints have fallen into. You must 'work out your own salvation with fear and trembling', yes, but it is never imposed from the outside; it works out from the inside.

You see the danger? The Roman Catholic type of piety is always in grave danger at this point. The life is determined by the priest, or by certain books and writings, and these are imposed upon people; but that also happens to many people in Protestant circles. They take a decision in a meeting, perhaps, and then they are given a list of rules that they must keep because they are told to: it has become the thing to do. They exchange one pattern of behaviour for another.

Now there is a danger of being misunderstood at this point; I am well aware of it. Nevertheless, this is one of the most essential points of all. I have known so many Christians, young Christians in particular, who appear to be true Christians but who later reveal that they have never been Christians at all. I have known many people who, in their student days, were members of Christian Unions, and were carried along by the momentum of the excitement and the movement and the activity, and appeared to be wonderful Christians. But then they left the university and went out into life, and once they had lost all that was round and about them as students, they had nothing. They fell away completely and even scoffed at the Christian faith and ridiculed it: I have known many instances of this. It is what is known as the leakage that takes place in evangelistic work, particularly among students.

Now this is just a solid fact and I am giving you the explanation. They had a system imposed upon them, they conformed to a society to which they belonged, and were carried along by something entirely outside themselves. But when a man or woman has this fountain inside them, it does not matter whether they are in a Christian society or not, the fountain is in them, they work out their own salvation with fear and trembling because it is God who works in them both to will and to do.

This is taught throughout the New Testament. We read about 'the fruit of the Spirit' (Galatians 5:22) and about bringing forth 'much fruit' (John 15:5) – it is our Lord himself who uses this comparison. We are dealing with life here, not with mechanics, and if it is a question of fruit-bearing, then it is bound to come from inside outwards. You do not add fruit to a tree. No, no; it is the life that produces the fruit, and it takes time, and you get different stages: the bud, then the growth of the bud, and then the full maturity. That is God's way, that is life; not the imposing of things from the outside, not doing things because you are told to, but a desire created within. There, then, is one manifestation of this power, one way whereby we can test whether or not this power is in us.

But let us look at another manifestation. It is similar and yet there is a real distinction. Because this is the nature of the Christian life, it follows of necessity that it is not a life that we can control, rather, we are controlled by it. Religious people are always in control of themselves and their religion. That is a further characteristic of religion: you take it up, you do it. But here we are in an entirely different realm. Because this is inside us, because it is life, because it is a power springing up, it is in control of us.

How can I put this to you? This is indeed the most wonderful thing about being a Christian, and this is what guarantees the final perseverance of the saints: we are not in control. 'I live; yet not I' – that is it – '. . . and the life which I now live in the flesh I live by the faith of the Son of God, who loved me, and gave himself for me' (Galatians 2:20). It sounds contradictory and yet, again, experientially there is no difficulty about this at all, and every one of us at this moment knows this. Are you in control or are you being controlled? Are you in control of your life, or do you say with that centurion who came to our Lord, 'I am a man under authority' (Matthew 8:9)? The Christian is always a man or woman under authority. There is always this power, this life, springing up and working within.

Now I want to make this point clear so I am going to put it like this – I have found this a most valuable test, and, incidentally, an excellent ground of assurance of salvation. It works like this. This life within you is a well. You have drunk the water and it becomes within you a well of water springing up. You experience this energy, this power, this bubbling quality, this dynamic; yes, and sometimes that makes you very unhappy. By that, I mean that in a backsliding condition you may want to revert to the life of the world. Going out with your old friends may seem interesting and attractive once more, and that is what you would like to do. But this other power is there inside you, working in you, and you are annoyed, you wish you had never known anything about it. It is a nuisance. It is spoiling life and you resent it. You struggle against it and do your utmost to silence it, to explain it away. You are glad to read in the newspaper that some critic has said this or that, or some church dignitary seems to have denied the whole of Christianity. 'Ah,' you say, 'this is it. I've been too narrow.' But the more you do that the more this other power works within you and you cannot silence it, you cannot stop it. It goes on and it nags at you and it troubles you and you are in a conflict. Now this is an absolute proof that there is this life of God within you, that there is a power working within you.

Now let me give you my authority for saying this. Listen to the apostle Paul putting it to the Galatians:

This I say then, Walk in the Spirit, and ye shall not fulfil the lust of the flesh. For the flesh lusteth against the Spirit, and the Spirit against the flesh: and these are contrary the one to the other: so that ye cannot do the things that ye would. (Galatians 5:16–17)

'But surely,' you may say to me, 'many an unconverted person has this kind of conflict?'

No, not this kind of conflict. Many a moral man knows the trouble he gets with his conscience, and is unhappy after he has fallen into sin, and experiences remorse. But that is on a very different level from this. The word used here is the word 'lusteth'. This is a tremendous power; it is not merely that you are aware of your conscience speaking to you, there is an intensity about it all, you are aware of a vigour and there is a conflict within you.

Now James puts that even more strongly when he says, 'Do ye think that the scripture saith in vain, The spirit that dwelleth in us lusteth to envy?' (James 4:5). That is the translation of the Authorized Version but it is generally agreed that the true idea there is that the Spirit that has been put within us as Christians – this water that we have drunk and that has become a well of water within us – the Spirit that dwells in us is anxious about us and in a most jealous manner lusts, as it were, for our entire sanctification. What a wonderful thought it is that God has put his Spirit in us and the Spirit now is anxious for our perfection and is even jealous! He knows the devil. The world, the flesh and the devil are fighting, and he knows that the flesh itself is on the side of the world and the devil, and therefore there is this lusting of the flesh.

The idea, the picture, is that of a parent looking on at a child and being concerned and anxious that the child should do well – this kind of anxiety. This 'lusting' is as strong and as powerful as that. Now this is the power of the well of water that is within us springing up into everlasting life. It is God working in us both to will and to do 'with a jealous envy', so great is the concern of the Spirit. And Christians, I say, are aware of this, aware that they are not really in control of themselves, that they are being controlled by this Other. They can fight against it, they can quench the Spirit, they can grieve the Spirit, but the Spirit is always there.

And so we can go on and look at this as it is put by John in his first epistle. These verses are often misunderstood: 'He that committeth sin is of the devil; for the devil sinneth from the beginning. For this purpose the Son of God was manifested, that he might destroy the works of the devil.' Now then – 'Whosoever is born of God doth not commit sin' – why not? – 'for his seed remaineth in him: and he cannot sin, because he is born of God' (1 John 3:8–9). That is a perfect statement of the point I am making. 'He that committeth sin' – why does he do that? Here is a natural man, living a life of sin. Why? Because he is 'of the devil'. What you do is the result of what you are. You commit sin because you are *of* the devil, that is the nature that is in you.

Our Lord put this quite explicitly to the Pharisees and scribes when he said, 'Ye are of your father the devil, and the lusts of your father ye will do' (John 8:44). The nature must express itself, it must come out. This is true on both sides. A life of sin is not something that is added on, it is the expression of the person. 'For as he thinketh in his heart, so is he' (Proverbs 23:7). Actions come from the inside. Again, let me quote the words of our Lord. People always misunderstand this. 'For', our Lord says, 'out of the heart proceed evil thoughts, murders, adulteries . . .' (Matthew 15:19).

The trouble with the Pharisee is always that he is concerned about the outside and that which goes in, that which he takes in. But it is the heart that is wrong, the heart is the polluted fountain (not the fountain of the Spirit but another one). 'He that committeth sin is of the devil; for the devil sinneth from the beginning. For this purpose the Son of God', says John, 'was manifested, that he might destroy the works of the devil.' So, then, this becomes true: 'Whosoever is born of God' – this is the place where you start. You do not look at a man's actions, you say, 'What is the life that is in him? Is he born of God?' 'Whosoever is born of God doth not commit sin' (1 John 3:8–9).

Obviously, that does not mean that he never commits a single act of sin. The tense of the verb used there is the continuous:

he does not go on sinning. There is the contrast with the unbeliever. The unbeliever lives a life of sin; the believer does not live a life of sin. He may occasionally fall into it but he does not go on living such a life. 'Whosoever is born of God doth not commit sin' – why not? – 'for his seed remaineth in him.' There is a seed of new life in this man. Now John prefers to work with this idea of a seed of life. It is the same truth, using a different comparison. And this is one of the greatest and profoundest sources of assurance and comfort and consolation. Here is a man, he is born of God, very well. But he is in this sinful world and there are the world, and the flesh, and the devil, and he gets attacked and he may fall into sin. But he cannot fall away, 'his seed remaineth in him'. He will not be allowed to. He may for a while, but he cannot go back to that life that is of the devil. In chapter 5, John puts this still more explicitly:

> *All unrighteousness is sin: and there is a sin not unto death. We know that whosoever is born of God sinneth not; but he that is begotten of God keepeth himself, and that wicked one toucheth him not. And we know that we are of God, and the whole world lieth in wickedness. (1 John 5:17–19)*

That is it. The man who has this life in him does not remain in wickedness – he never can. This seed, this life of God, stays in him. That evil one cannot touch us in the sense of ever getting us back into his embrace and under his control. No, no; the Christian is under the control of the Spirit of the living God. As I have said, Christians are no longer in control of themselves, but are being controlled. They do not have to force themselves to live the Christian life. They are being forced to live the Christian life by the power that is within them. All you and I can do is this: we can either yield to that power or else we can resist it, we can quench it, we can disobey. And if we do we will be miserable. When Christians go back to sin they are miserable wretches and they continue like that; they are not allowed to enjoy it, there is this power that is within them. This is very wonderful. It is wonderful in pastoral experience to see a backslider restored.

All this is implicit in this idea of the well of water springing up, the power that is working within us. And this is the way in which the New Testament preaches the doctrine of sanctification. The New Testament is not always urging us to do this or that; it does not keep attacking us individually and on particular points. If you want that sort of approach, you have a religious, and not a Christian outlook. All I am here to do is to tell you that if you have the life of God in you, and you sin, you are a fool because you are asking for misery and you will get it, and you will go on living in hell, as it were, until you obey this power that is working in you. It will bring you back, though to do so, it may knock you down, it may take your health from you, it may make you lose your money. So if you are a child of God, well, then, do not be a fool, do not resist the Spirit, you will only bring trouble on yourself.

> O Love, that wilt not let me go,
> I rest my weary soul in thee;
> I give thee back the life I owe,
> That in thine ocean depths its flow
> May richer, fuller be.
>
> *George Matheson*

He will follow you all your way – 'The Hound of Heaven' – think of any illustration you like. This is the truth. And it all comes under the general principle that we are not in control of this life, it is in control of us.

So I make this next point, which is simple and obvious. The kind of life that is lived by the Christian is of necessity, therefore, never mechanical and it is never legalistic. The terms that are used in the New Testament are so wonderful – the word 'living', the word 'lively'. 'If thou knewest the gift of God, and who it is that saith to thee, Give me to drink,' says our Lord to this woman, 'thou wouldest have asked of him and he would have given thee *living* water.'

Or listen to Peter writing to people who are passing through a very difficult time:

Blessed be the God and Father of our Lord Jesus Christ, which according to his abundant mercy hath begotten us again unto a lively hope [a living hope, a bubbling hope] by the resurrection of Jesus Christ from the dead, to an inheritance incorruptible, and undefiled, and that fadeth not away, reserved in heaven for you, who are kept by the power of God through faith unto salvation ready to be revealed in the last time. (1 Peter 1:3–5)

If you read those epistles of Peter, you will find that he is very fond of emphasizing this 'living', 'lively', 'bubbling', 'sparkling' quality; and it is right. Again, that is one of the best ways of testing whether we are just religious or whether we are Christians. The religious person is always mechanical, always legalistic, knows exactly, has it defined, knows how far he can go, knows where to stop, and just lives a 'square', mechanical sort of life that keeps you just within the law; so nice, so moral, so clean so good! Ach! What a contrast with Christianity! This is life! This is not mechanics, this is not law, this is not legalism. Christians live above the law, they fulfil the law because they are living in a realm above it, not just ticking off whether they have done this and have not done that.

The Pharisees knew exactly what they were doing. Our Lord's parable of the Pharisee and the tax collector going up to the Temple to pray puts it perfectly. The Pharisee can get up and recite exactly what he does – fast twice in the week, give a tenth of his goods to the poor. He can tell God exactly when he prays and for how long (Luke 18:10–14). What a tragedy! What a small life it is! There is no liberty, there is no abandon. It is not living. Religions are always dead, and that is why they are always hopeless, and that is why they never help people when they need them most of all. Religion always lets you down at the point of your greatest need. Nor can you help others if you have only got religion.

But let me say one other thing. It follows on directly and it is marvellous. I want to end by stressing the greatness of the power that is within us. 'The water that I shall give him shall be in him a well of water springing up into everlasting life.' Now this power is a variable quantity; it varies from person to person – another most important point. Christians are never identical. If you show me a church of people who are all the same, I say it is not a church, it is a religious gathering. Any teaching or system that makes everybody the same, doing the same things in the same way, is never Christianity, because it is never of God. How often have I said this: no two flowers are identical! They may appear to be, but if you examine them, you will find they are not. And no two Christians are identical; there is a wide variation in the amount of the power. The apostle Paul has put this perfectly, of course, in his great illustration of the body in 1 Corinthians 12. There are 'comely parts' and less comely parts – they are all essential, they are all in the body, they all have their function, and, ultimately, in the sight of God, they are all one. But there is the variation and the foolish people at Corinth had not grasped this principle, so they were quarrelling over gifts.

But that is not what I am interested in now. I want, rather, to establish the fact that Christian people experience variations in the degree of this power. But let me add also that there are variations in the power in the same person. Are you not aware of that? Do you know what you are going to be like when you wake up tomorrow morning? If you do, you are not a Christian. We do not control this, as I am emphasizing. What we do does affect our experience of this power, but we do not control it. If I disobey, if I rebel against the power that is in me, if I quench the Spirit, or if I grieve the Spirit, then it makes a difference. But it is a temporary, and not an ultimate, difference. The point I am establishing, however, is that even granting all that, you and I are not at the centre of control and we never know what that power is going to be.

I say it again, to the glory of God, this pulpit is the most romantic place in the universe as far as I am concerned, because I never know what is going to happen when I get here – never. My anticipations are often falsified on both sides. Both sides! This is wonderful! The temptation to a preacher is to think that if he has prepared what he regards as a good sermon, there will be a wonderful service, but it can sometimes be very bad. On the other hand, the poor man may have had a very difficult and trying week, he may have been ill, a thousand and one things may have happened to him, and he may go into the pulpit in fear and trembling, feeling that he has not done his work and has nothing. Yet that service may be one of the most glorious he has ever had the privilege of conducting. Why? Because he does not control the power; it varies.

And not only in preaching, but in daily life and experience. We do not control the well of water that is in us, it controls us; so the power, of necessity, varies from time to time even in the same person. Show me a person who is always the same, always on the same level – I doubt whether he is a Christian at all. Show me a preacher who is always at the same level – he is not much of a preacher. A great preacher will sometimes be a very bad preacher. It is because there is this other element, the element of the Spirit, the unknown, the unseen, the authority, the power. A man relying on his own ability can always operate on a certain level, but he is always on that level. But here there are variations; you are up, you are down, you are on top of the mountain, you are down in the depths. But, oh, the glory of the possibilities of this power, of this water bubbling up into everlasting life!

Let me just quote a few passages to show the sort of thing I am talking about. Here is the height of the power. Fairly soon after the Day of Pentecost, the apostles are on trial. When they are prohibited to preach, Peter gives the immortal answer, 'We cannot but speak' (Acts 4:20). That is the power. A man never says a thing like that. 'We cannot help speaking!' Why not? Not because they had decided they were going to preach, they were not those sorts of people; this man Peter was the man who, in order to save his life, had denied his Lord just a few weeks back. He had been afraid of the authorities and terrified of being arrested. He now faces the Sanhedrin and he says, 'We cannot but speak'! It is no use telling us to stop, we cannot stop, we cannot help ourselves.

Or listen to the apostle Paul putting it in his way: 'The love of Christ constraineth us' (2 Corinthians 5:14)! He is like a man in a vice, it has been wound up, it is being pressed upwards. 'Woe is unto me, if I preach not the gospel!' (1 Corinthians 9:16). You do not 'decide' to do these things in cold blood, you do not do them mechanically, but you are aware of this tremendous pressure, the power – 'The love of Christ constraineth me' – a man under pressure, and he cannot desist.

Or listen to the apostle Paul writing to the Colossians: 'Whom we preach [the Lord Jesus Christ], warning every man, and teaching every man in all wisdom; that we may present every man perfect in Christ Jesus' – then listen – 'whereunto I also labour' – now here is the secret: 'I labour'. Of course he does all he can, his preparation, his activities, his travelling – 'striving' – that is still stronger, striving goes beyond labouring – 'according to the working, which worketh in me mightily' (Colossians 1:28–29). Can you not see it? He is like a volcano. There is a power, there is a fire, within him, moving him, energizing him, carrying him along irresistibly in the performance of his great and his high calling.

Jeremiah speaks of the same power: 'a fire in my bones'. He had decided not to speak again because every time he spoke he got into trouble. 'But,' he said, 'his word was in mine heart as a burning fire shut up in my bones' (Jeremiah 20:9).

My dear friends, do you know anything of this power working in you? People in times of revival know it tremendously in their personal experience. But there are variations, do not be discouraged if it may be low at the present time. Examine yourself, make sure you are not quenching or grieving the Spirit. But even when you have done all that, there is no guarantee that you will get the power. This idea that teaches, 'Do this and you will get that', is not Christianity; you do not control it. There has been a foolish false teaching for 80 years or so that has told people, 'Be willing to be willing and you will get it. Do this – surrender and you have got it.' You have not! You can do everything and still be lifeless. *His power*! 'His power that worketh in me mightily' – 'shall be within you a well of water springing up into everlasting life'. The possibilities are glorious; they are endless! Realize that; seek them, and do not be satisfied until you know the mighty power of the life of God working in your life, lifting you up, above, outside yourself. And then what you do will not be mechanical works, but will be the fruit of the Spirit.

16

Mind, Heart and Will

Jesus answered and said unto her, If thou knewest the gift of God, and who it is that saith to thee, Give me to drink; thou wouldest have asked of him, and he would have given thee living water . . . Whosoever drinketh of this water shall thirst again: but whosoever drinketh of the water that I shall give him shall never thirst; but the water that I shall give him shall be in him a well of water springing up into everlasting life. (John 4:10, 13–14)

We are considering together the main characteristics of the life that is given us by the Son of God, this 'gift of God', and we are now dealing with the particular characteristics of this life. So far we have seen that it is inward, and also that it is a power within us, a power that is working within in a mighty manner, and we must never forget that.

But now I want to take this teaching a step further and point out that this power that works within us, this 'well of water springing up into everlasting life', changes our lives in a radical manner. These points, you notice, follow logically one upon the other, and it is important that we should take them in that way.

If this power that is working in us is the power of God – and we have seen that it is – then it is obvious that it must change us radically. It is not superficial, not on the surface, it must produce the profoundest change conceivable – and this is confirmed by the terminology that is employed in the New Testament concerning this power.

One of the terms used is 'regeneration'. Now there is nothing profounder than regeneration. The Christian faith is not something that merely makes us a bit better than we were, it does not just improve the surface appearance. No, no! It is *regeneration.* You are 'generated' anew and afresh. In other words, and to use a more frequent term, it is *rebirth.* Rebirth is the essence of the teaching in the third chapter of John's Gospel. Here, our Lord, interrupting the speech of that great teacher, Nicodemus, said, 'Ye must be born again' (John 3:7). Nicodemus had dropped into the customary fallacy of thinking that our Lord had just got something extra to give, something that he, Nicodemus, could add on to what he already had. No, no, said our Lord. You do not understand. You are quite wrong. You have nothing. You need to be born again. You must go back to the very beginning. The foundation needs to be changed.

The Christian life is as radical as that. But the difficulty is that people, as we have seen, fail to realize this; they will turn Christianity into a religion or into a philosophy, something that we add on to our lives. But that is quite wrong. The apostle Paul compares this new birth to a 'new creation'. He says: 'Therefore if any man be in Christ, he is a new creature [a new creation]: old things are passed away; behold, all things are become new' (2 Corinthians 5:17). And in Romans chapter 16, making the same point, he says that this life is comparable to a death followed by a resurrection: the end of one life, the beginning of another:

'Likewise reckon ye also yourselves to be dead indeed unto sin, but alive unto God through Jesus Christ our Lord' (Romans 6:11). The reference is to our Lord himself, crucified, dying upon the cross and his body buried in a grave, then the mighty resurrection in that new, glorified body.

And that, says Paul, is what happens to a Christian. We have been crucified with Christ, we have died with him, we have also risen with him in newness of life. Now it is impossible to conceive of any stronger comparisons or analogies than this – a death, a resurrection out of death. But that is the language that is used in the Scripture in order to bring out the radical character of the change that takes place when someone becomes a Christian.

There is another way of putting this that I myself am very fond of and that Paul constantly uses in the sixth chapter of Romans, as he does in other places. 'Ye were . . . ye are!' 'But God be thanked, that ye were the servants of sin, but ye have . . .' (Romans 6:17) – you have, you have received, you are. And this is not confined to the apostle Paul. The apostle Peter says to those Gentile people who had become Christians, 'Which in time past were not a people, but are now the people of God' (1 Peter 2:10). Here is the contrast – something that you were, something that you are, that you have become. The point is that there is a complete contrast. The New Testament uses an almost endless variety of expressions to describe this great change that takes place within us – and this makes it all the more important that we should grasp the point.

Another way in which this change is put is in terms of a contrast between living a life 'after the flesh' and living a life 'after the Spirit': 'For they that are after the flesh do mind the things of the flesh; but they that are after the Spirit the things of the Spirit' (Romans 8:5). And then Paul adds: 'But ye are not in the flesh, but in the Spirit, if so be that the Spirit of God dwell in you'

(Romans 8:9). But perhaps it can all be summed up by putting it like this: when you become a Christian, you receive a new heart. It is nothing less than a change of heart.

Now it is very important that we should always remember that the Bible uses the term 'heart' in a very special way. When we hear this word, we tend to think immediately of the affections, the emotions, the feelings; but Scripture uses the term in a much profounder sense. It includes the feelings but it contains much more than the feelings. In Scripture, the heart stands for the centre of the personality, the very core of one's being. We all have a centre. We have various faculties, we have the body and its propensities and characteristics and we have our temperaments and so on, but there is something at the centre that controls all this, and that is what the Scripture means by the heart. It is the very spring of life, that which controls who the person is and what the person does.

The older theologians had a very good term to express the centre of the personality – I know of no better one, that is why I use it. They talked about one's 'disposition' and said that what happens when a man or woman becomes a Christian is that there is a profound and radical change in their disposition, that they have received a new disposition. I have sometimes used an illustration to bring out this point and I think it is helpful. Think of it in terms of management. Think of a man running his own business. He perhaps employs a number of others to help him, but he owns the business; he has the direction and the control; he is the ultimate authority and he gives out the orders. Then his business is bought up or taken over by another firm. He may still continue as a manager, and the employees are there as before, but there is an essential difference, there has been a change at the centre of control.

The image that our Lord uses is: '. . . the water that I shall give him shall be in him a well of water springing up into everlasting life.' There will be a new disposition and this will govern everything else about this person. In other words, then, we must realize that there is a change of the whole of the personality.

Now I could easily show you that it is the failure to realize this that has accounted for many of the heresies and freak religious movements of the past. It is the failure to realize this that tends to lead us all astray. We want to be put right intellectually only, or in the realm of the feelings only, or in the realm of activity only: but that is not Christianity. And it is when the personality is dealt with in a piecemeal manner rather than as a whole that you have something that is spurious.

So the general statement is that this life, this well of water that is put into us, this life of God in the soul, will manifest itself in the whole of our personality. We must therefore consider what these manifestations are. But let me add this, lest someone be discouraged. It is my business, of course, to represent this new life at its maximum, at its best and highest. The New Testament itself always does that. But do not let yourself think that you are not a Christian simply because you find that you do not have one hundred per cent of what I have described. All I am concerned about is this: Are we able to say that on the whole this is true of us? If this essential change has taken place, it is bound to manifest itself in these various ways. But, of course, there are variations in the degree to which it does so. The Scripture itself teaches us this when it says that we are born 'babes in Christ', and then grow to be 'children' and after that 'young men', then adults and finally 'old men'. There is a progression, a maturing; there is a development as one goes on in the Christian life under the instruction of Scripture and the influence of the Holy Spirit. But in the veriest babe there is this essential life and it always shows itself.

And so we can analyse this new birth in the following way. First, there is obviously a profound change in the minds of Christian people, in their understanding. Again, here is something that is illustrated and emphasized in many places in the New Testament. It is one of the big differences between a Christian and a non-Christian. There is a different mind, a different understanding, a different outlook. Our Lord himself, for instance, puts it like this in his great high priestly prayer when he is praying for these men whom he is going to leave behind him to carry on his work. He says:

I have manifested thy name unto the men which thou gavest me out of the world: thine they were, and thou gavest them me; and they have kept thy word.

These are men who have been given to him out of the world; they are separated people. And our Lord says that they have this characteristic: 'they have kept thy word'. And he continues:

Now they have known that all things whatsoever thou hast given me are of thee. For I have given unto them the words which thou gavest me; and they have received them, and have known surely that I came out from thee, and they have believed that thou didst send me. I pray for them: I pray not for the world, but for them which thou hast given me; for they are thine.

He then sums it all up at the end of that same prayer when he says:

O righteous Father, the world hath not known thee: but I have known thee, and these have known that thou hast sent me. (John 17:6–9, 25)

Now there, you see, is the big differentiating point. Here are people who have this understanding concerning him and his purpose in the world, which the world in general does not know or recognize. This is a vital matter, and, if I may say so, in my pastoral work, as people come to me in difficulties about their spiritual or their Christian lives, I am constantly finding myself having to quote these statements. People say to me, 'You know, I don't think I'm a Christian after all. I had some sort of an experience, I was forced under pressure in a meeting to say certain things, but I don't think that I have ever really been a Christian.' And they are distressed about this. How can one help them?

Well, I find that one of the best ways of all is to show them that they have a new mind, a new understanding. I generally start by putting it to them like this. I say, 'Why have you come to see me? Why are you troubled about this? Can't you see that you are doing something rather exceptional in this modern world? Think of your friends and associates, think of your fellow students or your friends at work, are they concerned about this? Are they questioning somebody like me because they are troubled and want to know whether or not they are Christians – is that their attitude?'

And they smile at me. 'Well, no,' they say.

'Of course not,' I say. 'They ridicule the whole thing and probably think you are a little bit mad for being troubled about such things.' In this way, I immediately establish that there is a difference in outlook between them and other people. Then I take them on, of course, to the second chapter of the First Epistle to the Corinthians where these truths are put so plainly and clearly. The apostle is reminding the Christians in Corinth that the wisdom that he is talking about in the gospel is a mystery – 'the hidden wisdom'. He says:

Which none of the princes of this world knew: for had they known it, they would not have crucified the Lord of glory. But as it is written, Eye hath not seen, nor ear heard, neither have entered into the heart of man, the things which God hath prepared for them that love him. But God hath revealed them unto us [to Christians] by his Spirit: for the

Spirit searcheth all things, yea, the deep things of God . . . Now we have received, not the spirit of the world, but the spirit which is of God; that we might know the things that are freely given to us of God. Which things also we speak, not in the words which man's wisdom teacheth, but which the Holy Ghost teacheth; comparing spiritual things with spiritual.

Then the crucial verse:

But the natural man

– that is, the non-Christian. Those who are not Christians may be very able, very moral, but they do not have the Spirit in them, they do not have the well of water, they do not have the new life. A non-Christian may be a 'natural man' at his very best, but here is the truth –

receiveth not the things of the Spirit of God: for they are foolishness unto him: neither can he know them, because they are spiritually discerned. (1 Corinthians 2:8–10, 12–14)

Now there it is. I say to these people, therefore, who come to me in trouble: 'You are concerned about this?'

'Yes,' they say.

'You are in trouble and anxious about these things?'

'Yes.'

'You want to know these things?'

'Certainly.'

'Well, then,' I say, '"the natural man receiveth not the things of the Spirit of God: for they are foolishness unto him: neither can he know them." Are these things foolishness to you?'

'No, no,' they say.

'Very well,' I say, 'you are not a natural person, and if you are not a natural person, you must be a spiritual person, there is no other possibility. You are either natural or spiritual, you are either in the flesh or in the Spirit, and the proof of your being a spiritual person is that you do not regard these things as foolishness but you are anxious about them.'

And then Paul goes on to say:

But he that is spiritual judgeth [hath understanding of] all things, yet he himself is judged of no man. For who hath known the mind of the Lord, that he may instruct him? But we have the mind of Christ. (1 Corinthians 2:15–16)

That is a magnificent statement, and is perhaps the clearest of all the statements with respect to this matter. But let nobody think that this is just Pauline teaching. The apostle John says exactly the same thing. Here he is as an old man writing his farewell letter to Christian people, and he is worried about them because certain false teachers – antichrists – have gone abroad. There were false teachers in the church even in the first century. Let me say once more that there is nothing so fatuous and ridiculous about people who pride themselves on their modernity as their ignorance and their failure to realize that they are but the modern counterparts, and very pale imitators, of the false teachers of the first century – the antichrists. But ultimately John is quite happy about the Christians he is writing to. He says this:

They went out from us, but they were not of us; for if they had been of us, they would no doubt have continued with us: but they went out, that they might be made manifest that they were not all of us. (1 John 2:19)

Here are people who belonged to the church but they have gone away and are now teaching heresy and thereby, says John, they are giving proof that they did not really belong to us. But then he goes on:

But ye have an unction from the Holy One, and ye know all things. I have not written unto you because ye know not the truth, but because ye know it, and that no lie is of the truth. (1 John 2:20–21)

John says, 'Ye have an unction.' What does that mean? Well, it is not any natural ability. It is something they have been given from the Holy One, from the Holy Spirit within them. In verse 27, John repeats this, and is it not reminiscent of our Lord's words to the woman of Samaria, 'The water that I shall give him shall be in him a well of water springing up into everlasting life'?

The anointing which ye have received of him abideth in you, and ye need not that any man teach you: but as the same anointing teacheth you of all things, and is truth, and is no lie, and even as it hath taught you, ye shall abide in him. (1 John 2:27)

Now that is a perfect way of putting this very point about the change, the radical change, in the mind and understanding. This is the first profound manifestation of this new life that is within. We can enforce it still further by putting it in terms of certain great contrasts. The apostle Paul does this in the Epistle to the Ephesians. Listen: 'This I say therefore, and testify in the Lord, that ye henceforth walk not as the other Gentiles walk' – how do they walk? How is the world living today? What is the difference between a Christian and a non-Christian? What is the effect of having within you this well of water, this life of God, this new disposition that governs everything and especially your mind? Well, here it is – 'in the vanity [emptiness] of their mind, having the understanding darkened, being alienated from the life of God through the ignorance that is in them, because of the blindness of their heart' (Ephesians 4:17–18). Could anything be clearer?

The trouble with people who are not Christians is that their understanding is darkened, they are alienated from the life of God.

Why? Well, 'through the ignorance that is in them'. And that is the whole explanation of the state of the world. But that is no longer true of the Christian. You are not to be like those people in any respect, says Paul. Why? Because your minds have been enlightened, you have received this unction, this anointing. You have new life in you. You have 'put off concerning the old man' and have been 'renewed in the spirit of your mind' (Ephesians 4:22–23).

So how does all this show itself in actual practice? It can be put like this: a Christian is someone who knows what the truth is. Our Lord says to this woman of Samaria, 'If thou knewest the gift of God, and who it is that saith to thee.' She did not know, but the Christian, by definition, is one who does know. Christians know the truth about the Lord Jesus Christ, they know the truth about themselves. Christians know that they are sinners, condemned sinners, under the wrath of God, who do not deserve anything but punishment and retribution. They know this, they see it quite clearly, and they see the blessed truth that God has provided the way of salvation even in his only begotten Son, and that he saves by dying on the cross on Calvary's hill. They know what the truth is and they have a measure of understanding concerning it.

Now I am taking it for granted that we are all familiar with these great doctrines of the faith. If any of you are not, I counsel you to come on Sunday night, when I shall be preaching more evangelistically and putting these things more plainly. If you are in any doubt or trouble about yourself, come then and you will have the gospel direct and plain. But the point I want to establish at the moment is this: Christians not only know this teaching and see it, they see its inevitability. By that, I mean that their old difficulties have gone and so has their old opposition.

You know what I mean, do you not? You have known what it is to stumble at these truths and to be always arguing against them and fighting them. But the moment you became a Christian, all that came to an end. Now I am not saying that Christians understand everything. Of course they do not; they have to grow. But there has been a shift, a change in their whole position. That is what matters. So that now, though they still fumble and stumble and often still do not understand and have many questions, they are on the side of truth; they are no longer against it. Before, they were always trying to turn it down, putting their catch questions and arguments, watching every word, trying to trip up the preacher, or anybody putting forward the Christian faith. But they are now in an entirely different position. They want to know and to understand; all their sympathies are on this side, and when they come across a difficulty, they do not immediately say, 'Ah, there's nothing in it after all.' No, no! They say, 'No, I'm defective somewhere here, there must be an explanation.'

Let me give you just one illustration. Take the great doctrine of the death of Christ, the doctrine of the atonement. It has always been a great stumbling block to the unbeliever. The apostle tells us that it was a stumbling block to Jews, and to Greeks it was foolishness. And the modern man, the intellectual, finds the whole notion quite immoral. Thereby, of course, he just tells us that he is not a Christian, and that he is not a Christian because he does not see his own need. But the moment people become Christians, their root difficulty with regard to the atonement vanishes completely. Why? Because they are, by definition, men and women who have been enlightened; they have come to see that they are sinners, and hopeless, condemned sinners, who can do nothing at all. They have some glimmer of understanding of the righteousness and the holiness and the justice of God; that no longer troubles them, they are not opposed. They feel that the glory of God is that he is essentially different from us.

Then the question is: How can such a God forgive such creatures as we are? And the answer is in the atonement. It is a mystery, it is wonderful, it is amazing. Christians do not understand it fully but they can see now that there was no other way, that there is an inevitability about it. They are no longer against this truth. They want understanding, they want help, they do not resent it or constantly try to turn it down. Now Paul sums up this change in that extraordinary statement at the end of 1 Corinthians chapter 2: 'We have the mind of Christ.' What a statement! We used to have the mind of the world, we now have 'the mind of Christ'.

So I put this to you as a general question: Which side are you on? Let me put it still more plainly: What is your prejudice? Are you prejudiced against this truth or are you prejudiced in its favour? When men and women have this new life put into them, this well of water springing up into everlasting life, their whole disposition, their prejudice, is changed radically. They are delivered 'from the power of darkness', and have been 'translated into the kingdom of his dear Son' (Colossians 1:13). Or as Paul puts it in Romans 8:5: 'They that are after the flesh do mind the things of the flesh; but they that are after the Spirit the things of the Spirit.' Now this word 'mind' means 'are interested in', 'concerned about', 'delight in'. That is the Christian. Is this true of us? If it is not, then we are not Christians.

You can, I repeat, be a very good person; you can be doing a lot of good; you can want to make the world a better place; you may be marching and protesting about a thousand and one things; but all I say to you is that you are not a Christian. Christians 'mind' these things of the soul and of the Spirit. These have the priority. This is what controls their entire outlook. And you have either got this or you have not. If you have not, I say again, you are not a Christian.

You can never produce it by your own efforts. It is the water that he has to give, and all you and I can do is to drink the water and then it becomes in us 'a well of water springing up into everlasting life'.

This is the secret and the explanation of some of those amazing romantic stories that we can read of in the lives of the saints, the profound change that they underwent. It is all seen and exemplified to perfection in the apostle Paul himself, who puts it like this: 'I verily thought with myself that I ought to do many things contrary to the name of Jesus of Nazareth' (Acts 26:9). That is what he was. He now becomes 'the apostle of Jesus Christ' and he glories in him and 'determined not to know any thing . . . save Jesus Christ and him crucified' (1 Corinthians 2:2). What a profound change in the mind, the understanding, in the whole outlook and orientation!

But, secondly, there is an equally profound change in the heart. Again, you see, this is quite inevitable. If people are Christians, their feelings and their emotions are bound to be engaged. There is no such thing as a theoretical Christian; it is a contradiction in terms. That is inevitable because if you really believe the truth I have been referring to, you cannot remain unmoved, it is impossible. Of course, you can see these things intellectually and subscribe to them – I am not talking about that – I am talking about really believing, really being governed by them.

Is not this a note that is lacking today? And it is because it is lacking that we tend so often to produce an artificial joviality and try to manufacture bright services and so on. What a travesty! If the truth is in you, the truth will move you. 'God be thanked,' says the apostle, 'that ye were the servants of sin, but ye have obeyed from the heart that form of doctrine which was delivered you' (Romans 6:17). Of course! Christians rejoice in the truth, they do not subscribe to it reluctantly or apologetically or half-heartedly, it is everything to them. This is the biggest thing for them. They are moved by it to the very depth of their being. That is why the apostle Paul, this giant intellect, who in his epistles writes and handles these marvellous periods, with profound logic, will suddenly burst out, smash his own grammar, forget form, as his heart begins to speak and he indulges in some great apostrophe: 'God forbid that I should glory, save in the cross of our Lord Jesus Christ' (Galatians 6:14). That is why Paul is always talking about glorying and rejoicing.

This, again, follows inevitably. I am tempted to put it like this. Do you come to listen to the exposition of God's word as a matter of duty? Do you come reluctantly? Do you come half-heartedly? Or do you come keenly, enthusiastically, excitedly, wanting to get more and more of it, rejoicing in it and knowing that there is nothing in the world that is comparable to it? There is nothing that has done so much harm to Christianity as a formal religion that is observed as a matter of form, part of the week's programme, Sunday morning service on condition that it is not too long. Out upon the whole suggestion! That is not Christianity at all. That is religion, that is law. We are reminded that we are not under law but under grace, and this is one of the ways in which you test that.

Is your heart, in the sense of your feelings, your emotions, engaged? The apostle John puts this perfectly. In his first epistle, he has a number of tests that he applies to people that they may know whether or not they are Christians, and this is one of the best: 'His commandments are not grievous' (1 John 5:3). If you find the commandments of God grievous, you had better examine yourself again. Why are they not grievous to the Christian? Because they are inevitable. Christians are men and women who have a love for God and a love for the Saviour. They say, 'God so loved the world [he so loved me], that he gave his only begotten Son, that whosoever believeth in him should not perish, but have everlasting life' (John 3:16), and believing that, their hearts overflow with praise and gratitude and thanksgiving. This must follow as the night follows the day.

If you believe that '[God] spared not his own Son, but delivered him up for us all, how shall he not with him also freely give us all things?' (Romans 8:32), then, again, your heart wells up in gratitude and in praise and in thanksgiving, and you are filled with joy. Peter defines the joy for us: 'Whom having not seen,' he says, referring to the Lord Jesus Christ, 'ye love; in whom, though now ye see him not, yet believing, ye rejoice with joy unspeakable and full of glory' (1 Peter 1:8). That is the Christian. Christians find themselves bursting out and saying, 'Thanks be unto God for his unspeakable gift' (2 Corinthians 9:15), and with Peter, 'Blessed be the God and Father of our Lord Jesus Christ, which according to his abundant mercy hath begotten us again unto a lively hope by the resurrection of Jesus Christ from the dead' (1 Peter 1:3).

My friends, are your feelings engaged? Are you moved by the truth that you believe? There is a new emotional aspect to the life of those who are Christians, and unless you have been moved emotionally, you are not a Christian. It is contradictory to the Christian position for a man to be able to preach about these things without feeling or emotion, with a kind of detachment as if he were reading an essay, concerned about the form of his address rather than the substance. Ah, the perfection that denies the true Christianity – how terrible that is! No, no! There is a freedom here, there is a joy, there is an abandon. George Whitefield always used to say to ministers that a man should never preach except he preach 'a felt Christ'. Is it possible for a man who preaches the truth about Christ not to feel it? It is impossible. No, no; really to see him and to know him and to believe him, you must have 'a felt Christ'; the feelings are engaged as much as the intellect and the understanding.

And, thirdly, this also applies to the will. Again, note the inevitability. It is obvious. Those who believe these things are moved by them and want to do something about them. They have a desire to obey, and this desire results from the understanding and the feeling. It is not theoretical, it is not just a point of view, it is not imposed upon them. No, no! They see the whole. They reason like this: 'I believe that Jesus Christ died for me on the cross. Why did he do that? He died that I might be forgiven, he died to reconcile me to God. But was that all? Has he just provided me with some kind of insurance so that now I can go on sinning as much as I like, knowing that I am covered by the blood of Christ?'

That is the very question Paul asks: 'Shall we continue in sin, that grace may abound?' (Romans 6:1). If you say that, you have not understood the gospel at all. Paul continues: 'God forbid. How shall we, that are dead to sin, live any longer therein?' (Romans 6:2). Or, as he puts it to Titus. '[Christ] gave himself for us, that he might redeem us from all iniquity, and purify unto himself a peculiar people, zealous of good works' (Titus 2:14). He died that we might be forgiven, but he died to make us good also. His whole object is to destroy the works of the devil, to produce a people worthy of their Father who is in heaven.

So the moment men and women have this new life in them, this well of water springing up, they do not live the Christian life reluctantly, they do not object to the commandments. That is the whole difference between being religious or moral or ethical, on the one hand, and being truly Christian, on the other. Moral people obey grimly. They force themselves. It is a rigid discipline, a kind of stoicism. But Christians are entirely different, their attitude is positive. They see why all these things have happened, they desire to be good, they want to please God, they want to show their gratitude.

This is the change that has taken place in the realm of the will. Christians are not fighting against the gospel, they are not moving as near as they can to the world without getting over the border and being punished. No, no! They want to be as far away from the world as they can, they want to grow in grace and in the knowledge of the Lord, and they are aware of a new ability within them. When people become Christians, this change takes place in their wills. The trouble with the 'natural man' is that his will is in a state of bondage, but when men and women receive this new life, their wills are set free.

This is put so plainly by the apostle in the Epistle to the Romans. 'Sin', he says, 'shall not have dominion over you' – why not? – 'for ye are not under the law, but under grace' (Romans 6:14). You see the difference? Sin used to have dominion over you. The natural man is under the bondage and the serfdom of sin and of Satan; he is in a state of bondage. But the Christian is not. Paul says in Romans 8:15, 'For ye have not received the spirit of bondage again to fear; but ye have received the Spirit of adoption, whereby we cry, Abba, Father.' And in Romans 8:2, 'The law of the Spirit of life in Christ Jesus hath made me free from the law of sin and death.' That is the argument. Paul says in Romans chapter 7:

When we were in the flesh, the motions of sins, which were by the law, did work in our members to bring forth fruit unto death. But now we are delivered from the law, that being dead wherein we were held; that we should serve in newness of spirit, and not in the oldness of the letter. (Romans 7:5–6)

And he makes exactly the same point in that great moral ethical appeal at the beginning of Romans 12 – watch the word 'therefore':

I beseech you therefore, brethren, by the mercies of God, that ye present your bodies a living sacrifice, holy, acceptable unto God, which is your reasonable service. And be not conformed to this world: but be ye transformed by the renewing of your mind, that ye may prove what is that good, and acceptable, and perfect, will of God. (Romans 12:1–2)

This, then, is what happens to anyone who receives this new life. The entire personality is changed, there is a new disposition. It is the disposition that governs the mind, the heart, and the will in every person, every human being. In someone who is not a Christian, the disposition is evil, and the mind and heart and will are working against God, against their own best interests, governed by the world, the flesh, and the devil. But those who drink of this water receive a new life and a new disposition, they are given a new mind, a new feeling, a new understanding, and it is all working in the direction of God and of the soul and of holiness and of heaven, and of a joy that is unspeakable and full of glory.

Have you this new life in you? Have you the new disposition? Are you essentially different from the person who is not a Christian, the person you once were yourself? God give us grace to answer this profound question in the only way that matters, enabling us to say, 'I was!' but now, 'But by the grace of God I am what I am' (1 Corinthians 15:10).

17

'The Life of God in the Soul of Man'

Jesus answered and said unto her, If thou knewest the gift of God, and who it is that saith to thee, Give me to drink; thou wouldest have asked of him, and he would have given thee living water . . . Whosoever drinketh of this water shall thirst again: but whosoever drinketh of the water that I shall give him shall never thirst; but the water that I shall give him shall be in him a well of water springing up into everlasting life. (John 4:10, 13–14)

We have been considering the particular characteristics of the great life offered us by our Lord. We have seen, first, that it is a 'heart' religion, and, second, that it is a mighty power that takes up the whole person – mind, heart and will. The whole personality is involved. It is a total change that can only be represented by referring to it as 'regeneration', a new birth, a new creation.

But we do not stop even there because we must again take this a step further. The text demands this, insists upon it, particularly as we consider it in the light of other, and perhaps even more explicit teaching, elsewhere in Scripture. In this passage, our Lord is putting this new life as a picture to the Samaritan woman. She does not understand. We have seen from the record how she stumbles and asks her questions, so our Lord puts it very generally to her. The next step, therefore, in this analysis is to see that what he is talking about is more than power. It is a power, as we have been emphasizing, a power that changes the whole of the personality; but it is more than that. It is, indeed, a *life*, and Christians are aware of a new life within them.

But the counter distinction that I have in my mind is that our Lord is not just talking about some urge to a new life, or a new way of living. We ended last time by saying that obviously this 'well of water' that our Lord gives will lead to a new way of living – that is because it affects the will. The truth perceived moves the heart, and that in turn moves the will. So Christians do practise and live a new and a different kind of life, but what makes them do that is not merely a power that urges, it is not merely a suasion. There is an element, of course, of moral and spiritual suasion in it but it is more than that. And I am trying to establish that we must realize this further truth because, after all, one of the most glorious aspects of the Christian life is that it is not merely a power in the sense of a dynamic. There are powers, such as machines and so on, that can stimulate us; electrical vibrations can put a kind of energy into us and tone us up. But it is not like that; it includes that, but that is the result of an actual life that is within us. We must use the terms that are found in the Scriptures themselves. It is a new life within. And, still more incredible and amazing, it is a *divine* life.

I have already referred to the book that greatly influenced Whitefield and the Wesleys 200 years ago, a book by old Henry Scougal, a Scotsman who lived towards the end of the eighteenth century. It was called *The Life of God in the Soul of Man* – that, he said, was Christianity. And that was what awakened these great men of God to the fact that they had never been Christians. Though they had been brought up in religious homes, they realized that they had never really had this life; they had been living in a certain way, but it had been a religion based upon their activities. But now Henry Scougal convicted them. And the writings of William Law were used much to the same end, although they were not as good and as scriptural as the book by Henry Scougal. However, the truth that was brought home to them was that Christianity is nothing less than the life of God in the souls of men.

Now, of course, there are abundant statements of this truth in Scripture. We see one when our Lord was speaking to Nicodemus, where he says, 'Verily, verily, I say unto thee, Except a man be born of water and of the Spirit, he cannot enter into the kingdom of God' (John 3:5). And he goes on: 'That which is born of the flesh is flesh: and that which is born of the Spirit is spirit' (verse 6). Christians do not merely have a new outlook and a new disposition, they have new life in them. The new outlook is the result of the fact that they have been 'born of the Spirit'.

The apostle Peter, in his second epistle, makes the same point in different language and in very striking terms. In verse 2, he prays that 'grace and peace [may] be multiplied' to these Christian believers, and continues:

According as his divine power hath given unto us all things that pertain unto life and godliness, through the knowledge of him that hath called us to glory and virtue: whereby are given unto us exceeding great and precious promises: that by these ye might be partakers of the divine nature. (2 Peter 1:3)

That is it – 'partakers of the divine nature'. And the apostle John in his first epistle makes the same point when he talks about the 'seed' that remains in the believer, and not only the seed. He says:

These things have I written unto you that believe on the name of the Son of God; that ye may know that ye have eternal life, and that ye may believe on the name of the Son of God. (1 John 5:13)

And John has just said that this life is in the Son: 'He that hath the Son hath life; and he that hath not the Son of God hath not life' (verse 12).

Now these are all statements that bring home to us this great and staggering teaching that the power that works in us, transforming us entirely in the mighty way we have been considering, is the power of an endless life; it is the power of divine life, so that we are 'partakers of the divine nature'. This, of course, is a great mystery; our Lord said that to Nicodemus: 'Marvel not that I said unto thee, Ye must be born again' (John 3:7). Nicodemus was foolish enough to try to understand it, and many of us have repeated his error, but it cannot be understood. It has often been compared – and I think rightly – to our Lord's own incarnation. He was 'conceived of the Holy Ghost'. He derived his human nature from Mary, his mother, but he was born of the Holy Spirit, conceived by the Holy Spirit, born a man in that way. And, therefore, it is right to say that, in a sense, this is comparable to what happens to us. It is an operation of the Holy Spirit; we are 'born of the Spirit'. There is a new birth and a new being, and we are made 'partakers of the divine nature'.

Now the term 'partakers of the divine nature' eludes our understanding: we must be careful that we do not imagine that this means that we become divine. Let me put it like this: we are told that at the very beginning of creation God created man in his own image and likeness. That is the idea that we must keep in our minds. It does not mean that when man was created, he was created a god. He was not. He was man – perfect man. The meaning of the words 'created . . . in the image of God' is that God gave to man certain characteristics of his own divine nature and being. This, of course, differentiates man from the animals. That is what is meant by 'the image', and it is that image that has been defaced and partly lost by the Fall. So man has lost these particular characteristics that he had originally that made him like God.

Now in the rebirth that is what we regain. This, again, is said by the apostle Paul in the Epistle to the Ephesians. He is reminding these Gentile people who had been born again, and had now become new beings, that they must not go on living as they had before and as other Gentiles still were. Why not? And this is how he puts it:

> *Put off concerning the former conversation the old man, which is corrupt according to the deceitful lusts; and be renewed in the spirit of your mind; and that ye put on the new man, which after God is created in righteousness and true holiness. (Ephesians 4:22–24)*

That is it! This new person is a new creation.

Now in the original creation, the man, Adam, in his perfection was righteous. God gave him an 'original righteousness', an original holiness; he was free from sin. And what is given to us in the rebirth – and this is the real meaning of the words, 'partakers of the divine nature' – is not that we become gods, nor that we become divine, but that we receive again this original righteousness, this something that is in God himself and that he puts into us, 'righteousness and true holiness' or 'holiness of the truth' (Ephesians 4:24). And so it is right to say that we are 'born of the Spirit'. And, indeed, in his first epistle John goes so far as to say this about our Lord, 'as he is, so are we in this world' (1 John 4:17). And, of course, implicit in all this is the notion that we become 'the children of God' (1 John 3:10; Romans 8:16).

Now that does not only mean that God takes an interest in us comparable to the interest of a father in his children – it goes beyond that. We are 'the children of God' in a deeper sense, and, because of that, we are 'heirs of God, and joint-heirs with Christ' (Romans 8:17). And all that is implicit in this statement here that our Lord makes to the woman of Samaria. It is a power, yes, but it is the power of this life, this principle, this divine nature – 'partakers of the divine nature'.

How frequently we fail to realize this! Indeed, probably from day to day we none of us realize this as we should. We know that we are changed; there was no difficulty about agreeing with everything I was trying to say when we were considering the change in the mind, the outlook, the orientation in the desires and the affections and in the will; that is all right. But we must go beyond that. And it is, I am persuaded increasingly, because we as Christian people do not realize these profundities concerning ourselves, because we do not realize what we are as Christians, that the church is as she is and her witness is so weak and ineffective. This is the key to true Christian living and to rejoicing in Christ. It is only as we realize these truths that we shall become people whom God can use to his glory and praise.

Too often we are apologetic for our Christianity and are almost ashamed of it in our work or professions. If ever you feel at all ashamed of your Christianity, it is for one reason only – you do not realize this truth. If you were a member of the royal family, you would not try to hide it, and we are told here that we are members of the family of God. This is the great contrast that Paul is so fond of making: 'Ye are no more strangers and foreigners, but fellow-citizens with the saints, and of the household of God' (Ephesians 2:19). We are children of God! God is our Father in a sense that he is not the Father of those who are not Christians.

This, then, is what our Lord is saying to the woman of Samaria, and we have been looking at it broadly and generally. But the

Scriptures are more specific – and we come here to the fourth characteristic of this life. They actually go on to say – and this is all a part of what it means to have this well of water within us 'springing up into everlasting life' – that not only are we partakers of the divine nature, but that in addition God dwells within us. That is why old Scougal's title to his book is so good – *The Life of God in the Soul of Man*. Now this, again, is an exposition of the great, true, mystical teaching of the Scripture. I have referred to false mysticism, but there is a true mysticism, and this is the mysticism that tells us that the Christian is one who is joined to the life of God because of God dwelling in his or her soul.

This is divided up like this. We are told that the Holy Spirit dwells within us. This is made plain in many passages. A famous one, of course, is in this same Gospel of John, where our Lord is now saying to the religious public what he says here privately to the woman of Samaria:

> *In that last day, that great day of the feast, Jesus stood and cried, saying, If any man thirst, let him come unto me, and drink. He that believeth on me, as the scripture hath said, out of his belly [out of his innermost parts] shall flow rivers of living water.*

Then John explains:

> *(But this spake he of the Spirit, which they that believe on him should receive: for the Holy Ghost was not yet given; because that Jesus was not yet glorified.) (John 7:37–39)*

Now that is a great statement of this truth. Then, later, our Lord, giving this final teaching to his disciples, puts it like this:

> *If ye love me, keep my commandments. And I will pray the Father, and he shall give you another Comforter*

– our Lord was a Comforter while he was here, now he is going to give another Comforter –

that he may abide with you for ever; even the Spirit of truth; whom the world cannot receive, because it seeth him not, neither knoweth him: but ye know him; for he dwelleth with you, and shall be in you. (John 14:15–17)

There it is put plainly and clearly that the Spirit dwells within us.

Now when we come to the exposition of that teaching in the Epistles, we find the apostle Paul saying this plainly and clearly. Writing to the Romans, he says, 'So then they that are in the flesh' – they are not Christians – 'cannot please God. But ye are not in the flesh, but in the Spirit, if so be that the Spirit of God dwell in you' (Romans 8:8–9). What could be plainer than that? Again in verse 11, he says, 'If the Spirit of him that raised up Jesus from the dead dwell in you' – well, then, the argument is that – 'he that raised up Christ from the dead shall also quicken your mortal bodies by his Spirit that dwelleth in you.'

But a still more specific passage is in the First Epistle to the Corinthians. The apostle there is dealing with sins in the flesh – fornication and so on – and this is his argument:

What? know ye not that your body is the temple of the Holy Ghost which is in you, which ye have of God, and ye are not your own? For ye are bought with a price: therefore glorify God in your body, and in your spirit, which are God's. (1 Corinthians 6:19–20)

The Holy Spirit dwells in us, in our bodies; our bodies are the temple in which he resides and in which he dwells.

So there it is beyond any doubt or question whatsoever; and James, whom people tend to dismiss lightly as if he were not a spiritual writer, makes exactly the same point: 'Do ye think that the scripture saith in vain, The spirit that dwelleth in us lusteth to envy?' (James 4:5). I have already expounded the latter part of that verse, but now I am simply emphasizing the words, 'Do ye think that the scripture saith in vain, the spirit that dwelleth in us . . .' He does! And, indeed, Galatians 5:17 makes the same point: 'The flesh lusteth against the Spirit, and the Spirit against the flesh' – the Holy Spirit who is within us as believers.

So here is this tremendous statement that the Holy Spirit does not merely influence us. He does, but, more, he dwells within us, he tabernacles within us in our lives. That is why we have the teaching about being careful, therefore, not to grieve him, or hurt him, or offend him and hinder him, or quench him, or resist him. 'The Holy Spirit dwelleth within you.' The apostle produces that as an argument for us to use in the time of temptation.

But, in exactly the same way, we are told that the Lord Jesus Christ also dwells within us. There is no higher teaching than this, but it is a part of New Testament teaching and the danger is that in our slick and glib way of reading the Scriptures and reading little notes, or taking a whole chapter in a Bible lecture or something like that, we reduce all these things and regard them merely as phrases. But these are solemn facts, these are truths that are actually put before us. So listen to what our Lord himself is recorded as saying in the fourteenth chapter of this great Gospel. He says, first of all, in verse 19:

> Yet a little while, and the world seeth me no more; but ye see me: because I live, ye shall live also. At that day ye shall know that I am in my Father, and ye in me, and I in you.

Then in verse 23:

> Jesus answered and said unto him, If a man love me, he will keep my words: and my Father will love him, and we will come unto him, and make our abode with him.

There is the statement. Our Lord repeats this at the end of the high priestly prayer, where he is talking about the unity that should exist among Christians:

> *I in them, and thou in me, that they may be made perfect in one; and that the world may know that thou hast sent me, and hast loved them, as thou hast loved me. (John 17:23)*

But this teaching did not end with our Lord himself; the apostles are given enlightenment and understanding. Paul writes to the Ephesians: 'If ye have heard of the dispensation of the grace of God which is given me to you-ward: how that by revelation he made known unto me the mystery . . .' (Ephesians 3:2–3). Christ has enlightened him; the Spirit works in him. So he puts it in his characteristic way again in the eighth chapter of Romans, and it is exactly the same teaching:

> *But ye are not in the flesh, but in the Spirit, if so be that the Spirit of God dwell in you. Now if any man have not the Spirit of Christ, he is none of his. And if Christ be in you, the body is dead because of sin; but the Spirit is life because of righteousness. (Romans 8:9–10)*

You notice, 'if Christ be in you.' Not only the Spirit, but also the Son, are in us, as the children of God. And again, in writing to the Corinthians, who had been falling into errors and going astray in so many ways, Paul exhorts them to examine themselves. He puts it like this: 'Examine yourselves, whether ye be in the faith; prove your own selves. Know ye not your own selves, how that Jesus Christ is in you, except ye be reprobate?' (2 Corinthians 13:5). Now you see that he does not say, 'Do you not know that as Christians you are those who believe in the Lord Jesus Christ and know certain things about him, and are trying to put his teaching into practice through the Spirit who is having an influence upon you'? No, no! Paul says, 'Know ye not your own selves how that Jesus Christ is in you, except ye be reprobate?' What could be more specific than that? Nothing more specific, perhaps, and certainly nothing more moving. And I suppose that in a sense there is nothing that rises higher than Galatians 2:19–20:

> *I through the law am dead to the law, that I might live unto God. I am crucified with Christ: nevertheless I live; yet not I, but Christ liveth in me: and the life which I now live in the flesh I live by the faith of the Son of God, who loved me, and gave himself for me.*

Now you must not reduce that to an influence; Paul goes beyond that. He says, 'I live; yet not I, *but Christ liveth in me.*' And we find exactly the same truth in Ephesians 3:17, where the apostle prays: 'That Christ may dwell in your hearts by faith; that ye, being rooted and grounded in love' and so on. And, again, there is a staggering statement in the Epistle to the Colossians, where Paul, again talking about this great privilege that has been given to him, says:

> *Whereof I am made a minister, according to the dispensation of God which is given to me for you, to fulfil [fill out] the word of God; even the mystery which hath been hid from ages and from generations, but now is made manifest to his saints [you and me!]: to whom God would make known*

– listen! –

> *what is the riches of the glory of this mystery among the Gentiles*

– notice the language! There is something wrong, Christian people, that we can be dull and apathetic, that we are not on our feet rejoicing with our faces shining in this evil world! It is a glory, and it is a rich glory. What is it?

which is Christ in you, the hope of glory. (Colossians 1:25–27)

Some have tried to reduce those words to mean, 'Christ among you'. That is included, but it cannot stop at that, it goes further. It is, 'Christ in you, the hope of glory'. And the hope of glory rests upon the fact that Christ is in us, that he is dwelling in us. That is the guarantee. We have been born again, we are partakers of the divine nature. The basis of 'the hope of glory' is that Christ is in us. What a glorious mystery! It is not surprising that the apostle's language seems to fail him, and he talks about 'the riches of the glory of this mystery'.

And, again, Paul reminds the Colossians:

If ye then be risen with Christ, seek those things which are above, where Christ sitteth on the right hand of God. Set your affection on things above, not on things on the earth. For ye are dead, and your life is hid with Christ in God. When Christ, who is our life, shall appear . . . (Colossians 3:1–4)

So it is clear that not only does the Holy Spirit dwell within us but also that our Lord and Saviour Jesus Christ, the Son of God, dwells in us. But in the twenty-third verse of the fourteenth chapter of John's Gospel that I quoted just now, did you notice how our Lord went even further? One almost hesitates to say such a thing, but I am here to read the Scripture:

Jesus answered and said unto him, If a man love me, he will keep my words: and my Father will love him, and we will come unto him, and make our abode with him. (John 14:23)

And remember Revelation 3:20: 'Behold, I stand at the door, and knock: if any man hear my voice, and open the door, I will come in to him, and will sup with him . . .' – eat and have fellowship with him. Here it is: God himself, God the Father, dwelling within us. And we find the same teaching in the high priestly prayer: 'I in them, and thou in me, that they may be made perfect in one' (John 17:23). Our Lord constantly repeats this. He has given them the glory that the Father had given him (verse 22). He is in us, and since the Father is in him, the Father is in us.

And this is what our Lord is putting in general to the woman of Samaria. He is saying: You have no idea – 'If thou knewest the gift of God . . .' And it is because people outside do not know that this is Christianity that they are not interested in it. And it is because we who are inside do not know this as we should that we are as we are, and are such poor representatives of this glorious Christian gospel. The life of God in the soul!

Now do not try to understand this – it is the highest teaching. Paul constantly talks about it as a mystery, and it is. The term 'mystery' in the New Testament always means something that is beyond the reach and the grasp of human understanding but which is 'made known'. This does not mean that it is a mystery to us in an ultimate sense. We have been let into the secret. It means something beyond human understanding, which God in his infinite grace has made known, 'revealed'. But it still is a mystery in the sense that we cannot understand it, we cannot work it out in detail, and we must not try to do so. We just know that it is true, we believe it; and, as we believe it, we increasingly enter into the experience of it.

A good deal of this is expressed in our greatest hymns, which are almost invariably the hymns of the eighteenth, and not the nineteenth, century. Nineteenth-century hymns are generally saccharine and sentimental.

> A heart resigned, submissive, meek,
> My great Redeemer's throne,
> Where only Christ is heard to speak,
> Where Jesus reigns alone;

A humble, lowly, contrite heart,
Believing, true, and clean;
Which neither life nor death can part
From him that dwells within.
                              Charles Wesley

It was this realization, first in Whitefield, then in the two brothers
Wesley, that led, as I have mentioned, to the great Evangelical
Awakening of the eighteenth century. The Lord Jesus Christ dwells
in the heart. And so we get a prayer offered by Charles Wesley:

Love divine, all loves excelling,
Joy of heaven, to earth come down,
Fix in us thy humble dwelling,
All thy faithful mercies crown.
                              Charles Wesley

Now I often listen to congregations singing that second line and I
find that they almost forget the comma. They sing it like this:
'Love divine, all loves excelling, Joy of heaven to earth come
down.' No, no; it is a request, it is a plea: 'Joy of heaven, to earth
come down – fix in us thy humble dwelling.' That is the meaning.
And it is only those who know that he is already there who offer
that prayer. They are praying for the certainty of it, as Paul is in
Ephesians 3. Christ was in the hearts of these Christians
in Ephesus, and Paul is praying that they may know that, that they
may be able to comprehend that more and more, 'with all the
saints', that they may have an active realization that Christ is
'dwelling in their hearts by faith'.

And that is the burden of the teaching in the third chapter of
Ephesians, which ends in that staggering, almost bewildering
statement, 'that ye might be filled with all the fulness of God'. The
apostle actually uses that language. That is what he is praying for

these Ephesians. You find this put in a negative way in that well-known hymn of poor William Cowper when he was in one of his periods of depression, with a sense of desertion. He cries out in his agony and says:

> Return, O holy dove, return,
> Sweet Messenger of rest;
> I hate the sins that made thee mourn
> That drove thee from my breast.
>   *William Cowper*

You see the teaching? This is Christian mysticism, this is the Christian life at its acme, at its highest: the realization that God dwells within, God the Father, God the Son, God the Holy Spirit. And our Lord puts that in these words to the woman of Samaria: 'The water that I shall give him shall be in him a well of water' – it will become a well of water – 'springing up into everlasting life.'

And, of course, the inevitable result of this is the point that I am putting next in order, which is my fifth particular test that we should apply to ourselves, and that is a sense of surprise, a sense of amazement and astonishment. More and more I would say that this is the ultimate test. Are we surprised at ourselves? If we are not, I do not think we are Christians. If you can explain yourself, you are not a Christian. Of course, as a religious man or woman you can explain yourself. Your religion is, as I have been pointing out, something you do, something you control, something that you handle. Moral people, religious people, always know exactly what they are doing and there is no mystery in their lives at all. They are in charge, everything that they have is less than themselves. But here, by definition, if the life of God is in the soul, it is something surprising, and those who know this are astounded that they should ever be in this position at all. Notice how the apostle Paul constantly says this:

> *I am the least of the apostles, that am not meet to be called an apostle, because I persecuted the church of God. But by the grace of God I am what I am: and his grace which was bestowed upon me was not in vain; but I laboured more abundantly than they all: yet not I, but the grace of God which was with me. (1 Corinthians 15:9–10)*

He cannot get over this, in a sense, he cannot believe that this is true of him. We have already read Galatians 2:20: 'I live; yet not I, but Christ liveth in me.' Did you notice it again in that third chapter of Ephesians as the apostle explains why he is a preacher? 'I Paul, the prisoner of Jesus Christ' (verse 1). He tells them of this great privilege that has been given him: 'whereof I was made a minister' (verse 7). He has this mystic secret.

> *That the Gentiles should be fellowheirs, and of the same body, and partakers of his promise in Christ by the gospel: whereof I was made a minister, according to the gift of the grace of God given unto me by the effectual working of his power. Unto me, who am less than the least of all saints, is this grace given. (verses 6–8)*

Paul cannot get over this. He is astounded at it. Or, again, notice how he puts it in writing to Timothy:

> *According to the glorious gospel of the blessed God, which was committed to my trust. And I thank Christ Jesus our Lord, who hath enabled me, for that he counted me faithful, putting me into the ministry; who was before a blasphemer, and a persecutor, and injurious: but I obtained mercy, because I did it ignorantly in unbelief. And the grace of our Lord was exceeding abundant with faith and love which is in Christ Jesus. This is a faithful saying, and worthy of all acceptation, that Christ Jesus came into the world to save sinners;*

of whom I am chief. Howbeit for this cause I obtained mercy, that in me first Jesus Christ might shew forth all longsuffering, for a pattern to them which should hereafter believe on him to life everlasting. (1 Timothy 1:11–16)

Now, again, this is but an expression on the part of the apostle of the fact that he is amazed that this should have happened to him. And what is it? It is that Christ is in him, and that Christ is using him thus to his glory and to his praise. John is saying the same thing in those two verses at the beginning of the third chapter of his epistle:

Behold, what manner of love the Father hath bestowed upon us, that we should be called the sons of God: therefore the world knoweth us not, because it knew him not. Beloved, now are we the sons of God, and it doth not yet appear what we shall be: but we know that, when he shall appear, we shall be like him; for we shall see him as he is. (1 John 3:1–2)

Now that is fact; it is staggering; it is amazing. Beloved, realize it, says John, even as he himself realized it and was amazed.

This is the experience of the saints throughout the centuries, and it is put perfectly in that well-known hymn of Charles Wesley:

And can it be, that I should gain
An interest in the Saviour's blood?
Died he for me, who caused his pain;
For me, who him to death pursued?
Amazing love! How can it be,
That thou, my God, hast died for me?

Almost incredible!

And, finally, use this test. Men and women of whom Scougal's words are true, those who have the life of God in the soul, are aware of this difference in themselves, and they are aware that they are different from who they once were, and different from those who do not have this life of God. Now this is not Pharisaism; the Pharisee is proud that he is different because he is such a wonderful man. But that is not the feeling of the Christian. Christians know that they have done nothing; the difference is because of what God has done to them I believe that this is the explanation of our Lord's teaching in the tenth chapter of Matthew's Gospel. He says:

> *Think not that I am come to send peace on earth: I came not to send peace, but a sword.*

This is a staggering statement and people often do not understand it.

> *I am come to set a man at variance against his father, and the daughter against her mother, and the daughter in law against her mother in law. And a man's foes shall be they of his own household. (Matthew 10:34–36)*

How do you explain that? Here is the explanation: the moment you receive this life of God in your soul, you are made different. Though you are related to those people still in the flesh, not only do you know that you are different, they, too, know it, they sense it immediately. They do not understand you now. If you merely 'take up' something, well, then, they can understand it and explain it, but this they do not understand. And you cannot expect them to.

That is why, when Christian people come to talk to me about this kind of difficulty that often arises when one member of a family alone becomes a Christian, I always exhort them not to be harsh, not to be impatient. These family members cannot help it; they do not understand it; it is impossible. They are like Nicodemus. So I say: Be patient, bear with them and pray for them. You have a new nature, the divine nature, and this inevitably shows itself in your life.

'He that is spiritual judgeth all things, yet he himself is judged of no man' (1 Corinthians 2:15).

And so Peter's words are perfectly true. Listen:

Forasmuch then as Christ hath suffered for us in the flesh, arm yourselves likewise with the same mind: for he that hath suffered in the flesh hath ceased from sin; that he no longer should live the rest of his time in the flesh to the lusts of men, but to the will of God. For the time past of our life may suffice us to have wrought the will of the Gentiles, when we walked in lasciviousness, lusts, excess of wine, revellings, banquetings, and abominable idolatries.

Then:

Wherein they think it strange that ye run not with them to the same excess of riot, speaking evil of you. (1 Peter 4:1–4)

There it is. Peter says, in effect, 'You know, because you are different, your friends and relatives do not understand you; they think it strange that you are not prepared to run with them now in the way you used to, and they speak evil of you. What is happening? Oh, they are just letting you know that they realize that you have the life of God in your soul, they see the difference and do not understand you.'

So one of the tests that we apply to ourselves to know whether this well of water is within us springing up into everlasting life is just this: Do we know that we are different? Are we amazed at it? And do other people prove it to us by telling us that we are different, perhaps even 'speaking evil' of us because we can no longer live the kind of life they still live?

Here are some of the particular tests, then, that we apply to know whether we are 'partakers of the divine nature'.

18

Never Thirst

Jesus answered and said unto her, Whosoever drinketh of this water shall thirst again: but whosoever drinketh of the water that I shall give him shall never thirst; but the water that I shall give him shall be in him [become in him] a well of water springing up into everlasting life. (John 4:13–14)

We have been looking at the characteristics of the great life that is offered to us in the Christian gospel in order that we may be able to test ourselves. Christianity is not theoretical. It is not just espousing a teaching or taking up a point of view. It is a life. That is the whole point of what our Lord is saying here. If it is a 'well of water' within us, the life of God in the soul, then it must express itself. And therefore if we would know for a surety whether or not we are Christians, we can test ourselves by observing the characteristics of this life that he gives us and asking ourselves whether we are aware of the manifestations of this life in our own lives.

Now having done that in general, we come to another important aspect of this statement of our Lord: 'But whosoever drinketh of the water that I shall give him shall never thirst.' This is a staggering statement – 'shall never thirst'. You see the contrast that our Lord makes: 'Whosoever drinketh of this water shall thirst again.' This is the element of complete satisfaction that our Lord claims for the life that he came into the world to give. There are many statements of this teaching, not only in the Gospels but also, subsequently, in the New Testament Epistles. 'I am come', says our Lord, 'that they might have life, and that they might have it more abundantly' (John 10:10).

Here is a subject that obviously needs our close attention: it is a further test that we can apply to ourselves. Bishop Westcott says of this phrase 'never thirst' that it is a very remarkable expression, and we must give it its full value. Somebody has suggested that it should be translated like this: 'Whosoever drinketh of the water that I shall give him shall never, no, never, be thirsty any more', and even that is not quite strong enough.

This term 'never' is found several times in John's Gospel. In the eighth chapter we find the words:

Verily, verily, I say unto you, If a man keep my saying, he shall never see death. Then said the Jews unto him, Now we know that thou hast a devil. Abraham is dead, and the prophets; and thou sayest, If a man keep my saying, he shall never taste of death. (John 8:51–52)

And in the tenth chapter there is the same thought: 'And I give unto them eternal life; and they shall *never* perish, neither shall any man pluck them out of my hand' (verse 28). That is: 'They shall never perish, no, never, never perish.' It is the same expression exactly. In chapter 11 we again find it: 'Jesus said unto her, I am the resurrection, and the life: he that believeth in me, though he were dead, yet shall he live: and whosoever liveth and believeth in me shall *never* die' – never, no, never (verse 25). And once more in the thirteenth chapter when our Lord was proposing to wash the disciples' feet, and Peter said, 'Thou shalt *never* wash my feet' (verse 8).

But perhaps the most interesting example of the use of this term is to be found in the First Epistle to the Corinthians. Paul has been dealing with the question of meats offered to idols. The stronger brethren had come to see that there was nothing in this at all, but the weaker brethren were still troubled when they saw fellow Christians eating this meat. So the apostle finishes by saying this: 'Wherefore, if meat make my brother to offend, I will eat *no* flesh *while the world standeth*, lest I make my brother to offend' (1 Corinthians 8:13).

Now it is remarkable that the translators of the Authorized Version, the very people who translated the statement 'shall never thirst', when they came to translate exactly the same word in 1 Corinthians 8:13, should translate it, 'no . . . while the world standeth'. And there is no doubt at all but that the latter is altogether better because it brings out the strength and the force of the meaning. The translation 'never' is really not strong enough. Of course, if you put its full value into the word 'never', I suppose it tells you everything; the language that our Lord used, and the repetition of the words, do bring out this additional emphasis. But to make clear the literal meaning, we could translate verse 14 like this: 'Whosoever drinketh of the water that I shall give him will by no means thirst unto the end of the age'; or, to use the words of the translators of the Authorized Version, 'Whosoever drinketh of the water that I shall give him, shall not thirst while the world standeth'; or, 'while the world is in being and in existence'; or, 'While the world continues to be and to stand, he shall never thirst.' As long as the cosmos is in existence, as long as this particular age is in existence, whoever drinks of this water shall never thirst. Now what could be stronger than that?

And yet, after all we have seen, this is something that we should expect. It is quite inevitable and logical. We have seen already that if we drink this water, it becomes in us a well of water springing up into everlasting life, and that this is God's action in us: it is the result of the miracle worked in us by the Holy Spirit. This is Christianity. It is not something we add on, not something we do, but something done to us. It is 'regeneration', being 'born again', it is being 'created anew', it is becoming 'a new creation'. These are the terms, and it is all done by God himself. And, supremely, as we have seen, he puts something of his own being into us, we are 'partakers of the divine nature'.

So, in the light of that, it would be a contradiction in terms to say that you can be a partaker of the divine nature and yet go on thirsting. It would mean that God's work was incomplete, that it was not perfect, that elements were still lacking. But, as we know, everything that God does is perfect. We are told that when he originally created everything, the whole universe, including human beings, he looked at it all 'and, behold, it was very good' (Genesis 1:31). Of course! And the work that God does in the soul in regeneration is equally perfect. So our Lord here makes this claim for it: 'Whosoever drinketh of the water that I shall give him shall never thirst.'

We can, then, immediately say two things. First, that the ultimate truth, the ultimate characteristic, of this life is its all-sufficiency, the complete satisfaction that it gives. And, secondly, at the same time, this also becomes the ultimate test that we apply to ourselves to discover whether or not we have received this life.

Oh, let me go on emphasizing this. I am not here to talk about these truths theoretically, but because, to me, the most wonderful thing in the world that can happen to men and women is that they receive this life; and not only that, but the most terrible thing that

I can conceive of is that people should mistake something spurious for this glorious reality. There is no greater need in the church at the present time than to have men and women who are filled in this way. We do not call for busy people, or for activists, we call for people who have this life within them. These are the true evangelists, wherever they are. In all their circumstances, this life will show itself and be obvious to all. So the question we put to ourselves, therefore, is this: Have we obtained this complete, final satisfaction? Do we 'never thirst'?

Now it is important that we should be clear, therefore, as to what the expression 'never thirst' means. There is a very real danger of our so misinterpreting it that we depress ourselves, and we must not do that. There is a way of looking at this that could make us feel that we are not Christians at all, and that would obviously be wrong. What, therefore, does our Lord mean?

It seems to me that the best way of expounding this phrase is to take it together with the statement that is found in Philippians chapter 3. The apostle here is talking in terms of what he desires. He says:

> *Yea doubtless, and I count all things but loss for the excellency of the knowledge of Christ Jesus my Lord . . . that I may win Christ, and be found in him, not having mine own righteousness, which is of the law, but that which is through the faith of Christ, the righteousness which is of God by faith. (Philippians 3:8–9)*

Then in verse 10, he says:

> *That I may know him, and the power of his resurrection . . .*

In verse 12, he gives us certain negatives:

> *Not as though I had already attained, either were already perfect: but I follow after . . .*

before again repeating, in verses 13 and 14:

> *Brethren, I count not myself to have apprehended: but this one thing I do, forgetting those things which are behind, and reaching forth unto those things which are before, I press toward the mark.*

Now there is on the surface an apparent contradiction between the two statements: 'Whosoever drinketh of the water that I shall give him shall never thirst' and, 'That [my desire is] I may know him . . . Not as though I had already apprehended, either were already perfect.' Are they contradictory? And, of course, the answer is that they are not, they fit in perfectly together. Here is the great apostle Paul at the height of his experience, in his maturity, expressing this desire, this longing, to know Christ more and more. He has not apprehended as he wishes to apprehend. He is trying, he says, to 'apprehend that for which also I am apprehended of Christ Jesus' (verse 12).

So how do we resolve the apparent difficulty? The answer is that it is the difference between 'thirsting' and 'desiring more' of this life, of this water. The very expression 'to thirst' implies a very deep need. There is an element in thirst of profound dissatisfaction, of exhaustion and emptiness. There is an element of pain in it. I turned up the Oxford Dictionary on this and it describes 'thirst' in these terms: 'The uneasy or painful sensation caused by the need of drink.' Westcott says, 'Thirst is the pain of an unsatisfied want.' And that is a very good definition.

Now our Lord is saying that the Christian will never again experience thirst. He will never have this sense of utter exhaustion, this painful sensation of need – never again. He says that Christians will never be empty or exhausted; they will never be in dire trouble or be desperate; they will never be in despair; they will never be, as it were, almost at the point of death, feeling that they are going to die. Our Lord uses the word 'thirst' in its full and right meaning and this is what we must grasp.

The term 'never thirst' does not mean, however, that the Christian is one who knows full satiety. Nor does it mean that Christians will not know any variations in their life and experience and will never desire more – the apostle himself says that he does, as we have just seen. Indeed, we can go so far as to say that the only people who do ever desire more of this living water are those who already have it, and that is why they desire more. This aspect of it can be put in terms of growth. If you are not alive, you cannot grow. But where there is life, there is the possibility of growth; and there should be growth. So the very fact of growth, and the desire to grow, is a proof that there is life within. So we must regard this teaching mainly from the negative standpoint as meaning that once we have received this life, we will never again be empty or desperate or exhausted – never. And this can never be put too strongly.

There is, therefore, no incompatibility between these two statements, no contradiction between them. The Christian, while never empty, should always be desiring to have more and more of the fullness. Christians may at times feel that they are comparatively empty, but they are never completely so. They may look at others or read the biography of a saint and say, 'What have I got?' and yet they know they have something. Their very appreciation of what the other has, and their desire for it, is that which is within them crying out for more. So you must give the correct meaning to this word 'thirst'.

Now I suggest that perhaps the best way of all of knowing the difference between thirsting, on the one hand, and desiring more, on the other, is by understanding what the apostle tells us about himself in a bit of autobiography in the Second Epistle to the Corinthians. He makes a tremendous statement:

For God, who commanded the light to shine out of darkness, hath shined in our hearts, to give the light of the knowledge of the glory of God in the face of Jesus Christ.

That is what he is glorying in – it is another way of talking about this 'well of water within'. The apostle goes on:

But we have this treasure in earthen vessels, that the excellency of the power may be of God, and not of us.

Then his next words show us the difference between 'never thirsting' and yet 'desiring more':

We are troubled on every side

– now watch his negatives –

yet not distressed; we are perplexed

– things are happening; he does not understand them and at times he does not know what to do. You remember the famous account of his vision at Troas (Acts 16:6–10). Paul was in great perplexity, and this happened to him on many an occasion –

but not in despair

– you see, he does not thirst. There is great need but he is not thirsting –

persecuted, but not forsaken; cast down, but not destroyed. (2 Corinthians 4:6–9)

Now there, I think, is the perfect exposition of this question of 'never, no, never, thirst again'. Here is the apostle surrounded by trials, troubles, tribulations, everything, as it were, going against him, but in spite of it all he brings out these positives. 'Do not misunderstand me,' he says. 'We are troubled on every side, yet *not distressed,* we are perplexed, but *not in despair . . .*' He has taken of this water, he has drunk of it and he never thirsts again.

Christians, in other words, may be perplexed, they may be in trouble, they may be in difficulties, but they are never frantic. They never again search about violently for satisfaction; they never reach the point at which they wonder whether they will find satisfaction again – never. This is the vital distinction. There are certain things that can never happen to Christians again. Why? Because their great central need has been satisfied once and for ever. That is the assertion, and that is what we must hold on to. Many things may happen to Christian people. It may be that through their neglect, through their laziness, their lack of diligence or through their sinning, the water in the well, as it were, becomes muddy, filled with a lot of mire, and sticks and stones, and other people may say that the well is finished. At times, they themselves may be tempted by the devil to think exactly the same thing. But the point is that it will never be dry – never.

Whatever may happen to Christian people, they will never find themselves having to ask where they can find water, they will never become prospectors, or send for a prospector, and think about digging another well in order that they may find satisfaction. Christians at their worst, in the depth of backsliding – and Christians can backslide, and backslide so far that the world is convinced that they have never been Christians at all, or that, if they ever have, they have ceased to be, having sunk to the most awful depths – will still always know that all they must do is clear out the well and get rid of the mud and the stones and the filth and all that has been clogging up the outlet of this well of water that they know is within them.

In the depths of their backsliding, Christians always know that they are children of God, that is why they are wretched and miserable. They do not have to seek for truth elsewhere, they know it is there, they know that they are responsible for their condition, and that all they must do is repeat the action that Isaac the son of Abraham had to take on one occasion when he came to the valley of Gerer: 'Isaac digged again the wells of water, which they had digged in the days of Abraham his father; for the Philistines had stopped them after the death of Abraham' (Genesis 26:18). Isaac did not have to dig new wells. All he had to do was get rid of the filth that the Philistines had thrown into the wells. He knew that once he had got rid of the filth he would find the water in all its old pristine purity, bubbling up as in the days of Abraham. And backsliders do exactly the same thing; they never thirst. They have the water in them and they know it is there, and all they must do is repent, and 'do works meet for repentance' (Acts 26:20).

There, then, is the way in which you interpret this word 'thirst'. It does not mean that you are always at the same dead level. The cults teach that sort of thing, and that is where they differ from this Christian teaching. There are people who say that once they became Christians they never afterwards had problems or troubles or doubts. That does not conform to what one reads in the Scriptures, nor in the lives of the saints. There are variations. 'Never thirst again' does not mean that you are immediately put on to that topmost position and remain there. No, it is compatible with Paul's 'that I may know him'. I long to know him: I feel I do not know him as much as I should.

So here is our Lord's great statement that we must consider. He says, 'Whosoever drinketh of the water that I shall give him shall never thirst.' Now this is true of the entire personality. We have already seen that this power within produces a *total* change, a change in the whole person. It is equally important for us to see that the satisfaction that it gives is a satisfaction that is likewise complete, and this, again, is one of the claims we make for this glorious gospel. Everything else gives us only a partial, temporary satisfaction. There is nothing else under heaven that can satisfy the complete, the total person. And it does so unfailingly and for ever.

What do I mean? Well, we must take it again in the same way. When we were talking about the power working within, transforming and changing us, I said it changed our mind, our outlook, our heart, our sensibilities, our affections and our will. And this is exactly how I want to show the satisfaction that we receive.

First – now listen to this claim I am making – when we receive the life of God in our soul, we get complete intellectual satisfaction. Now that is a big claim and yet, thank God, it is nothing but the simple truth. If you do not have final satisfaction intellectually, are you a Christian? Humanity always thirsts for intellectual satisfaction. One of the greatest characteristics of man is intellectual curiosity. Man looking at life, looking at everything that he knows of, wants understanding, wants explanation, so he begins to think and to meditate, and to put up theories. That is the meaning of philosophy: it is the love of wisdom in order to have understanding. That is why people engage in all kinds of research: the moment they begin to think at all, they find themselves up against the great mystery of the world in which they live. What is this world? Where has it come from? What is its meaning?

And then life: look at life – flowers, animals, human beings. What is this mysterious thing that we call life? Where has it come from? People want to know. Then, of course, there are human beings themselves. What is man? There is the question. These are subjects that have aroused intellectual curiosity from the very beginning and men and women have been seeking for explanations.

And then they have to go on, of course, if they are true thinkers. What is this thing that we call 'evil'? Why is there so much failure in life? Why am I a failure? Why are you a failure? Why do we fall? Why are most people fundamentally unhappy? Why do they have to seek ways of relieving the unhappiness of which they are conscious? What is the explanation? People have been grappling with these problems, these questions, from the very beginning.

And then people are aware of the fact that they are 'here today and gone tomorrow' and after they have gone there will be others and there were people here before them. So what is this sequence? What is history? What is the meaning of history? Is there any meaning in it? What is this whole business of time? How does one understand time – the great problem at present? And then, of course, suffering, the extraordinary suffering in the world. Pain! Humanity has grappled with these various problems all along.

And, finally, of course, death; there it is, 'the last enemy'. Yes! The last mystery, too! It is the end of life in this visible world. What then? Ah! That has occupied the minds of these thinkers and they have grappled with it. And what lies beyond death? Eternity! And behind everything, God, this being. Is he there? Who is he? What is he? You have a consciousness of him; no one has ever been born without a consciousness of God – it is universal. In the most primitive tribes there is a consciousness, an awareness, of a supreme being. The clever people try to explain it away but it is in them, it is in everybody. There is a universal God-consciousness in the whole of humanity. These are the questions that agitate the minds of men and women.

And here is the claim that our Lord is making and I am privileged to preach it now in his holy name. The world has no answer to these questions. It has done its utmost; it is still doing its utmost. It is no nearer to giving satisfaction than it was in the great flowering of Greek philosophy five centuries before the birth of our Lord and Saviour. The world goes through phases in this quest for knowledge, for understanding. There is a sense in which this is quite amusing, were it not so vitally important and, in a sense, tragic. I am old enough to have seen the fashions in philosophy. One teaching becomes the craze and everybody is taking it up, and it is wonderful – it does not last, another comes. Each one claims to be able to answer all the questions but it never does. Indeed, we can go further; no teaching ever will. If philosophers could solve our problems, the Son of God would never have come into this world. He came to give light: 'I am the light of the world,' he said (John 8:12; 9:5), and he alone is the light. And here is the claim that he is making to the woman of Samaria; it is the claim that we make in his name. The only answer is the answer that is to be found in him, and it is, I emphasize, a complete answer.

Now I want to add a few words here in parenthesis. I am speaking to people who in name, I have no doubt, are evangelical people and evangelically minded. I think the greatest charge that can be brought against evangelicals in the last 90 years or so, since the seventies of the nineteenth century, is that we have grievously failed at this point. We have tended to reduce this glorious gospel, and the life that it gives, to just a question of forgiveness, as if everything happens when a person takes a decision, as though that is the beginning and the end of the gospel. The glory, the bigness, the greatness, the complete intellectual satisfaction, has not been preached and expounded as it should have been. Indeed, evangelical people have often been charged, and I am afraid it has been a true charge, of being afraid of the intellect.

There were men 40 years ago – I knew some of them and have read their books – who definitely used to advise young Christians not to read theology, as it was dangerous. So the impression was given that to be evangelical meant to commit intellectual suicide. To be an evangelical you had to stop thinking and adopt a formula and that put you right. That is a travesty of the gospel! The gospel of our Lord and Saviour, and that alone, gives complete intellectual satisfaction. There is nothing more glorious about it than the way in which it takes up the whole person and gives a perfect understanding of all things. That is the claim.

Does this mean that every one of us, therefore, has complete understanding of everything? Of course not. All I am saying is that the explanation is given. Many of us, like those Hebrew Christians about whom we read in the Epistle to the Hebrews, are 'dull of hearing', and we are 'babes', and we have not 'exercised' our senses (Hebrews 5:11–14). We have been content with just a first experience of conversion and we have never grown, we have never even read, we have not thought. Shame on us! With all this wealth before us, all this amazing teaching, all this intellectual comfort, all this profound Christian philosophy! But that is entirely due to us, you see. Our Lord is saying that he is the light of the world. He is claiming that there is in this book that we call the Bible complete satisfaction intellectually, that here there is understanding of all these problems that are agitating the minds of men and women.

In other words, the Christian message is called *truth* ; it is not only something you experience. It is that, as we shall see, but I never start with that; and if you start with experience, you are going against the Scriptures. This is truth, and the only experience that is of any value is the experience that is based upon truth. The cults can give you experiences, but the only experience that is valid is that which our Lord gives, and it results from the truth that he himself introduces to us: 'I am the way, the truth, and the life' – that is it – 'no man cometh unto the Father, but by me' (John 14:6). The apostle tells Timothy to pray 'for kings, and for all that are in authority' (1 Timothy 2:1–2). Why? Because, he says, '[God] will have all men to be saved, and to come unto the knowledge of the truth' (1 Timothy 2:4) – and Christianity is primarily 'a knowledge of the truth'. And so it comes to us in terms of this great and glorious revelation.

What do I mean by this? Let me just give you some headings that you can work out for yourselves. Take the various problems that I have mentioned. Where have they come from? What is the explanation of their origin? You are familiar with some of the theories that have been put forward. There are people who speak of the theory of evolution as if it were an established fact, and yet increasingly scientists are admitting that it is not and that it is most inadequate. I venture the prophecy that it will soon be utterly discredited, in spite of the vogue that it has had for over a hundred years, since Darwin published his book in 1859. No, there is only one adequate explanation for the origin of the world, it is the one that is given at the beginning of the book of Genesis, the first book in the Bible: 'In the beginning God created . . .'

Now I am not saying that this statement is one that you can comprehend, but it is something that you can understand, it is a satisfactory explanation and it is the only one. But then that leads me on to ask the question: Well, if you say that God has created everything that is, who is God? How can I know him? And here again the philosophers have been busy but they have failed completely. The apostle Paul is able to say of them, 'the world by wisdom knew not God' (1 Corinthians 1:21). They could not get further than 'the unknown God' (Acts 17:23).

There is only one who can really teach us about God: it is this blessed Lord and Saviour. 'No man hath seen God at any time; the only begotten Son, which is in the bosom of the Father, he hath declared him' (John 1:18). This is the only way to know God. It was when 'the world by wisdom knew not God, it pleased God by the foolishness of preaching to save them that believe' (1 Corinthians 1:21). There is no knowledge of God apart from him who says to the woman of Samaria: Take this water and you will have complete satisfaction. 'He that hath seen me hath seen the Father' (John 14:9). There is no other way; by knowing him, one knows God and knows God as one's Father.

And it is the same with the knowledge of man. You cannot understand man except in terms of the biblical explanation. You cannot explain man biologically, you cannot explain him materialistically, dialectically, economically, or in any other way. There is only one way to explain the greatness of man. What is it? It is that he is made in the image of God. The smallness, the despicable aspect of men – what is it? It is the doctrine of the Fall, man's disobedience and rebellion against God. You do not begin to understand the state of the world unless you accept this biblical explanation. Evolution tells you the world is getting better and better. It obviously is not. Why not? Evil! The devil! Sin! The forces of hell working against God! That is why the world is unhappy, that is why men and women are unhappy, with a sense of guilt and an accusing conscience. These are facts of experience, yet psychology cannot explain them – the rival theories of psychology contradict one another. No, here in the Bible is an adequate, and the only adequate, explanation.

And when you come to consider the way of deliverance from it all, oh, how much more evident is it that there is no satisfaction anywhere except in this message. Can you find peace of conscience by searching for it? Can you find rest for your soul? Can you know that your sins are forgiven? There is no other way. Here it is, and it is complete, absolute, perfect. 'Whosoever drinketh of the water that I shall give him shall never thirst.'

Our Lord's claim is not an idle claim. There is here in this revelation, and particularly and specially in him, the answer to all our questions. 'All the promises of God in him are yea, and in him Amen, unto the glory of God by us' (2 Corinthians 1:20). These words really mean just this: in him is the answer; here is the satisfaction. I do not stop thinking when I become a Christian, indeed, it is the other way round. In a sense, I start thinking and I am now able to face all the questions, and I know that there is always an answer.

19

Full Satisfaction – of the Intellect

Jesus answered and said unto her, Whosoever drinketh of this water shall thirst again: but whosoever drinketh of the water that I shall give him shall never thirst; but the water that I shall give him shall be in him a well of water springing up into everlasting life. (John 4:13–14)

In our last study, we saw that if Christians are ever conscious of a lack – and they often are – they always realize that it is entirely due to themselves. It is due to their own failure in some shape or form to partake of this well of water as they should, to avail themselves of it, or, because of sin, they have allowed the well to become almost invisible as a result of all the various things that have cluttered up its mouth. But they are always certain that it is there, they have never sought it in vain. They know that there is always a sufficiency for their every need.

Indeed, as the apostle Paul puts it, in a passing word, as it were, to the Philippians: 'Let us therefore, as many as be perfect, be thus minded: and if in any thing ye be otherwise minded, God shall reveal even this unto you' (Philippians 3:15). He says, in effect, 'There you are, you were satisfied, as it were, for the time being, but there is just something else you are not quite clear about. It is all right, that will be revealed to you.' Christians have this certainty, this consciousness, that there is nothing that they can ever need but that it is already supplied, and supplied with a great and a wonderful superabundance, in our blessed Lord and Saviour.

And now we are emphasizing that this is a sufficiency for the whole person: the mind, the intellect, the heart and affections, the sensibilities. Whatever the circumstances, the whole person is always fully and completely satisfied. And we are beginning to work this out in detail. We have started with the intellectual satisfaction that is given by this gospel and its teaching – teaching from our Lord himself and the life that he imparts to us. We must start here because, after all, the greatest gift that God has given to men and women is the gift of mind and the gift of understanding. It is perhaps this more than anything else that differentiates man from the animals. So we must be able to establish that the gospel, this life, gives complete intellectual satisfaction.

In a hurried word at the end of the last study, I pointed out how this life given by our Lord immediately provides satisfaction with regard to the first great problem that confronts us all, and that is our awareness of failure, our awareness of deep dissatisfaction. We do not understand the world and life and ourselves and our misery, our unhappiness, we do not know anything about God. We have a con-sciousness of God, but we cannot find him, and we are concerned how to be reconciled to him. These are the first fundamental human needs, and in a hurried, glancing word I just reminded you of how all that is dealt with here in the gospel, and only here, and dealt with perfectly, fully and all sufficiently. There is only one way of salvation, only one deliverance. It is not arrogance to say this, it is just to be truthful.

But we do not stop at that, and, indeed, we must not. We are concerned to show the fullness, the all-sufficiency, of our Lord's words 'shall never thirst'. So we do not stop at entering into the Christian life and having a knowledge of sins forgiven, we must go beyond that. Let me show you in two further ways the intellectual satisfaction given by the gospel. One is that our minds cry out for greater understanding: questions come up, difficulties arise and doubts may assail us, and we want to answer them. Any Christian who thinks at all, while thanking God for the knowledge of sins forgiven and a general new outlook, will still have questions and look for answers. And, as I say, there is the devil, the adversary, who hurls doubts and questions and queries at us. Not only that, there is false teaching, false teaching in the church. The New Testament has a great deal to say about that. There is much false teaching at the present time and we want to be able to deal with these issues. All this is a part of the desire for intellectual satisfaction, and our emphasis is that the gospel is able to give satisfaction by answering these questions.

The second way of showing you the greater fullness and all-sufficiency of the gospel and its way of life, is just by calling your attention to the fact of the Bible. There is, perhaps, no better way of demonstrating the complete intellectual satisfaction that is given by the Christian faith than by considering the Bible itself. Now what is the Bible? You may think that is a foolish, almost ridiculous, question to put to Christian people on a Sunday morning, but I suggest that it is not, and that oftentimes much of our trouble arises because we have never really considered this question. Or let me put it in a different way: How do you as an individual Christian use the Bible?

Now I have often found that there are many people – I am talking about Christians, those who have come into the Christian life – who read the Bible because they have been told to do so, it is a duty. They have never read it before, but now they have become Christians – ah, one of the things a Christian does is read the Bible! So they join some scheme or other and they begin to read it.

Other people read the Bible in what may be described as a purely devotional manner. Their attitude towards it seems to be this: they have now 'got' what was necessary, they are converted, they are born again, they have new life, they have become Christians. So they regard the Bible as a book that is here to help them, it is an aid to their devotional life. They feel they have got everything, really, and all they need to do now is just keep this life going. As you keep your physical body going by eating and drinking day by day, so you just keep on nourishing this life that you have received.

Now I want to suggest to you that while the second is legitimate and while, in a sense, the first is right, to read the Bible solely for those two reasons is not only inadequate, it is almost a misuse of the Bible; at least, it is a failure to realize what the Bible is and why it has ever been given to us.

So what is this book? Now, again, there is a teaching at the present time that is very popular in the Christian church and, unfortunately, it seems to be gaining a certain amount of approval and currency among evangelical people. It is a view of the Bible that says that the Bible is the account of the experiences of various individuals in the past, and in particular of the Jewish nation. It records the experiences of the patriarchs, and people such as David and the prophets, and also of the Children of Israel in general, and shows the attempts of those people to explain and to expound their experiences.

Well, now, it is my business to show that that is a complete misunderstanding of the true nature of the Scripture. That view turns the Bible into a human book: people's experiences. Those who hold this view grant that the experiences were given by God, although they would tend to say that even so, they were mainly the result of human seeking and searching, but as regards these records, they are nothing but human documents written by men at various times. That is why, they say, you find errors in the Bible. They have come about in an attempt to explain the experiences; experience is the big thing, the Bible is just the attempt to expound it.

No, no! There is only one word that must be used to define what the Bible is and that is *revelation*. The Bible is not about discovering anything, it is not man attempting to do anything. The first truth about the Bible is that it is God's revelation to human beings, God making truth known to us; that is what it is. God taking the trouble to call certain people, to equip them and to endow them with the necessary faculties, then to make known to them knowledge pertaining to truth, and enabling them to write this revelation in an accurate, indeed, in an infallible manner. That is what the Bible claims for itself: 'All scripture is given by inspiration of God' (2 Timothy 3:16). If you prefer it, you can translate that, 'All scripture is God-breathed.' The apostle Peter says, 'Holy men of God spake as they were moved by the Holy Ghost' (2 Peter 1:21) and 'No prophecy of the scripture is of any private interpretation' (2 Peter 1:20). There are many similar passages and this is the claim that the writers always make for themselves.

Now this, you see, is a most important matter. Here, I say, God has been pleased to give us knowledge, to give us truth. He has taken all this trouble to deal with the people and to prepare them and then to equip them and to endow them and to give them knowledge of the truth, which they pass on to us. Why is this? Well, in order that we might have knowledge. What knowledge? Knowledge concerning God himself. That is what you find in this book. What does anyone know, really, about God apart from this?

Oh, I know you can know something about God if you look at him and his work in nature and creation. You are familiar with the arguments, so called, for the being of God – the demonstrations and proofs of the being of God. All right; grant them their full value. You can deduce, you should be able to deduce, the hand of God from nature and creation. Paul argues this in Romans 1:18–20. Modern scientists, some of them, have had the sense to say that. Sir James Jeans said that having studied science for all the years that he had done, he had come to the conclusion that there must be a great mind at the back of it all and that this must be the mind of a great mathematician. All right, you deduce all that, and you can also do so from history and from providence. You can use purely philosophical reasoning to argue for the existence of God, for instance, that if there is bad and good and better there must be a best, there must be perfect. All right! I will grant you the maximum value to all those arguments, but still I say that when you have done all that you have only, as it were, 'touched the hem of his garment', even if you have done that. You have learned a few things, but you have no real knowledge of God. And this is true, of course, of necessity. The very character of God's being, the nature of God, makes it quite impossible for finite, sinful beings ever to come to an adequate knowledge of God by their own efforts and endeavours. Of course they cannot.

But, you see, this is the glory of it – that God has been pleased to make himself known to us, he has 'revealed' himself; and not only that, he has told us what he has done. But, and this to me is most thrilling of all, here in the Scriptures, God not only tells us what he has done, he even takes the trouble to tell us why he has done it, and why he is going to go on doing certain other things. Now we are meant to know all this; this is a part of the intellectual satisfaction, the fullness in the realm of the understanding, that is given by the gospel. 'Whosoever drinketh of the water that I shall give him shall never thirst.'

Now this is, of course, the sort of claim that is made in so many places in the Bible. There is perhaps no more wonderful statement of this truth than at the end of the second chapter of the First Epistle to the Corinthians, where Paul says:

> *The natural man receiveth not the things of the Spirit of God: for they are foolishness unto him: neither can he know them, because they are spiritually discerned. But he that is spiritual [the Christian] judgeth [has an understanding] all things, yet he himself is judged of no man.*

Then the question:

> *For who hath known the mind of the Lord, that he may instruct him? But we have the mind of Christ. (1 Corinthians 2:14–16)*

Now this is a staggering claim. We have the understanding, says Paul, we have the mind of Christ. He allows us to share his own understanding of these mysteries and 'immensities and infinities'. This is the claim – complete, full, intellectual satisfaction.

Now this, of course, astonishes the non-Christian most of all. His view of Christianity is that it is based on a refusal to think. The typical modern sophisticated person thinks that those of us who are still Christians believe as we do because we are wearing blinkers, burying our heads in the sand, not facing the facts, not reading the clever articles in the Sunday newspapers, and not listening to the learned discussions on the television. And when we say that we have this full and complete understanding, we are regarded almost as psychopaths. And yet, you see, it is our bounden duty as Christians to make this great claim.

The person – 'the natural man' as Paul calls him – who regards us as people who refuse to think, has no understanding. The reason the apostle gives for this lack of understanding is that Christianity is a mystery. In the New Testament, the term 'mystery' means 'something that is beyond human comprehension and understanding' and, of course, God is a mystery to the natural man. 'Great is the mystery of godliness' in every respect (1 Timothy 3:16). It must be. It is entirely supernatural, beyond man and his highest reach.

Now, as the apostle argues, the natural man, of course, cannot possibly understand the message of the gospel, and regards it as foolish. We must not be surprised at that and it must not trouble us. I never can understand the kind of Christian who seems to be terrified and almost cast into despair when he is reminded that all the great scientists and philosophers today are non-Christians. He should not be troubled. The greatest scientist, the greatest philosopher, has no advantage over Tom, Dick and Harry in these matters; none at all. In fact, he may well be at a disadvantage because he is foolish enough to trust his own faculties in the way that the other does not. However, the point is that nobody can understand; this is beyond, this is a mystery.

Now I can give a simple illustration. There are many people who are tone deaf. They get nothing out of music, and to them the most glorious music is nothing but a painful noise. They cannot help it, they are lacking in this faculty. Now you do not say that they are unintelligent because they are not musical. You may have highly intelligent people who get nothing out of music but annoyance. And there are others who similarly have no appreciation of art, or to whom science means nothing, and so on. It is not a question of ability. You need the requisite faculty, and you have either got it or you have not.

Now it is the same with Christianity, only infinitely more so, and so it comes to pass that very able people, great people, judged by natural human measures, know nothing about the gospel and regard it as foolishness. Not only should this not surprise us, still less depress us, it is something we should expect. But – and this is what the apostle glories in, and you and I ought to glory in – the moment you become a Christian, then you are able to understand these truths. 'We have received,' says the apostle Paul, 'not the spirit of the world, but the spirit which is of God; that we might know the things that are freely given to us of God' (1 Corinthians 2:12). That is it. And the moment someone has this spirit, then, 'he that is spiritual judgeth all things' (verse 15) – that is, the spiritual person has an understanding of these truths that are foolishness to the wise and prudent. They are revealed by the Spirit, even unto babes. Therefore, we are to rejoice in this understanding. 'Whosoever drinketh of the water that I shall give him shall never thirst [never thirst intellectually].' 'We have the mind of Christ' (1 Corinthians 2:16).

Now I am concerned to emphasize this because I have a feeling that so much of the trouble in the church today is due to the fact that this teaching has been neglected and ignored, perhaps most of all by those of us who are evangelical. We have been so afraid of higher criticism and philosophy and so on that we have tended to retreat into some corner where we say that nothing matters but experience.

Now let us be clear about this. I am concerned to show the fullness of the glorious gospel, and if it does not include the realm of the intellect, well, then, it does not have the all-sufficiency of which I am speaking. That is why we say that Christianity is not only an experience. You notice how I put it – I say it is not 'only' an experience. Thank God, it is an experience, it is a powerful experience, a well of water springing up. We have spent many Sunday mornings demonstrating that, and if you do not have an experience of this living water, you are not a Christian. But now I have to emphasize that Christianity is also an understanding, an understanding that is given to us, that explains what has happened to us and why it has happened and how it has happened.

Why is this so important? Well, because this is the way in which you always show, not only the complete superiority, but the complete difference between this and everything else that is offering people satisfaction and help. I am referring to teachings such as the cults, which offer people happiness and peace and joy, and you will find people testifying that they have had these experiences. That is how the cults succeed. Do you think Christian Science, for instance, would ever had succeeded as it has done and become the wealthy corporation that it is, with its buildings and literature and so on, were it not that people get up and testify that it has made all the difference in the world to them, that they have become new people? Other people, hearing this, say, 'That's just what I want! I'm a worrier'; or, 'I'm unhappy. I can't sleep'; or, 'I'm ill – here's the answer.' And they claim that they get the experience they are looking for.

Then there are perversions or misuses of the gospel, which go by names such as 'positive thinking'. And there is also the misuse of the Scripture by preachers who give nothing but psychological teaching dressed up in scriptural terms and terminology, and bring in the name of our Lord while denying the essence of the faith. Now all these claim to give people experiences – and this is the danger, they delude people. That is why we must be careful to say that Christianity is not only an experience.

Now, as I have already said, Christian people themselves have often over-emphasized experience, and it has often been done in a spirit of fear. Let me give you two illustrations. In the middle of the last century, particularly after Darwin had published his famous book *The Origin of Species* in 1859, a great attack was made upon the Scripture, on the inspiration of the Scriptures, by the so-called higher-critical movement. Now a number of very good people were frightened by this. They said that science was now rising and shaking the very foundations of the faith, and they asked: How are we going to defend the faith? They had their experience, what they called the 'faith experience', and they knew Christianity was true, but the question was, how were they going to defend it?

It seemed to them that there was only one way. They said, 'All right, you can say that the whole of Genesis is wrong, the first chapters particularly. You can prove that Abraham was never a man, that he was just a group. But let the higher critics, the scientists, say whatever they like, we have faith experience and that is what matters.' And they thought they were defending the faith by saying that. But far from defending it, they were virtually denying it because they did not demonstrate that it gives full intellectual satisfaction so that we are afraid of nothing – not science, or philosophy, or anything else that can raise its head against this precious truth.

I remember a man once speaking in a meeting – I had the misfortune or the difficulty, at any rate, of having to speak in the same meeting, but fortunately I followed him – who put the case like this. He said he had read a novel, I think it was, or had been to the cinema, and the chief character was a poor old lady who spent most of her time sitting in the corner. There in the corner she sat holding a very old, shrivelled, yellow document. It was yellow because of age and shrivelled because of age. But as she held it and looked at it, she would smile. As I remember it, the poor old lady believed that this was a letter she had received about 70 years before from her lover. Now she had had many afflictions in life and many troubles, but as long as she could hold this letter in her hand, she was perfectly happy. Actually, said the preacher, she was wrong, but why should you bother to tell her that it was not her lover's letter? Why should you be concerned to point out the error? Why tell her that she was unscientific and inaccurate? The document did the trick, and made her happy. Now that is the kind of argument that has been put forward. Though critics may declare the Bible to be riddled with errors, the faith experience still remains.

I remember another occasion some 30 years ago when I was at a conference of ministers in Oxford. We were having a discussion together, I remember very well, on a Monday night, and the question came up about the veracity of the Bible and the whole foundation of the faith and our authority and basis for standing where we stood. And I remember that a number of men, who thought they were on my side, gave me the greatest difficulty in the discussion because they said to the others, 'You can say what you like about your science and your criticism and so on and I cannot answer you, but it is all right because you can never touch my experience.' Now I say that they put me into difficulties for this reason: I felt that they were selling the pass. That was not the way to argue for the faith at all because they were delivering themselves over entirely to the psychologists and to these other people I have already mentioned. They were saying precisely what psychologists say about us.

Psychologists say, 'All right, we don't quarrel with you for being Christian; if it makes you happy, carry on. Anything that makes people happy – let them do it; it will help them. We're not against it. What we object to is your saying that we should be Christians, too, and your attempts to base Christianity upon what you claim is solid fact and truth.'

Now, then, the answer to all that is that the Christian is not only someone who has an 'experience' but also someone who has understanding. God has given us this book, the Bible, to give understanding. We know what we believe; we can give explanations. We have an answer to doubts, we have an answer to criticism, we have an answer to heresies. There is no need for us to be afraid, there is no need for us ever to apologise. The Bible has been given to us in order that with the understanding that comes through it we might be able to deal with all these questions that assail us.

Now, then, how does the Bible answer these questions? Well, you see, here is a great book, 66 different books all in one. I have never called this book 'a library of books'. It is not, because it is only one book. Nothing is more marvellous about it than its unity, its consistency. It has only one great message from beginning to end and it is this message about God and his great plan and purpose. You see, the Bible tells us this. It is no use going to people and saying, 'You know, if you become a Christian, you would be as happy as I am and you would have this, that and the other.'

'All right,' someone replies, 'I know, my Christian Science friend said that to me yesterday.'

Then where are you? No, no, my dear friend, thank God for your experience, but oh, look at this! This is God – the plan and purpose of God! In 1 Corinthians 2, Paul says:

We speak wisdom among them that are perfect: yet not the wisdom of this world, nor of the princes of this world, that come to nought: but we speak the wisdom of God in a mystery, even the hidden

*wisdom, which God ordained before the world unto our glory.
(1 Corinthians 2:6–7)*

Now this is Christianity, this is what you and I are to be talking about. Christians are not people who are always talking about themselves and their experiences; they should be talking about God and what God has done. Their little experiences are only minute illustrations of this wonderful thing 'which God ordained before the [foundation of the] world unto our glory', and it is revealed here. That is what the Bible is. It is the revelation of all this.

So, you see, the Bible starts with creation. Now, my dear Christian friend, do not start with your experience. Always start with God. That is what the Bible does and you have no right to start anywhere else. You have no right to start in Matthew, you must start in Genesis because that is where God's revelation begins – creation! The Fall! The promise of redemption! Here you stand back and look at this great plan of God for the redemption of the world.

In the Old Testament we are shown the preparation for this redemption. Having announced that he is going to bring this about, God then lets us know how he began to prepare for its actual coming. And he got men to write all this, told them the facts, gave them the information, guided them by his Spirit. So there is the account of the Flood: judgement, the saving of this one family, the family of Noah, the selection of Shem out of Noah's three boys, Shem, Ham and Japheth. Then the great call of Abraham, beginning the nation, followed by Isaac, Jacob, the formation of the Children of Israel, and the giving of the Law. What is the purpose of the Law? It is God revealing himself as a holy God, and preparing a holy people for himself. And God's purpose is to redeem us from all sin and iniquity, and to prepare for himself 'a peculiar people, zealous of good works' (Titus 2:14).

Now I am not saying this, it is the Bible that says it, and why does the Bible say it? Why did God cause men to write this? The answer is that you and I might *know* it. Not that we might just go about the world saying, 'I've had a marvellous experience, you know, and you can have it.' All right: but you must tell them what it is, where it has come from, how it has come. Here is the answer – in the Bible. The understanding, the intellectual comprehension, is given to us by God, and it is part of the fullness of the living water.

Then we come on to David, the choice of David and the promise to him that the great Messiah will come from him, from his seed. After David there are the great prophetic messages looking forward to this Coming One, pointing forward. What amazes me is that anybody can find the Bible a boring book! As you read all this you feel the thrill that these men felt as they were given this revelation and set it forth. Of course, quite often, they set it forth in historical terms: in terms of a contemporary difficulty or problem or stress. But through all that you see the purpose. Do not get distracted by the clothing; do not miss the wood because of the trees. Start with this great comprehensive picture and then see the outworking in all these detailed ways and in the variety of customs that are characteristic of the Old Testament. The author of the Epistle to the Hebrews sums it up as 'at sundry times and in divers manners' (Hebrews 1:1); different times, different places, different forms, but all always the same message.

Then we come on to the New Testament. We start with the Gospels, and we read about the birth of the babe. Who is this? The one who had been prophesied! The Messiah who had been promised! But he has come! We read about him, what he was like, how he was born, how he grew and developed, what he did, what he taught, what he promised – all this. We read about it, and, of course, having started in Genesis, we see that he is the fulfilment of all that had been promised; we see that he is the very acme of God's plan made before the foundation of the world; we see it all fitting into a great whole.

And then we go on to the Acts of the Apostles, and what do we find there? Well, we find the fulfilment of some of the promises given by the Lord Jesus Christ. He had said to his disciples: You need not depend upon my physical presence. I am going to leave you, but do not be troubled; I will send you the Spirit, the Holy Spirit, 'He will guide you into all truth' (John 16:13). The Spirit will give you understanding, he will give you power and ability to teach and to expound these subjects.

What is the Acts of the Apostles? It is the fulfilment of that promise; the Holy Spirit came down on the Day of Pentecost, and these men who had fumbled and stumbled suddenly had understanding and spoke authoritatively and with great power, and tremendous things happened. The book of Acts is a thrilling account of that. It is all a part of this process, this sequence, 'the wonderful works of God'.

And then we come to the Epistles, and what are they? Well, these are but grand expositions of all this – that is why they were written. Take, for instance, the first eight chapters of the Epistle to the Romans, what are they? Well, there is only one answer. There the apostle expounds God's great plan and shows how it is worked out. The first three chapters of the Epistle to the Ephesians do exactly the same thing and so do the first two chapters of the Epistle to the Colossians.

Have you ever stood back and looked at these great chapters and asked yourself: What is this about? What is it for? Have you noticed the explanations, have you noticed the arguments, have you noticed the reasoning? The eleventh chapter of the Epistle to the Romans is perhaps a perfect illustration of what I am trying to say to you. The apostle takes up a question. He says: If all that I have been saying is all right, well, then, what about the Jews? They are outside the church, they are not Christians.

Here was a problem that was troubling the minds of Christian people. They had been saved, they were born again, they had got their experience, but people came to them and said, 'Look here, there's something wrong somewhere. You say all this, but your God has gone back on his own promises. He said the Children of Israel, the Jews, were his people, but they are outside the church, your church is mainly Gentile, how do you explain that?' And Romans chapter 11, indeed, chapters 9 and 10 as well, are the apostle's answer. But I want to emphasize this point: notice the way the apostle argues, the way he reasons – 'If this, then that' – all the logic that is brought to bear. This is part of Scripture, this is revelation. God has taken the trouble not only to tell us what he has done, but also to say why he has done it, how he has done it.

And so we come to understand why the only way of salvation is that which is in Christ. It is argued out, it is made plain and clear. The Epistles show why Christ had to come, why no man could ever save us, why salvation had to be through the incarnation of the eternal Son. The apostle Paul explains why our Lord died on the cross on Calvary's hill. So many Christian people do not know why he died. If you ask them, they do not know or they are muddled. But here we are told why he died, and the Christian must know why the Son of God had to die on Calvary's hill. 'There was no other good enough to pay the price of sin.' He is the Lamb of God slain from the foundation of the world. All that is expounded and explained here.

And then the Epistles go on to explain how the perfect work of Christ in salvation is applied to us by the Holy Spirit. They even take you through the steps and the stages. Listen to this in Romans

8 – what a wonderful statement it is of all this: 'We know that all things work together for good to them that love God, to them who are the called according to his purpose' (verse 28). How do you know that? Here you are, you are in trouble. Do you know that 'all things work together for good to them that love God, to them who are the called according to his purpose'? How can you know that? Here is the answer:

For whom he did foreknow, he also did predestinate to be conformed to the image of his Son, that he might be the firstborn among many brethren. Moreover whom he did predestinate, them he also called: and whom he called, them he also justified; and whom he justified, them he also glorified. What shall we then say to these things? (Romans 8:29–31)

Now this is part of Christianity, and if you and I do not know something about this and cannot state it, oh, what small Christians we are, what little life there is in us! We are meant to know the steps and the stages and the outworking of this grand pattern and scheme – God's foreknowledge, his election, justification, sanctification, glorification. It is here; it is unfolded to us so that we not only know that something has happened to us, we have an understanding of what has happened and why it had to happen to us, and what will happen to us.

So as you study this book, you get this great, final and full satisfaction in every way. Are you rejoicing in this? Is this the way in which you use your Bible? Do you just read the little portion prescribed in some daily notes and then dash off, feeling you have done it? Shame upon us! Have you seen the whole? Are you working it out in its parts and portions? And, above all, I ask: Are you revelling in it? Here is the test. Someone who knows how to read the Bible always ends with these words:

O the depth of the riches both of the wisdom and knowledge of God! how unsearchable are his judgments, and his ways past finding out! For who hath known the mind of the Lord? or who hath been his counsellor? Or who hath first given to him, and it shall be recompensed unto him again? For of him, and through him, and to him, are all things: to whom be glory for ever. Amen. (Romans 11:33–36)

20

The Authority of the Bible

Jesus answered and said unto her, Whosoever drinketh of this water shall thirst again: but whosoever drinketh of the water that I shall give him shall never thirst; but the water that I shall give him shall be in him a well of water springing up into everlasting life. (John 4:13–14)

The apostle Paul, in writing to the Ephesians, prays that ultimately they 'might be filled with all the fulness of God' (Ephesians 3:19). And in dealing with this and in showing how it is true that the gospel really does satisfy the whole person in every respect, we have naturally started with the intellect and with intellectual satisfaction. But though we start with the intellect, we are not going to stop there, because the gospel is equally satisfying for the heart and every other aspect of one's personality. We started with the intellect because this is God's greatest gift to men and women; it is the way in which we differ from animals. God made man in his own image and likeness, he gave him the power of reason and of understanding and of appreciation.

There are many reasons why it is very important that we should understand something of the complete intellectual satisfaction that is given by the gospel. If we fail at this point, we may be in danger of misunderstanding the faith. In referring to Paul's epistles, the apostle Peter says, 'in which are some things . . . which they that are unlearned and unstable wrest, as they do also the other scriptures, unto their own destruction' (2 Peter 3:16). This is due to a lack of understanding. They have not used their minds as they should and so have found themselves in grievous trouble. There is a great warning running right through the Bible with regard to this, especially in the New Testament.

Let us be clear therefore. The gospel, the way of salvation in Christ Jesus, is not merely meant to give us relief, it is not merely meant to give us help or experiences. Thank God, it does do that. We all need forgiveness of sins and deliverance from the power of sin; we need help, we need experiences, and the gospel gives all this. But even this is not its primary object. We tend to think that this is the purpose of the Bible because we are all governed by our feelings and moods and states – we do not like to be miserable, we crave for relief, for peace and joy. It is very natural. But we must be careful that we never say that the whole business of the gospel is just to give us some kind of relief. It is not. That is incidental.

No, the primary object of the gospel is to reconcile us to God. 'God was in Christ' – why? To deal with our aches and pains and little illnesses and pinpricks? Not at all – 'reconciling the world unto himself' (2 Corinthians 5:19). That is the big, the great thing, and that is the most essential truth for us. It is our whole standing before God, our whole relationship to him, that matters primarily, and all these other benefits are, as it were, added on to us. As our Lord said, 'Seek ye first the kingdom of God, and his righteousness; and all these things shall be added unto you'

(Matthew 6:33). But the danger always is that we tend to give the whole of our attention to eating and drinking and the various reliefs that I have indicated.

If we do not sort our priorities out into the right order and proportion, we shall go astray, as the Scriptures tell us. So while we thank God for every blessing, as we shall be seeing, we must start with the intellect. In other words, the primary business of preaching and of teaching, the primary business, indeed, of the whole of Scripture, is to bring us to a knowledge of the truth. This is what we tend to forget. In his First Epistle to Timothy, the apostle Paul tells Timothy to teach people that:

Supplications, prayers, intercessions, and giving of thanks, be made for all men; for kings, and for all that are in authority; that we may lead a quiet and peaceable life in all godliness and honesty. For this is good and acceptable in the sight of God our Saviour; who will have all men [all kinds of people] to be saved, and to come unto the knowledge of the truth. (1 Timothy 2:1–4)

The importance of knowing the truth is emphasized in the whole of Scripture. That is why preaching and teaching has such importance in the Bible; and that is why we as Protestants, evangelical Protestants in particular, are so opposed to the kind of service that puts the sacraments forward and discounts preaching and teaching. It is always a bad sign when the church gives increasing attention to forms and ceremonies, and to the service as such, rather than to the exposition of the word of God. As I am trying to show, this needs to be emphasized especially at this present time, when the whole tendency is to go back to that which, by the Spirit of God, the Protestant fathers and the Reformers were given to see was a departure from the New Testament order. And we must be careful lest, unconsciously, in our subjectivity and in our concern about our own moods and feelings, we also return to forms and ceremonies. There is a terrible danger today of going astray, of becoming heretics, and, still more, there is a danger of confusing this gospel with the cults and their message.

The Christian gospel is not a mere matter of moral uplift and the sort of teaching put forward by proponents of positive thinking, psychology and the cults. They are always just out to give us ease and relief in some shape or form. They have no truth. They want to help us, and that is why they appeal to people, especially people in trouble, people who are neurotic, those who are crying out for relief. There is nothing wrong in this, but it differs from the gospel in that first and foremost the gospel brings us to a knowledge of the truth and reconciles us to God. The ease and relief that people are seeking are an outcome of that, the fruit, as it were, the incidental consequence.

So that is why we start with the fullness of satisfaction that is given to the intellect, to the understanding and, as I have shown, this is brought about supremely by the Bible itself, which is God revealing himself and the truth concerning his ways. And we saw that God not only tells us what he has done, and what he is going to do, but also tells us how he has done it. He gives us an understanding of it. And that should thrill us all.

You see, according to the apostle Peter, we should all of us be ready at all times to give a reason for the hope that is in us (1 Peter 3:15), so it is important that we should enter into an understanding of the truth not only for our own satisfaction, but also in order that we may help others. When people are shattered by things that happen to them, or when they get frightened by the state of the world and are filled with forebodings, yet see that we remain calm and quiet, they say, 'Why are you different? Is it merely that you have decided to adopt some psychological device and tell yourself that you need not worry about anything; there is always a silver lining to the cloud; things will soon be all right again? Are you just playing tricks with yourself and refusing to face facts in that way, or can you give a reason for the hope that is in you? And none of us can give a reason for the hope that is in us unless we have an understanding of the truth as it is revealed in the Bible as a whole, this great revelation of God and his ways with respect to men and women and especially with respect to his dear Son, our blessed Lord and Saviour. That, then, immediately gives us satisfaction.

But I am concerned that we should see the fullness of this intellectual satisfaction, so I now want to show it in a slightly different way. This is that the gospel, and the gospel alone, satisfies our desire for authority. Now here is something that humanity has always desired. People want some certainty, they want something on which they can rest. Life is precarious, uncertain. This was true of people when they lived a nomadic life and were hunters, and it has been true ever since. Though people now build cities and have fortifications, life is still full of uncertainty. To anybody who thinks at all, life is a great mystery. There are billions and billions of viruses. You never know what is going to happen. And men and women want some assurance, some authority – but where are they to get it? So they ask their questions: How can I be sure? How can I know what is right?

Now here is a very important point and it is a part of the glory that belongs to the gospel that it, and it alone, gives us the authority we stand in need of. There is no authority and final satisfaction to be found in philosophy, still less in science, the god of the present time. Alas! There are those, even in the church, who are foolish enough to turn from the gospel, the only sure authority, to philosophy, 'the thinkers', they say, and especially to science, the scientists, who seem to know and understand. People are ready to trust them and will hang on their every word and commit themselves to them. But I repeat that there is no authority to be found there, and this for a number of reasons.

First of all, before we have even listened to what they have to say, we know that all that philosophers and scientists can put before us, apart from certain well-established facts, is mere speculation. It is all theory; it is only human effort and endeavour, human attempts to solve the mystery and arrive at final assurance. We immediately know, therefore, that there is a very serious limit because of the obvious inadequacy of human ability and understanding.

And this, in the second place, is made still more evident to us when we are confronted by the rival theories. There is nothing so futile or so foolish as to think that all people who are not Christians believe the same thing. They do not, of course. There are schools among the philosophers, there are schools and rivalries among the scientists, they contradict one another fundamentally. There are two famous scientists in this country at the present time quarrelling even about the very origin of the universe! I remember reading, a couple of years ago, an article, I think it was by Miss Marghanita Laski, a well-known atheist. She wrote that you must not talk about 'the typical unbeliever', and said that she could not write for *the* unbeliever because there was no such person. Unbelievers differed and disagreed among themselves. That is perfectly true. And so, without even looking at the details of what they say, you see at once that they can have no authority and you cannot rest your weary soul there.

Now there is nothing wrong with science as long as it confines itself to science, as long as it examines and investigates and reports actual findings, facts that can be seen and touched and felt and weighed and handled. I am talking about science when it attempts to explain the whole of life to us and to say dogmatically, 'There is no God! Miracles cannot happen!' and so on. That is no longer science, that is philosophy. While science deserves much credit, its whole trouble is that it fails most of all at the most crucial and vital points in life. It can give a lot of knowledge and information, but our problems are finally the problems of human beings themselves: What are they? What is their purpose? What is life? What is death? Scientists and philosophers can talk dogmatically and they do, of course, but it is all theory. They do not know. They have told us nothing about death and what lies beyond.

When we come to the most fundamental problems of all, everything that opposes the Christian message, and is supposed to give us scientific and solid assurance fails us, and fails us completely. It was no accident that the great German philosopher Goethe cried out on his deathbed, 'More light!' He had not got it, he was in the dark. He was as much in the dark as the greatest ignoramus lying on his deathbed.

And not only that, further proof that there is no authority in these realms comes from the fact that they are always changing. And they not only change, it is a part of the scientist's boast that they do. These are the people who are always talking about 'the advance of knowledge', 'modern thought', 'the modern man' — and implicit in their very statements, in their slogans, in their clichés, is a tremendous and a terrible confession. They all tell us that they are the ones who are right, they are the ones who have arrived at true knowledge, everybody in the past was wrong, yet in the past, a hundred years ago, two thousand years ago, the same sort of people were speaking with equal dogmatism and authority.

Now it is important that we should know all this. I am referring especially to the type of uninformed, illiterate Christian who is afraid of science and of philosophy, who apologizes for the faith and is ready to accommodate it to some scientific discoveries. This is a denial of the truth and when you do this you are robbing yourself of one of the most glorious aspects of the Christian faith.

I can easily prove this to you. Look, for instance, at the change in the attitude of scientists towards the atom. I was taught in my scientific training that the atom was indivisible, the smallest piece of matter. I was taught it with absolute authority. But we know today that that is nonsense, and the atom is a whole world of life and of activity. And then there is the change in the understanding of light, and we have the new physics, and so on. Everything has changed. How can you place yourself in the hands of such a supposed authority? There is no authority there; you are on a sliding scale. If you really accept this modern attitude, you are bound to say that however good modern theories may be, it is certain that in a few years they will have to be discarded because they have been proved to be wrong. As today that is said about the past, so in the future it will be said about the present.

Those, then, are some of the reasons why you will never find authority in science or philosophy – it is impossible. But here in the gospel we come to something absolutely different. Why? Because it is from above. It is from God. This is not human speculation, not men and women making theories, it is God teaching us, God revealing himself to us. We are in an entirely different realm. This is the claim: 'All Scripture is given by inspiration of God' (2 Timothy 3:16). It is 'God-breathed'. The biblical writers do not claim that they are recording their own ideas or suppositions or insights; they say their messages were 'given', they were 'revealed'. Now I must not keep you with quotations. Study the Bible yourself and keep your eye on that very point. It is the whole essence of this position that there is certainty in the Bible.

But we see this still more clearly, of course, when we come to our Lord himself. Take, for example, the third chapter of John's Gospel and our Lord's words to Nicodemus. Nicodemus was a great teacher, a great man, but when our Lord told him about the rebirth, Nicodemus did not understand.

> *Nicodemus answered and said unto him, How can these things be? Jesus answered and said unto him, Art thou a master of Israel and knowest not these things? Verily, verily, I say unto thee*

– here it is –

> *We speak that we do know, and testify that we have seen; and ye receive not our witness. If I have told you earthly things, and ye believe not, how shall ye believe, if I tell you of heavenly things? And no man hath ascended up to heaven, but he that came down from heaven, even the Son of man which is in heaven. (John 3:9–13)*

Now there is the authority. Here is one standing among men and saying, 'I know!' Why does he say that? He says: I know for this reason – I have seen him.

The Lord Jesus Christ does not speculate about God, he declares him: 'No man hath seen God at any time; the only begotten Son, which is in the bosom of the Father, he hath declared him' (John 1:18). Why? Because, he says, he has come down from heaven: 'No man hath ascended up to heaven, but he that came down from heaven, even the Son of man . . .' (John 3:13). Human beings do not know anything about God. How can they? God is in heaven, he dwells in a light that is unapproachable. Human beings cannot understand themselves and their own world, still less God. No, no; the only authority we can have on ultimate questions is the authority of one who has looked into the face of God and has 'come down' to tell us. That is exactly what our Lord claims: 'We speak that we do know, and testify that we have seen.'

So we are in an entirely different realm here. Our Lord says exactly the same thing, as we have seen, to the woman of Samaria: 'Ye worship ye know not what: we know what we worship' (John 4:22). 'We know'! He speaks with the authority of one who has come from heaven, from the unseen into the seen. He is just a carpenter, he has not been to the schools, and yet he speaks with authority. He says, 'I am the light of the world' (John 8:12).

Here, then, is one who speaks with authority and he proves his right to do so by his miracles, by his prophecies, by all that he did, ending supremely with the great fact of the resurrection. So the authority, the question of authority, comes back to the whole question of the person of the Lord Jesus Christ himself. He is unique. This is his claim. He has dwelt with God, he was God, he has always been with God: he knows and he has come down to tell us.

And then we look back at the Old Testament and we find that this person believes it, he accepts it, he speaks of it as 'God's word' and says 'the scripture cannot be broken' (John 10:35). So as we face this question of authority, our real question concerns the person of the Lord Jesus Christ, and if we believe in him as the Son of God, then we know that this is God's word, this is our sole authority, and it speaks authoritatively because it has all come from God.

Now that being the case, immediately we have satisfaction, we have authority. We are not dependent upon changing human ideas and the so-called advance of knowledge. No, no; we have an absolute statement, we have one from eternity speaking in time and revealing the mind of God.

And that tells me not only that this is true, but, further, that it always will be true – and to me this is most marvellous of all. This – I am thinking of the whole Bible – is true, it has been true; a hundred years ago it was true, a thousand years ago, two thousand years ago it was true, and because of that it always will be true. Now there is no difficulty at all in proving this – and it is one of the things in which we should glory together. There is no new truth about man or about life or about death or about God – none at all. Now this is the kind of thing, of course, that the world does not think of – and, unfortunately, many foolish Christians do not think of, either. They accept the thinking of the world: the advance! 'We *know*.' But we do not! We know nothing more about man nor about any of these great, ultimate questions than our forefathers did – nothing at all. Here it is in the Bible, and it is exactly the same truth that it has always been. There is no change, no modification whatsoever. This is very wonderful to me, and it is why I often thank God that I am preaching today and not a hundred years back.

'What?' says somebody. 'Would you prefer to preach in 1967 rather than in 1867?'

Oh, yes, most definitely. This is a day of great opportunity. The poor preacher of a hundred years ago must have been in considerable difficulty, in fact, we know he was. That is why they sold the pass, so many of them. The world was so steady and steadfast: *pax Britannica*! The Victorian era! Knowledge and science growing, and man advancing. Why, everything seemed to be on man's side and those so-called 'great Victorians'! I must restrain myself – poor bemused and deluded fools as most of them were in their pride of knowledge and understanding. They were the people who talked about the world advancing and developing. Parliament of man! The federation of the world! War to be banished! The world to be made paradise by political enactments, acts of Parliament. There was nothing to stop us, everything was moving forward. Of course, we know today how utterly illusory it all was. The modern world proves that the Bible is true, that the Bible is the only authority.

A hundred years ago they read in the Bible – they did not believe it, they said it was wrong – that man in sin will always behave in the same way, that man in sin is a fool, that man in sin is a rebel, that man in sin always brings misery down upon himself, whatever the appearances may happen to be; and this twentieth century has proved that. It is more patently true today than it was a hundred years ago. Man has shown that the Bible is right, that the Bible is true. Your morning newspapers are proclaiming the truth of the Bible, the whole world is proclaiming that truth. For all these centuries, this book has gone on saying the same things about God and man and the relationship between them and it is as true at this moment as it has ever been. You see, here is authority and the modern world is proving it. There is nothing more futile than trusting to man and his knowledge and his wisdom and his speculation.

But I anticipate one question here. Someone may say to me, 'Well, what about science? Are you really saying that you are putting the Bible before science?'

This is a very popular question, is it not? We obviously cannot deal with this adequately in a glancing word in a sermon, it would take a book: but there is no difficulty. There is no difficulty in principle in dealing with this. There is no contradiction whatsoever between the teaching of the Bible and science. Now notice what I am saying. I have already told you what I mean by science. Science is just the collecting of facts and putting them in order. That is the business of science.

'All right,' you say, 'but are you maintaining that the scientist doesn't have a right to speculate?'

I will grant him that. I will grant him the right to speculate as long as he tells us that that is what he is doing, that he is no longer dealing with facts, but is putting up a theory, putting up a supposition, which he intends to test. I know that is of value – that is how you get your inventions. That is perfectly all right as long as scientists do not make dogmatic pronouncements as if they were facts. As I said, the moment they do that, they cease to be true scientists, and become philosophers.

Let me make one other qualification. I draw a distinction, also, between the teaching of the Bible and what the Christian church has sometimes taught. It is essential to define this teaching accurately, just as it is essential to define science accurately.

Why do I say this? It is because historically the church, the Roman Catholic Church in particular, has blundered by making dogmatic pronouncements in the realm of science, causing a great deal of confusion. The simple answer to that is that she had no right to do so, she was not expounding the Bible at that point. What she was doing was expounding the philosophy of Aristotle, as worked out still more fully by Thomas Aquinas and by others, on which so much of her teaching has always been based. And it was when she began to do that that she went wrong, and science was able to prove that she was wrong. But science was not proving that the teaching of the Bible was wrong, merely that the speculations of certain Christian thinkers, who had become more philosophical than biblical, were wrong. So my fundamental proposition is that there is no contradiction between the teaching of the Bible and the teaching of science.

Now many people are worried, of course, by the early chapters of Genesis. They say, 'Surely, you can't believe that any longer? You must accept the theory of evolution.'

Now these people do not say the 'theory' of evolution, they tend to say the 'fact' of evolution, and that is where they go wrong. No scientist, no teaching of science, can tell us with any authority whatsoever how things came into being. They can speculate, they can put theories forward, but they do not know – nobody was there. And they are in the difficulty of having to say that this is something that seems to have happened once and for ever, and why it did, and so on; and they do not know. It is all speculation. Nobody knows what happened in the intervening period. They know what is happening now, and what they tend to do is to extrapolate (that is their new word) back to what happened at the beginning. They say, 'Because we observe this now, it must always have happened.' But they have no right at all to say that. That is sheer supposition.

All I am trying to tell you is that science is in no position at all to disprove the teaching of the early chapters of Genesis that the world was created in six days and that man was a special creation and did not evolve through the millennia, eventually becoming man out of the animal. That is all theory and speculation, it is a contradiction of the Bible, and it does not prove anything at all. In the Epistle to the Hebrews, we are given the answer to all that: 'Through faith we understand that the worlds were framed by the word of God, so that things which are seen were not made of things which do appear' (Hebrews 11:3). And the attempt on the part of people who call themselves believers in theistic evolution is no better than non-theistic or atheistical evolution because it is still introducing the theorizing of men into the plain record of God. And the whole of our salvation, in a sense, depends upon a correct understanding of Genesis, because I am told by Paul, 'As in Adam, so in Christ' – he draws a parallel.

I am trying to show you that in the Bible there is complete intellectual satisfaction, that as this is true today, and as it has always been true, we need be in no fear whatsoever with regard to any future discoveries. I make bold to assert this: scientists will never discover anything that will in any way invalidate the authority of the Scripture. They will never be able to do so because the facts of creation can never contradict the facts of revelation, and this is because it is the same God who is at the back of both.

And, indeed, I can give you some evidence to support what I am saying. I say we need not be 'afraid' of discoveries. I would venture to prophesy that discoveries will continue, as they have done hitherto, to prove and to support the teaching of the Scriptures. Take what we read in 2 Peter 3:10 about the elements melting with fervent heat. Until comparatively recently that was regarded as nonsense by the wise and prudent, the philosophers and the scientists, but when the first atomic bomb was exploded, people began to see that there was something in this. That is exactly what happens when these atomic bombs are released – the elements melting with 'fervent heat' in the great atomic explosion. I need say no more. All I am trying to show you is that the Bible gives complete and entire intellectual satisfaction and that we need never be afraid of anything that may be discovered.

I have a feeling that there are very many Christians today who go to bed every night in fear, afraid they are going to read the next morning that some scientist has looked down a microscope and proved the whole of the Bible to be wrong. Oh, shame upon us Christian people! You need have no fear whatsoever; it is impossible. As the Bible has gone on through the ages, it will go on: it is the truth of God.

Now another great argument to support the truth of the Bible is, of course, the argument of prophecy; for instance, among other prophetic examples that I could give you, God revealing the birth of Christ, with all the various details, eight centuries before it happened. Have you considered this? What a proof it is that the Bible is the word of God and not human speculation.

And then think of the whole question of the witness of the apostles. Peter writes:

> *I will endeavour that ye may be able after my decease to have these things always in remembrance. For we have not followed cunningly devised fables, when we made known unto you the power and coming of our Lord Jesus Christ, but were eyewitnesses of his majesty. For he received from God the Father honour and glory, when there came such a voice to him from the excellent glory, This is my beloved Son, in whom I am well pleased. And this voice which came from heaven we heard, when we were with him in the holy mount. (2 Peter 1:15–18)*

Here is the evidence, here are the witnesses. This is not mere hearsay, this is not a novel, this is not imagination and fantasy, this is not human theorizing and speculations, not, 'cunningly devised fables' – 'we heard . . . we were with him.' The witness! Here is the authority, and it is because of all this that we can say without any fear whatsoever:

O Word of God incarnate,
O Wisdom from on high;
O Truth unchanged, unchanging,
O Light of our dark sky!
William Walsham How

It is the only light. It is unchanged. I am preaching the very same gospel, the same truth, the same message, that men preached a thousand years ago, the message that has always been preached: exactly the same message. What have I said that is in any sense different? Nothing at all! I have simply been showing the fallacy of modern thought. My message is not based on modern thought: it is the Bible. I am simply expounding it. A man a thousand years ago, though he would not have been able to use the same illustrations, would have preached the same message. 'O Truth unchanged, unchanging' – there is no need to modify it in any respect whatsoever. There is nothing that modern people know that needs us to qualify anything at all in the Bible. Take the Bible as it is. Differentiate between it and the speculations of able men in the church.

And that brings me to just a final word: the lasting and the increasing interest that the Bible always gives us. This is another great desire in the human heart – we want something to interest us. By nature we get tired of things, we get tired of everything, do we not? We always want something new. We are all by nature like those Athenians of whom we are told they 'spent their time in nothing else, but either to tell, or to hear some new thing' (Acts 17:21). Everybody wants a change, on every level, including almost the animal level. People get tired of drinks, they want a new one; they change the form of leisure, sport and entertainment. It was once cinemas, it is now bingo. Humanity is always dissatisfied and restless.

And, of course, it is exactly the same with the most sophisticated people. It is especially typical of those who are most intelligent and enlightened. They take up a theory, they are very intrigued, they say, and they rush after it – it is all the vogue. It is soon dropped! Something else comes and that is taken up. 'Have you heard of this? There's a new teacher, he has a wonderful teaching. This is quite something', and off they rush. The history of civilization is the history of changing fashions in the realm of thought and in almost every other conceivable respect.

Let me make a confession. By now, I have been trying to preach this message for 40 years, and I find it much easier as I go on. Do some of you think that because I have been here

29$^{1}/_{2}$ years that I must be finding it difficult to have something fresh to say? Let me assure you that my difficulty is the difficulty of having enough time to say what I want to say about all that I find here in the Bible! You are aware that that is my difficulty, are you not? All right! But it is nothing in me. It is this book; it goes on before me and opens out. I am ready for next Sunday, I do not mind telling you. I am already prepared for next Sunday morning and next Sunday evening – indeed, and Sundays after. This book is endless. It is an ocean, a mighty ocean, God's truth, God himself revealing himself.

And so you see what are we doing? Well, in the last study, though I did not use this comparison, this is what I was doing: I took you through the whole Bible. I was looking at the Bible through a telescope – and it is all right, you can do that, you should do that. But you do not stop at that. Having looked at it telescopically, you then begin to look at it microscopically. I am often reminded of this: it is what I used to do in medicine, and medical people are still doing it, especially those who work in laboratories and examine specimens. This was the method that we were always taught: we were given something and first we looked at it in general; then, having done that, we cut it into pieces and we put each section under a microscope.

How did we then use the microscope? Well, this is how we were taught, and this is how medical students are still being taught. We started with a fairly low magnifying power in order to have a general view of the section that we intended to examine in detail. Having done that, we put the microscope on a higher power to get still more detail, and then higher still. And now laboratories even have electric magnification, so that you can almost see things that are invisible.

And it is like that with the Scripture; you see the whole message of the Scripture, then you see the parts and then the portions of the parts. And it is all wonderful, it is all a miracle. It is all God in almost every detail; it is God everywhere. And so it comes to pass that it is endless, it is always enthralling, it is always exciting, it is always stimulating, it is always new, it is always amazing, it is always more and more marvellous. And it must be this, because ultimately it is all but a part of the knowledge of God.

Men and women will never get tired of this knowledge. It will always satisfy them as long as they live and cause their minds to expand and to develop and to reach out, and it will be the same even in eternity. That is why no one ever has been or ever will be bored in heaven. Heaven is going on to all eternity to know more about God: God the Father, God the Son, and God the Holy Spirit. It is an endless sea! It is as infinite as God himself! Oh, the fullness of the satisfaction that comes to the minds of those who drink of this water that the Lord Jesus Christ offers them! 'Whosoever drinketh of the water that I shall give him shall never thirst; never, no, never.'

21

The Sufficiency of the Bible

Jesus answered and said unto her, Whosoever drinketh of this water shall thirst again: but whosoever drinketh of the water that I shall give him shall never thirst; but the water that I shall give him shall be in him a well of water springing up into everlasting life. (John 4:13–14)

In our consideration of these great verses, we are now concerned with truth. The Bible is not just some sort of agency that offers us happy feelings. All our experiences, as we saw in the last study, are a result of coming to an understanding of the truth. So we must start there, and the truth, obviously, presents itself primarily to the mind. So we are looking at this glorious sufficiency that we have in the Bible for the mind and the understanding.

Here in this one book, the Bible, God has treasured up his wisdom for us. This is not an ordinary book: it starts with revelation. God has given the knowledge, the information; he has chosen men to write it and to report his message infallibly under the influence of his Holy Spirit, and so we have it here. And, as we have been seeing, the Bible not only tells us about salvation, but also how it works, how it has been planned.

We saw in the last study that the Bible satisfies our desire for authority, a desire that is common to the whole human race. We ended on the note that the Bible not only holds our interest, but also always increases it. To me, there is nothing more pathetic and tragic than Christians who are always looking back to their first experience, always repeating that, as if nothing had happened to them since. As you go on in this Christian life, it becomes increasingly more wonderful, more enthralling, more stimulating, more exciting, because it is eternal truth. You go on and on into it and there is no end to it.

That is the point at which we have arrived, but we do not stop there. The next thing I want to note is that the Bible satisfies our desire for system and for wholeness. This, again, is one of the fundamental desires of the human nature. And this, of course, is what is meant by philosophy. The love of wisdom springs from the desire to have a comprehensive understanding. Man – intelligent man – has always looked at his universe and at himself and has tried to understand it. What makes man man is that he is concerned about this, and philosophy is his endeavour to reach this understanding.

We have an innate feeling that there must be some wholeness, some explanation, there must be something that holds everything together. I put it like that in order to emphasize the difference from certain schools of modern thinking that teach the exact opposite and tell us that life is all the result of accident and chance. Man has been searching throughout the centuries for a system – a system of truth – something comprehensive, all-inclusive, a wholeness. One school of thought is associated with the name of Field Marshal Smuts, who was a great philosopher as well as a statesman. His view, his teaching, was called Holism.

But in spite of all these endeavours, people have never been able to arrive at a comprehensive system of thought. All they have done is discover bits of knowledge, bits of information, here and there. They have tried to put them all into one piece, they have tried to complete the jigsaw puzzle, as it were, but they have never succeeded. There are always portions that they cannot fit in, that they cannot reconcile. What they discover there is contradicted by what they know here. Human knowledge is always fragmentary, even at its very best, and try as they will, people can never arrive at the wholeness, the fullness, the perfection they are searching for. But – and this again is one of its central glories – that is precisely what the Bible gives us.

Now this is something in which we should rejoice and of which we should be increasingly aware. No greater disservice is done to the Bible than to represent it as a book that tells us about how our sins can be forgiven – that one bit of information – and after that as a book to be used mainly to stimulate our devotional life. That is a very serious misunderstanding. It is such a misuse of the Bible that it really almost contradicts its teaching.

Of course, the Bible does tell us how our sins can be forgiven. Thank God that it does. But it does not stop at that. The Bible is concerned not only about my soul in particular – thank God, I say again, that it is interested in that – but it does not stop at me and my little needs and aches and pains. The Bible is interested in the whole cosmos, the entire universe; there is nothing that it does not take in. The apostle Paul writes: 'That in the dispensation of the fulness of times he might gather together in one all things in Christ, both which are in heaven, and which are on earth; even in him' (Ephesians 1:10). This is the astounding thing about this book, about this revelation of God, which centres upon the blessed person who is talking to the woman of Samaria. It is all in him. He is the light of the world, and all we have here is what has been given through him.

Now we must remember that while there is a great deal of particular and detailed teaching in the Bible, while there is what might be called 'bits and pieces', nevertheless, the great characteristic of the Bible is that in addition to the portions, there is the whole. The author of the Epistle to the Hebrews puts it like this:

God, who at sundry times and in divers manners [in parts and portions, in bits and pieces] spake in time past unto the fathers by the prophets, hath in these last days spoken unto us by his Son [in his Son], whom he hath appointed heir of all things, by whom also he made the worlds. (Hebrews 1:1–2)

There it is again, always starting from the particular, the bits and portions, and then coming to the whole, this Son by whom he made all things and who sustains all things. Now this satisfaction for the mind is a most wonderful aspect of our Christian life. I do not have just a bit of something here and another portion there, but these are parts of a whole and I can look at the whole as well as at the parts.

When I am asked, as I often am, about reading the Bible, the answer that I always give is there is a sense in which you cannot understand any particular potion of the Bible until you have grasped the message of the whole Bible. Of course, you will never know the whole until you have gone through the parts, but that is the way to do it. You go through the parts, and perhaps for a while you may feel lost, but go on: read the whole Bible. Always read the whole Bible as frequently as you can, I would say at least once a year. Then you have the whole and the more you understand the whole, the more you will understand the parts. That is one of the thrilling things about the Bible.

Let me explain this. The Bible gives us this understanding that we crave for in two main ways. It has its plain, direct, explicit teaching: statements, propositions. There are large numbers right through the Bible, particular statements with which we are all familiar: 'God is love'; 'God so loved the world, that he gave his only begotten Son'; and so on. But the danger is that we tend to stop there. Of course, we start with the plain statements, we are bound to. Growth in spiritual understanding and knowledge is exactly the same as the growth of a child in the natural realm. The child has to start with simple elements – letters, then words, then sentences and so on. But the point is that you must not stop at the letters, you must not stop at the words, you must be more and more interested in the sentences, in paragraphs, in a book, and on and on it goes.

The second way in which the Bible gives us the understanding and knowledge that we innately stand in need of, and ever crave for, is by giving us knowledge that we *deduce* from the general teaching of the Scripture. Let me give you an example that I think will put it quite plainly. Take the doctrine of the blessed Holy Trinity: God the Father, God the Son and God the Holy Spirit, three eternal Persons and yet but one God. Now the doctrine of the Trinity is not stated explicitly anywhere in the Scriptures. But as we read we find this: God the Father, God the Son, God the Holy Spirit. There are ample statements about these three Persons, and yet the Bible also asserts that God is one. There is only one Godhead. And by putting these together, we arrive at the doctrine of the Trinity. That is just one example, and there are others that I could give you.

Now as we read the Scriptures, we are meant, under the influence and inspiration of the Holy Spirit, not only to take in and to grasp and to rejoice in the direct biblical statements, but also, as our minds are enlightened, to arrive at other doctrines by deduction. This is, I repeat, not only a vital, but also a very thrilling matter. Let me put it like this – and this is where one begins to see the wholeness – as we read the Bible, we come across great particular truths – teaching about the nature of God, about sin, about man, about salvation and so on. This is generally called *biblical theology*. Are you frightened of the word 'theology'? Well, if you are, there is something wrong with you! Theology means 'the knowledge of God' and that should be the greatest desire of every Christian. How can we arrive at a knowledge of God? Only by reading what God has been pleased to reveal about himself. It helps the mind that these great statements should be given a particular form – and that is what is meant by a *doctrine*. So we have the doctrine of God, the doctrine of salvation and so on.

The business of theology is to help us in these matters. That is why God has raised up teachers and instructors – theologians – who can teach the doctrine. They help us because the more we know about these doctrines that are revealed here, the more we shall rejoice before him and marvel and be filled with a sense of amazement.

But then we take a further step, using the mind that God has given us – it is all submitted to the Spirit, we do not go outside the Spirit at all – but now we find that we can take these great doctrines and see that there is a system in all this. So we arrive at *systematic theology*, which means the great doctrines of the Bible put in a logical, reasonable order. This has been done throughout the centuries. In a way, the great creeds and confessions of the church have been efforts to do that very thing. And, indeed, very often in the New Testament itself we see clear evidence that the teachers of the early church, who did not have books as we have now, would produce a form of words, a kind of formula, which they taught the people to say. One great example is 1 Timothy 3:16 – 'Great is the mystery of godliness: God was manifest in the flesh, justified in the Spirit, seen of angels, preached unto the Gentiles, believed on in the world, received up into glory.' Now that is obviously a primitive confession. That was the early church's way of making a systematic theology.

In other words, in the Scriptures there is a great line, a great chain of thought, which we can work out. To me, there is nothing more satisfying, more thrilling, than to have some glimpse of an insight into this. So we look, we stand back, and there we start with the everlasting and eternal God. 'In the beginning . . .' That is the beginning always. Here it is in the beginning of Genesis, the beginning of the Bible. It is of necessity the beginning. We are in this mysterious universe and we say, 'I want to have understanding. Is there any plan? Is there any system, any wholeness?'

Well, here is the answer: God! And the great truths about God. One of our hymns talks about 'his wise decrees', and, as the apostle Paul reminds the Ephesians, these things were done, 'before the foundation of the world' (Ephesians 1:4) – before time.

This is how we find this completeness, this wholeness, this fullness of understanding of the whole cosmos. The world is not an accident. Things have not just happened, come into being somehow, anyhow. No, no! God, the three Persons, in his wisdom and his understanding and purpose conceived the creation of the whole universe. There it is, and as we think about this, we are working out our systematic theology, the great doctrine about God, God the Father, God the Son, God the Holy Spirit.

So the creation of the universe; and then the creation of man. But then we come to the condition of man, humanity as it is now. What is this? And the Bible has its answer: the doctrine of the Fall.

And so we are taking these subjects in an intelligent, intelligible order. And there is an order in these matters. The teaching is here in the Scriptures, but it is not put in a systematic order. You get one revelation here and another there, and we are meant to take all these and to put them into this great order. Indeed, the more I read the Bible, the more I see the order coming out everywhere.

So having seen why man is as he is, we ask the question: What can be done for him? And in comes the great doctrine of salvation, again involving the person of the Son, the miracle of the incarnation, the virgin birth. What he did. What he said. That leads to the crucial doctrine of the cross – what he was doing there, the meaning of that, the way of salvation ordained by God. The Lamb of God slain before the foundation of the world, here, in actual practice. His death, his resurrection – and so it continues – his ascension, his return to heaven.

So the work of salvation is completed, but how am I to partake of this? Here it comes – the work of the Holy Spirit, this dispensation to which you and I belong, all mediated through the Spirit and applied through him. And even the steps and stages of that are given to us in detail: the calling and the setting apart, the justification, the sanctification, the glorification. This is all a part of this great system. And then, of course, the ultimate end of it all when this Son of God will return to this world and complete the work and establish his eternal kingdom.

Now that is what I mean by systematic theology, this wonderful arrangement and order. The plan, you see! People are so ignorant about these matters; there are those who have been foolish enough to talk about the cross of Christ as if it were an afterthought, saying that something had to happen because the Jews in their folly had rejected their own Messiah. 'Afterthought'? The Bible teaches *forethought*! Before the foundation of the world, in every single detail, there was this perfect plan. And now God in his grace has been pleased to give us the revelation of it so that we can stand back and look at it. And we end by saying, 'I am a part of that!' and begin to realize what it means to be a human being and to be a Christian, and we are filled with rejoicing and with praise.

To give you an illustration of what I am trying to say, let us look again at the first chapter of the Epistle to the Ephesians. What a chapter it is! The apostle is doing there the very thing that I have been trying to do in my feeble manner, and he succeeds; he gives just a glimpse of this grand sweep of it all. This is one of the most difficult chapters to read aloud in the whole of the Bible. Did you realize that from the beginning of the third verse to the end of the fourteenth verse there is just one sentence! We do have, unfortunately, full stops in the various versions, but in the original, from the words: 'Blessed be the God and Father of our Lord Jesus Christ' right until the end of the fourteenth verse, 'unto the praise of his glory' there is just a single sentence – but what a sentence! Into that one sentence Paul has crowded it all, this whole great and eternal purpose.

Paul begins –

God . . . who hath blessed us with all spiritual blessings in heavenly places in Christ: according as he hath chosen us in him before the foundation of the world . . . having predestinated us unto the adoption of children by Jesus Christ to himself, according to the good pleasure of his will . . .

On he goes. Then he says, in verses 7 and 8 –

In whom we have redemption through his blood, the forgiveness of sins, according to the riches of his grace; wherein he hath abounded toward us in all wisdom and prudence.

Now then, in verse 9 –

Having made known unto us the mystery of his will, according to his good pleasure which he hath purposed in himself

– before the foundation of the world, he has purposed it all 'in himself', but it has pleased him now to make this known. And all I am trying to urge upon you is the vital importance of giving yourself to this; and the more you do so the more you will be satisfied. You will find that it really does cover everything. But what is this 'good pleasure which he hath purposed in himself'? Well, there it is in that tenth verse –

that in the dispensation of the fulness of times

– by which Paul means that at an appointed time, which was known to God before he ever created the world, he will wind it all up again –

he might gather together in one all things in Christ, both which are in heaven, and which are on earth; even in him

– everything will be wound up and brought to a glorious consummation in him. That is a great summary of this wonderful and amazing system. Now all this is not merely for the intellectual entertainment of the Ephesians, nor is what I am trying to do for your intellectual entertainment. But if you really do want intellectual entertainment, read your Bible and listen to its exposition. See how everything else is dwarfed by it and seems so trivial and piecemeal; the pompous human philosophies – how ridiculous they look. Here it is, the whole cosmos is involved.

But watch how the apostle goes on. In verses 11 and 12, he says –

In whom also we have obtained an inheritance

– who is he talking about? It is the Jews. There is the great plan. Here is humanity and it is divided into Jews and Gentiles. This is not our division. God has done it. God made a nation for himself: the Jews. Paul is saying that the Jews first had obtained an inheritance. He continues –

being predestinated according to the purpose of him who worketh all things after the counsel of his own will: that we should be to the praise of his glory, who first trusted in Christ.

In Romans 1:16, Paul says, 'to the Jew first, and also to the Greek'. We find this teaching everywhere. There are bits and portions here and there but it is all part of this great plan of God.

Then in verse 13 of this first chapter of Ephesians, Paul says –

In whom ye also trusted

– who are the 'you' here? The Gentiles. Jews first, then Gentiles. They are brought in, in exactly the same way, and thus the whole of humanity is brought into God's salvation.

And in verse 14, Paul finishes by saying that we have received the 'earnest' of all this by the Spirit –

until the redemption of the purchased possession, unto the praise of his glory.

Very well, Paul says, there it is, that is the truth you need to understand. So he continues, in verses 15 to 20 –

Wherefore I also, after I heard of your faith in the Lord Jesus, and love unto all the saints, cease not to give thanks for you, making mention of you in my prayers

– he is praying for them. What is he praying?

that the God of our Lord Jesus Christ, the Father of glory, may give unto you the spirit of wisdom and revelation in the knowledge of him: the eyes of your understanding being enlightened

– Paul is saying, 'Oh, if only you saw it!' He is an apostle, of course; he has been dealt with in a special manner. He tells them that in the third chapter. He writes of how the Lord appeared to him and gave him a dispensation of the grace of God, 'that I should preach among the Gentiles the unsearchable riches of Christ' (3:8). He is not boasting. He is saying: I am an apostle. I have been given this revelation. He has appeared to me, he has taught me. He has sent me to teach you and this is what I'm doing. I want you to see it. If only you saw these things –

that ye may know what is the hope of his calling, and what the riches of the glory of his inheritance in the saints, and what is the exceeding greatness of his power to us-ward who believe, according to the working of his mighty power, which he wrought in Christ, when he raised him from the dead

– and which he is now exercising in you until he brings this church that he is forming to an absolute final completion – 'the fulness of him that filleth all in all' (verse 23).

There it is. Is it not wonderful to be able to look at something like this, especially at a time of uncertainty and confusion such as this present age? Who can find sense anywhere? It is only to be found here. There is a hymn, written by a man who was not a biblical writer, that expresses it and there is no more glorious way that I know of:

The Lord is King! Lift up thy voice,
O earth, and all ye heavens, rejoice!
From world to world the joy shall ring,
The Lord omnipotent is King!
Josiah Conder

This is the biblical way of giving us this fulness of intellectual satisfaction. We have our troubles and problems, of course we have, and I would like to show you how they are all dealt with. But this is the way to begin, my dear friend: put yourself into the right setting, put yourself into the right context. If you are in trouble, do not look at yourself, look at God, and realize something of this glorious and eternal truth.

Then, having done that, you can proceed to my next point, which is that the Bible and its amazing revelation then goes on to deal with our particular intellectual problems. This, again, is essential because we are in the flesh, we are in the world, we are very frail creatures. Extraordinary things are happening round and about us and men and women are perplexed and bewildered and are always asking: Why? Why does this happen? Why is that allowed? These are certainly a part of the trouble, and if this salvation and this Saviour cannot answer my questions and solve my needs in this matter of my intellectual problems and difficulties, then is he right to say, 'Whosoever drinketh of the water that I shall give him shall never thirst'? And the answer is an eternal 'Yes!' He answers everything.

Now we must be clear about this, and the more we understand it, the more we will rejoice in the fullness of this great salvation. So I start with this – and, again, in dealing with particular problems, I must emphasize the importance of order – the first thing that the Bible teaches us is that there is order in the universe. If you do not believe the revelation of the Bible, you will not believe that, and there are foolish people today who believe that all that we see is the result of blind, purposeless, mindless chance, a view that is surely monstrous and ridiculous. A famous old American preacher said recently – he at any rate had seen this clearly – that you cannot explain the universe by saying that it came about by accident or chance. As he said, you cannot explain even the works of Shakespeare in that way; these are not words that have just fallen together somehow or another.

No, no; there is only one satisfactory explanation and that is that there is a mind behind the universe. This does not go far enough by way of explanation, but that much at any rate is plain and clear: this is not an accident, there is order, there is arrangement. We see it not only in plants and creatures and the whole order of the seasons, but, especially, in human beings and in the gifts that they have.

Now this is always a great way of starting. If you take the position of these so-called scientific humanists, these atheists, Sir Julian Huxley and others, who say quite plainly and specifically that there is no order whatsoever in the universe and it all came about capriciously, by chance, and there is no discernible purpose, either in creation or history or anywhere else, then you do not know what may happen. The world may decide to move upwards, it may do the exact opposite; it may, indeed, go both up and down! And if there is no purpose, then, obviously, there is no explanation for anything at all.

But starting, as we do, with God the Creator and with an ordered universe, and a purpose and a plan, we can confront the problem of pain and of suffering that agitates the minds of people. There are those who say they cannot believe in God when they see pain or when they see suffering, malformed children. They say, 'I cannot believe that a God of love could possibly be responsible for this or even allow it.' You are familiar with all these arguments that people bring forward.

Now I want to show you that if you take the humanist position, or the position of so-called Scientism, which simply means the opinions or the philosophy of certain scientists, then you are left without any explanation at all. If it is all an accident, then accidents are to be expected, they must happen, and it is these accidents that give rise to pain. Then those who take this view are foolish enough, because of their theory of evolution, to say that there will be fewer and fewer accidents. But actually, when we look at the world, it seems that they are increasing. So people do not understand and are completely bewildered.

But when you come to the Bible, you find an explanation. Where have pain and suffering come from? There is no difficulty here as regards the biblical teaching: they are entirely due to man's original rebellion and sin, to the fall of man. That is the simple answer. Adam and Eve were put into a place called Paradise and there was no pain there, there were no problems. The man and woman were perfect and their surroundings were perfect, and if they had continued to obey God and to share their life with him, the world would never have known all this suffering.

There is a mystery here: Why did God allow evil? I shall tell you the answer later on when I deal with what may be called 'residual problems', but here is an immediate and adequate explanation: man has brought all this upon himself. And it is a part of his punishment; it is not all automatic, though a lot of it is. If you put your finger in the fire, you will get pain; commit sin and you will suffer for it. 'The way of transgressors is hard' (Proverbs 13:15). The poor fellow who got drunk last night is unhappy this morning and in pain. That is cause and effect.

But pain and suffering are not only the result of cause and effect; they are also partly the general punishment of sin. The biblical teaching is that all pain and suffering are the result of man's disobedience and rebellion, that God is not only a God of love but also of justice and of righteousness, that he is the moral Governor of the universe, and judgement is a part of his manifestation of himself.

Now there is a broad, general explanation, which immediately satisfies people. But then, as has often happened, you may go on and put certain questions. I am now referring to Christian people. It does seem at times as if godly people suffer more in this world than the ungodly, and that has often worried the saints. They see ungodly people flourishing while they themselves are in trouble. What is the answer? Well, the Bible has many, many answers; the book of Job was written to that end, it is the whole thesis of that book. And Job explains the problem perfectly. Do not forget to read that book right through; watch, as James says, 'the patience of Job' (James 5:11), and see how 'the LORD blessed the latter end of Job more than his beginning' (Job 42:12). Job came out of all his trials and tribulations a much bigger and a much richer and a much fuller man. God used that suffering to teach his servant and to lead him on.

Psalm 73, also, is entirely given over to this problem of the success of the ungodly while the godly suffer. And what a wonderful explanation it gives! The psalmist is worried and perplexed and beginning to complain about God; he is in intellectual confusion, as we all are, until he goes into 'the sanctuary of God'. What does he find there? He finds the Scriptures, he finds exposition, he finds preaching, he finds understanding: 'Then understood I their end' (verse 17). It is all right, he says. What a fool I was! He has a perfect answer and he goes on his way rejoicing.

Then Psalm 119! Here again is a man who has been in trouble, who has been ill and so on. But afterwards he says, 'Before I was afflicted I went astray . . . It is good for me that I have been afflicted' (Psalm 119:67, 71).

My dear friend, one of the most marvellous things we discover in this world is that what we formerly regarded as being entirely bad is often for our good. We are such fools, we will not be taught, so God as our Father chastises us. 'Whom the Lord loveth he chasteneth, and scourgeth every son whom he receiveth . . . If ye be without chastisement . . . then are ye bastards, and not sons,' says the writer to the Hebrews (Hebrews 12:6, 8).

Can you not see that it is because of sin that all this suffering has come in? But God even uses all this to our perfection: 'We have had fathers of our flesh which corrected us . . . after their own pleasure' – but here is God correcting us, not for his pleasure but for our good – 'but he for our profit, that we might be partakers of his holiness' (verses 9–10). He is bringing us to glory, he wants us to have this understanding. Many people have thanked God for an illness or an accident or a loss or some suffering because it has brought them into a deeper and a greater knowledge of God. Oh, yes, says the apostle Paul, this is what he has discovered: 'All things' – all things! – 'work together for good to them that love God, to them who are the called according to his purpose' (Romans 8:28). Paul says 'all things', and he could not have used a more inclusive word. There is literally nothing of which this is not true.

Have I told you of the illustration that an old preacher once gave of that verse? I think it is a good one. He took out his watch and he opened it and said, 'If you have a watch, open yours and there you will see it; one wheel is turning this way, and the other is turning that way. They seem to be working at cross purposes, but they are not. That is how the pins are sent round and forward. It appears to be a mass of contradictions. But it isn't. Everything has been made by a watchmaker and he knows that this wheel turning like this is going to move that one like that, and so each one moves the other, and the watch goes on and keeps time.' 'All things work together for good to them that love God.' No one can say that but the man or woman who has this enlightenment and this instruction. They do not always understand it at the time but they know within themselves that this is true, and as they go on living, they find it is true and they thank God for it.

So at the end of 2 Corinthians 4 we find one of the most glorious things the apostle ever wrote, and, my dear friends, this is the test of our Christianity. Can you join him in saying this? He has given the Corinthians a terrible list of his troubles and trials and tribulations, enough to crush a man and to finish him once and for ever. But then he stands back and looks at it all and says: 'Our light affliction, which is but for a moment, worketh for us [produces for us]' – listen! – 'a far more exceeding and eternal' – somebody says it should be translated 'an exceeding exceedingly abundant' – 'weight of glory; while we look not at the things which are seen, but at the things which are not seen: for the things which are seen are temporal; but the things which are not seen are eternal' (2 Corinthians 4:17–18).

The Bible teaches me that I am a stranger and a pilgrim in this world. I am only here for a while. Now people who are not Christians do not know that; to them, this is the only world, this is the only life, and if things go wrong in this world, they have lost everything. When they die, they end; their life has been in vain; they have no comfort or consolation. They are failures. But Christians say: This, our light affliction, is only for a moment. We are only in this world a very limited time.

This time seems to be extending. It was 'three score years and ten' but people are living longer, are they not? But, you know, when they get to 90, it is marvellous. Thank God, there are two, at least, in this congregation who are nearly reaching that age at the present time. God bless them and keep them. Nevertheless, there is a limit. Paul says, 'for a moment', and I know that this life is but my preparatory school, this is only a stage of transition. There awaits me the everlasting and eternal glory. I expect a world like this, a world of sin and of shame, to be a difficult and cruel world. Look how it treated the Son of God. But it was only for a while. He has finished with it. He has entered again to the glory that he shared with God from the foundation of the world. He has but gone to prepare a place for me so that where he is I shall be also.

And, therefore, as I look at the problem of pain and of suffering – and you can throw in the problem of war – I find that the Bible, and the Bible alone, has the explanation. 'From whence come wars and fightings among you? come they not hence, even of your lusts that war in your members? Ye lust, and have not' (James 4:1–2). You are all against one another. War! It is caused by nothing but by lust. Why does God allow war? Because he is teaching us what fools we are, and what we bring down upon ourselves because of our folly. Do not blame God for war. All these evils are the result of human folly and sin and rebellion. But the scientists, the humanists, do not understand and they die in despair, feeling that all they have worked for has gone. The First World War shook most of them, the Second World War shook practically all of them and they were left speechless, hopeless. The League of Nations had failed; everything fails. Of course! The Bible is not surprised at all this, it anticipates it, it prophesies it, but it also shows us that there is an ultimate that is beyond it all.

And so in these various ways with regard to these particular problems, the Bible gives us complete and entire satisfaction and understanding.

22

A Purpose for Life and Death

Jesus answered and said unto her, Whosoever drinketh of this water shall thirst again: but whosoever drinketh of the water that I shall give him shall never thirst; but the water that I shall give him shall be in him a well of water springing up into everlasting life. (John 4:13–14).

The majority of people today who are outside the church will tell you that this is because of what they call 'miserable Christians'. They think the Christian life is a life that is almost to be despised. If we are giving them that impression, it is quite clear that we are not only missing the glory of this life ourselves, but we have not even understood it as we should. That is why it behoves us to examine a statement like this in John 4:13–14 and not just slide over it. We must see whether it is true and how it is true; we must ask whether we can substantiate it and whether we are experiencing something of it.

So we are doing that, and we have started with the complete and full intellectual satisfaction that this gospel gives. We must start there, as we have been seeing, because the truth comes to the mind, and if it fails us at that point, then it will fail us elsewhere. We do not start with feelings, we start with the mind. Feelings, the will, everything follows from that. If we do not say that, then we have no test to apply to agencies that can give experiences and affect feelings. We have seen that the gospel gives us a great comprehensive view of the way of salvation and the reason for it. We have seen also that it satisfies our craving, our longing, for authority, and in our last study we saw how it satisfies our desire for system, for wholeness, for completeness, and how, as the result of that, it also deals with so many of our intellectual problems. We have indicated some of them – the problem of pain, the problem of suffering, the problem of war. People are in difficulties about them, and if we cannot show that the gospel deals with these matters in a satisfactory manner, then how can it be true to say that 'Whosoever drinketh of this water shall never thirst'?

But let me give you another illustration. There is the great problem of life itself. What is the meaning, the purpose, of life? Now here, surely, at this present time, is a most urgent question. Is it not becoming increasingly evident that the tragedies that one reads of and hears of in the papers and elsewhere are so largely due to the fact that people see no point in living, and do not know what to do next? There is a fundamental lack at their very centre as to life itself. There is nothing new about this; when it has thought about it, humanity has always been in difficulty about this question, but it is particularly urgent, it seems to me, at the present time. It is of the very essence of the modern problem. In other words, as Christian people, when we find non-Christians who are interested in life – people who call themselves humanists and moralists and so on – we have to point out to them that while they are but tinkering with the symptoms and manifestations, they will get nowhere. We must show them that it is the disease that matters, and that this disease is the fundamental failure to know and to understand the purpose of life.

Now many people regard life in the way described so eloquently by Shakespeare:

> To-morrow, and to-morrow, and to-morrow,
> Creeps in this petty pace from day to day,
> To the last syllable of recorded time;
> And all our yesterdays have lighted fools
> The way to dusty death. Out, out, brief candle!
> Life's but a walking shadow; a poor player,
> That struts and frets his hour upon the stage,
> And then is heard no more: it is a tale
> Told by an idiot, full of sound and fury,
> Signifying nothing.
>
> *Macbeth Act 5, Scene 5*

How prevalent that view is at the present time! Life is a vain show, nothing in it. 'Let's eat, drink and be merry for tomorrow we die.' Let us be clear about this. This is not merely true of the so-called 'giddy youth', but also of many others who have never read or thought at all about these matters. There is a grave danger that we will take a wrong view of today's adolescents. They are inheritors, let us not forget that; they are inheritors of a tradition, and much of what is true of them is the result of the failure of those who went before them.

I have often said from this pulpit that the people who deserve to be blamed above everybody are many of what are called 'the great

Victorians', the people who lived towards the latter end of the nineteenth century. We are now but reaping the end result of their concessions with regard to the Scriptures and their failure truly to understand the nature of the Christian gospel. They went on using biblical terms but they evacuated them of their meaning, and the hopeless view of life that we see today is the result. It is found in some of the most sophisticated people, people in the very highest seats of learning. I well remember reading during the last war the autobiography of R. R. Marrett, the head of Exeter College, Oxford. I have never forgotten the words that he uttered there. He told us how he was completely shattered by the Second World War – these were his words as I remember them:

> But to me the war brought to an end the long summer of my life. Henceforth I have nothing to look forward to but chill autumn and still chillier winter; and yet I must somehow try not to despair.[1]

Now there it is; culture, thought at its best, philosophy, with all that it has to offer, but no understanding – hopelessness, emptiness. The 'hope' of the Victorians was the especial failure of this era. It was a fact that they were fooled by appearances; everything seemed to be so secure, so firm, so solid. But this century has shown that there was no foundation for their optimism, that you cannot build on human greatness – financial, military, or any other sort.

And the result is that today people are bankrupt. They do not know how to live, and do not know why they should go on living. The consequences are quite inevitable. People turn to pleasure in various forms. But they soon get tired of the more innocent pleasures and have to experiment with others, and so they go from

---

[1] R. R. Marrett, *A Jerseyman at Oxford*, Oxford University Press 1941.

drink to drugs, and it goes on and on and on. This is all but a manifestation of a central emptiness, the absence of a foundation. The whole of life is some sort of iridescent bubble that people keep going by their own breath. But as they get older and more tired they cannot do it, and it finally bursts and there is nothing. Now this, I say again, has worried humanity from the very beginning; it is the quest of philosophers and others: What is life? What is its meaning? What is its purpose?

Now I am here to say that there is only one answer and it is the answer that is to be found here in the Bible. The world is in the condition that I have described because it does not believe in God, and because it does not believe in God, it cannot understand itself, it cannot understand life, it cannot understand all the things that finally matter. Not believing in God, it does not know anything about his purpose, it does not understand history, and, above all, it does not realize that God is behind and above history, that he has his hand upon it and is controlling it, bringing all things to pass according to his own eternal will.

The Bible gives a full explanation of the state of the world. I have often said that if I had no other reason for being a Christian or for believing the Bible – and thank God I have thousands of greater reasons – this, to me, would be more than enough. I know no other book that really tells me the truth about myself and about life. But here I see it all plainly and clearly, and I see that the Bible teaches that there is a purpose in life, a purpose and an object in history. People look at the world and life around them and say that it is senseless, that there is no meaning, and this, as I have often reminded you, is granted by all the humanists, both classical and scientific.

Mr H. A. L. Fisher, a great historian at Oxford, said that he had studied history all his life but could not see any end or purpose.

Sir Julian Huxley, a scientific humanist, said exactly the same thing. Now that is because they are looking at segments, they do not see history as a whole. They are immersed in wars and fightings and advances and retrogressions, and they come to the conclusion that there is no true and ultimate development. But you cannot read the Bible for any length of time without discovering that there is a great central purpose predetermined by God. If you regard the origin of life as an accident, then you will inevitably have to think of the remainder of life as a series of accidents. But life is not an accident. God made this world, he had an object and a plan and he will carry that out; nothing can stop it.

Well, then, you say: What about all the things that happen?

Now the Bible has an answer. It says that God's will takes two forms. There is his *directive* will, and there is his *permissive* will: both are of God. God has chosen to work in this way. He need not have, but he did, and is continuing to do so. And the moment I understand that, I am not surprised by all that happens.

God has a purpose, of course, in his permissive will. We do not see it all but we certainly see parts of it very clearly. God permits us to do many things in order to teach us the truth about ourselves. I grew up in an agricultural district – there is a great advantage in that. I remember very well how at times boys would come down to work for the old farmers, sometimes boys from schools here in London and from other institutions. And these boys, because they had come from the town, regarded every farmer as a clodhopper, an ignoramus who knew nothing. They knew everything about farming as well as about everything else, and they were not ready to listen to instruction, they did not want any information, they knew it all. And the philosophy of the old farmers, I used to find, was always this: 'He'll learn!' And these boys did learn, after many painful experiences of being thrown by horses and sticking forks into their feet instead of into the earth and so on. That was a learning process.

Now that is the way in which God permits so many things. We say: Why does God allow this? And the answer is that he allows it in order that we may see what fools we are. It is his only way of bringing us to see that we do not know quite as much as we thought we did. We know too much to listen to God, we know too much to listen to his Law, we do not need his instruction, we say it is démodé, entirely of the past, and we smile in derision. Very well, says God, carry on – carry on! All that is stated perfectly in the second half of the first chapter of Paul's Epistle to the Romans: 'God gave them over to a reprobate mind' (verse 28), and thereby he brings them to their senses.

These truths are taught quite plainly in the Bible. God has a positive purpose that he brings to pass in spite of us. Read your Bible from beginning to end and you will see God's advancing purpose, all that he said being brought to pass, and then, by the side of that, this permissive aspect. And as you look at it at first, you see a mass of contradictions. But it is not. It is all being directed. One of the psalmists, inspired by the Spirit, puts it like this: 'Surely the wrath of man shall praise thee' (Psalm 76:10). Of course! Take this century with its two world wars and its tragedies. What is this? I say that it is the wrath of man, and it is praising God. It is showing that what God in his word has said about humanity is true. It has completely exploded the false optimism of the Victorians, along with every other form of false optimism and idealism. The 'wrath of man' is praising God: all things do and all things finally will.

So I see the great message of the Bible: life has a purpose. And I see that by nature I had not realized this and had been fighting against it, and that is why I got disappointed and unhappy and felt that life was vain and useless. Oh, there have been some great tragedies in this respect. I remember how, over 30 years ago, we all read of a surgeon here in London, one of the best surgeons, at the top of his profession, who had suddenly given it all up to become just a ship's doctor on ordinary pleasure steamers. Why had he done this? Well, he was an ambitious man and he realized he had enemies who had thwarted his ambition to get to a certain high position in the profession, so he had given it all up in disgust.

Now that, again, is man, the natural man, in many ways at his best but lacking this fundamental understanding. He is disappointed and he gives up. He falls into cynicism and into a kind of despair. But the moment one's eyes are opened to this Christian teaching, one sees everything in an entirely different light. The moment men and women become Christians, they not only become children of God, they also begin to see God's purpose and understand that they are a part of it, they are sharers in it. So the whole of life takes on an entirely new aspect.

This is just what the apostle Peter is saying in his first epistle. He says: Do you realize who you are? You are:

> *a chosen generation, a royal priesthood, an holy nation, a peculiar people*

– a people for God's special possession. What are you here for? –

> *that ye should shew forth the praises [the excellencies] of him who hath called you out of darkness into his marvellous light: which in time past were not a people, but are now the people of God: which had not obtained mercy, but now have obtained mercy. Dearly beloved, I beseech you as strangers and pilgrims, abstain from fleshly lusts, which war against the soul; having your conversation honest among the Gentiles: that, whereas they speak against you as evildoers, they may by*

your good works, which they shall behold, glorify God in the day of visitation. (1 Peter 2:9–12)

What a picture! Can you not see? Life, according to Peter, is a kind of royal march, a great crusade; you are pilgrims, you belong to God, you are God's own special people. You are his nation, as the Jews were his nation under the old dispensation. Christian people are God's nation, the holy nation, at this present time. What God said of the Jews before giving the Ten Commandments, he now, through his servant Peter, says of Christians. And our calling now is – oh! – not just to live anyhow, somehow, eating, drinking and doing what the world does, having our ambitions and being thwarted, and being cast down and made miserable, and saying, 'Is there anything in it? Is there any point? Is it all just "a tale told by an idiot, full of sound and fury, signifying nothing"?' Of course it is not! We have a great object in living; we are here to show forth his praises, the praises of God; we are here to live to the glory of God. God made the whole world to manifest his own glory and now we become sharers in this great task. What is the chief end of man? It is 'to glorify God, and to enjoy him for ever' (the Westminster Catechism). We are to make these truths evident and plain.

Not only that, God has a great purpose of redemption and we are to take part in that. The purpose of redemption is not carried out only through preachers, it is to be carried out through every one of us. As we live and mix with people, we 'shew forth the praises of him who hath called [us] out of darkness into his marvellous light'. Remember, then, that dignity has been bestowed upon us. We do not regard ourselves as just animals, a little more intelligent than most other animals. No, no; the image of God has been renewed in us, we have been created anew after the pattern of God's dear Son. The Son came into the world to carry out the purpose of redemption, and he continues this work in us and through us.

So the whole of life changes. We become interested in other people in a new way: we have something to tell them; we can really deal with their problems. We see them unhappy, we see tragedies. All round us we see breakdown in marriage and in every other respect. People do not know what to do and the world has nothing at all to offer them. Read the family histories and the personal stories of all the clever people and you will soon see that they have nothing to offer at this point. But you and I have everything to offer. Life becomes exciting, it becomes full of interest and opportunity, it becomes thrilling. We can really help people. We do not merely pat them on the back and say a comforting word and send them away thinking what nice people we are. That does not help, it does not change anything. No, we have something to say to them that can change them and make them masters of their circumstances instead of victims. We really can show them this. In other words, we are participators in God's great programme and sharers in this great ministry. We are guardians and custodians of the faith. And as we are doing all this, we know that we are going on steadily day by day and hour by hour to the glory that God has prepared for us and that awaits us.

This is the whole picture of the Christian life. Isaac Watts puts it in these words:

The men of grace have found
Glory begun below;
Celestial fruits on earthly ground
From faith and hope may grow.

This is the truth by which we must test ourselves. Our Lord says, 'Whosoever drinketh of the water that I shall give him shall never thirst.' In other words, we will never be at a loss to know what to do with the next hour, we will never be bored, we will never say, 'My time has come to retire and now what am I going to do with myself?' They 'have found glory begun below'. They have the Bible, the study, the fellowship of the saints, and all this work outside the church.

And the opportunities have never been greater. Oh, the world is in a sad condition today. Let us not speak of the world in derision, let us speak with sorrow and sympathy. Our Lord looked out upon the people and he saw them 'as sheep not having a shepherd' (Mark 6:34) – and that is the simple truth. People are trying to find sustenance and failing, they are hounded by dogs and marauders. Here they are, and there is nobody who can help them except the Christian – nobody at all. Nobody else has any light to give. But we have it! And this, I say again, transforms our whole view of life, our whole existence while we are still left in this world.

And then we see death in an entirely new manner: it is transfigured. 'For to me to live is Christ, and to die is gain,' said Paul (Philippians 1:21). Why? Because it means that we go out of this world, which, though now we are living in it as princes and are marching to Zion, is nevertheless a land of sin and woe, of trial and problems, of pain and suffering. So we look forward to the glory that awaits us. And here it is – and seeing it, our whole attitude towards life in this world is transformed. We have an understanding that nobody else has and it gives life not only meaning, but also makes it great and glorious.

Shall I put it in the form of a question? Are you tired? I mean by that, are you tired of life? Are you weary? You should not be, my dear friend, if you are a Christian. The tragedy of this age is that young people are tired, they are old. They have exhausted the possibilities of life, so they are toying with things that promise to take them out of it by drugging them. Oh, how tragic that is!

But the Christian does not suffer from that. As Paul puts it in 2 Corinthians 4:16: 'Though our outward man perish' – and that is bound to happen, the body will go on decaying and death is facing us all – 'yet the inward man is renewed day by day.' And so I challenge you as a Christian in this way: your body is getting older but you ought to be getting younger. Are you feeling younger than you were? Are you conscious of increasing youth because of the vigour and the power that the Spirit of God puts in you? '. . . our inward man is renewed day by day', and as you go nearer to the glory and see it more and more clearly, your vigour increases. That is the Christian. Christians do not tire out, fade out. No, not at all.

Now this is the whole picture of the Christian as given in the Bible. This is the life that our Lord lives. Life, I say, becomes a grand march.

> We're marching to Zion . . .
> The beautiful city of God.
> Come, we that love the Lord,
> And let our joys be known . . .
> We're marching through Emmanuel's ground.

This world does not belong to the financiers or to the clever people. This world belongs to Emmanuel, the Son of God.

> We're marching through Emmanuel's ground
> To fairer worlds on high.
>
> *Isaac Watts*

Christian people, are you rejoicing in this? Is this your conception of your life in this world? Is this what has happened to you since you have taken of this water? Do you have fullness of life in your understanding and in your living as you go forward on your heavenly journey?

This world is 'Emmanuel's ground', but we, because of the effect of sin and the Fall and shame, have become 'strangers and pilgrims' in it. We do not live to this world only, we do not settle in it. We realize we are journeymen and are moving on. We are away from home, as it were. 'Our conversation [citizenship] is in heaven; from whence also we look for the Saviour' (Philippians 3:20). Now this is the view of life that is given me. It is the reverse of cynicism, the reverse of just cleverness. It is big, it is clean, it is holy, it is triumphant, it is filled with a sense of glory. And there are anticipations of it even in this world of time.

> The men of grace have found
> Glory begun below.
>   *Isaac Watts*

But then I go on to the next point, which is this: the Bible, having told me that this is the nature of my life in this world, then goes on to deal with the next problem that arises, which is, of course, how to live in this world while I am here. I have told you this in general, but, of course, we want to know in particular because we are confronted by different situations and choices: Is this right? Is that right? Should I or shouldn't I do this? Problems still confront us. There is nothing automatic about the Christian life. You start with the general view but that does not then settle every question as if it were a sort of ready reckoner. You cannot just turn up the right page and find the answer. We know we cannot do that, and yet we long for teaching and guidance on how to live.

Here, of course, is another major and mounting problem. Almost every day the papers refer to a new aspect of it. Why? Because what is being queried at the present time is the very category of morality itself. Is there such a thing as morality? Is there any code of behaviour? We are living in an age when the cult of self-expression is dominant and many philosophers are telling us that our behaviour is our own private business and that nobody else has a right to interfere. It is this view that accounts for the lawlessness and increasing crime at the present time. Then people go on to say that what you privately decide is governed by one thing only, and that is whether or not it gives you pleasure: so you become a hedonist.

In other words, authority is not recognized, there are no sanctions, there is no discipline, no law. This is the height of modern sophistication. Again, this is most important. It is very easy to look at some of these poor young people, who in many ways have never had a chance, and curl up your lip as you look at them and dismiss them with contempt. But let us remember that the philosophy underlying what they are doing is supplied by some of the ablest people in the country, some of the leading philosophers. This view that denies external moral sanctions or the right of anybody to tell anybody else what to do, that says that in this life it is every man for himself, that says that there is no law, no discipline, no punishment – this has been exalted into a philosophy. And we see how it is being carried out, we see the results. But these philosophers cannot see this. On the one hand, they go on asserting their great new view of liberty, as they call it, and then, on the other hand, there are these mounting problems. They cannot see the connection between them and call us philistines if we point this out to them. But it is not we who are saying these things, it is the Bible.

In other words, everything is fluid. Ideas change from generation to generation. What one generation says is derided and dismissed by the next as old-fashioned, out of date. You become a back number, 'square', whatever they may choose to call you. Everything is relative; nothing is fixed. One age condemns sexual perversions, another says they are wonderful, much better than heterosexual love, and so on. And not only that, there are different schools of thought. Philosophers are not agreed among themselves, and they are all equally dogmatic. You are familiar with all this.

But, above all that, even those who still believe in morality and in a measure of discipline and control are just as useless because they simply exhort us to live up to standards that by nature we cannot attain to. There is not much idealism in the modern world, it is cynicism now, but even idealism is quite useless; it is as useless as cynicism. It is no use saying to people, 'This is what you ought to do', the trouble is, they cannot. 'To will is present with me; but how to perform that which is good I find not' (Romans 7:18). This is where your idealistic systems all break down. Without Christ, the highest morality is as useless as the most profligate sin. What we need is not instruction, it is power. Morality fails and the world is as it is because human beings lack power. Even someone who knows what is right cannot do it.

This is the essence of this moral problem of how to live in this world. And there is only one answer; the answer given here: 'Whosoever drinketh of the water that I shall give him shall never thirst' at this point, too. Why? Well, here is the biblical scheme of things in this respect – you start with God, not with yourself. You do not start with your own likes and dislikes. You ask: Where has the world come from? Where has humanity come from? What is this that one is conscious of? God!

Then human beings made in the image of God – their reason, their understanding, their fears, their sense of guilt. Where do they come from? Conscience! What is the conscience? Where has that come from? You cannot say that it has developed because it is there in the most primitive people; everybody, every human being, has a sense of right and wrong. The most primitive races have this sense, they all have a fear of punishment. Not only that, the most primitive societies develop codes and rules. Whatever makes them do it? They have not had teaching, they have not had culture, they have never read, they have never listened to a lecture, yet they have all developed these codes.

That is the question, and there is only one answer: they all have a memory of the original law that God put into the heart of human beings and subsequently in a written form gave only to the Children of Israel. There is no other adequate explanation. So now I begin to see that there is a moral system, there are moral ideas. And then when I look at the Bible, I see that God has revealed all this. It is all here, this view of man as a responsible being, not an animal, but someone who was given an original righteousness, someone who was meant to correspond to God. And something in me says, 'Yes, I have a feeling that there is that in me and here I am told that God has given it to us all.

Then I see the Law, the Ten Commandments given through Moses, and I see that it is essentially right and good, that any society governed by the Ten Commandments will be a good, a happy society, and I find that is true with even minor regulations. I remember as a medical student having to listen to a man lecturing on certain aspects of certain diseases, and I remember him telling us that Moses was undoubtedly the first and perhaps the greatest of all the medical officers of health that the world has ever known. Where did he get his knowledge from? How did he anticipate so much that has been discovered since? And the answer of the Bible is that God revealed it.

And then in the Sermon on the Mount I find our Lord's exposition of the Law, and there I see life as it should be lived – a big life, a great life. Not just doing what I want to do and letting other people suffer; not just being the creature of my own lusts and passions and living like an animal. No, no; consideration for others: 'Love your enemies . . . do good to them that hate you' (Matthew 5:44). It is a great life, it is grand, it is uplifting, it is something that moves me.

And then I look at him who exemplified it all, the spotless, perfect Son of God. I say, 'Here is man as man ought to be; that is what I ought to be. I am beginning to see a reason for living a good life.' And the Bible goes on to give me motives for doing so. The Christian life is not just a series of arbitrary laws; it is not a form of legalism. The Bible does not come to us as a kind of collection of instructions and maxims and admonitions. No, no; it gives us a great view of ourselves under God, of what we are meant to be doing, and then it says: This is the way to do it.

Read the second half of all the New Testament epistles and you will find they are all arguments, they are all reasons. They say, 'Realize who you are.' Again, Peter has said it all: 'Dearly beloved, I beseech you as strangers and pilgrims, abstain from fleshly lusts, which war against the soul . . .' (1 Peter 2:11). In other words, Peter does not say, 'Now look here, don't commit sins of lust because you will get certain diseases if you do and you will suffer for it and your children may suffer.' That is morality. Morality just talks about the thing itself and the consequences of certain actions. Peter does not, the New Testament does not. The New Testament says: Realize who you are – 'a royal priesthood, an holy nation, a peculiar people' (1 Peter 2:9). Because of that, 'abstain from fleshly lusts, which war against the soul'.

Why should I live a good life? Is it simply to be moral and decent and better than somebody else? No, no; that is pharisaism, that is the antithesis of this Christian life. Why should I live this good life? Because I am a child of God, I am a child of the heavenly Father; so are we all. And we are here in this world 'to shew forth the praises of him who hath called [us] out of darkness into his [most] marvellous light' (1 Peter 2:9).

Not only that; I have to give an account to him, I have to go home and he will look at me, as the parent looks at the child coming home from the party – How did you behave yourself? What impression did you give of the family? And then I know that if I have done anything approximating to what I should have done, there is the great 'recompence of the reward' (Hebrews 11:26), the 'Well done, thou good and faithful servant' (Matthew 25:21). And he does not merely ask me to do these things, he has given me a new nature, a new heart, a new desire. He has put his Spirit within me and the power of the Spirit is in me:

> He breaks the power of cancelled sin,
> He sets the prisoner free.
> *Charles Wesley*

'If the Son therefore shall make you free, ye shall be free indeed' (John 8:36). God even goes beyond that to this: he makes this good life something that I love. 'His commandments are not' – no longer – 'grievous' (1 John 5:3). I see them as the pattern that God has set for the one he has made in his own image and likeness; and so I say with the psalmist: 'O how love I thy law!' (Psalm 119:97). It is not against my nature but is now something I want to live, I want to exemplify, in order that I may promote the glory of God and win my fellow men and women to him.

23

Conscience Answered

Jesus answered and said unto her, Whosoever drinketh of this water shall thirst again: but whosoever drinketh of the water that I shall give him shall never thirst; but the water that I shall give him shall be in him a well of water springing up into everlasting life. (John 4:13–14)

We are examining this great and glorious statement and have started with the intellectual aspect of the gospel. We have already seen many, many things – how the gospel gives us a general understanding with regard to our very being and existence, with regard to the universe in which we live, and to the problems that arise in connection with life, such as the problems of pain, of suffering and of war. We find on examination that full satisfaction is given in answer to the problems that trouble and perplex our minds.

And now we come to another aspect of the mind, and that is the conscience – the problem of its accusations. The conscience puts questions to our understanding, it raises difficulties, and one of our greatest problems is what to do with an accusing or troubled conscience. Oh, the unhappiness that this causes!

I always feel that one of the best ways of considering this question is in terms of the problem of praying and of going into the presence of God. It is then that conscience tends to be most alert and most powerful in its accusations. We can deal with other people very well, they are not the problem. The greatest difficulty we all have is to live with ourselves, and that means, partly, living with our own consciences. We can always answer the problems of other people, it is much more difficult to answer our own. The moment we go into the presence of God, or try to, conscience comes with its accusations. And then behind conscience there is the devil, 'the accuser of our brethren' (Revelation 12:10).

So this question – whether we can go into the presence of God at all – constitutes one of our greatest needs. This is what we need to know. The question comes in many different ways and it is put many times in the Bible in most eloquent language. Job puts it once and for ever: 'How should man be just with God?' (Job 9:2). Here is the question. See how it is raised in the biographies of people in the past, and, of course, we all ask it in our own lives. How can I know my sins are forgiven? How can I face God? And, ultimately: How can I die and face God at the bar of eternal judgement? These are the various ways in which this central problem of conscience tends to present itself.

Now there are those who want to suggest to us that there is a very simple answer to all this and that, indeed, our trouble over conscience is an indication of morbidity, not to say some psychological or even psychopathic condition. They say, 'You shouldn't be troubled like this.'

Why not?

'Well,' they say, 'God is love and is not that the final and full answer? Because God is love, there's no need to be concerned about the accusations of the conscience. Of course God forgives everybody and everything; he would not be love if he did not. So stop thinking! You've become morbid, you've become introspective and unhealthy. Just realize that God is love and that is enough.'

But unfortunately it is not enough for us; it certainly is not enough for anyone who has ever read the Bible. The people who talk so glibly about the love of God are generally people who are very ignorant about the Bible. They are basing what they say on their idea of God; they just think that God must of necessity be like that. It is a philosopher's idea of God. But that, of course, is of no value to us because we can always answer by saying, 'How do you know that? You say that, but can you prove it? Can you demonstrate it?' There seems to be so much in the world, as we have been considering, that contradicts that idea of God, that what they say does not really help us. It is especially unhelpful when we turn to the Bible, where alone we have true teaching and knowledge concerning God. Here we are told that God is love, but we are also told that he is holy, that he is righteous; we are taught about the various attributes of the being and character of God. So merely telling me that I should rest on the fact that God is love does not satisfy me.

And it is exactly the same in the case of those who tell us to rely upon the fact that occasionally we feel happy and feel that we are forgiven. That is all right, we all know about that. But then we know that feelings are so treacherous. We may be happy singing hymns in the atmosphere of a church, and we say, 'Well, yes, I'm a Christian after all, I enjoy this.' But then on Monday morning all the doubts and uncertainties and questionings may return along with the accusations of our conscience. So we cannot rely upon our feelings. No, we need something deeper, we need something greater. We need a satisfaction that is complete and cannot fail. We need something that will indeed conform to what our Lord says here, that will put us into a state in which we shall 'never thirst' with regard to this particular question of conscience.

So, then, in order to see how it is that only the gospel and our Lord himself deal with this, we must, once more, state the problem. Those who are not even aware of it are ignorant. People who are not aware of problems are ignorant people. There are those who say they have never known any difficulty about prayer. I always have a feeling that such people have never prayed in their lives. Prayer is not easy. Prayer is the most difficult thing that a person can ever engage in. The saints of the centuries had to learn how to pray. You remember the disciples saying to our Lord: 'Lord, teach us to pray' (Luke 11:1). Have you ever realized the difficulties in prayer? The people who tell you that prayer is quite simple tell you to relax in a comfortable chair and start listening to God. But that is not the teaching of the Bible – far from it.

No, no; let me remind you of some of the difficulties. I have mentioned one, the most vital of all – the character, the being, of God himself. 'God is light, and in him is no darkness at all' (1 John 1:5). He is righteous; he is holy; he is just. '[Thou] canst not look upon iniquity,' says Habakkuk (Habakkuk 1:13). All this is revealed in the Bible, in the Old Testament and the New. It is here that God tells us about himself, about his holy character and the kind of life he expects from men and women whom he has created. God's character is revealed supremely, of course, in the Law that he gave to Moses. The Law is there, and you cannot say, 'But the Law doesn't matter – only the love of God!' It is that God of love who gave the Law. You cannot take any one attribute in the being of God and say that is the whole.

And not only the Law. If you read the Old Testament, you find that some of the greatest characters there have been humbled and trembling in the presence of God. Moses at the burning bush, we are told, 'hid his face' (Genesis 3:6). Of course he did. And when the people were given the Law on Mount Sinai, the very mountain was quaking and they were filled with terror (Exodus 19:16). The Old Testament is full of this. 'Who shall ascend into the hill of the LORD? or who shall stand in his holy place?' (Psalm 24:3). 'Who among us shall dwell with the devouring fire?' (Isaiah 33:14). And Isaiah, one of the greatest and holiest of the men of the Old Testament, gets a vision of God, just a glimpse, as it were, and his response is, 'Woe is me! for I am undone; because I am a man of unclean lips' (Isaiah 6:9). Why does he say this? It is because he has come somewhere near the presence of God and, as the author of the Epistle to the Hebrews puts it, we must 'serve God acceptably with reverence and godly fear' – why? – 'for our God is a consuming fire' (Hebrews 12:28–29).

Above all, we find this teaching given by our blessed Lord himself. First of all, watch him as he prays to God; this is how he prays: 'Holy Father' (John 17:11) – though he is the Son of God. And when he responds to the disciples' request to teach them to pray, this is how he begins: 'Our Father which art in heaven, Hallowed be thy name' (Luke 11:2). That is our Lord's own teaching. So this notion that there is no difficulty about prayer, that it is quite easy and quite simple – 'pray when you like' – is a contradiction of the teaching of the whole of the Bible and, above all, of the teaching of our blessed Lord and Saviour himself concerning the nature and being of God. This is the first problem, this is the first difficulty about prayer. How can anyone go into such a place?

But this difficulty becomes much more acute when the accusations of conscience begin. There is the being of God; then I look at myself and conscience reminds me of my past sins. Conscience is a very accurate recorder and has a memory that never fails. It can remember words and actions from years and years ago, and it brings them back, raises them up and sends them in a horrible panorama before our eyes. And we have no answer; these are true: our sins, our failures. Conscience brings us to the condition of the Prodigal Son: 'Father, I have sinned against heaven, and in thy sight, and am no more worthy to be called thy son' (Luke 15:21). Or to the position of David. Having come to a realization of his terrible sin, David writes Psalm 51, and says, 'Against thee, thee only, have I sinned, and done this evil in thy sight' (Psalm 51:4). It is no use talking about the love of God, says conscience, this is what you have done. You have forfeited the love of God, you have sinned deliberately against the love of God. You cannot dispute it, you cannot deny the facts. Here is the record – there it is before you.

And then, on top of this, and from this subjective standpoint, the most difficult thing of all is the sense of pollution, the sense of uncleanness, the sense of unworthiness; and nothing makes one so conscious of this as to be in the presence of God. We know this in a measure as we come into the presence of saintly, holy people; they always make us feel that we are vile, that we are unclean. A man or a woman who has never felt unclean is just not a Christian; it is impossible. You see it in the Scriptures, and you feel it. The apostle Paul expresses this in the seventh chapter of the Epistle to the Romans: 'For I know that in me (that is, in my flesh) dwelleth no good thing' (Romans 7:18). Is that hyperbole? Is that exaggeration? Is that just a bit of rhetoric on the part of the preacher? No, no; Paul means it, he knows it – and do we not all know something about this? The hymn writer knows it:

Eternal Light! Eternal Light!
How pure the soul must be,

When placed within thy searching sight,
It shrinks not, but with calm delight
Can live and look on thee.

The spirits that surround thy throne
May bear the burning bliss;
But that is surely theirs alone,
Since they have never, never known
A fallen world like this.

O how can I, whose native sphere
Is dark, whose mind is dim
Before the ineffable appear
And on my naked spirit bear
The uncreated beam?

Thomas Binney

How can I? Here it is, this sense of unworthiness; not merely that one has done things that are wrong, there is something worse than that. It is the heart, the nature, that ever created the desire to do them. Again, Psalm 51 is a wonderful exposition of that. David is aware of the need of a clean heart: 'Create in me a clean heart, O God; and renew a right spirit within me' (Psalm 51:10). And the realization of this pollution and uncleanness and unworthiness almost makes us feel that God cannot forgive us, that God, to be consistent with himself, cannot forgive the sins we have committed. He can have no fellowship, no dealings, no communion, with people of such a character and of such a nature. And so, like the wandering leper, we feel we can do nothing but spend the rest of our existence crying out in agony, 'Unclean! Unclean!'

That is what conscience does to us, especially, I say, as we try to enter into the presence of God; and, of course, the whole time, as I have already indicated, there is the accuser of the brethren, there is the devil, reminding us of these things, pressing them home; the devil as an angel of light (2 Corinthians 11:14), the devil quoting Scripture, as he did to our Lord himself. Satan is an expert, he knows all the Scriptures. We begin to feel we are all right, and then he will bring up a scripture and it seems to cast us down again into utter condemnation and we feel that we are completely hopeless. The devil puts us there, in this position where the Law of God is thundering against us with its terrifying accusations, and we really feel that we cannot give an answer.

There is the problem. Is there a satisfactory answer? Is there any way of receiving assurance that I am forgiven, that I can enter into the presence of God and have fellowship and communion with him?

Now here is one of the most glorious aspects of the gospel; it is the beginning, the very first step. It is one of the things our Lord has in mind as he is speaking to the woman of Samaria, this woman who at this very moment is living in adultery: 'Thou hast had five husbands; and he whom thou now hast is not thy husband', and he tells her that he can give her full satisfaction in this respect. She can not only be forgiven, she can know that she is forgiven; she will never thirst again, she will never be in trouble again with regard to her conscience.

But this is our message: not only can our Lord do this, but he alone can do it. It is interesting to see how at the present time a series of men are confessing their utter bankruptcy with regard to all this. Some of them do not recognize the category of morality, but they do admit honestly that they are miserable. They cannot find peace; there is no peace anywhere. 'Peace, perfect peace, in this dark world of sin?' The world at its best, philosophy, cannot provide it. It is completely bankrupt. Here, and here alone, can we receive this fullness of satisfaction with regard to the forgiveness of our sins and the possibility of communion with God.

How does it happen? Well, let me remind you on this Palm Sunday morning.[1] The glory of this gospel is that it is not merely a teaching. It is a teaching, but it is a teaching based upon facts, upon historical events. I say that, do I not, every Palm Sunday, every Good Friday, every Easter Sunday morning, every Whitsunday morning, every Christmas morning! My dear friends, the glory of the gospel is that it is based on facts, that it is history. That is what makes it unique.

And the facts are these: that this person who is talking to the woman of Samaria is none other than the eternal Son of God. That immediately gives me a sense of relief and peace. I know that other people cannot help me. Why not? Because they have all sinned. They may say, 'Ah, you know, God is love, and it's all right,' but I reply, 'You are not in a position to speak to me, you are a sinner yourself. You are saying that to cheer yourself up; you are playing a psychological trick on yourself, and you know no more than I do. We are all faced with the same revelation.'

But then I am confronted by this unique person, the Son of God himself: 'If thou knewest the gift of God,' he says to the woman, 'and who it is that saith to thee, Give me to drink; thou wouldest have asked of him . . .' Thank God, I know who he is; he is the Son of God. Then my question is: What is he doing in this world? Why did he ever come into it? And the answer is that he is 'the gift of God'. This is the gospel: 'God so loved the world, that he gave his only begotten Son, that whosoever believeth in him should not perish, but have everlasting life' (John 3:16). 'But when the fulness of the time was come, God sent forth his Son, made of a woman, made under the law' (Galatians 4:4). He was in

---

[1] 19 March 1967.

the world because God himself, the one I am concerned about, sent him there.

But why did God send his Son into the world? The answer is implicit in those words that I have been quoting; but perhaps a still more specific statement is in the Epistle to the Romans: 'For what the law could not do, in that it was weak through the flesh, God sending his own Son in the likeness of sinful flesh, and for sin' – which means, 'on account of sin', in order to do something about sin – 'condemned sin in the flesh' (Romans 8:3).

So I am beginning to feel that my problem has been dealt with, the problem of sin – in me, in the whole of humanity. People of the world cannot solve it and cannot do anything at all about it, but God sent his Son into the world especially on account of this problem. Here is one who came from the outside, from the glory, from eternity, into the world to deal with the problem of human beings in sin. I see that he is man, but I see that he is more than man; I see these indications of his glory, I see his miracles, his signs. He is man, he is God. He came into the world, the Son of God. The Word was made flesh in order to deal with the problem of my sin.

How did he do that? Well, I follow him. I look at his life. Do that this Palm Sunday and these next days. Go through the Gospel stories again reminding yourself of all that you read of there, and what do you find? First, you find that he rendered a perfect obedience to his heavenly Father. He kept the Law of God perfectly. Not one of us can keep it. We have all broken it. That is the argument of the third chapter of the Epistle to the Romans: 'Therefore by the deeds of the law there shall no flesh be justified in his sight: for by the law is the knowledge of sin' (Romans 3:20). What the Law does is give me knowledge and information concerning sin and my own failure, and under the Law the whole world lies guilty before God. But here is one who never failed in any single respect. The Law of God, which we have all broken, he honoured absolutely, completely and perfectly; no one can bring a charge against him.

Now this is vital and all-important for me. I must keep the Law, God has said that. If I do not, I am under the condemnation of the Law and the punishment it metes out is death and separation from God. And I cannot keep the Law. But I am beginning to see life, I am beginning to see hope. Here is one who himself honoured and kept the Law of God. But still I am left with my major problem. I have sinned. My past sins I cannot remove, I cannot make atonement for them, I cannot do anything at all about them. Does he help me here? I have seen that he kept the Law. That is all right for him, as it were, but what about me?

Ah, now, you see, we come to Palm Sunday, the triumphal entry into Jerusalem, and all that followed after it. 'He stedfastly set his face to go to Jerusalem' (Luke 9:51). He knew he had got to die. He could have escaped it all. He said so. He could have commanded twelve legions of angels and gone to heaven without dying; there would have been no difficulty whatsoever. But he did not, he deliberately went to the cross. He said that he had come into the world in order to go there. This was the hour, he said, for which he had come. It was the hour of his glorification. It was all deliberate.

What does this mean? What was happening on the cross on Calvary's hill? What is the meaning of the death of the Lord Jesus Christ? And this is the most astounding thing of all. It was here that he dealt with my ultimate problem, the problem of my guilt. How did he do that? Well, this is what he says himself: he came 'to give his life a ransom for many' (Matthew 20:28). The apostles, according to the light and the instruction that he himself gave them and then worked out still more clearly by the operation of the Holy Spirit within them, say this: 'Whom God hath set forth to be a propitiation through faith in his blood' (Romans 3:25) – and this is the most amazing thing ever said. A propitiation is a peace offering, it is something that is offered to God in order to satisfy his holy demands, the demands of his justice and righteousness. And Paul is saying that God himself provided the propitiation that he himself needed, and it was his own Son, bleeding and dying upon the cross on Calvary's hill.

The apostle puts it like this in 2 Corinthians 5:21: '[God] hath made him [Jesus Christ] to be sin for us, who knew no sin' – he was innocent, he was pure, he had kept the Law, but he was 'made sin', 'made a sinner'. How? By our sins being laid upon him – 'that we might be made the righteousness of God in him.' This is the message – that God has taken your sins and mine and laid them upon him. He has *imputed* them to him. He has put them on his account. These are the terms that are used right through the Bible. It is foreshadowed in the Old Testament in all the offerings of bulls and goats and lambs. All that is just a prefiguring of this ultimate offering – 'the Lamb of God, which taketh away the sin of the world' (John 1:29). Or as Isaiah puts it, 'The LORD hath laid on him the iniquity of us all' (Isaiah 53:6). That is what happened. God smote him: 'We did esteem him stricken, smitten of God' (Isaiah 53:4). The Father did this to the Son.

What was God doing? He was punishing our sins in the person of his Son. The Son came into the world in order to take our sins upon himself. God was punishing our sins there, in him who had not sinned. As Peter puts it: 'Who his own self bare our sins in his own body on the tree, that we, being dead to sins, should live unto righteousness: by whose stripes ye were healed' (1 Peter 2:24). That is the sole explanation of the cross on Calvary's hill. He died because he was bearing the punishment meted out to our sins, and he was laid in a tomb; but he rose!

And what was the resurrection? It was God declaring to the whole world that he was satisfied with the offering of his Son. It was God pronouncing absolution of sins. It was God declaring his utter satisfaction. And then the Son ascended, and he entered into heaven, presenting himself and his own blood as this offering unto God, and there it was accepted: '[He] sat down on the right hand of the Majesty on high' (Hebrews 1:3); and he is there at this moment ever living to make intercession for us (Hebrews 7:25) for whom he died and bore the penalty. So this is the answer that is given in the whole of the Bible to the question raised by my conscience and by my awareness of sin.

How, then, do I receive this for myself? Well, God applies it to me now by his Holy Spirit. We are told that as God has laid my sins upon his Son, he now puts upon me the righteousness of his Son. It is all there, again, in 2 Corinthians 5: 'God was in Christ, reconciling the world unto himself, not imputing their trespasses unto them' (2 Corinthians 5:19). This is often put in terms of clothing – he has put this great 'robe of righteousness' of the Lord Jesus Christ upon me. God looks at me now and he sees me clothed in the righteousness of Christ, who has obeyed the Law absolutely, without any mistake, without any shortcoming; we are 'made the righteousness of God in him' (2 Corinthians 5:21). And so God declares all who believe on the Lord Jesus Christ to be just. As the apostle says, 'Therefore we conclude that a man is justified by faith without the deeds of the law' (Romans 3:28).

Now that is the great declaration of the gospel. That is the message that the Son of God himself is preaching there to the woman of Samaria. That is the message of the gospel at this very moment to anyone who listens to it and is ready to receive it. But does this completely satisfy me? That is the question. Does it cover my every question? And the answer is a glorious and eternal 'Yes'!

Here is the way to get assurance of faith; here is the way to know the joy of salvation: 'The kingdom of God is not meat and drink; but righteousness, and peace, and joy in the Holy Ghost' (Romans 14:17). Are you rejoicing in the knowledge of your sins forgiven? Christian people, are you happy? Do you know that you have access to God and that you are his children? This is the way to obtain that access, and we are all meant to enjoy it.

How does the gospel do this? First of all, it answers my first terrifying question about God himself. How can a God who is holy and righteous and true – a God who gave the Law and who says, 'The soul that sinneth, it shall die' (Ezekiel 18:4), and, 'The wages of sin is death' (Romans 6:23) – how can this holy God possibly forgive me? He is the righteous God who cannot contradict himself, the God of whom the apostle Paul says to Titus, 'God, that cannot lie' (Titus 1:2). He is the just God, who says: I must punish sin, I cannot pretend I have not seen it. I can have no dealings with people until sin has been punished.

And the answer is here. As Paul, as we have seen, puts it in Romans 3:

> *Whom God hath set forth to be a propitiation through faith in his blood, to declare his righteousness for the remission of sins that are past, through the forbearance of God; to declare, I say, at this time his righteousness: that he might be just, and [at the same time] the justifier of him which believeth in Jesus. (Romans 3:25–26)*

The death of Christ shows that God is just – my sin has received the punishment that God said he would mete out to it. As Paul puts it at the end of that third chapter of Romans: 'Do we then make void the law through faith [by this gospel]?' – No! – 'God forbid: yea, we establish the law' (verse 31). The death of Christ on the cross established the law of God. It declared the righteousness and the justice of God. And because he has punished sin, and established his eternal righteousness, he can with justice and righteousness forgive me. He can look upon me, the sinner, and justify me, and smile upon me.

And so my first and greatest question is answered. The throne of God that hitherto has been to me a throne of justice, has become the throne of grace. The Law of God is satisfied. God himself has satisfied his own Law in the person and in the death of his Son. So I can sing:

> The terrors of law and of God
> With me can have nothing to do;
> My Saviour's obedience and blood
> Hide all my transgressions from view.
> *Augustus Toplady*

There is no difficulty. Because God himself has done this, I know it is true and right. The Law has been honoured completely; it cannot condemn me.

And then, because my past sins have been forgiven, I feel I am now in a position to go into the presence of God. Ah, yes, but wait a minute: my pollution, my unworthiness – what can I do about this? Well, here is the answer. I have a robe of righteousness upon me. It is not mine. God does not see me, he sees me clothed with the righteousness of his dear Son. I do not go alone, I go through him. He is my High Priest. He is there to present me and my prayers. He 'ever liveth to make intercession' for me (Hebrews 7:25).

> A debtor to mercy alone,
> Of covenant mercy I sing;
> Nor fear, with thy righteousness on,
> My person and offering to bring.

That is it! It is his righteousness that is upon me. Or, as Count Zinzendorf put it in the hymn translated by John Wesley:

> Jesus, thy blood and righteousness
> My beauty are, my glorious dress;
> Midst flaming worlds, in these arrayed,
> With joy shall I lift up my head.

This is the glory of the gospel – I can approach the throne of grace with assurance, with boldness, because I am coming to God in the dress that he himself has put upon me. It is he who has made it possible. I am simply doing what he has told me to do.

I still have my conscience and it continues to speak, but I can now answer it. What is my conscience that it thinks to condemn me, if God has already absolved me? God is greater than my conscience, he is greater than my heart: 'God is greater than our heart [conscience], and knoweth all things' (1 John 3:20). I can quote God against my own conscience, and what I say is this:

> Jesus, my great High Priest,
> Offered his blood and died;
> My guilty conscience seeks
> No sacrifice besides.
> His powerful blood did once atone
> And now it pleads before the throne.
>
> *Isaac Watts*

My conscience is satisfied. It is answered by what my great High Priest did for me when he offered his blood and died.

But there is still one enemy left – the devil, with his subtlety, his ingenuity, his power and his malignity. He still comes, and I know that I am not strong enough to deal with him myself – he has defeated all humanity. The only one Satan has never defeated is this blessed Son of God who rode into Jerusalem on that ass. And so I can turn to my Lord and say:

Be thou my shield and hiding place
That, sheltered near thy side,
I may my fierce accuser face
And tell him, thou hast died.
Philip Doddridge

'They overcame him by the blood of the Lamb, and by the word of their testimony' (Revelation 12:11). The devil cannot answer; he is silenced; he is dumb. As I shelter by the side of Christ, this bully, this ultimate fiendish, devilish, high spiritual bully, cannot any longer cause me to quake or to fear. Instead of being frightened and whimpering and running away, I can face him and cause him to flee by telling him that Christ has died for me, that the blood of Christ is on me, and that I am accepted by God.

As I take the water of life that our Lord offers me, as I drink in this message and this truth, I am put into a position in which I can answer the whole universe, and I defy the whole universe to bring me under condemnation. And I say with Paul:

What shall we then say to these things? If God be for us, who can be against us? He that spared not his own Son, but delivered him up for us all, how shall he not with him also freely give us all things? Who shall lay any thing to the charge of God's elect? It is God that justifieth. Who is he that condemneth? It is Christ that died, yea rather, that is risen again, who is even at the right hand of God, who also maketh intercession for us. Who shall separate us from the love of Christ? shall tribulation, or distress, or persecution, or famine, or nakedness, or peril, or sword? . . . Nay in all these things we are more than conquerors through him that loved us. For I am persuaded [I am certain], that neither death, nor life, nor angels, nor principalities, nor powers, nor things present, nor things to come, nor height, nor depth, nor any other creature [not the whole creation] shall be able to separate us from the love of God, which is in Christ Jesus our Lord. (Romans 8:31–35, 37–39)

God himself is for us. He has proved it in the person of his Son: his birth, life, death, resurrection, ascension – ever living to make intercession for us. He is there, he will always be there, and therefore we are eternally and everlastingly safe. 'He is able also to save them to the uttermost that come unto God by him' (Hebrews 7:25). Oh, the glory of the gospel that satisfies the demands of my conscience and gives complete satisfaction to my mind as I consider the greatest question of all – my relationship to God, the possibility of fellowship with him while I am left in this world, and the glorious hope of spending my eternity in his holy presence.

> Oh how shall I, whose native sphere
> Is dark, whose mind is dim,
> Before the ineffable appear,
> And on my naked spirit bear
> That uncreated beam?
>
> There is a way for man to rise
> To that sublime abode:
> An offering and a sacrifice,
> A Holy Spirit's energies,
> An advocate with God.
>
> These, these prepare us for the sight
> Of holiness above:
> The sons of ignorance and light
> May dwell in the eternal light
> Through the eternal love!
>
> *Thomas Binney*

Blessed be God for such a gift. 'He that drinketh of the water that I shall give him shall never' – no, never – 'thirst again.'

24

Death Defeated

Jesus answered and said unto her, Whosoever drinketh of this water shall thirst again: but whosoever drinketh of the water that I shall give him shall never thirst; but the water that I shall give him shall be in him a well of water springing up into everlasting life. (John 4:13–14)

We are considering the all-sufficiency of the gospel. Let me give you a better translation of our Lord's words in John 4:14: 'Whosoever drinketh of the water that I shall give him shall never, no, never, thirst: never, no, never, as long as the world stands.' Whoever takes of this water, takes the life that he has come to give, and shall never thirst, shall never know again any final or ultimate need or emptiness. This is the great claim that we make for the Christian gospel and we have been investigating it. We have been asking: Is this true? We have started with the mind and the intellect, and last time we were considering the great questions and accusations that are put to our minds by the conscience. And we saw that there is no answer except the answer that is given us in the Lord Jesus Christ and his blessed gospel.

But we must agree that the ultimate problem of all problems is that of death, the problem of the grave and of what lies beyond – if anything does. The apostle Paul said, 'The last enemy that shall be destroyed is death' (1 Corinthians 15:26), and it is indeed the last enemy. These other problems that we have to confront come and go – scientific questions and problems, the problem of pain and suffering, political problems, the problem of war – all these may or may not be urgent, but there is one that is inevitable, inexorable, ineluctable – the problem of death. No one can evade it. And, of course, we are bound to be concerned about it. Here we are in life, full of activity and interests – then death. Is there any purpose in it? Can it all just end here, all the pother and all the trouble and all the agony and all the suffering – does it all finish? And what then . . .?

And so the ultimate test of the truth of this gospel that we preach, the test to apply to this statement of our Lord – 'Whosoever drinketh of the water that I shall give him shall never thirst; no, never thirst' – is the question: Does it help us and does it give us satisfaction face to face with this last, this ultimate, question of death? Well, we meet together on Easter Sunday morning and that is the answer to the question. The gospel never fails us – it does not fail us here. It is here, indeed, that it shines out, perhaps, most gloriously of all.

But, again, let us look at this in the words the Lord used to the woman of Samaria. I put the general proposition to you in these terms: It is the gospel, and the gospel alone, that deals with the problem of death and the life beyond. I am making an exclusive claim. 'Whosoever drinketh of this water shall thirst again' – there is no answer here – 'but whosoever drinketh of the water that I shall give him shall never thirst.'

Now the problem of death has been the problem of the ages. The literature of the world deals constantly with it. The author of the Epistle to the Hebrews expresses it in these words:

Forasmuch then as the children are partakers of flesh and blood, he also himself likewise took part of the same; that through death he might destroy him that had the power of death, that is, the devil; and deliver them who through fear of death were all their lifetime subject to bondage. (Hebrews 2:14–15)

That is it. Death has been a cause of bondage for the human race from the beginning. Read the literature of ancient Greece with its mythology and you will find that the Greeks of classical times were tremendously concerned about this question. Those great men, the Greek poets and philosophers, applied their minds to the question of death and found no answer. All they had to tell us was something vague and indefinite – the River Styx and some misty Elysium. They did not know, it was all poetic imagination and fancy. There is no satisfaction from them.

And when you come to the so-called great religions of the world, it is no better – they also just do not know. At best, they offer you some sort of absorption into the absolute. Some believe you must keep coming back to this world in a series of reincarnations in order to get rid of this body and then eventually your spirit is absorbed into the ultimate, the absolute, some Nirvana. All they can offer are speculations, which are not satisfactory, and which do not answer our questions. That is why all those so-called religions are profoundly pessimistic, and hold their people in a thraldom of pessimism.

And when you come to consult the great poets, you find that they often have wonderful insights into this life, but when they face the problem of death, they fail as much as all the others. Let me take perhaps the greatest – Shakespeare. He put it once and for ever in those immortal words spoken by Hamlet:

To die, – to sleep, –
To sleep! perchance to dream: – ay, there's the rub;

For in that sleep of death what dreams may come,
When we have shuffled off this mortal coil,
Must give us pause:
. . . who would these fardels bear
To grunt and sweat under a weary life,
But that the dread of something after death, –
The undiscover'd country, from whose bourn
No traveller returns, – puzzles the will,
And makes us rather bear those ills we have
Than fly to others that we know not of?
Thus conscience does make cowards of us all.
> *Hamlet, Act III, Scene 1*

There is no knowledge, there is always this terrible possibility – what if? And there you have it at its best and highest in the realm of the poets: there is no answer.

And then you turn to the realm of general philosophy and science – I am not thinking of the Greeks now but of the subsequent philosophers coming right up to modern times. Of course, there is a lot of talk, a lot of dogmatic talk, but they cannot prove anything. A scientist may say, 'Death is the end' – but it is only his opinion, based on nothing, and, indeed, there is disagreement among the scientists themselves. We know, for example, that people such as the late Sir Oliver Lodge had a firm belief in an afterlife. In other words, there is no answer from scientists.

Let me give you one quotation from the man who is regarded as the greatest living philosopher, the greatest philosopher, they say, of the twentieth century. These are the words of Bertrand Russell:

> We stand on the shore of an ocean, crying to the night and to the emptiness. Sometimes a voice answers us out of the darkness, but it is the voice of one drowning, and in a moment the silence returns. The world seems to me quite dreadful.

That is it! Let us grant that Bertrand Russell is the greatest philosopher of the twentieth century, certainly a great intellect; but when he confronts this question, he just does not know. And there have been similar evidences recently of able old men, who have made their contribution to literature and so on, but who, faced with this question, know nothing – nothing at all.

And when we come even to the realm of spiritism, we still see the same ignorance. Even if we grant that spiritism and the investigations of the Society for Psychical Research have produced certain valid evidence of an existence beyond this life, we have to conclude that what they produce is totally unsatisfactory as has often been pointed out. The evidence is generally in terms of some Red Indian, some ancient Chinaman, or something of that sort. Surely the most we can grant for it – and, of course, as Christians we are in no difficulty about this – is that they do establish that there is another realm, an unseen, a spiritual realm.

Now we do not need the evidence of Spiritualists, we do not need their proof, we already believe on the grounds that I am going to give you. All I am saying is that even if you give this evidence its maximum value, all it can do is give you some vague indication that death is not the end, that there is something beyond it. It does not tell you what it is. There are those of us who believe that all the phenomena of spiritualism can be explained very simply in terms of evil spirits, and I do not hesitate to say that that is the ultimate answer. That is why an element of sport and of mockery is generally associated with it, and that is why the Bible tells us not to touch it – not only because it is unnecessary but because it can be dangerous.

So there is no help from any of these directions. But let me go even one step further. If you turn to the Old Testament, you will find that even the Old Testament is not clear on the subject of death, though there are some striking, glorious statements here and there. On the whole, the Old Testament is alarmed by the thought of death. It says, for example, 'A living dog is better than a dead lion' (Ecclesiastes 9:4). There was an uncertainty, there were only glimpses, adumbrations. Even the Old Testament does not get beyond that. It has faith that someone is coming who will deal even with death, but it is looking forward, it does not have a living and a clear faith.

But the moment we turn to the New Testament, we find that the position is completely changed. That is why the New Testament is the most lyrical, the most exhilarating, the most cheerful book in the whole universe. Here is a book of triumph, a book of joy, a book of everlasting and eternal hope. It is said, and it is true, that whenever the Christians in the early church met one another, especially on Easter Sunday morning, it was their custom to greet one another with these words – 'Christ is risen!' And that is typical and representative of the Christian hope and the difference that this person who is talking to the woman of Samaria has made to this world. He is able to say, 'Whosoever drinketh of the water that I shall give him shall never [no, never] thirst' – not only in life, but even in death.

Christ and his gospel give us the only satisfactory answer even with regard to this last, this ultimate question. So let us discover how our Lord does this. This is the whole purpose of meeting like this on Easter Sunday morning. Of course, we do not confine this teaching to this day, we are not tied to any calendar; it comes in every Sunday. But we are particularly concerned about it this morning because of the historicity at the basis of all that we believe and hold.

How, then, does our Lord give us the answer to the problem of death? We start by pointing out that he does this in himself. He does it by his very presence in this world, before anything has been said by him or before anything has happened to him. His very coming into this world already answers all our ultimate questions, because he is unique. All of us, from the least, in the world's eyes, to the greatest people the world has ever known, are born from men and women, and we understand them all. We agree that some have greater qualities and abilities than others, some have faculties that are more highly developed, but they are simply ourselves writ large, they belong to us, and that is why none of them can help us. But here is one who is in a category on his own – he has come into this world from the outside; he has come from the eternal realm. That babe lying in the manger in Bethlehem really answers this question about death. He is a visitor from eternity who has entered into time. 'The Word was made flesh, and dwelt among us' (John 1:14). He has tabernacled for a period in this world, but he is the Word: 'In the beginning was the Word, and the Word was with God, and the Word was God' (John 1:1).

Moreover, the moment we begin to listen to him, we are struck by one thing, and it struck the people at the time. We read at the end of the Sermon on the Mount that the people who had heard him looked at one another in astonishment, 'For he taught them as one having authority' – authority! – 'and not as the scribes' (Matthew 7:29), and that was the quality that always characterized him. He did not speculate, he did not say, 'It's possible', 'Perchance it may be true.' No, he spoke about God and about the eternal unseen world with ease and with a strange authority.

Now that is based on what we read in the third chapter of this Gospel of John, the words that our Lord spoke to that great man Nicodemus. Our Lord said:

If I have told you earthly things, and ye believe not, how shall ye believe if I tell you of heavenly things? And no man hath ascended up to heaven, but he that came down from heaven, even the Son of man which is in heaven. (John 3:12–13)

That is the explanation. Our Lord is talking about something he knows. 'We speak that we do know,' he said to Nicodemus, 'and testify that we have seen; and ye receive not our witness' (verse 11). This is the essence of his position. Here he is, he belongs solidly to history – Jesus of Nazareth. This year is dated 1967 because of this person who appeared on the stage of history. No one else has ever been able to speak as our Lord did to Nicodemus. He spoke as one who had come from the realm beyond the veil, which is hidden to us. He came out of it into our world, and he went back again into it.

This is seen in all our Lord's teaching. He kept on saying that he had come from the Father. He said to the religious leaders: 'Ye are from beneath; I am from above' (John 8:23). And you cannot explain him in any other terms. He was a carpenter. He had never had the training of the Pharisees. He had never been to the schools, to the academies, he was not a Greek philosopher. And yet we are told, 'The Jews marvelled, saying, How knoweth this man letters, having never learned?' (John 7:15). He was able to speak about God and heaven and man with ease and authority. And the only explanation is that what he said about himself was true: he was 'from above'. He was from the Father and was returning to the Father.

And when we come to this whole question of death and what lies beyond it, there are his specific teachings. There are many that I could quote to you, I am only giving you some typical examples. Do you remember his story about Dives and Lazarus? He is not using his imagination but is talking about a realm that he knows of. He knows about 'Abraham's bosom'; he knows that 'there is a great gulf fixed' between the abode of the blessed and the abode of the others. He knows that there is a place of torment and a place of bliss, and that there is no traffic between the two. He does not speculate, he does not indicate possibilities, he speaks authoritatively, and he calls upon his listeners to accept his teaching (Luke 16:19–31).

Then on another occasion, some clever people came to him with their catch questions – there were people like that in the first century as there are today! There is nothing new about the clever questions that are put by the clever people on the television and the wireless. These people are pale imitations of some of these really clever men who were alive in the days of our Lord. Listen to this: 'The same day came to him the Sadducees, which say that there is no resurrection' (Matthew 22:23). You see, there is nothing new about denying the resurrection. My dear friends, if we do nothing else, let us get rid of the notion that it is modern knowledge or modern science that makes it difficult for people to believe the gospel. That has nothing to do with it. The Sadducees did not believe in the resurrection nearly two thousand years ago. This was their question:

Master, Moses said, If a man die having no children, his brother shall marry his wife and raise up seed unto his brother. Now there were with us seven brethren: and the first, when he had married a wife deceased, and, having no issue, left his wife unto his brother: likewise the second also, and the third unto the seventh. And last of all the woman died also.

Now here is the clever question, you see; this really does knock the bottom out of all this belief in a resurrection!

Therefore in the resurrection whose wife shall she be of the seven? for they all had her.

Can you not hear the laughter and clapping of the crowd! But listen to our Lord's authoritative reply:

Jesus answered and said unto them, Ye do err, not knowing the scriptures, nor the power of God. For in the resurrection they neither marry, nor are given in marriage, but are as the angels of God in heaven. But as touching the resurrection of the dead, have ye not read that which was spoken unto you by God, saying: I am the God of Abraham, and the God of Isaac, and the God of Jacob? God is not the God of the dead, but of the living.

And here is the footnote:

And when the multitude heard this, they were astonished at his doctrine. (Matthew 22:24–33)

Of course they were! He did not hesitate, he did not speculate. Here was one who knew what he was talking about.

And then think of that scene upon the cross: two thieves, one each side of our Lord, and one of them, in a spirit of repentance and shame, said, 'Lord, remember me when thou comest into thy kingdom.' And without a moment's hesitation, though he was enduring the agony of the cross, he turned to this man and said, 'To day shalt thou be with me in paradise' (Luke 23:42–43). Do you feel the authority? He was dying, but he knew!

Now those are samples of our Lord's teaching. But beyond this, beyond the teaching, are evidences that, again, show us the reality of this other realm. Look at his miracles! What were these? He said they were manifestations of 'the finger of God'. He said they meant that 'the kingdom of God is come upon you' (Luke 11:20). This was the power of the world to come. You cannot explain him in any other terms. The miracles were all demonstrations of the realm of God and the supernatural and the eternal.

And then you remember what happened on the Mount of Transfiguration. Our Lord took Peter and James and John with him up on top of the mountain. Suddenly they were overshadowed by a bright cloud, and when they looked at him they saw that an amazing change had taken place. He had become transfigured before them. His face shone like the sun, and his clothes were shining beyond anything that a fuller could ever produce. Then Moses and Elijah appeared and spoke to him and there was a voice from heaven saying, 'This is my beloved Son, in whom I am well pleased; hear ye him' (Matthew 17:1–8). These men never forgot this transfiguration. They saw him, this Jesus whom they had been accompanying, transformed, glorified, with a radiance of heaven shining from him and all through him, and they heard the voice of attestation from heaven.

Now I say that they never forgot this and I have evidence to prove what I am saying. Peter, an old man, at the end of his life, writes his last letter, and he says:

I think it meet, as long as I am in this tabernacle, to stir you up by putting you in remembrance; knowing that shortly I must put off this my tabernacle, even as our Lord Jesus Christ hath shewed me. Moreover I will endeavour that ye may be able after my decease to have these things always in remembrance. For we have not followed cunningly devised fables, when we made known unto you the power and the coming of our Lord Jesus Christ, but were eyewitnesses of his majesty. For he received from God the Father honour and glory, when there came such a voice to him from the excellent glory, This is my beloved Son, in whom I am well pleased. And this voice which came from heaven we heard, when we were with him in the holy mount. (2 Peter 1:13–18)

Now all this is a demonstration and proof of the reality of that life: it proves that our Lord came from it and that he spoke with knowledge and certainty concerning it. But then he was arrested and in apparent utter weakness he was condemned to death. He was crucified on a tree and he died. They took down his body and they laid it in a tomb, and they put a stone in front of it, sealed it and set soldiers to guard it.

But that is not the end of the story. We would not be here this morning if it had not been for this tremendous fact of the resurrection, a literal rising from the dead. The tomb was empty. As has often been said, the resurrection of our Lord is the best-attested fact of history. Then he began to appear to chosen representatives. But there was obviously a great change in him – some of his followers did not even recognize him. Something comparable to what had happened on the Mount of Transfiguration only still more so, had taken place. He could come into a room when all the doors were shut; yet he said he was not a ghost, and demonstrated that by eating broiled fish and honey. A spirit could not have done that. This was the resurrection of the body. Here was one who had risen from the dead.

Now the preaching of the resurrection is not speculation, it is not an idea suddenly thought of by some of his followers. Indeed, after his crucifixion, his own chosen followers were utterly cast down and completely disconsolate. They had lost all hope – until they saw him! This is what put them on their feet and transfigured them and transformed them. It was the literal fact of his rising out of the grave from the dead and appearing for forty days among the chosen witnesses who are listed in that great fifteenth chapter of 1 Corinthians. It was this that turned the unhappy, frightened apostles into bold, confident men. It was all the result of the resurrection. This is history, this is fact – not speculation.

And then he gave them his teaching, and we find the meaning of the resurrection, its message for the early Christians and its message for us. This is how our Lord fulfilled the promise that he gave to the woman of Samaria. Even face to face with death and the grave, we are never at a loss, we are never uncertain, we never thirst. This is the great message of the whole of the New Testament, especially the Acts of the Apostles and the Epistles.

What did the first apostles preach? 'Jesus, and the resurrection' (Acts 17:18). They were in trouble because of that, they were thrown into prison because of it. It is put perfectly by the apostle Paul in his second letter to Timothy. Writing of the Lord Jesus Christ, Paul says, '[He] hath abolished death, and hath brought life and immortality to light through the gospel' (2 Timothy 1:10). What does that mean? Let me give you some headings to guide your meditation this day and during the rest of your life. This is the truth to live by, this is a living faith, this is the way to be triumphant in life and death.

He has 'abolished death'! Now 'abolish' is not perhaps the best translation. The Greek word means, 'made ineffective', 'made powerless', 'broken its power', 'nullified', or perhaps, best of all, 'defeated'. He has defeated death! How has he done that? By actually rising from the dead. That is the final conquest of death. Death had hitherto held everybody in its grip, no one had ever risen from the dead.

'Ah,' you say, 'what about the case of Lazarus?'

That was not resurrection, that was resuscitation: he died again. Our Lord was the first to rise from the dead, the first to burst asunder the bands of death, the first really to conquer death – 'the firstfruits of them that slept' (1 Corinthians 15:20). He has literally, actually, conquered death. He rose the other side of it and still appeared in this world.

But, in addition to that and because of that, he has removed, for all who believe in him, the terror of death and its power over us. Read 1 Corinthians 15 where the apostle Paul puts it perfectly and wonderfully. How is it that we are able to smile in the face of death and no longer be afraid of it? The apostle gives us the explanation:

'The sting of death is sin; and the strength of sin is the law. But thanks be to God, which giveth us the victory through our Lord Jesus Christ' (1 Corinthians 15:56–57).

And this is how he won the victory. The trouble about death is this sinfulness of ours. 'The *sting* of death is sin' – thoughts of that unknown country, the idea of God, the idea of judgement, the idea of retribution. We know we are guilty. We try to explain our guilt away psychologically, but we cannot. The psychologists themselves are in trouble. Here it is – 'and the strength of sin' – the thing that gives power to it, the thing that makes it condemnatory – 'is the law [of God].'

But our Lord, by rising from the dead, gave proof positive that he had satisfied God's Law. It was God who condemned him as a sinner because he had taken our sins upon him on the cross on Calvary's hill; it was the same God who raised him from the dead, and thereby declared that he was satisfied: 'Who was delivered for our offences, and was raised again for our justification' (Romans 4:25).

And so Christians are no longer afraid of death; they do not die; they 'fall asleep' (1 Thessalonians 4:13–14). The sting has been taken out of death. In a physical sense, Christians die, but they do not taste the bitterness of death. The horror and the condemnation and the realization of their folly – they are spared all that. As our Lord put it in the account of Lazarus and Dives, 'and was carried by the angels into Abraham's bosom' (Luke 16:22).

But our Lord has not only removed the terror of death and the grave from us, he has also guaranteed our rising. This is the wonderful teaching! He has risen, and all who believe in him will rise also. We are in him, in a sense, we are already risen with him:

For we know that if our earthly house of this tabernacle were dissolved, we have a building of God, an house not made with hands, eternal in the heavens . . . For we that are in this tabernacle do groan, being

burdened: not for that we would be unclothed, but clothed upon . . .
(2 Corinthians 5:1, 4)

That is the teaching.

And as the apostle Paul puts it in his first chapter of the Epistle to the Philippians, Christ's rising from the dead has changed the whole aspect of death for Christians. He says, 'For to me to live is Christ, and to die is gain.' Then he continues, 'I am in a strait betwixt two' – to stay here is better for the Christians in Philippi, but as for Paul himself, he says – 'having a desire to depart, and to be with Christ; which is far better' (Philippians 1:21, 23). Death has no terror. Death is now just a little rivulet that separates this land of sin and woe from that 'land of pure delight where saints immortal reign' (Isaac Watts).

And, ultimately, we await the resurrection of the body. The Spirit in us is a guarantee that our bodies will be raised. Paul again puts it in incomparable language in the eighth chapter of the Epistle to the Romans, where he says, 'Ourselves also, which have the firstfruits of the Spirit, even we ourselves groan within ourselves, waiting for the adoption' – what is that? – 'to wit, the redemption of our body' (Romans 8:23). This is coming!

> *If the Spirit of him that raised up Jesus from the dead dwell in you, he that raised up Christ from the dead shall also quicken your mortal bodies by his Spirit that dwelleth in you. (Romans 8:11)*

It is certain. Christ is risen! We are risen in spirit, and we will rise in the body. He guarantees this. What has happened to him will happen to us.

So Paul, in one of the most amazing things, in a sense, that he ever said, tells the Corinthians that even death has now become our servant: it is part of our possession. He says:

Therefore let no man glory in men. For all things are yours; whether Paul, or Apollos, or Cephas, or the world, or life, or death, or things present, or things to come; all are yours; and ye are Christ's; and Christ is God's. (1 Corinthians 3:21–23)

There, then, is the difference his resurrection has made to all who believe in him. 'He hath abolished death.' He has defeated death. But beyond that, he has 'brought life and immortality to light through the gospel' (2 Timothy 1:10). I have not time to deal with this as I would like to, but if you are not thrilled at the thought of this, and at the very sound of it, I take leave to ask you to examine whether you are a Christian at all! 'He has brought life and immortality to light' – life! Not merely continuous existence. That is not life; that is the existence that people have in this world. No, life! Full, living, full being, a real life! Oh, our Lord put it like this in some amazing words:

Let not your heart be troubled: ye believe in God, believe also in me. In my Father's house are many mansions: if it were not so, I would have told you. I go to prepare a place for you. And if I go and prepare a place for you, I will come again, and receive you unto myself; that where I am, there ye may be also. (John 14:1–3)

That is life! With him. And with him for ever and for ever. It is a glorified life. This mortal flesh cannot inherit immortality, this corruption cannot inherit incorruption. There is going to be a change, a transformation. He was changed himself – he arose in a glorified body. And our bodies will also be glorified. No longer will there be these old bodies; the body will be the same, but it will be transfigured, transformed, glorified. There will be no disease, no weakness, no decay. There will be an eternal, a spiritual, a glorified body – and oh! – the glory and the wonder of it all! There will be no sighing there, there will be no sin, there will be no sorrow, there will be no weeping, there will be no parting, there will be no death. It is an entirely new realm and an entirely new kind of life:

> There shall we see his face
> And never, never sin!
> There, from the rivers of his grace,
> Drink endless pleasures in.
>
> *Isaac Watts*

That is what he has opened for us. He has brought this to light – real life!

Oh, listen to this from the book of Revelation:

After this I beheld, and, lo, a great multitude, which no man could number, of all nations, and kindreds, and people, and tongues, stood before the throne, and before the Lamb, clothed with white robes, and palms in their hands; and cried with a loud voice, saying, Salvation to our God which sitteth upon the throne, and unto the Lamb.

And there they are praising him.

And one of the elders answered, saying unto me, What are these which are arrayed in white robes? and whence came they? And I said unto him, Sir, thou knowest. And he said to me, These are they which came out of great tribulation, and have washed their robes, and made them white in the blood of the Lamb. Therefore are they before the throne of God, and serve him day and night in his temple: and he that sitteth on the throne shall dwell among them. They shall hunger no more, neither thirst any more; neither shall the sun light on them, nor any heat. For the Lamb which is in the midst of the throne shall feed them, and shall lead them unto living fountains of waters: and God shall wipe away all tears from their eyes. (Revelation 7:9–10, 13–17)

That is it! That is life! He has brought it to light. You and I shall be glorified. This is what Paul means when he talks in Romans 8 about 'the manifestation of the sons of God':

I reckon that the sufferings of this present time are not worthy to be compared with the glory which shall be revealed in us. For the earnest expectation of the creature waiteth for the [glorious] manifestation of the sons [children] of God. (Romans 8:18–19)

The whole creation is going to rejoice in it and partake of it.

But, above all this, we shall see him face to face; we shall see him as he is. Beyond even that, we shall see God! 'Blessed are the pure in heart: for they shall see God' (Matthew 5:8). That is what our Lord has opened for us. And do you know what will happen when you see God? Let the apostle Paul give you the answer. Here he is at the end of his life, writing his last letter:

For I am now ready to be offered, and the time of my departure is at hand. I have fought a good fight, I have finished my course, I have kept the faith. Henceforth there is laid up for me a crown of righteousness, which the Lord, the righteous judge, shall give me at that day: and not to me only, but unto all them also that love his appearing. (2 Timothy 4:6–8)

Not only seeing God, but hearing the words, 'Well done, thou good and faithful servant' (Matthew 25:21), and God will put the crown of righteousness on our brows – even on ours! And we shall share the bliss, the joy, the glory, of eternity with God the Father, God the Son and God the Holy Spirit. There we shall be 'lost in wonder, love and praise'.

He never fails. He gives full satisfaction – in life, in death and for ever. We shall spend our eternity singing together in great unison: 'Thou art worthy . . . for thou wast slain, and hast redeemed us to God by thy blood' (Revelation 5:9).

25

Guidance

Jesus answered and said unto her, Whosoever drinketh of this water shall thirst again: but whosoever drinketh of the water that I shall give him shall never thirst; but the water that I shall give him shall be in him a well of water springing up into everlasting life. (John 14:13–14)

We have been looking together at various aspects of life as we live it, as we know it and as we have to contend with it, and we have seen that a satisfaction is always given in the gospel that is to be found there alone.

But I move on now to a further question, because it is one that often perplexes people. And, again, we are able to say, and must say, that our Lord's claim fails if he himself, his teaching and all that he gives us cannot help us at this point, too. I am referring to the question of guidance. Now I am not talking here so much of guidance in a moral and ethical sense – which we have already dealt with – as guidance from a more general aspect, guidance with respect to what we are to do in particular circumstances.

We are all very familiar with this problem – here are certain possibilities before us, what are we to do? Perhaps there is no problem that brings people so frequently to the minister of the gospel in his pastoral office as just this question. We want to do the right thing, but the question is how to discover what that is. Now our Lord says, 'Whosoever drinketh of the water that I shall give him shall never thirst,' which we have interpreted as meaning, 'shall never be in any kind of final perplexity, shall never be beside himself, shall never be torn asunder'. And that includes the whole question of guidance.

Now, once more, the world patently cannot help us here. The best it can offer us is worldly wisdom: 'An eye to the main chance'; 'Do the best you can for yourself', and so on. But most people find that unsatisfactory. Many therefore talk about 'luck', they talk about accident and chance, they consult astrologers, fortune-tellers, they dabble in spiritism. Now all this, of course, just shows that there is no satisfactory answer in the world. Yet people display a longing for some authoritative answer, for some certainty, in these matters.

Now we grant that there is an average kind of person who goes through life fairly well, who 'muddles through', and things, on the whole, do not cause them much difficulty. That is very often because such people do not think, they are just content with their given lot. Their whole outlook is narrow and small. Think of the millions in this country and in every other country who live like that. They go to work, because without money you cannot have a house, you cannot have food and drink, you cannot bring up a family. But there it is, they fit into this little life that goes round in a circle – 'nine to five' – and nothing bigger is ever a consideration.

But the moment people become Christians, all sorts of other possibilities open out before them. And, indeed, it is right and true to say that when one does become a Christian, one is confronted by new problems, one can no longer go on living a mechanical life, there are new considerations, new thoughts, new possibilities, new questions. In other words – and many of you, I know, have had this experience – the first thing that happened when you became a Christian was that you asked yourself: 'Is my job, or the work that I am doing, right for a Christian?' Now that is the sort of problem that we are considering.

The world, then, really cannot help us, so what is the teaching here? Can our Lord's claim be substantiated? I suggest that it can, and that there are principles that we can follow. This is a very difficult and large subject, and I can only lay down certain general guiding principles, but I, personally, find them more than adequate and have often found them to be equally helpful to others.

The first proposition we lay down is this: in the spiritual realm there is no such thing as automatic or mechanical guidance. I have to start with this because many people have gone astray at this point. They have misunderstood certain statements of Scripture, taking them to mean that the moment you become a Christian you no longer have any problems or difficulties about what to do; you are given direct and immediate guidance that is always right, and you will never go wrong again.

But we must correct that immediately. If you read the beginning of Acts chapter 16, you will find there a final and sufficient answer to such a wrong idea. Here is the apostle Paul, of all men, with his great experiences and with his knowledge of the Lord, and this is what we are told:

Now when they had gone throughout Phrygia and the region of Galatia, and were forbidden of the Holy Ghost to preach the word in Asia

– the apostle Paul and his companions were anxious to preach in Asia. They clearly believed that it was the right thing to do and they

were going ahead, but 'were forbidden of the Holy Ghost'. Now
the apostle was a great evangelist. He had been called to evangelize
and preach, to found churches and establish them. The world was
his parish and he had felt that it was right to go into Asia, but he
was not allowed. Then the same thing happened again –

> *after they were come to Mysia, they assayed to go into Bithynia: but the*
> *Spirit suffered them not. (Acts 16:6–7)*

In both instances, the apostle had to be restrained, in some
striking manner, by the Holy Spirit. The only deduction that can
be drawn from that is that guidance is clearly not automatic or
mechanical. We must never think it is. I could keep you by giving
you examples from history, from the history of the church in
particular, of great tragedies that have happened because very
good, sincere and honest people have gone astray in this very
respect. There is always the danger of identifying our wills with
the will of God.

Then, on top of that, of course, there is the teaching in the New
Testament about the influence of 'evil spirits'. The people who are
most prone to the kind of danger to which I am referring are those
who are most concerned about living a truly spiritual life. They are
interested in the doctrine concerning the Holy Spirit and in all the
activities of the Spirit. They are not cold, detached intellectuals
who are merely interested in abstract truth. No, no; these are
spiritual people and they want to live life on a high spiritual level.
So they put themselves, as it were, at the disposal of the Spirit, and
their danger is to forget that in doing that they are partly also
putting themselves at the disposal of evil spirits. So we read these
exhortations in the Scriptures: 'Beloved, believe not every spirit,
but try the spirits whether they are of God' (1 John 4:1); 'Prove all
things; hold fast that which is good' (1 Thessalonians 5:21).

So you can see immediately that there are many great dangers just at this point of knowing God's guidance, and as this has been the experience of Christians throughout the history of the church, and is still the case today, it is very important that we should consider this subject. Some of the freak religious movements that arose in the past, especially during the last century, and particularly in the USA, were characterized by this very belief in immediate, infallible guidance, and tragedies often resulted.

So we go on to a further classification of this whole matter and I would suggest that we can divide this question of guidance into two main groups – the exceptional and the usual. We must do this because, clearly, this distinction is drawn in the Scriptures themselves, both in the Old Testament and the New. There is such a thing as exceptional guidance – it is very wrong to exclude it. We find it described in the Old Testament and in the New in terms of 'visions'. We read quite a lot about dreams in the Old Testament – not so much in the New – and there are visions in both Old and New Testaments. People were directed to do things through a vision and in that vision they were given guidance. And, similarly, guidance came to people through dreams. This is something that we must recognize.

Now it is very interesting to me to see how that one paragraph in Acts 16 deals with both the exceptional and the usual forms of guidance. Have you ever noticed this striking contrast? The apostle and his companion had been prohibited by the Holy Spirit from going to Asia and Bithynia and, as the result of that, they had to go down to Troas. They had not been able to go there, they had not been able to go here, and so they just went straight on and came to Troas, and as that happened to be a seaport, they could not go any further. Now here was the question: What were they to do? And you remember the answer that was given – 'the man of Macedonia'. This was a vision:

> *A vision appeared to Paul in the night; There stood a man of Macedonia, and prayed him, saying, Come over into Macedonia, and help us. And after he had seen the vision, immediately we endeavoured to go into Macedonia, assuredly gathering that the Lord had called us for to preach the gospel unto them. (Acts 16:9–10)*

Now this is quite exceptional. The apostle Paul, in the course of living his Christian life, and filled with the Spirit, had thought that he ought to go to Asia, and then to Bithynia – but no, he was wrong. Then he was given this vision in the night and he 'assuredly gathered', he was certain, that this was God's will. This is the way in which the gospel first came to Europe. It was a new departure, and God gave his servant a vision in order to show him what to do.

Peter, too, had a vision, similar in general, though not in the details. For Peter, it was with regard to his going to preach to the household of Cornelius. This was a tremendous thing for a Jew to do. Though Peter had been baptized with the Spirit on the Day of Pentecost, he was still tending to think in Jewish terms, so how could he preach this message to Gentiles? But God gave him a vision of a sheet coming down filled with all kinds of animals, clean and unclean, and then gave the command, 'Rise, Peter; kill, and eat.' Peter's immediate objection was that he had never eaten anything unclean. But in that vision Peter was given guidance, understanding and instruction (Acts 10).

Now exceptional guidance is always clear, unmistakable and assured. There are many illustrations in the lives of the saints and in the lives of men and women of outstanding qualities whom God has raised up in connection with the life of the church. There was, for instance, the guidance given to Hudson Taylor as he was walking on a beach in the south of England, in which he received the whole conception of the China Inland Mission. Now I am emphasizing that this kind of guidance is exceptional because there is a certain type of person who is always trying to live in this realm of the unusual. A man once wrote a book with the title *Ten Thousand Miles of Miracles in Great Britain*. His life was supposed to be a series of miracles. But that is a contradiction of terms: miracles are not as common as that, so what happened to him was obviously not miraculous. He was thinking in a loose kind of way. No, miracles are unusual, and this kind of guidance is exceptional. But God forbid that anybody should understand me to be saying that it does not happen. It does. Thank God, it does! It has to happen at times. There are situations such as those I have described, and it may be a time such as this, when we are in need of something exceptional.

Let me give a final illustration before we move on. The kind of distinction between what I am calling the usual and the exceptional is the difference between the regular work of the Holy Spirit in the church, and revival. Revival is not perpetual. By definition, it is not. Revival is exceptional and it comes in God's own time. And it is exactly the same with this immediate, unmistakable guidance that enables someone to say, 'I gather assuredly that this is what God is calling me to do and I'll go and do it,' exactly as Paul went from Troas and landed in Samothracia and went through Neapolis to Philippi, bringing the gospel into Europe.

So let us turn now to the usual, to that which is more customary. This is what applies to most of us in our daily lives. Now the following, it seems to me, are the biblical principles with regard to this matter. First, we start with a general doctrine of vocation, a doctrine of calling. This was one of the grand discoveries made by

Martin Luther. At the time of the Reformation, he was given to see that God calls people who are not in the ministry or in the priesthood, that there is a calling and a vocation even with regard to such an activity as sweeping a room.

Now this is the general doctrine. It declares that God knows us individually, and is concerned about us individually, that he endows us with different capacities and faculties and calls us to different tasks, to different callings. This is clearly taught in the Scriptures. For instance, in Ephesians 4, Paul says with regard to the church that '[God] gave some, apostles; and some, prophets; and some, evangelists; and some, pastors and teachers' (verse 11). All this goes under the general heading of vocation. In Romans 13:1–7, we find that Paul says, 'the powers that be are ordained of God', and people are called to these tasks. It is very important to start with that general principle, based on the fact that God is our Father, that he has numbered the very hairs of our head and knows all about us and is concerned about us. We must always keep in our minds this truth that God has a purpose for every one of us. It is a general principle, a general, overarching idea.

Then, secondly, these general biblical principles with regard to life are applied to our daily lives. We must not be absurd about this, of course; the Bible has no detailed instructions for the scientist on how he is to work in his laboratory or what he is to do next. That is not what I mean. I mean that in this book, in the Scriptures, we are given certain broad principles with regard to our conduct. We are given them not only in a moral and ethical sense, but also in a more general sense and they combine with our common sense to produce what we may call the 'enlightened common sense' that should characterize every single Christian. As we have been showing earlier, when we are born again, there is not a part of us that is not affected. By nature, we all have an element of judgement and of wisdom and of common sense, but when we become Christians, that is all heightened. We no longer have the world's version of common sense – 'rule of thumb' and so on – but an 'enlightenment' – everything in us is sharpened by the Holy Spirit, every faculty is influenced by the Spirit in this general way.

So, then, these two come together – the teaching of Scripture and enlightened common sense and understanding, so that if you have a feeling that you ought not to be doing something, then, if it is something that the Bible prohibits, you need not consider it any further. You know you must not do it, you know it is an attack of the devil.

Now there are people who have got into trouble over this matter; let me give you one illustration. I remember very well in the early days of the last war reading an article by the late Dr C. S. Lewis, who had just become a Christian. As an unbeliever he had been a lecturer, a professor in English literature in Oxford, and he wrote that when he became a Christian, he at once began to feel that he could no longer go on being a teacher of English literature; what has English literature got to do with the Christian faith, with the spiritual life? He had a feeling that he must give that up and do something more specifically Christian. Now I have no doubt that there are many who have had this exact experience, in fact, I know there are. There are people who have been teaching various subjects and have become Christians and have said, 'How can I go on teaching that any longer?' There is this feeling that we tend to get in our early days in the Christian life that we must all be doing something that is specifically Christian. But that is a fallacy.

The teaching of the Bible is that we are to do all things to the glory of God (1 Corinthians 10:31), and general culture comes under that heading. It is wrong to regard anything that is not specifically Christian as therefore valueless for the Christian; there is a place for general culture. Now, of course, the Christian will always know the limits in these matters, but as Dr C. S. Lewis came to see, his feeling had been quite wrong. So he went on with his work as a professor of English literature.

Now it is only an understanding of the biblical teaching that leads us to draw that kind of distinction. You can glorify God in art, in music, in so many realms of life. Anything that is wrong, of course, does not glorify God, so is excluded. The Scriptures show that. But if it is not wrong, it comes under the heading of all things bringing glory to God. And that is what I mean by saying that the general principles of biblical teaching plus an enlightened common sense and understanding are the basic way in which we proceed with regard to the great question of guidance.

But having put it like that very broadly and generally, I must move on to my third point, because we are not left with just the general teaching and our enlightened understanding, there is something more here – there is an inward leading. And it is at this point that so many of us have so often been in trouble. By 'inward leading' I mean a pressure on one's spirit. Something comes to you; you have not sought it – it came to you and you tried to dismiss it, but it keeps coming back. There is a kind of pressure urging you, as it were, to do something, to take up something, or to proceed to a given place and do something in a given direction.

Now this again is plainly taught in the Scriptures and it is exemplified constantly in the lives of God's people throughout the centuries. But at this point also danger again comes in. There is the danger of fanaticism, or of exaggerating or misunderstanding this inward leading, or of turning it into something that is isolated from the teaching of the Scripture, something that is infallible and immediate and direct. This has brought many people into trouble and into distress, so what do we do about it? We begin by recognizing this inward leading. There is nothing more valuable, nothing, in a sense, that is higher than this in the realm of experience, except that which is quite exceptional; but how do we avoid the danger of misinterpretation or of fanaticism?

Again, the Scripture provides certain tests. The first is that God's leadings always conform to certain patterns. That is what is so marvellous about the work of the Almighty. Look at the flowers, look at the seasons; God's work is always on a pattern. And if you find that you seem to be having a leading that does not fit into the general pattern found in the Scriptures and in Christian biographies, you should always be suspicious of it. The devil tries to counterfeit this, but he generally overdoes it, he makes the leading too dramatic, too wonderful. You remember how he tempted our Lord to go and throw himself down from the pinnacle of the Temple – that kind of exaggeration is the mark of the devil always. God's leadings are more rational, they fit into this general pattern.

Secondly, God's leadings never suggest that we should do something that is against God's own laws and ways. Let me give you two examples. I remember reading about a woman in the early centuries of the Christian church, a very godly, spiritually minded woman who believed in the leading of the Spirit. She believed the whole teaching of the Bible and was anxious to give herself and her best to God and to be doing God's will. Now this good woman reached a stage in which she believed that God was calling her to leave her husband and her children to go and live a monastic life. She really believed that she had received a direct leading of the Spirit. She was genuine and was prepared to make the sacrifice. And so that is what she did. Mark you, her heart was breaking as she was doing it, and the record even tells us that as she was going away and could hear the crying of her little children, though it was breaking her heart, she felt it was well-pleasing to God and the pain was the measure of her obedience.

But she was completely wrong. Why? She was wrong because she was violating one of the very principles of God's own teaching. A woman is never called upon to leave her husband and her children in order to serve God. It is plainly contradictory of God's laws with regard to marriage and the family and the home and the subjection of the wife to the husband and many other principles that I could enumerate. But that is the kind of tangle into which the devil in his malice can lead us; that is one of the ways in which he can lead us astray. So the principle I am laying down is that God's inward leading never blankly contradicts his plain teaching in the Scriptures with regard to certain fundamental matters.

Let me give you another illustration. I once knew a bank manager who felt that he was called of God to give up his work in the bank and become a preacher, an evangelist and perhaps a pastor. Now he had a wife and two daughters, and they were entirely opposed to this idea, but in spite of that, he went ahead, causing his family great misery. Large numbers of people regarded this man as someone who had done something very fine. They said, 'This is what Christians should do.' But I dissent entirely from that view. My principle, which I have often had to apply, is that when a man in such a position comes to talk to me, the first thing I always ask him is this: 'Is your wife in agreement?' I ask that because a man must never divorce himself in any sense – you cannot divorce yourself and please God. You cannot divide yourself from your wife, you cannot leave her. The man and wife are one: 'They twain shall be one flesh' (Matthew 19:5). They have been united by God, you cannot break that. There is to be this consensus, this agreement.

This principle that the guidance of God will never lead us to break any of his own ordinances is vital and can be applied along a very wide range of issues – including the order of creation, under which we put marriage, family, the home and so on. There is consistency always in God's guidance.

The final way in which I would illustrate this principle of consistency is that God never acts in what I may call – I cannot think of a better term – a freakish manner. Now people who claim guidance often do behave in a very freakish way. I can deal with this by repeating a story of something that once happened to the great Charles Haddon Spurgeon. A man came to him at the end of a service and said that the Spirit had told him that he was to preach in Spurgeon's Tabernacle the following Thursday night. He was certain of this. Now Mr Spurgeon's answer was not only full of common sense, but also full of biblical teaching and understanding. He said, 'Well, it is a very strange thing that the Spirit has not told me that,' and so the man did not preach in Spurgeon's Tabernacle on the following Thursday!

You see the principle that is involved? If it had been the leading of the Spirit that this man should preach in Mr Spurgeon's pulpit on that Thursday night, it is clear and obvious from God's way of acting that he would also have told Mr Spurgeon. Mr Spurgeon, without saying it, was applying that rule. There is a general consistency about God's way of guidance, and recognizing that is how we defeat the devil. The devil's counterfeits always overdo it, they are too clever, too wonderful, they always have this odd, freakish element and do not conform to the wholeness, the amazing pattern, that is ever the characteristic of God's dealings with us.

So, then, we have the Scriptures, we have enlightened common sense, we have an inward leading, which we can check: we must 'prove all things' (1 Thessalonians 5:21), and 'try [test] the spirits' (1 John 4:1). Do not assume that because you like the idea that comes to you, it must be the Spirit – prove it!

And then, what else? Well, according to the teaching of the Scripture, when we are seeking guidance, other people can be of help to us. What are pastors and teachers for? They are to give guidance, they are to give instruction and help, it is a part of their function, part of why they were ordained of God. Christ has set them in the church to give answers, to give help in these matters. Therefore, talking together about these questions is something that we are exhorted to do. We do not just take a stand on our own opinion. If we do not acknowledge and respect those who are called and ordained of God to lead us and guide us, then we are breaking God's Law, and Christ's own law for the church. We are to respect those who are set over us in these matters of the faith. And then together with them, perhaps, those who are not pastors and teachers but are spiritually minded, can also help us. We seek the mind of God together, we discuss the questions we have in the light of the scriptural teaching and we pray together.

Now, of course, all these ways of finding God's guidance have their risks, and one of the dangers that a pastor always has to guard himself against is that of becoming other people's conscience. There are people who are in perplexity and they would make the pastor their conscience; they say, 'Tell me what to do.' Now the pastor must never do that. He can give advice, he can give his knowledge of the Scriptures and scriptural principles, he can consider the circumstances, he takes the story as it is told him into consideration, but he must never become anybody's conscience.

And, indeed, I also want to emphasize your side of that statement. You must never allow anybody else to become your conscience. I have often had people come to me who are in trouble because they went to a missionary meeting where the terrible need in a certain country was put before them and pressure was brought to bear upon them. The principle that was put forward was, 'the need is the call'. 'Here is the need,' they were told, 'what are you going to do about it?' And they were made to feel that they were almost criminals if they did not stand up immediately and say they were ready to give themselves in response to the missionary call.

Now that to me is sheer false teaching. To start with, the need is not the call, otherwise every Christian would be in whole-time service in some part of the world. Look at the need today, we would all be having to go out as missionaries. The need is not the call because that contradicts the whole doctrine of vocation. But it is still worse when emotional and other forms of pressure are brought to bear upon people. This is thoroughly bad. God does not lead like that. It is all done with a very good motive, but it often leads to muddle and to tragedies, even on the missionary field.

That, then, is the whole principle of how other people can help but of the need to take care lest such help be abused or we make a wrong decision through our lack of understanding. Now I come to certain final general rules that I have found to be of considerable value in my own life and in my attempts to help others.

First, never try to anticipate God's leading. That is, do not sit down and start putting questions to yourself, such as: Is it right to be doing this? Ought I to be doing it? The rule is this: Go on with your work and if it is not God's will that you should be doing it, he will stop you. Do not anticipate him. Do not put theoretical questions to yourselves. Do not create problems. Go on living your life; go on living the Christian life. Follow the teaching of 1 Corinthians 7:20: 'Let every man abide in the same calling wherein he was called.' Go on with that; that is your business and mine.

Then, secondly, tell God, and tell him this honestly – and this to me is perhaps the most important principle of all – that you put yourself entirely in his hands. The moment you become a Christian, you should do that. You cannot believe in Christ as simply your Saviour; you cannot divide him. He is your Lord always. To say that you can take him as your Saviour without taking him as your Lord is, again, a contradiction of plain biblical teaching. You should put yourself unreservedly in God's hands and tell him that your one desire is to know his will and to do his will. If you can say that honestly, then there is a sense in which you have done everything you can do. Say that, then leave it to him. If you say that to God, you have no right to take it back to yourself – leave it with him. But you must be honest, you must be able to say, 'I want to know your will, and I want to do your will and to live to your glory.' Say that, give yourself entirely to him, then go on with your work.

Then, thirdly, watch for openings and at the same time watch for closings. I am again referring to what happened to Paul in Acts 16:6–7. You go on doing your work, but you are a spiritually minded person and while you are not creating the problem, or thinking theoretically, you always have your eyes open. God approaches us and speaks to us, as we have been seeing, in many different ways. A door appears to be opening and you will probably come to the conclusion, 'Here it is!' but suddenly it is shut! Watch for that. In other words, never force a door open. If it is merely ajar, do not pull it open; never be violent. Never force in any sense but just be watchful.

And that leads me to the next point, which is this: be prepared for delays and for testings. Oh, this is a tremendous thing! God tests us! It is his way of training us, it is his way of enabling us to grow. So nothing is more important than that we should be patient. Is that not one of your biggest problems? We are in such a hurry. God is never in a hurry and the more Christian we become, the less we shall hurry. There are foolish people who have talked at different times about evangelizing the whole world in this generation, or something like that. Nonsense! They were proved wrong in the past, and those who say that kind of thing today will equally be proved to be wrong. Be prepared for delays, disappointments, discouragements. You say: 'Here it is at last!' And then you find it is not. It is all right; be patient.

Then I come to what I have had to say more frequently than anything else in this pastoral context. Make sure of Philippians 4:6–7:

> *Be careful for nothing [in nothing be anxious]; but in every thing [all things] by prayer and supplication with thanksgiving let your requests be made known unto God. And the peace of God, which passeth all understanding, shall keep your hearts and minds through Christ Jesus.*

Never be anxious! In nothing be anxious! Never be tense, never be worried, never be troubled, never be frantic, never be divided – never.

Now I generally put that to people like this. They come and they put their position to me, and they are perplexed and troubled. Sometimes they give me the impression that I have only to say, 'Do this!' and they will do it. I will not say that, I am in no position to do so. I cannot be their conscience. I do not know the will of God for people. What I say is this: 'Look here, you're worried about the wrong thing; you're worried about what you are supposed to be doing, what you ought to be doing. Is it this or is it that? But what you ought to be worried about is this: Have you got the peace of God which passes all understanding?

Now that is a paradox, is it not? But I mean this: Whether or not you are to go to Japan or to India is not the question. Though you do not know where you are to go, or what you are to do, or whether, perhaps, you are to stay doing what you are now doing, does not matter. What is important for you is that you should *always* enjoy the peace of God which passes all understanding (Philippians 4:7). Whatever the position, if you concentrate on that, you will find that it will solve most of your problems of guidance, because that will lead you to stop analysing and considering and weighing and measuring and always coming back to the same uncertainty. Leave it all with him and be concerned about this relationship to him.

And then my final principle is this: Never move; never do anything until the last signal falls. The final signal is that you are unanimous. I have talked about the unanimity of the family. I am now talking about *your* unanimity. Listen to this:

Hast thou faith? have it to thyself before God. Happy is he that condemneth not himself in that thing which he alloweth. And he that doubteth is damned if he eat, because he eateth not of faith: for whatsoever is not of faith is sin. (Romans 14:22–23)

These words just mean that however pure your mind may be about something, if there is doubt and hesitation, do not move – your head and your heart must be unanimous. When God guides, he guides the whole person, there is no division, no uncertainty. God persuades the mind and the heart, and they act in a great and a wonderful unison – 'whatsoever is not of faith is sin'. In this passage, Paul is talking about eating meat that had been offered to idols, but that is only an illustration. It does not matter what it is, if there is a doubt in it, or something is restraining you, do not move, wait until the final signal drops, then move on, and you will be moving on in the direction of God's will.

You can always be certain, my dear friend, that if you have fulfilled honestly these conditions I have been laying down to you, then even if you find that you have done something that is wrong, you will never suffer for it. God is your Father, and a father does not punish a child when he knows the child is doing his best – at least, not if he is a father worthy of the name. God is our Father, and if you and I have honestly sought his will and have been concerned about honouring and glorifying his great and holy name – even though we may prove to have been wrong and to have been misled, he will not punish us; indeed, he will even be able – as he is able – to take our very mistakes and turn them into blessings; he will honour our desire and our faithfulness to him. So you need never worry, you need never be anxious; even then you will enjoy 'the peace which passeth all understanding', for you will have had a vision of his heart of love such as you had never had before, and he will enfold you in his arms as his fallible child who nevertheless loves him and is anxious to promote his glory.

Well, that is more than enough – that is the final thing. And so you see our Lord's claim is fully justified in the matter of guidance as in all others: 'He that drinks of the water that I shall give him shall never thirst, no, never, as long as the world stands.' Those who drink this water know that they are right with God and that 'all things work together for good to them that love God'.

26

The Secret Things of God

Jesus answered and said unto her, Whosoever drinketh of this water shall thirst again: but whosoever drinketh of the water that I shall give him shall never thirst; but the water that I shall give him shall be in him a well of water springing up into everlasting life. (John 4:13–14)

As we have been considering these words together, we have seen that the world cannot meet our needs, it cannot solve our problems, it cannot give us that which we fundamentally long for. But our Lord says that he can and he will, if we but take of this water that he has to give. So we are examining this statement, testing ourselves and our own experiences, and we have started with the mind, with the intellect and the understanding. Our Lord claims that he can give complete satisfaction to our minds – these minds with their questions.

We have examined this from various aspects and have found that it is true with regard to life in general, with regard to the way of salvation and to problems that arise, such as the problems of pain, suffering and war. Our Lord answers the accusations of conscience and he answers our questionings about death and the grave and what lies beyond. He has conquered even this last enemy, and has 'brought life and immortality to light through the gospel' (2 Timothy 1:10). In our last study, we looked at the question of guidance, a very vexed question that tends to agitate us all, and we found that there again, in his way, as revealed in the teaching of the Bible, he gives us the satisfaction that we stand in need of.

Well, now, having gone through all that, it seems to me that we have reached the point when we can consider what I would regard as the final problem. I say 'final problem' in a general or generic sense because I want to consider with you some questions that we may put together under the heading of 'Residual problems and difficulties'. I could look at these individually, but in order to save time and to advance with this great theme and show how our Lord satisfies the heart and the will as well as the mind, I am putting them all together.

What do I mean by 'residual problems'? Well, I am thinking of a subject such as this: God himself! We talk about God, but the being and the nature of God and the eternity of God are a problem to the mind. Then there is the whole problem of the origin of evil. Many people are troubled and agitated about that. Where did evil come from? How is evil possible? How is it compatible with a holy God and with what we postulate with respect to him? Linked to all this is the mystery of God's ways, God's dealings with humanity in general, and with men and women as individuals: it is a great problem. How are we to understand God's ways, how reconcile them with other aspects of the truth concerning him? You are familiar with these questions.

To take some specific questions, there is the problem of why it is that some people are saved and become Christians and some do not. This often worries people. What determines why some are believers and some are not? Then many people are troubled about the condition of the lost: eternal punishment, hell, God's punishment of sin. How do you reconcile that with the love of God? And there is the problem of why some people die young and others live to an old age. Why is it that very often those who seem to be evil go on living a long life, while the good die young? But perhaps beyond all these there lies the question: What happens after death? Heaven! What is heaven like? What happens there? Why are we told so little about it?

I could add to the list, but I am simply picking out typical problems that so often trouble the minds of men and women. Sometimes people say that these questions prevent them from being Christians, while at other times it is Christians who raise these questions because of what has happened to them or because somebody has put the question to them in an argument. Every pastor, every minister, knows what it is like to be plied with such questions.

Now all these questions have an element in common – they are all in the realm of the ultimate, they all belong to that realm that is above us. I need not waste any time in pointing out how the world quite obviously cannot help us here. The world is either not interested or, when it is, only adds to the difficulties and exaggerates them and aggravates the problem. The world does not understand. It is very good at asking questions – but there is nothing clever about asking questions; any fool can do that. The world never gets beyond that. It can raise the difficulties, it can show you the problems and it does so constantly. But it cannot bring us anywhere near even to the beginning of an understanding. It gives no satisfaction at all.

But here is the question: Does our Lord satisfy us here? Can he who says, 'Whosoever drinketh of the water that I shall give him shall never thirst' give satisfaction even with regard to these residual problems?

Now we know that he can. But can we demonstrate it? Moreover, are we ourselves able to say, 'Yes, I am satisfied even here'? To help one another come to that satisfaction, and to strengthen one another, let us proceed to see how our Lord does this. I would put the answer under two main headings. The first is general, and the second is detailed or particular.

Now I start with the general answer because it is very important that we should be clear about certain things. The first point is a negative. The Bible is the Lord's book, it is his word, it is here that he gives satisfaction to the mind and to the understanding, but – and I start with this as a general proposition – the Scriptures do not give us complete, detailed answers with regard to all these questions. To me, it is tremendously important that we should always be ready to say that, and we must not be afraid to say it, we must not even say it reluctantly. Christian people often get into trouble because they seem to think that they should have a detailed answer to every single question that is put to them. But that is not the case. The Bible does not pretend to put us into that position.

In other words, as I have said before, we must never regard the Bible as a sort of ready reckoner – here is the problem, you just turn up some verses and there is the answer. That is never true of the Scripture. It has, as we have been seeing, its didactic teaching, its explicit statements, which are clear and unmistakable; other questions it deals with more generally, leaving us in the realm of principles. And there is a good reason for that, as we shall see.

But I hasten to another negative. Because we do not have complete and detailed answers, we must not think that we can then swing or fly to the other extreme and be obscurantist. This is equally important. Obscurantism means that you refuse to think, you refuse to employ your understanding, you just dig in your heels, as it were, and become irritable. It means you refuse to consider any questions and even resent them, merely making dogmatic statements such as, 'This is what I say,' or, 'This is what the Bible says.' It is burying your head in the sand, refusing to employ the gifts that God has given you to understand the teaching of the Scripture. Obscurantism does great harm to the Christian faith. People who become obscurantist and make dogmatic statements without being able to give reasons for them have to adopt this stance because they really are in trouble, and are unhappy. So they retreat and erect a barrier round themselves. They are not satisfied, and they most certainly do not help anybody else; indeed, they tend to hinder them.

We must avoid the two extremes of trying to give detailed answers to everything or of answering nothing. We cannot answer everything, but we do not retreat into a kind of castle of obscurantism and lose contact with the world that is round and about us. But what is our Lord's method? How does our Lord give satisfaction when we are faced with these residual problems?

Well, in the first instance, it seems to me, our Lord immediately takes the excitement out of these problems, and this is wonderful, as I hope to show you. I am sure that you are familiar with the way in which people come with this kind of problem and look worried: 'I don't see this, I can't understand that, and I don't know how these can be reconciled.' They are troubled and disturbed. And our Lord's method always is to remove completely this worry, agitation and confusion. As far as our intellects are concerned, we are no longer like the Scripture's description of the sinner: 'like the troubled sea, when it cannot rest, whose waters cast up mire and dirt' (Isaiah 57:20). There is immediately a balance and a poise that go a long way in the direction of this final satisfaction.

So there it is in general, but let us work this out together in detail. How does our Lord do this? First, he always deals with our spirit, and this is the key. The real trouble in connection with these various problems is always, ultimately, in the realm of the spirit, our heart, if you like, in the biblical sense of that term; and our Lord gives us satisfaction by putting that right.

Now this, of course, is something that happens inevitably at conversion, and it is a proof that we are truly converted. When the Holy Spirit deals with us, he humbles us. You cannot be a Christian without being humbled. Every man and woman who has been regenerated has been humbled. The Spirit does this by convicting us of sin. Our Lord made this quite clear more than once. He said, 'Except ye be converted, and become as little children, ye shall not enter into the kingdom of heaven' (Matthew 18:3). That is how he put it to Nicodemus, who asked, 'How can these things be?' (John 3:9). Nicodemus wanted to understand. 'How can a man be born when he is old?' (verse 4). Here it is, this agitation, this trouble, this excitement. You remember how our Lord treated Nicodemus? He humbled him!

Verily, verily, I say unto thee, Except a man be born again, he cannot see the kingdom of God . . . Except a man be born of water and of the Spirit, he cannot enter into the kingdom of God. (John 3:3, 5)

He must be humbled and become as a little child:

Marvel not that I said unto thee, Ye must be born again. (John 3:7)

This is an essential part of the whole process of conversion and, remember, it happens to the mind, it happens to the whole personality. We are humbled, our spirits are put right in the sense that we are laid low.

Now you see the value of this when dealing with these residual problems. Through the word, the Holy Spirit tells us and shows us the truth about human nature, about ourselves – not, in the first instance, about our own individual problems, but about human beings in general, man as man. This is the first thing we all need. Most of the troubles in the world are due to the fact that man has a wrong idea about man. We are living in an age when man is worshipping man; man has become the God, he is the arbiter of everything. It is his understanding that controls everything. So the first thing that is necessary is that we should have a true conception of man. And what we are told about him is that he is finite. Even at the beginning he was finite; even when perfect, he was still finite. He was not God, he was only a human being.

This is a tremendous fact. We must realize that man at his best is limited. There is an essential qualitative difference between God and man, and man, therefore, by definition, even when in a state of perfection, can never span the infinite, the absolute and the eternal. And the moment you realize that, you are well on the road to dealing with these residual questions and problems that we are looking at.

But when you understand further that man is fallen and that as the result of the Fall, he is not only finite but is also sinful, then your whole condition is being put right. You are reminded, in other words, that the original sin was a desire to be God. That was the temptation that the devil brought to the woman: 'Ye shall be as gods' (Genesis 3:5) – you will have complete understanding. That is what man wants and he is in trouble about the residual problems and questions because he thinks that he has it in him to understand. This great man, this great brain! Why, there is nothing he cannot do! But the moment we are dealt with by the Spirit and through the word, we see that man is a fool, that he has lost his understanding of this essential, eternal difference, and that his greatest trouble, and the cause of his original fall, was and has always been his presumption, this desire to know things that are beyond him. As the result of the Fall, his understanding is darkened, it is sinful. Whether he likes it or not, that is the simple truth, and his world proves it, of course.

There, then, is the condition of fallen man. He is annoyed about this. His greatest trouble is intellectual pride. You see that in so-called civilization – the history of civilization. It is a manifestation of human pride, and especially intellectual pride. Never has this been clearer than during the present twentieth century as a result of so many discoveries, inventions and great advances. Man believes now more than ever that he has it in him to encompass all knowledge. There must be nothing that he cannot understand, and he will not believe until he does understand. This, I say again, is the original sin, and it has polluted the minds and understanding of all the progeny of the first man and woman.

But as Christian people, what we must remember in particular is that even though we are born again and are new men and women in Christ Jesus, the besetting sin for most of us is still intellectual pride; it is still the danger of presumption, it keeps on creeping back. In a sense, that was the great trouble with the church at Corinth; it is, at any rate, the problem that is dealt with in the first four chapters of 1 Corinthians. Though the Christians in Corinth had believed the gospel under the teaching of Paul, other teachers had come and had brought in an additional element – philosophy, a Greek idea of wisdom – and the Corinthians were ready to take it up. Of course, they said, Paul is just a simpleton, 'his bodily presence is weak, and his speech contemptible' (2 Corinthians 10:10) – he was not eloquent and he did not talk philosophy as Apollos did and so on. So they were being led astray by this very sin, though they were Christians.

Intellectual pride is always the danger, and so I emphasize our Lord's humbling of us, and put it first, because it will control everything else. Our spirits are put right when we realize how small and how finite we are, how ignorant we are, how little we know really in an ultimate sense. The teaching that he gives keeps us low, brings us down, and then we are already almost 75 per cent on the road to dealing with these residual problems.

But then – and you may query the order in which I have put these points, but I have done so to be experiential – I put, secondly, the teaching that our Lord gives us concerning the greatness of God. You cannot consider man without this. I have already mentioned it in dealing with man, but the Scripture is full of it. This is what it says to us: God is in heaven, and you are upon earth: be careful. Be careful! Indeed, the answer to these residual problems is, in a sense, just the being of God. If we only knew more about God, we would talk much less, we would have fewer problems, we would be silenced.

It is terrible, is it not, how glibly we talk and argue about God. We have all done it. I remember years ago doing this for many, many hours, and there would be men smoking pipes and saying this and that about God, and about predestination and election, lounging in chairs and getting up and laughing and joking about God! The mystery is that we are here at all, that he has not blotted us out of his sight for our arrogance. But he knows that we are ignorant; he understands our frame.

Oh, let me put this to you as it is put in the Scriptures. The trouble with all our thinking, and especially our agitation over these particular problems, is that we are wrong at the beginning. It is our attitude that is wrong, and the moment our attitude is put right, all is well. This can be illustrated from other realms of life. We often read that in a debate in the House of Commons the temperature was rising, tempers were beginning to fray and everybody was up in arms and shouting. Then somebody who was more of a statesman than a politician would get up and take the heat out of the discussion. Now that is always a great contribution to a discussion because when the heat rises you are no longer arguing about the original problem, but are now dealing in personalities, and all sorts of issues have come in that have nothing to do with the primary question. And it is similar here. So you must start with God and with man and that takes the heat out.

That is what our Lord does. We see a good illustration at the end of the eleventh chapter of the Epistle to the Romans. The apostle Paul has been dealing with a great problem, an extremely difficult problem for Jews who had become Christians. The question is: How can the promises of God to Abraham be reconciled with the fact that the Jews are rejecting the gospel? And what Paul does – and it is so typical of his method and of the whole method of our Lord through his servants – is reason it out. He argues it out in detail in chapters 9, 10 and 11. But notice the conclusion at which he arrives:

O the depth of the riches both of the wisdom and knowledge of God! how unsearchable are his judgments, and his ways past finding out! For who hath known the mind of the Lord? or who hath been his counsellor? or who hath first given to him, and it shall be recompensed unto him again? For of him, and through him, and to him, are all things: to whom be glory for ever. Amen. (Romans 11:33–36)

And, you know, there is a sense in which I ought to pronounce the benediction at this point – 'Amen'! But, no, the Scripture gives us reasons and I must go on. Yet that really is the answer.

Or take it as it is put in the Old Testament, in the book of the prophet Isaiah. It is the same argument exactly – it runs right through the Bible. We need to be put right, so we find this:

> *For my thoughts are not your thoughts, neither are your ways my ways, saith the LORD. For as the heavens are higher than the earth, so are my ways higher than your ways, and my thoughts than your thoughts.* (Isaiah 55:8–9)

There it is! God is in heaven; we are on earth. 'The LORD reigneth; let the people tremble . . . let the earth be moved' (Psalm 99:1). 'No man hath seen God at any time; the only begotten Son, which is in the bosom of the Father, he hath declared him' (John 1:18).

This is how our Lord deals with these various questions and problems. But then he goes on, he does not leave us at that. Thank God, he gives and he gives abundantly, superabundantly, always. Take this question concerning heaven and heavenly things. People are often troubled and ask about heaven: Will we know one another there? What happens? Is everyone in the same position? A thousand and one questions are raised. So how does our Lord deal with queries like this? Well, there is perfect satisfaction here. If you listened to what he tells you about these matters, you would soon stop raising your questions, for you would realize that here we are in a realm that is so transcendent and so glorious that it is entirely beyond our thoughts, and, indeed, entirely beyond our imaginations.

People often say, 'Here's the revelation that God has given us, but why is there so little about heaven?' They would like to know what it is like there, what we are to look forward to. Dear me, they should not be in trouble; they should thank God that we are told so little. Do you know why? Well, I can tell you. Heaven – the glory – is so wonderful that if our Lord had described it in our language and our categories, his words would have detracted from it. Our language is fallen; it is utterly inadequate. So the Bible gives us pictures, it gives us symbols. People often become obscurantist about these or literalize them and take a stand on them. That is not the way. These are pictures, representations. We are told that we only see now 'through a glass, darkly' (1 Corinthians 13:12); we see 'as in a glass the glory of the Lord' (2 Corinthians 3:18). We could not stand anything more. If you and I really saw heaven, we would be blinded, it might even kill us: we could not take it.

Towards the end of the third chapter of the Epistle to the Ephesians, Paul offers a prayer for the people, and it is always interesting to me to notice that the first prayer that he offers for them is this:

> *That he would grant you, according to the riches of his glory, to be strengthened with might by his Spirit in the inner man; that Christ may dwell in your hearts by faith; that ye, being rooted and grounded in love, may be able to comprehend with all saints what is the breadth, and length, and depth, and height; and to know the love of Christ, which passeth knowledge. (Ephesians 3:16–19)*

It always fascinates me that in this prayer, Paul's first request is that we might be 'strengthened with might by his Spirit in the inner man'. Why is this? It is because if we were not, we would not be able to stand this knowledge – 'the breadth, and length, and depth, and height'. It would shatter us. We need to be strengthened by the Spirit in order to get just a glimmering of a knowledge of this glory.

Heaven is so amazing, it is so wonderful, it is so altogether different and utterly beyond that we cannot understand it or have a detailed explanation. Oh, our vocabulary is inadequate, our terminology is not enough, our dictionaries are exhausted. It is an entirely different realm, and God in his grace conceals it, as it were, from us, gives us glimpses 'as through a glass darkly' – a picture, a vision, a glimmer of an understanding. Now that illustrates our Lord's whole approach to these questions.

As a result, we are bound to draw certain inevitable deductions, and, indeed, the Bible draws them for us. In the book of Deuteronomy, there is a specific statement that really is the answer to all our residual problems and questions. Remember it!

> *The secret things belong unto the* LORD *our God: but those things which are revealed belong unto us and to our children for ever, that we may do all the words of this law.* (Deuteronomy 29:29)

Now there it is; there is the fundamental answer: 'The *secret* things . . . those things which are revealed.' The secret things all belong to God; the things that are revealed belong to God – everything belongs to him. But he draws a distinction. There are things that he chooses to reveal to us, and there are things that he chooses not to reveal to us – and there is the complete answer.

'Why does he do this?' you say.

The answer is: Because he is God, and because he knows.

Oh, how poor we are at judging our own and one another's competence. It is the great lesson that every preacher and teacher has to learn. The danger for a young preacher, of course, is to give strong meat to people who can barely take milk, while there are others who go on giving milk to people who need strong meat. This is the whole question of the assessment of capacity. God knows what we can and cannot take, and he has drawn the ultimate division. And you come like the foolish waves of the sea dashing themselves against a rock; you can ask your questions, but you will only be thrown back, and all you will have at the end is mud and mire and dirt and wreckage.

But let us just work that out a little. Having started there, you can then understand, can you not, the argument of the apostle Paul in Romans chapter 9. Paul puts his great argument about election, giving the example of Esau and Jacob. God had said: 'Jacob have I loved, but Esau have I hated' (Romans 9:13) – here were two children in the same womb together:

(For the children being not yet born, neither having done any good or evil, that the purpose of God according to election might stand, not of works, but of him that calleth;) it was said unto her, The elder shall serve the younger. (Romans 9:11–12)

And Paul sums up his argument by saying, 'Therefore' – in the light of all he has been quoting and saying – 'hath he mercy on whom he will have mercy, and whom he will he hardeneth.' And the apostle continues, 'Thou wilt say then unto me' – people had said this many a time to the apostle. He did not need any imagination, they had been talking to him at the end of his sermons or his teaching and saying, 'Well, now, we don't understand this! If this is so, why that?' – 'Why doth he [God] yet find fault? For who hath resisted his will?' (Romans 9:18–19).

How is this right? How can it be fair? That is one of the ultimate residual questions, is it not? And here is Paul's answer in verse 20: 'Nay but, O man, who art thou that repliest against God?' In other words, your problem is not the problem of election, it is the problem of – God!

So it is not your question that matters. What really is important at this point is that you, little pigmy, ignoramus as you are, you who do not even understand yourself, should think you can stand up on your feet and say, 'I want to know from God'! There is only one thing to say to you: If you persist like that you will soon be destroyed:

> *Nay but, O man, who art thou that repliest against God? Shall the thing formed say to him that formed it, Why hast thou made me thus? Hath not the potter power over the clay, of the same lump to make one vessel unto honour, and another unto dishonour? What if God, willing to shew his wrath . . . (Romans 9:20–22)*

He is God! And that is not obscurantism, that is drawing a deduction from the being of God and the condition of man; and that is the way to deal with these questions. Election is one of those 'secret things' that we do not understand because obviously we are not meant to understand them. If we were meant to understand these secret things, God would have given us a revelation concerning them.

Now I want to bring this right home. It is the test of the Christian, ultimately, that we not only believe that there are 'secret things' that belong only to God, but that we accept that this is inevitable. Now we must come as far as that. I mean by that, that the moment we really look at all our residual problems and questions in the light of the everlasting and eternal God, and in the light of what we know to be so true about ourselves, then we see that this truth follows of necessity, and each of us says, 'I should never have thought anything else. There are bound to be issues that I can't understand. My mind is warped, it's sinful. My ideas of loving are wrong, there's a bit of lust mixed up with them. I can't think straight. I have no idea of justice. God is God and I am on earth! The ultimate mind and wisdom of God! I am not even going to try to understand, it would be foolish.'

But we should not only recognize the inevitability of this teaching, it should be something in which we rejoice. We rejoice that God in his infinite love and kindness and compassion has been pleased even to reveal anything to us. We do not deserve anything. We have forfeited every claim upon him. To me, there is nothing more wonderful than that God as our loving Father has let us into some of his secrets. Look what he has given us, look at the revelation!

People have a problem and say, 'I don't know the answer to that' – but look at all *this*, have you taken all this in? Have you encompassed all he has given you, all he has revealed? The moment you look at it like that, you begin to understand poor old Job. Oh, no, he is no longer 'poor old Job', not at the end. You remember the story – there he is, poor fellow, suffering agonies, this terrible condition of his skin, and those foolish friends, supposed comforters, aggravating it all. But at last God deals with him. He has allowed Job to say so much but at last God really deals with him and manifests himself to him, and Job therefore ends like this:

Then Job answered the LORD, *and said, I know that thou canst do every thing, and that no thought can be withholden from thee. Who is he that hideth counsel without knowledge? therefore have I uttered that I understood not; things too wonderful for me, which I knew not. (Job 42:1–3)*

Have you come to that, my friend? Job had very excellent reasons for speaking as he did in his agony. God, as it were, had handed him over for the time being to the devil to test him and to sift him. Look what he went through, but that is what he says. And on he goes:

Hear, I beseech thee, and I will speak: I will demand of thee, and declare thou unto me.

Then here it is:

> *I have heard of thee by the hearing of the ear: but now mine eye seeth thee. Wherefore I abhor myself, and repent in dust and ashes. (Job 42:4–6)*

And if you have not come to that with all these residual problems and questions, you have not yet drunk as you should have of the water that he giveth unto you, for the moment you drink it, this will be your experience, and thirsting will be at an end.

My dear friends, do you not realize that you are asking questions about things that even angels do not understand? Consider what Paul tells us in Ephesians 3:10. He is talking about God's great plan of salvation and he says:

> *To make all men see what is the fellowship of the mystery, which from the beginning of the world hath been hid in God, who created all things by Jesus Christ: to the intent that now unto the principalities and powers in heavenly places might be known by [through] the church the manifold wisdom of God. (Ephesians 3:9–10)*

Now the principalities and powers in heavenly places referred to there are not the evil powers, they are the good ones; these are the highest, most glorious angelic beings, who have always lived in the presence of God! But they need to be taught, they need understanding and wisdom, and God is revealing something new and fresh concerning his eternal wisdom to them through and by means of the church. And if they have not understood all this fully, who are you and I to try to understand!

But listen to Peter saying exactly the same thing:

> *Of which salvation the prophets have enquired and searched diligently, who prophesied of the grace that should come unto you: searching what, or what manner of time the Spirit of Christ which was in them did*

signify, when it testified beforehand the sufferings of Christ, and the glory that should follow, unto whom it was revealed, that not unto themselves, but unto us they did minister the things, which are now reported unto you by them that have preached the gospel unto you with the Holy Ghost sent down from heaven

– listen! –

which things the angels desire to look into. (1 Peter 1:10–12)

The angels of God are looking into this great mystery of God's eternal purpose, God's everlasting wisdom and they are amazed at it. And you and I are tempted arrogantly to ask our questions, 'I don't understand. If this, then why that?'

Here is your answer: 'I will lay mine hand upon my mouth'; 'I abhor myself, and repent in dust and ashes' (Job 40:4; 42:6). No, no; my dear friends, you must say:

My knowledge of that life is small,
The eye of faith is dim.

But here is the Christian answer:

But 'tis enough that Christ knows all
And I shall be with him.
Richard Baxter

'We walk by faith, not by sight' (2 Corinthians 5:7), and we are in his hand who knows all and will lead us through to the end. And so we make this kind of confession:

I cannot see the secret things
In this my dark abode;
I may not reach with earthly wings
The heights and depths of God.

So faith and patience wait awhile!
Not doubting, not in fear;
For soon in heaven my Father's smile
Shall render all things clear.

Then thou shalt end time's short eclipse,
Its dim uncertain night;
Bring in the grand apocalypse,
Reveal the perfect light.

'Then shall I know even as also I am [already] known' (1 Corinthians 13:12)! Are you content with that? Thank God, I am content. I want no more.

Stronger his love than death or hell;
Its riches are unsearchable.
The firstborn sons of light
Desire in vain its depths to see,
They cannot reach the mystery,
Its length, its breadth, its height.

Charles Wesley

And if they cannot, who am I to seek for this knowledge that belongs to 'the secret things of God'?

27

The Need for Emotional Satisfaction

Jesus answered and said unto her, Whosoever drinketh of this water shall thirst again: but whosoever drinketh of the water that I shall give him shall never thirst; but the water that I shall give him shall be in him a well of water springing up into everlasting life. (John 4:13–14)

The wonderful subject that we are looking at – and it is the great theme of the whole of the New Testament – is the fullness, the all-sufficiency, the never-failing character, of the Christian salvation, of the Christian life.

Now today this is questioned. The vast majority of people in this country regard Christianity as entirely outmoded, as ridiculous, finished, as no help at all, an anachronism in the modern world. So it is, therefore, our business, for our own sakes and for theirs, to show them how wrong and foolish they are, how they rob themselves of this amazing blessing that the Son of God came into the world to give us. We need to do this for our own sakes because if we are not sure of it, if we are not experiencing it, we shall be very poor witnesses, and, after all, the gospel has always spread mainly by means of the personal witness of Christian believers. It does not matter what the preacher may be like, if his people do not commend what he is saying, then his words will have very little effect.

So it is our duty, not only to understand this fullness, but to know and to experience it, and then others, seeing this in us, will be drawn to it. And never has the need of the world been greater than at the present time. Though in many ways we are living in discouraging days, these are also days of opportunity such as we have never seen before; as the bankruptcy of the world becomes more and more evident, so our opportunity becomes greater and greater.

But, my friends, the question is: Do we realize this? Are we ready for it? Are we enabled, because of our understanding and experience, to take up this great challenge given by our Lord and Saviour Jesus Christ? Now I do want to emphasize that. The trouble so often has been that Christian people come to the house of God only to receive – they just want satisfaction for themselves. That is all right, on condition that you go beyond that. You ought to be right in order to be able to help and influence others round and about you. The world is full of trouble and problems and anxiety and pain, not only on the big scale, but also in the smaller spheres of life, and men and women do not know where to turn. Here is our opportunity. That is why it is our duty to examine this full satisfaction that our Lord gives.

So far we have shown how our Lord's claim is substantiated when you look at it from the standpoint of the intellect. We have seen that it applies to the realm of thought. I can look at it, as it were, objectively, and I can see that there is a perfect system here.

And there is, of course; that is the astounding thing. Moreover, it is the only perfect system. It is possible for intelligent men and women to see that. They can see it clearly with their minds; they can see the whole Christian position. But that does not of necessity guarantee that they are Christians. They must know that it is true for them. Inherent in each of us is the desire for Christianity to be true for me in particular.

Now this is inevitably the case because, after all, no one is mere intellect. That is the fallacy that many fall into. Some define man as 'a reasoning animal', and they emphasize only the intellect. It is as if man were some kind of marvellous intellectual machine, almost as if he could be made by means of computers. Now computers can do very wonderful things, but a computer can never feel, it can never register sensation or emotion. And we must realize that human beings are not mere intellects, they also have hearts. One of the greatest intellects the world has ever known, the famous Frenchman Blaise Pascal, made a wonderful statement about this. One of the profoundest things he said, and he said many, is this: 'The heart has its reasons which reason knows nothing of.' For all that Pascal had a gigantic intellect, there was something deeper crying out for satisfaction, a satisfaction that he could never arrive at merely with his mind, though it could soar to heights far beyond not only the average, but also the greatest of people.

So because we have hearts as well as minds, because we have affections, feelings, sensibilities, as well as intellectual capacity, it is not enough that our minds alone be satisfied. It is not enough for us to believe that God does forgive sin; what every one of us wants to know is this: Are *my* sins forgiven? Now there is a vital distinction there. We can see intellectually that God is ready to forgive sins – God is love, and we see what God has done. So we know that God does forgive sins, he is a 'pardoning God'. But still there is that within us that cries out, 'Has he forgiven my sin?'

I remember a man who was dying a very slow and agonizing death, which took many months. He was a Christian, and a very able man, but he had not always responded to God as he should have done. He was a man who had tended to indulge his own eccentricities and oddities. That can be quite interesting, and it can amuse people, and you can be regarded as a character, but when you come to your deathbed, when you are left alone, as it were, it can land you in trouble, and this man was unhappy. He put it in a phrase one day to a friend, who repeated it to me, and I have never forgotten it. He said, 'I know the way of salvation. I know it up there.' And he pointed to his head. 'I know it perfectly. I see it. I have preached about it.' And he had, magnificently. 'But what troubles me,' he said, 'is this.' He pointed to his heart. 'Has it been registered here?'

Now this is true for all of us. Take some words that I read recently about Martin Luther: 'That Christianity is a matter of relationship rather than a matter of assent to truth, seemed basic to Luther.' This is a most important statement. This year we are celebrating the 450th anniversary of the famous occasion when Luther nailed his Ninety-five Theses to the door of the church, and it is right that we should commemorate that. But let us make use of this historic fact to remind ourselves of what really was the essence, the central point, of the Protestant Reformation. In a sense, it is all in that phrase that I have just quoted.

The Roman Catholic Church had virtually been teaching, as she still tends to do, that what makes someone a Christian is an assent to the dogma of the Roman Catholic Church. But Luther had become unhappy about this, it no longer satisfied him. There was a desire within him to know that he could stand before a holy, righteous God. The word that dominated the thinking of the young Luther was the word 'righteousness' – 'the righteousness of God'. This was what terrified him and caused him to pass through a long agony of soul. How could he stand before the righteous God? It seemed impossible.

Luther became a monk and fasted and sweated and prayed, but he was still no nearer finding an answer, indeed, he was further away. All that he did simply gave him a greater conception of God, and, as this quotation puts it, he knew that what really mattered was his personal standing before God. Salvation is a matter of personal relationship, not a matter of accepting a body of truth or of dogma; ultimately, it comes to that. And that is what accounted for Luther's long agony, his painful, painful struggle. He wanted this knowledge, this inner satisfaction, that his sins were forgiven, that he could have a righteousness that would be acceptable in the presence of God. And, as you know, one day he did receive this assurance. And that is what really led to the Protestant Reformation. It came out of the experience of Martin Luther. This assurance was what set him on fire and led to all the events that followed. Luther was only one of a number of people, but his experience is one of the most striking in the whole history of the Christian church.

And, in a measure, all of us have this desire for certainty, this desire for safety, for peace and for rest. We must of necessity face the fact that there is an affective side to our natures, which cries out for satisfaction. So if there is not an experiential side to the Christian faith, it has failed us; and if our Lord's great statement in John 4 does not include this, it is not comprehensive and is not satisfactory. Therefore we must consider it and see whether the Lord Jesus Christ himself and what he gives does satisfy the heart as well as the mind and the understanding.

Now in moving from the realm of the understanding to the realm of the heart, we are doing something that, in one way, is difficult, indeed, very difficult. The problem is in recognizing the limits, and seeing where one ends and the other begins. This is because one shades into the other and one influences the other. The heart and the understanding are, of course, intimately interrelated. Nevertheless, it is very important that we should differentiate between them. Not that we can make absolute divisions and distinctions, but, for the sake of clarity of thought and of understanding, it is helpful and essential to draw some lines and hold them in our minds.

There is clear teaching in the Scripture that our Lord can and does deal directly with the heart, the affections, the feelings, as well as with the mind. The normal manner is to deal with the mind and through that the heart, but – and, again, you see this in the history of the church and some of her great people – you will find that sometimes the heart is dealt with first, and the understanding follows. That is exceptional, but it does happen.

And that leads us to this great question – the place of feeling and of emotion in our lives and especially in our Christian lives. I want to introduce this subject now because I think it is one of the greatest causes of confusion at the present time. There are some people who make too much of feeling and of sensation – everything that we put together under the general heading of 'the heart'. There are many who live on their emotions and evaluate everything solely in terms of how they feel. They do not look at things objectively, they do not apply external measures of judgement, they just respond instinctually, intuitively; they are living, as it were, on a primitive level. This can have many causes; it can be due to sheer lack of intelligence. The younger we are, the more we live in the realm of feelings and instincts, of likes and dislikes, without applying much reason. This gradually changes as we get older, but if people are lacking in intelligence, they will tend to remain on this level. Experience teaches us that the less attention people give to training and developing their minds, the more they live in the realm of the emotions and feelings. That is one cause.

Another cause may be laziness. There are some people who live entirely on the emotional level simply because they are lazy. They do not like to use their minds, they do not like to think. This is very common, particularly in the realm of religion. This is astounding and is why I started with the intellect. There are people who object to having to think in connection with their religion. All they want is something that gives them a nice feeling. That is the explanation of much sacramentalism and a good deal of the ceremonial and the visual that is found in many churches. There is the desire not to think, but just to feel, to register sensations.

And this, I believe, is a charge that can be brought against this generation, speaking very generally. People do not like to read books as they used to, they do not like to read solid books, big books. Publishers tell me that they are having increasing difficulty in selling books, though they can sell booklets and pamphlets with comparative ease. People like everything short, snappy, tabloid, it is one of the characteristics of the age in which we are living. And let me be clear about this – this is sheer laziness. It would be wrong to try to excuse it in any way whatsoever. Shame on us that we who have such opportunities are not reading as our forefathers did. Very often they could not afford to buy books, yet nevertheless they would scrape and save out of their meagre wages in order to buy a book that would help them to understand the Bible and know God.

But there is another cause that is quite common at the present time, and this is perhaps the most serious. There is a kind of modern thinking, one type of modern philosophy, that can be called anti-intellectualist. And the extraordinary thing about it, and the amusing thing, in a sense, is that it is the intellectuals who teach it. Take a man such as the late Mr D. H. Lawrence: this was his creed. He said that the whole trouble with man was that he thought too much, and used his brains too much, and he must sink back to the animal level, and go back to nature.

It is said that the big mistake we have made in this century is the attempt to think and to reason and to plan. Man is, after all, nothing but a bundle of sensations, a reaction – I must not waste your time over this and yet it is important because it comes into the religious realm. This is true of so much modern poetry, is it not? It is no use trying to look for meaning or sense. You are not supposed to do that – it is the sound that matters, the sound of words, and the sound of the words is meant to do something to you. Do not ask for meaning, meaning is taboo. Do not ask for understanding. No, you react, you have a feeling, a sensation. That is said to be poetry.

So, for the reasons I have given there are many who, for varying degrees, make too much of feeling and exclude the intellect. But now I must consider the exact opposite attitude: making too little of feeling. In our realm, this is, perhaps, the more important and the commoner of the two. I am not sure but that at the present time the greatest problem of all confronting evangelicals is not this particular wrong attitude to the heart and feelings in connection with our Christian faith.

Now I am sure that part of the present reaction against the place of feeling and emotion in Christianity is due to a reaction, and, though it has gone too far, what I would regard as a very healthy reaction, against the sheer sentimentalism, the maudlin sentimentality, of the late Victorian and the Edwardian periods. There is also a further reason for the reaction against feelings, and one that I do not think is surprising in this generation. You always tend to get this when people's feelings and sensibilities have been subjected to terrible assaults. We have lived in a century in which there have been two dreadful world wars and there has also been the strain that we have been subjected to between these wars and after the last war.

The result of all this is that we are now in an age that more or less despises feelings so that we have reached a point where the feelings are almost entirely excluded. Have you noticed a new word that has gained a good deal of currency in the last few years – it is interesting and revealing – it is the word 'clinical'? When using that word people mean 'detached', 'objective', 'not involved', like the surgeon performing an operation; they mean, 'aseptic', perfect, mechanical, really. This is, incidentally, not a good use of the word 'clinical', but it is the word that is being used. This attitude is apparent in many areas – literature, novels, drama – and people are glorying in it.

Where does this come from? I have suggested that it is partly a reaction against the Victorians and also that it is a consequence of the terrible assaults that have been made upon us in this century. But it goes back even further – it is interesting to notice the elements that come into it. The man who, in a sense, started it all, and made this approach to life fashionable, was Thomas Arnold, the great headmaster of Rugby School, and he is still its greatest exponent. Arnold defined the perfect gentleman as a man who did not show his feelings. It is primitive people who show how they feel; the gentleman never reveals his feelings at all, no matter what happens. Of course, Thomas Arnold had a great illustration at hand in the Duke of Wellington, with the stories of his calm, cool indifference in battle. So this came in as a kind of philosophy – I shall not take time over that!

Much more important is the view that we must define as Stoicism. It is much older and there is much more to be said for it. Stoicism was a philosophy that was current at the time of our Lord and the apostle Paul: we read about Paul going to Athens and encountering 'certain philosophers of the Epicureans and of the Stoicks' (Acts 17:18). Stoicism was a teaching that said something like this: This is a hard and difficult and trying world, a world that makes assaults upon us – illness, accident, disappointment, the treachery of friends, death. If you want to go through life successfully, you must face this, and first you must put a curb on your feelings. If you allow your feelings to control you, then you will be defeated because one day you will be up on top of the mountain and the next day you will be down in the depth of a bog. If you do not want to suffer, if you do not want to be hurt, be balanced, be controlled and disciplined. Guard your feelings, hold them in check, keep a firm control over them with your will. Do not let things elate you too much because if you do, you will soon be disappointed, but, on the other hand, do not let things get you down too much, they are never as bad as they appear to be. Hold to a middle position, a mean, a balance. That was the philosophy of the Stoics, and notice that the motive behind it was to protect yourself from being hurt.

Now it is interesting to notice that there has been a marked recrudescence of Stoicism in this century. That very able man, Bertrand Russell, actually says in his autobiography that when he was quite young he came to the decision that he was going to protect himself against his own feelings because otherwise he could see what would happen. He says that he did this quite deliberately; he would not allow himself to be too happy, nor would he allow himself to be too miserable. So he developed a detachment, what some would call 'a scientific attitude'. It is not, but that is what they call it. That is nothing but sheer Stoicism. The point is that you are protecting yourself against your feelings because you know they will be assaulted in different ways, and you will suffer and be unhappy. The only way to prevent that is by suppressing your feelings. This philosophy is inculcated by people like Thomas Arnold and others who say that if you do show your feelings you are a fool, you will be laughed at. So you hold them down, put a band of steel about them, harden yourself. Whatever happens, you will not allow yourself to feel.

Now this is all wrong, obviously, because we must not crucify parts of our being in this way. We are all meant to express all aspects of ourselves, we are all meant to live a full life, and any teaching that denies that is going against our essential nature. When we come to the realm of the Christian faith, this view becomes still more serious, and, I repeat, I think it is one of our major problems. I remember a man coming to me who was delighted about a certain evangelistic campaign. 'Have you been?' he asked and when I replied, 'No, not yet,' he said, 'It's marvellous. Crowds of people go forward. No emotion, you know. No emotion. They all just went forward.' And he thought this was perfection – no emotion. People converted to God, people convicted of sin by the Holy Spirit, people regenerated, and 'no emotion'!

And that is the position, I think, at which we have arrived. But when we read the accounts of the early church, and the church throughout the centuries, we find a great deal about people weeping and glorying; we read about ecstasy. Why do we not see this today? Because we are living in an age when this worldly philosophy has been influencing the church. Everything has to be detached; it all has to be clinical; it all has to be kept at a distance, as it were.

Let me put it like this. How can the world help us with respect to this denial of the feelings? And the simple answer is that it cannot help us at all. 'Whosoever drinketh of this water shall thirst again' – and if that is not clear to you, you must be completely blind. The most dangerous and the most obvious and evident aspect of the modern world is its failure to help people in their hearts, in their feelings, in their sensibilities. Even at its best, the world has only been able to give temporary and incomplete satisfaction. It is all on the surface. I think this is alarmingly clear today.

Have you noticed the confusion in modern life, the blank contradiction in the modern outlook? On the one hand, there is the intellectualism that I have already been describing, the disdaining of the feelings, this clinical approach, and on the other hand, the 'pleasure mania', the constant craving for and living upon entertainment. Never has the desire for pleasure been more evident than at the present time. As I have said, people are reading less – why? Partly because they are being entertained more. And they not only crave pleasure and entertainment, they are indulging in it.

But still more than the pleasure mania, there is what can be described as sheer emotionalism. By that, I mean a kind of riot of the emotions, a working up of the emotions and a rejoicing in them. Where does this show itself? Well that, surely, was the main explanation of Hitlerism. Hitlerism was but a riot of emotions. Some of you remember – we heard it on the wireless – the shouting and the raving when Hitler appeared on the platform. It was quite genuine. The people felt that. But it had been worked up in various ways. There it was in Germany, a country famous for philosophy and for the intellect and for science. These were basic contradictions. What had happened? I think that these people had been repressed in the realm of their feelings. But the emotions werc there, and at last they found an outlet and burst through all the barriers like a veritable flood.

Today we are far short of something extreme and political like Hitlerism, but it is still very interesting that some of the most highly sophisticated people seem to enjoy most of all the most primitive kind of music. Have you noticed this? There are two types of music that are popular today: clinical, intellectual, clever, mechanical music that has no melody at all but is very clever technically – and the way it is done is marvellous – and, on the other hand, primitive music. And people say they like both. I am not surprised. There is something in them crying out for the two things. But what is interesting is that people are going back to the most primitive kind of music, and even further back, to that which is merely elemental. This is also happening, I understand, in dancing. But perhaps the most pathetic indication and example of this at the present time is the way in which these poor, modern, young adolescents indulge in frenzies of screaming. It is their response to a certain type of music and of entertainment and to certain persons.

But what is the explanation? That is what I am concerned about. I am not mentioning these things because I want to denounce them. I am not here to do that. I am sorry for people who manifest such emotions because I think the explanation is that it is all due to a lack of emotional satisfaction. There is that in human nature that cries out for emotional satisfaction and these primitive patterns of behaviour are an outlet for the cry in the heart for some satisfaction that the world cannot give. And people think, 'At any rate, I can express my feelings.'

And have you noticed the increase in violence? People like their novels to be violent, they like violence on their television screens. It is the same craving for something that is deeper than the mind, and the world is not giving it, so they get it in this way – violence! And the shouting at football matches – the cause is the same. This is the outlet for emotions that have been dammed down by a false philosophy.

And it is still worse, of course, when we come to the realm of drugs: not only alcohol but also drugs. It is no use just getting irritated and annoyed and condemning these practices. If we are Christian people, we should be concerned about those who are indulging in drink and drug-taking, and we should be asking: 'Why are they doing it? What are they after?' And there is only one answer: they want what they call 'kicks', and a 'kick' means emotional satisfaction. What is offered in the realm of intellect and of thought does not give this satisfaction, and the materialism that is so popular, the adulation of money, this does not satisfy either. You have to knock out your brain in order that your lower centres, as they are called, can come up and manifest themselves. And it is all caused, I say again, by a craving for a satisfaction for the heart and for the feelings.

And then, on top of that, some even turn to a new moral teaching that denies all morals and says, 'Don't listen to all that Victorian nonsense, let yourself go, do what you feel like doing, get satisfaction, that is the only thing that matters in a world like this.' It is called the 'new morality' and it is sometimes even preached in the name of Christianity.

Now there is the modern manifestation of this cry for satisfaction, but you can see what a subject it is, and how important it is for us all. I can sum it all up in the case of one person, who I think put this for us perfectly. I refer to the late Mr Aldous Huxley. Here was a dazzling intellect. In the twenties he said that nothing matters but intellect. So he wrote his brilliant books in which he said that science must be the answer to everything, thought was the solution, education and knowledge. He was the high priest of this way of thinking, the most brilliant of all. But in the latter years of his life, this man underwent a complete change. He began to write about mysticism, and he actually said: 'The only hope of the world is mysticism,' and he became a Buddhist.

But why did this happen to Huxley? It happened for the reasons I have been giving you. He saw that the intellect, however brilliant, was not enough, that there was something deeper, a heart crying out for satisfaction. He could not find it in all the intellectualism of the age in which he had been brought up and he felt that he had found it in mysticism. Now the form of mysticism that he adopted was one that virtually tells you to stop thinking; you just abandon yourself, hoping that ultimately you will be 'absorbed into the Absolute'. This is nothing but an interesting confession of the complete bankruptcy of the world.

'Whosoever drinketh of this water shall thirst again': and all that the modern world is offering to people who are craving for some satisfaction in their hearts simply aggravates the problem. A drug will give satisfaction to you for the time being; under the influence of the drug you feel marvellous, you feel you are in Paradise. But then the effect of the drug wears off and you are in a worse position, you feel horrible, you are in hell. So you have to get more and you increase the dose. It is the same with drink, the same with pleasure, the same with everything that the world has to give us; they make the problem worse and create fresh problems.

And this is where you and I come in. We have the answer for the world. Can we tell people in the world that there is full satisfaction without drugs, without drink, without all this anti-intellectualism, and yet without all this cutting out of the heart, without turning people into mere intellectual machines, without this dry, unmoving, clinical attitude towards life? That is the test for us. 'Whosoever drinketh of the water that I shall give him shall never thirst; but the water that I shall give him shall be in him a well of water springing up into everlasting life.' Oh, thank God, it is perfectly true.

Thou, O Christ, art all I want,
More than all in thee I find.
Charles Wesley

28

Moved by the Truth

Jesus answered and said unto her, Whosoever drinketh of this water shall thirst again: but whosoever drinketh of the water that I shall give him shall never thirst; but the water that I shall give him shall be in him a well of water springing up into everlasting life. (John 4:13–14)

We have seen that the gospel gives us entire intellectual satisfaction in a way that nothing else in the world can, and now we have moved on to consider the second aspect of the satisfaction that it gives, and that is the satisfaction that is offered to the heart, to the sensitivities, to the feelings. We have introduced the subject, and I felt it was essential that we should demonstrate its importance, especially for us as Christian people. The world today is perhaps less capable than ever of dealing with the feeling side of our make-up as human beings, and it is most important that we should emphasize our Lord's claim that he can give complete emotional satisfaction. One of the most wonderful and glorious aspects of this gospel is the way in which it deals with the whole personality: everything else is partial; everything else deals with us in bits and portions.

We can put this in terms of balance. The extraordinary balance of the Scriptures is always to me both remarkable and fascinating. We are all so unbalanced, we are creatures of extremes, we swing violently from one side to another. The most obvious example of that in this century is the attitude of people towards Mr Winston Churchill – vilified for so many years before the Second World War, regarded as a dangerous man and a warmonger, but after the war regarded almost as a superhuman being, almost a god.

We can also look at this balance in another way. Christian men and women as depicted in the New Testament never strike up attitudes. By nature, people are constantly posing and taking up positions. But Christians never do that because they have a fundamental balance, there is a wholeness. Another way of putting it is to say that Christians never follow fashions; everybody else does – in every respect. Fashions and changes in fashion are not confined to clothing; they are quite as amusing in the realm of the intellect. As one looks back across life it is really funny to remember the crazes, the movements and emphases, the excitements that are now long since forgotten, with people under the age of 30 knowing nothing about them. This is, of course, an expression of a lack of satisfaction. We have already considered the way in which people are always looking for something that will really give them the satisfaction that they long for. There is a new craze and they think they have found the answer. They are all out for it. 'Ah, here it is,' they say, and off they go. And then you find them doing perhaps the exact opposite at some later period. Civilization has been like this for many, many centuries, and is as far away from a final satisfaction as it has ever been.

But those who conform to the New Testament pattern never follow fashion, they never get excited about some new emphasis or teaching. That is always a characteristic of an unstable person.

It shows that there is a lack there somewhere, an imbalance. It is always the mark of those who have never drawn deeply of this water that the Lord Jesus Christ offers us, this 'eternal life' that he gives us and that satisfies the whole of the personality.

This is, therefore, a most important matter because we are meant to enjoy full satisfaction, and it is only as we do, that we shall be able to help others. If we are the victims of crazes and fashions and changes, and the striking of attitudes, then we shall not be able to give any help, but if people see that we are always balanced and equable, always in a position of poise, then they know that they can safely talk to us and consult us and bring their problems and their questions to us. So the question to which we must certainly address ourselves now is this: How does our Lord himself and his teaching deal with us in this matter of the emotions? What is the place of emotion in the Christian life? It is fascinating to trace just this very issue in the history of the church and to see how the church has fallen into error through always going to one extreme or another.

The first thing we must realize is that a mere assent to the truth, or an adoption of certain principles and teachings, does not make us Christians. People sometimes imagine that to agree to certain doctrines, and then to show great keenness in connection with them, makes them Christians. But it does not. That is, after all, one of the great differences between the cults and the Christian faith. The devotees of the cults take up their teaching and we are aware – we see a lot of this at the present time – of their keenness and their zeal. But that is, in a sense, where they betray themselves; they live on this enthusiasm. They have taken up a teaching, it is a limited one, they learn it parrot fashion, and repeat it like parrots, and they keep themselves going with this artificial keenness, and persuade themselves that they are very happy and that they have 'got it'. But if you examine them carefully, you notice that the whole time there is a fundamental lack of rest and of ease and of poise, because it is the enthusiasm that keeps them going, and the moment they stop, they seem to have nothing. Now that is different from the Christian position.

Or let me put it to you like this. There is a grave danger of our confusing the true Christian position with what I would call 'believism plus sentimentality'. You find people who have gone through some form of belief; they have heard a message and they are told that if they believe this and accept it, then all will be well. So they have believed, but they have not felt anything at all. They think that they should have felt something, but they have not. So what they do now is add sentimentality to this mechanical believism. This is something that they produce themselves, or others produce, in order to meet the innate desire for some satisfaction in the realm of emotion. What they believed has not moved them so something is manufactured.

There are many ways in which sentimentality can be produced. Sometimes the preacher or the evangelist does it by telling stories. They are very affecting stories, and because people find themselves weeping as they listen, they are satisfied. But the tragedy of that position is that what has made them weep is not the truth, but the story. Or maybe a religious novel, so called, or an affecting account of a true incident in the life of a missionary, produces a sentimental feeling. Again, as long as they can respond to this stimulus, they are satisfied.

Music is also used – and this is increasingly the tendency at the present time. The sentimentality of singing or the playing of a fiddle is added on. It is not great music, it is a sentimental type of music, and of course it gives a pleasurable feeling. And because it is performed in connection with a religious service or by

Christians, people imagine and persuade themselves that they are feeling the truth. But they are not. This feeling has no direct connection with what they have believed.

All I am trying to show you is that this is not our Lord's method, it is not the way of the New Testament. Feeling is not something that is added on to the truth, something that has to come as a kind of supplement to the truth. Or, to put it another way, we must be very careful to differentiate between emotionalism and the satisfaction that our Lord gives to the heart. Now here is another important distinction. How do you differentiate between a true emotion, and emotionalism?

First of all, the essential trouble with emotionalism is always that emotion is regarded as an end in and of itself. People want the emotion, their whole attention is placed on that to the exclusion of everything else. Because they make that initial error of isolating the emotions, the feelings, the heart, and because they concentrate entirely upon this and regard it as supreme, they have to adopt various ways and methods of producing what they regard as emotion. So they deliberately work it up; they have to create it, to manufacture it and stimulate it. And they do so by making a direct assault upon the feelings.

Now I am not questioning the sincerity and honesty of such people, I am not even querying their motives. I am simply putting what they do, and what they believe, over and against the teaching of our Lord himself and the teaching of the whole of the New Testament. They make this direct attack upon the feelings, and they generally do so by ignoring every other aspect of the personality for the time being. You are familiar with the many ways in which this is done.

Again, music is one of the methods most ready to hand, among the most primitive peoples and extending right along the line.

Music does appeal primarily to the emotions. I am *not* saying that there is no intellectual content in great music. There is. But there is a type of music that has no intellectual content whatsoever and is simply a direct assault upon the feelings. Then if you start clapping your hands or stamping your feet or moving them in a rhythmic manner, of course you are the whole time dealing with this realm of the emotions. And there is a great deal of that today.

There are even some who deliberately employ psychological methods, different coloured lights, for instance, to prey upon the emotions. Perhaps the most subtle attack upon the Christian faith at the present time comes from psychologists, and I am trying to show that very often good Christian people, in their ignorance of these matters, are simply playing directly into the hands of those who attack the Christian faith in terms of psychology. It is because Christians have never understood the place of emotion in the life of the Christian, and have substituted either a kind of flabby sentimentality, or a more active and vigorous emotionalism.

Now essentially emotionalism is emotion without any intellectual content. People deliberately abandon themselves. You will sometimes even see them leaning back and making an effort to 'let themselves go', as they say, and they are encouraged to do so. There is a teaching today that would even say that the intellect is a danger and a hindrance and you must avoid it. That is a terrible thing to say, and, of course, it is an entire contradiction of the whole teaching of the New Testament. And it all rises because of this desire for feeling.

True emotion always results from truth. It is kindled by truth, it is produced by it. That is always the order in the New Testament; as our Lord puts it to the woman of Samaria: 'If thou *knewest* . . .' It is because you do not know, it is because you do not understand, that you are as you are. This is the New Testament way. But with the other approach, a direct appeal is made to the emotions. And the subtlety of the devil comes in here. Because people are in a chapel or a church or a religious meeting, it is assumed that the feelings are the result of the truth. But they are not – and here, therefore, is a vital test that we must always apply: What is it that is moving me? Am I being moved by the truth, or am I just being moved by one of these agencies, such as lilting music or an affecting story?

A second, and definitive test, is that with emotionalism there is always an element of loss of control. Because it is divorced from the intellect and the mind and the understanding and the truth, emotionalism always has an element of excess. It is a form of intoxication similar to being under the influence of alcohol or a drug; the higher discriminating centres are eliminated, and so the more primitive and instinctual element comes to the surface. There are numerous examples in history of how innocent and good Christian people have gone into excess and brought the gospel into disrepute because they had not differentiated between a true emotion and emotionalism.

And another good test is this: emotionalism is always exhausting. It is bound to be because the mind and the will have not been affected but only the emotions. Emotionalism plays on one aspect of the personality and overdoes that. The result is that, as with artificial stimulants such as drugs and alcohol and so on, when the temporary stimulus has been removed and its influence has passed off, the person is in a state of exhaustion. Now that is a complete contrast with what we find described everywhere in the New Testament. Here you get true emotion, and true emotion, I repeat, is always the result of truth, this great truth coming to the mind, and coming with such clarity that the heart is moved and stimulated. And because it involves the mind and also the will, as well as the emotions of the heart, the whole person is involved.

And because of that, true emotion is always invigorating, it is always stimulating.

The next test is this, therefore: emotion always leads to action. This is one of the basic distinctions between true emotion and emotionalism. Because there is no element of truth or of understanding in what they are feeling, the poor victims of emotionalism are very often left not only exhausted but also with a failure in the realm of the will. So certain sins creep in, sins that always find their opportunity when the intellect is out of action and when the feelings are roused; and in this way the gospel is again brought into disrepute. But true emotion always moves and affects the will. It is deep, energizing, invigorating, and it moves the total personality. And so one desires with the whole of one's being to live to the glory of God.

Now this explanation, unfortunately, was essential. I did not want to give it, but I had to because the counterfeit is the greatest danger of all. I am simply trying to say that if I were asked to put in a phrase what is the greatest lack in the Christian church at the present time, I would say that it is our lack of real New Testament emotion. In contradistinction to these counterfeits that I have been describing, our Lord is talking about something that affects the whole person – the heart as well as the head. Indeed, I go as far as to say that unless our hearts as well as our heads are affected by the truth that we have believed, there is something wrong even with our belief and with our Christian position. Believism plus sentimentality does not make a Christian. Believism plus an ecstatic emotionalism does not constitute Christianity. There is no 'plus' in Christianity, it is all one, it is all part and parcel of the same thing; you cannot make distinctions – they are artificial.

So let us look at this: Do we agree that the heart is involved? Is it our own experience that our hearts are involved? This is a fundamental test of our whole position as Christians. The Bible is full of this. It gives great place to the heart, to the emotional side of our natures. The psalmists are very fond of expressing this. Psalm 4 puts it very well: 'Thou hast put gladness in my heart, more than in the time that their corn and their wine increased' (Psalm 4:7). Of course, farmers were always very happy when they had had a good harvest – when they had garnered in their corn and had good crops of grapes and wine had been produced, they had a great feast. Harvest was the outstanding occasion in the life of the Jew as a farmer. Yet this psalmist says that the Lord has given him a joy and happiness that entirely exceeds all the happiness that he has ever known as a farmer or as a man of the world.

We find this same rejoicing in many other psalms; one of the greatest examples, perhaps, is Psalm 107:

> *O give thanks unto the* LORD, *for he is good: for his mercy endureth for ever. Let the redeemed of the* LORD *say so, whom he hath redeemed from the hand of the enemy; and gathered them out of the lands, from the east, and from the west, from the north, and from the south . . . Oh that men would praise the* LORD *for his goodness, and for his wonderful works to the children of men! (Psalm 107:1–3, 8)*

Now that is typical of the psalms. The book of Psalms, remember, is a book of songs. The people sang the psalms, giving expression to the moving of their hearts, to their feelings. This is the great characteristic of the child of God, even under the Old Testament dispensation. This is yet more clear when we come to the New Testament, and it is what I want to put before you, my dear friends. Why is the world as it is? Why is the church as she is today? Why does she count for so little? I have no hesitation in answering that question: it is because we are so unlike the first Christians. Consider the position; look at the early church. There were only a handful of people, and unimportant people at that. They had no great learning, they had no great names, they had no wealth, they had nothing to recommend them – everything, apparently, was against them. And yet they shook that ancient world; they shook it to its foundations. This despised sect of the Nazarenes, these little Christians, became a dominant power in the life of the ancient world. Amid Greek philosophy and a world controlled by the power of Roman law, this power became dominating, mastering and conquering. How did they do it? What was the secret?

Now there is no question about the answer; everybody is agreed. Even secular, anti-Christian historians agree that Christians conquered the world by their sheer joyfulness, that this was their great characteristic. They began like that. On the Day of Pentecost, after Peter had preached to the people of Jerusalem, they were deeply convicted. Then this is what we read:

> They were pricked in their heart, and said unto Peter and to the rest of the apostles, Men and brethren, what shall we do? Then Peter said unto them, Repent, and be baptized every one of you in the name of Jesus Christ for the remission of sins, and ye shall receive the gift of the Holy Ghost . . . Then they that gladly received his word were baptized: and the same day there were added unto them about three thousand souls.

What sort of people were they? We are given a description of them. The first thing we are told is this:

> And they continued stedfastly in the apostles' doctrine and fellowship, and in breaking of bread, and in prayers.

But listen to this:

> And they, continuing daily with one accord in the temple, and breaking bread from house to house, did eat their meat with gladness and

singleness of heart, praising God, and having favour with all the people.
(Acts 2:37–38, 41–42, 46–47)

Now that is the Christian, and that is the Christian church – gladness, singleness of heart, praising God! This is what characterized the early church and made it irresistible in that ancient world; they were a rejoicing and a praising people. I could give you endless examples. Let me give you one from the end of the fifth chapter of Acts. All the apostles had been arrested, and not for the first time they were on trial. The members of the Sanhedrin, we are told, were cut to the heart and took counsel to slay them. The apostles would undoubtedly have been murdered there and then had it not been for a man whose name was Gamaliel. It was a near thing: they were face to face with death. But they were told not to preach about Jesus, and were released. Then this is what we read about them:

And they departed from the presence of the council, rejoicing that they were counted worthy to suffer shame for his name. And daily in the temple, and in every house, they ceased not to teach and preach Jesus Christ. (Acts 5:41–42)

Rejoicing! Going on with the thing they had been prohibited from doing, something irresistible driving them, filled with this spirit of rejoicing. It is always the characteristic of New Testament men and women.

Another example is the eunuch who Philip met, the eunuch from Ethiopia who had just been baptized. We read:

And when they were come up out of the water, the Spirit of the Lord caught away Philip, that the eunuch saw him no more: and he went on his way rejoicing. (Acts 8:39)

We find it also in the Philippian jailor. This man had been on the verge of committing suicide and then he believed, and we are told:

> *And he took them the same hour of the night, and washed their stripes; and was baptized, he and all his, straightway. And when he had brought them into his house, he set meat before them, and rejoiced, believing in God with all his house.* (Acts 16:33–34)

You see, it is universal; it is the great characteristic.

Just before the Philippian jailor believed and was baptized, there was something astounding. Paul and his travelling companion Silas had been arrested very wrongly, they had been scourged, their poor backs had been beaten with rods – an agonizing experience – and they had been thrown into the innermost prison and their feet put fast in the stocks. Everything was against them. But this is what I read: 'And at midnight Paul and Silas prayed, and sang praises unto God: and the prisoners heard them' (Acts 16:25). Singing in a prison! It had never been heard of before. Prisoners do not sing at midnight. And the other prisoners were there listening – what is this? What are these men? They are full of joy, praising God. They are singing, with their feet in the stocks, with agonizing backs, at midnight. 'Paul and Silas prayed, and sang praises unto God.'

That is Christianity, my friends, and I am suggesting to you that it is the absence of this joy that constitutes our essential problem. You see, this was not a concert that had been prepared in prison, it was spontaneous, nothing artificial, nothing manufactured, nothing organized. It was the spontaneous welling up of that which is within. The truth had captured them, moving them, so that whatever their circumstances they 'praised God, and sang praises unto him'.

Profound emotion is the whole characteristic of the New Testament. Again, look at it in the case of the apostle Paul.

When he met the Ephesians at Miletus, Paul reminded them of how he had conducted himself among them. He says:

Ye know, from the first day that I came into Asia, after what manner I have been with you at all seasons, serving the Lord with all humility of mind, and with many tears

– 'with many tears'! –

and temptations, which befell me by the lying in wait of the Jews. (Acts 20:18–19)

Let me put it to you like this. Can you read any one of Paul's epistles without feeling the tremendous emotion that is in them? Paul is interesting from every standpoint, but I am referring now to the very style of the epistles and not the content. Of course, at once you are aware of a giant mind, you are aware of a master thinker, a man who can organize his teaching, his truth: it is the sheer mastery that strikes you. But you do not stop at that; you immediately become aware of this other element, this emotion – the way that he is obviously moved and is having, as it were, to hold himself back. In addition to the reasoning and the logic, you see the emotion that comes surging through it all. The result is that in the epistles of the apostle Paul there are some of the most eloquent and moving passages that you will find in any literature whatsoever. Read Romans 8 again. Do you not feel the passion, the emotion, how he is thrilled with the subject that he is writing about?

And there are other examples. Take the fourth chapter of 2 Corinthians, where the apostle rises to a tremendous climax. He has been giving an account of his troubles and he says:

We are troubled on every side, yet not distressed; we are perplexed, but not in despair; persecuted, but not forsaken; cast down, but not destroyed; always bearing about in the body the dying of the Lord Jesus

– and on he goes. Then the climax –

For our light affliction, which is but for a moment

– that is not only reason. It is reason, but there is more than reason. He is ridiculing the affliction, he is standing up, he is rejoicing –

worketh for us a far more exceeding and eternal weight of glory

– language fails him there; he is moved, he is carried away, he is up in the heavens, as it were. Somebody has translated the words 'far more exceeding' as 'exceeding, exceeding abundant'. Language is inadequate. Paul is on the crest of a mighty emotion. Not emotionalism, not something worked up by some kind of trickery or organization or preparation. No, no; it is the sheer glory of the truth –

while we look not at the things which are seen, but at the things which are not seen: for the things which are seen are temporal, but the things which are not seen are eternal. (2 Corinthians 4:8–10, 17–18)

Or take Paul at the end of the third chapter of the Epistle to the Ephesians. He is praying for the Ephesians. What is he praying for? He says:

That ye, being rooted and grounded in love, may be able to comprehend with all saints what is the breadth, and length, and depth, and height, and to know the love of Christ, which passeth knowledge, that ye might be filled with all the fulness of God. Now unto him that is able to do exceeding abundantly above all that we ask or think . . . (Ephesians 4:17–20)

This is sheer emotion! This is mighty, majestic, true Christian emotion. It is the truth that moves the apostle and makes him write in this magnificent and glorious manner. And there are other examples that I could give you.

But this is not only a matter of Paul's style – he teaches it explicitly. This is something that he cannot avoid saying because it is so much a part of the truth, and so much a part of his own experience. Take the first four chapters of the Epistle to the Romans – what tremendous reasoning; what a demonstration of logic! Paul is out to prove that the Jews are as guilty as the Gentiles: 'For all have sinned, and come short of the glory of God' (Romans 3:23). In chapter 4, he takes up the case of Abraham and works that out. The reasoning is subtle: Where does circumcision come in? Where was the Law? And on and on he goes until he finishes at the beginning of chapter 5:

> *Therefore being justified by faith, we have peace with God through our Lord Jesus Christ: by whom also we have access by faith into this grace wherein we stand, and rejoice in hope of the glory of God.*

That is it! But Paul cannot stop at that, he is carried away:

> *And not only so, but we glory in tribulations also: knowing that tribulation worketh patience; and patience, experience; and experience, hope: and hope maketh not ashamed*

– why not? –

> *because the love of God is shed abroad in our hearts by the Holy Ghost which is given unto us. (Romans 5:1–5)*

Now there it is, you see, to perfection: rejoicing! The 'love of God shed abroad in our hearts'.

What is the meaning of 1 Corinthians 13? Its purpose is just the same – to show that if you do not have this love, nothing else matters.

> *Though I speak with the tongues of men and of angels, and have not charity [love], I am become as sounding brass, or a tinkling cymbal. And though I have . . . all knowledge; and though I have all faith, so that I could remove mountains . . . and though I give my body to be burned*

– it is no use. Believism plus zeal and enthusiasm and emotionalism and sentimentality, and even great sacrifices, are not the real thing. It is love that is real! Man can produce these other things, but it is only the Holy Spirit of God who can ever shed this love abroad in our hearts, and without this love all the rest is useless –

> *it profiteth me nothing. (1 Corinthians 13:1–3)*

Now this is but an opening out and a beginning of this great theme that we find running everywhere through the writings of this great apostle. Listen to him putting it again in perhaps the most lyrical of all his epistles, certainly, in many ways, the happiest of them all, the Epistle to the Philippians: 'Finally, my brethren, rejoice in the Lord' (Philippians 3:1). He thinks he is going to finish, but then he does not. He goes on to the fourth chapter! 'Rejoice in the Lord alway: and again I say, Rejoice' (Philippians 4:4).

My dear friends, are you rejoicing? Are you like these early Christians? This is the characteristic of Christians. They have not merely taken a decision and then have to do something else to give themselves a little bit of feeling. No, no! The truth has dawned upon them, captured them, captivated them, and has moved them to the depths of their beings, and they are rejoicing. 'We are the circumcision,' says Paul to these Philippians, 'which worship God in the spirit, and rejoice in Christ Jesus' – not merely believe, but *rejoice* – 'and have no confidence in the flesh' (Philippians 3:3).

So here is the question: Have you been moved by the truth? Does what you believe thrill you, move you to the depth of your being? Is your heart engaged? Your mind is, your will may be, but I am asking: Is your heart engaged? I am not asking: Is only your heart engaged, but is your mind engaged, is your heart engaged, is your will engaged? That is the Christian position – the complete personality captured, captivated by him. 'Whosoever drinketh of the water that I shall give him shall never thirst; but the water that I shall give him shall be in him a well of water springing up into everlasting life.'

29

Joyful Assurance

Jesus answered and said unto her, Whosoever drinketh of this water shall thirst again: but whosoever drinketh of the water that I shall give him shall never thirst; but the water that I shall give him shall be in him a well of water springing up into everlasting life. (John 4:13–14)

We have seen that the mark of the Christian is true, deep emotion. We see this in the Psalms: 'Bless the LORD, O my soul: and all that is within me, bless his holy name' (Psalm 103:1). We have seen that our Lord teaches this everywhere, and in the book of Acts, the first Christians were 'filled with joy'. We have observed, too, that the apostle Paul's great message to the Philippians is, 'Rejoice in the Lord alway: and again I say, Rejoice' (Philippians 4:4). This, says the apostle, is how Christian people are meant to be.

It is important to realize that in the New Testament Epistles, this teaching is not confined to the apostle Paul. I emphasize this because people are always ready to explain this rejoicing away in terms of temperament. So I want to call your attention just for a moment to the teaching of others. Take, for instance, what we read in the First Epistle of Peter. Peter, talking about our Lord Jesus Christ, says, 'Whom having not seen, ye love' – these people were strangers scattered abroad in various parts of the world; they had never seen the Lord – 'whom, though now ye see him not, yet believing, ye rejoice *with joy unspeakable and full of glory*' (1 Peter 1:8).

Philip Doddridge, the hymn writer, said that this 'joy unspeakable and full of glory' is a joy that is 'unspeakable' because it is already a foretaste of the joy of the everlasting glory itself: glorious beyond speech, full of joy. Christians know something about that, they have a foretaste of it, and that is what Peter says about the people to whom he is writing. He says it again in the second chapter of that First Epistle. In the Authorized (King James) Version, the translation is: 'Unto you therefore which believe he is precious' (1 Peter 2:7) – or, if you prefer it, 'Unto you therefore that believe is the precious one.' It is about him. He is the foundation that God has laid, and he is precious to those who believe in him. They love him with this 'joy unspeakable and full of glory'.

And the apostle John has precisely the same teaching. He puts it quite plainly in his first epistle. He starts off with this great testimony:

That which was from the beginning, which we have heard, which we have seen with our eyes, which we have looked upon, and our hands have handled, of the Word of life; (For the life was manifested, and we have seen it, and bear witness, and shew unto you that eternal life, which was with the Father, and was manifested unto us;)

– now –

that which we have seen and heard declare we unto you

– what for? –

> *that ye also may have fellowship with us: and truly our fellowship is with the Father, and with his Son Jesus Christ. And these things write we unto you, that your joy may be full. (1 John 1:1–4)*

Not only that your intellectual understanding may be full, but, in addition, that your joy may be full. This is John's whole object in writing this epistle.

This teaching on joy is the universal emphasis of the New Testament; and this is the standard by which we must measure ourselves. This was in the mind of our Lord when he said to this woman of Samaria, 'Whosoever drinketh of this water that I shall give him shall never thirst.' From the aspect of love, and the heart, and the emotions, there shall be perfect, full and complete satisfaction.

Here, then, is the question that people tend to ask: 'That's all right for New Testament times, but is it meant for all times?' People have often argued like this: 'Certain things happened in the time of the apostles, but we are not to expect them now.' There are people at the present time who exclude the miraculous in those terms. But they have no grounds whatsoever for saying that, and it detracts from the teaching of the Scriptures. The Spirit is Lord, and he chooses to give exceptional manifestations at times. But we must never say that it all ended with the apostles, otherwise we would be persuading ourselves that while the first Christians were meant to be filled with this joy, we are not, and we just have to go trudging along. What a travesty of the Scriptures it is to speak like that! It is entirely contrary to their teaching.

And not only that, examine the testimony of history and you will find how wrong that teaching is. Surely what we gather from the history of the first three or four centuries is that the joy that is taught and promised in the New Testament was exemplified constantly in the lives of the early Christians. Have you read something of the story of the martyrs and the confessors – those people who, at the very moment of being thrown to the lions in the arena, were thanking God that at last they would have the final crown, the crown of martyrdom? They rejoiced in it. 'The blood of the martyrs is the seed of the church.' Yes: people seeing this amazing joy were apprehended and convicted and wondered what it was, and began to make enquiries. This is undoubtedly the main factor in the way in which the early Christian church conquered the ancient world.

Now we must look at these issues historically, and it is the simple truth to say that unfortunately the Christian church herself began to depart from this very teaching, and, as she did so, she departed increasingly from the early Christian church in her life and experience. And so you get what are sometimes described as 'the dark Middle Ages' – and they were ages of gloom. But there were certain people who kept on appearing, even in those pre-Reformation times, who, having gone back to the Scriptures and having experienced their power through the Holy Spirit, knew something of this joy. Let us never forget those little groups that flourished before Luther and the Reformation – Waldensians, Brethren of the Common Life, and people like that in various parts of Europe. This irrepressible joy, this assurance, this happiness, this 'joy unspeakable and full of glory' was their characteristic.

And then we come to the towering figure of Martin Luther, and whatever you may say about him, you have got to grant him this – that above everything else he restored the note of rejoicing. He knew what it was to fast and sweat and pray; he knew what it was to be under a system that did not believe in assurance of salvation. That was the essence of his struggle. But at last the delivering word came: 'The just shall live by faith' (Romans 1:17). The 'gift of God'! This free gift of God's grace! It released him, and he began to sing, and he began to write his great hymns and tunes, and singing became one of the characteristics of the Protestant Reformation.

Let me give you a brief quotation. I was reading about Luther the other day and these words put it so well:

> His basic convictions were not arrived at in the ivory tower, but in the arena of life. It was his own personal experience of forgiveness in Christ which initially set his movement upon its course. Because it was the Scripture which finally brought him to this experience, he emphasized its authority; because his experience had come by faith rather than works, he emphasized faith; and because the church's uncertain testimony did not lead others to the same experience, he attempted to reform it.

Now the whole point of that quotation, and it is perfectly right, is that it was this experiential element that set the whole Protestant movement going. Of course, it was worked out theologically, but it was initiated by that astounding experience that came to Luther. It came in a flash, and his whole outlook was changed. He was released and he began to rejoice in his great salvation. This note of assurance was the great characteristic of the Protestant Reformation. It was equally true of John Calvin, temperamentally so different from Martin Luther. This is how Calvin puts it:

> Now we shall have a complete definition of faith if we say that it is a steady and certain knowledge of the divine benevolence toward us, which, being founded on the truth of the gratuitous promise in Christ, is but revealed to our minds and confirmed to our hearts by the Holy Spirit.

And it is a simple historical truth to say that the doctrine of the Holy Spirit was restored to the church largely by that man and his writings, and his emphasis upon the assurance that is given to the heart by the operation of the Holy Spirit.

Furthermore, as we trace the whole story of the church down the centuries, we find the same note of assurance, love and praise. Look through the hymn book, read the hymns, and you will find that this is the mark of all the greatest hymns. It is found in the hymns of Isaac Watts and of Charles Wesley, conceivably the two greatest masters of them all.

> Thou, O Christ, art all I want,
> More than all in thee I find;
> Plenteous grace in thee is found,
> Grace to cover all my sin.
> *Charles Wesley*

> O for a thousand tongues to sing
> My great Redeemer's praise.
> *Charles Wesley*

What is the value of one tongue? We need a thousand, and that is not enough.

> Join all the glorious names
> Of wisdom, love, and power,
> That ever mortals knew,
> That angels ever bore:
> All are too mean to speak his worth,
> Too mean to set my Saviour forth.
> *Isaac Watts*

We sing these hymns, but they are not merely lines of poetry, they are the expressions of the experiences of those men, and they are meant to be our experiences.

We see this, too, in the great movements of the Spirit, the tides of the Spirit in the church, the 'religious awakenings', or 'religious revivals'. Take, for instance, the Evangelical or Methodist Revival of 200 years ago. It does not matter which party they belonged to – the Calvinists or the Arminians – common to both was the original message, the message of assurance. It is the sole explanation of George Whitefield. Whitefield became the phenomenal preacher that he was when he received this assurance. When the Spirit sealed these certainties in his heart, he went forth as a flaming evangelist.

The same is true of John Wesley. He was an able and erudite man, very loyal and ultra-religious. But he was a very unhappy man, and though he made great sacrifices, trying, as it were, to earn his salvation, he could not get it. But then he crossed the Atlantic to go to Georgia to preach to pagans, thinking that he would add yet more to his merit. During that voyage there was a terrible storm at sea, and this proved to be a turning point in his life. Some Moravian brethren were on the same boat and he had noticed that they seemed to be very happy people, always praying and singing hymns. When the storm came, Wesley was terrified, but these people were still singing: the storm made no difference to them. That was what really convicted him. Later, when his heart was 'strangely warmed' in that little meeting in Aldersgate Street, this man's life was entirely changed, and he, too, became a great evangelist.

Now there, again, was a man who was essentially an intellectual, but he was useless until his heart was strangely warmed, and he was moved – until, as he puts it, 'I knew that my sins, even mine, were forgiven.' There is all the difference in the world between believing that God does forgive sins, and knowing that God has forgiven *my* sins, my personal sins. That is where the heart comes in. You can look on and see the truth objectively and accept it.

That does not make you 'rejoice with a joy unspeakable and full of glory'. The truth has to be applied, to become personal.

And this is the great note of that Evangelical Awakening – not only Whitefield and Wesley, but Howell Harris and Daniel Rowland as well. Whitefield and Howell Harris had heard of one another, and when they·at last met – in Cardiff, if I remember rightly, in 1737 – the first question that Whitefield put to Howell Harris was: 'Mr Harris, do you *know* that your sins are forgiven?' He did not ask him if he believed that but if he knew it. And Harris was able to testify gladly and joyfully that he had rejoiced in this knowledge for some two years.

Here, then, is the emphasis that comes out from all this history, and it substantiates the teaching of the Scriptures. So I move to my next point, which is that this joyful assurance is offered to us all. Now I have been giving you this evidence in order to prepare the way for this statement. The attempt is often made to deny this. People say, 'But this is not meant for everyone. We all have different temperaments. There are various psychological types – some people are stolid and quiet, calm and intellectual; others are emotional. And you would expect this sort of thing with the emotional type but not with the others.' That has often been brought forward as an argument and people evade the plain teaching of the Scripture by saying, 'Of course, I'm the phlegmatic, not the emotional type. It's all right, I don't object to it in others as long as they don't become a nuisance, but it's not for me.' So they shut out the possibility for themselves.

But, more than that, a kind of teaching has crept into the church that divides Christian people into two groups – the religious and the laity. This goes far back in the history of the church; the whole story of mysticism comes in at this point. The idea is that there are ordinary Christians, and unusual or extra-ordinary Christians; and these extra-ordinary Christians are people who give themselves to the cultivation of the religious life. That is the genesis of monasticism. The idea is that you cannot, while living your life in this world, come to the knowledge of God that gives you the ultimate state of contemplation, which leads to joy. You only arrive at this position after you have gone through various steps and stages in your journey along the mystic way. But, of course, you do not have time to do this while you are engaged in business or in a profession; you must give the whole of your life pursuit, which demands that you isolate, segregate, yourself, and become a monk or a hermit or an anchorite – 'the religious'. And only then, and at long last, you arrive at the mystic contemplation of God.

Now that, I repeat, is entirely contrary to the teaching of the Scripture, and it is most important that we should emphasize this. This is what Martin Luther discovered. I say 'discovered' but 'found to be true' is better. He did not arrive at it as the result of a process of thinking and reasoning and working it out. No, no; it flashed upon him, he saw it, and then he could work it out. And, as he said, it is as possible for a girl sweeping a floor to know this joy as it is for the monk in the cell; perhaps it is even more likely.

Now this is but a repetition and an outworking of a teaching that we find so plainly in the New Testament itself. Look at Peter preaching on the Day of Pentecost. He and the others had been filled with the Holy Spirit and it was obvious that something strange and marvellous had happened to them: they were transformed men with unusual powers and also with this joy. Then the people came together and Peter preached and we read that as he was preaching:

> they were pricked in their heart, and said unto Peter and to the rest of the apostles, Men and brethren, what shall we do? Then Peter said unto them, Repent, and be baptized every one of you

– not only some exceptional people –

in the name of Jesus Christ for the remission of sins, and ye shall receive the gift of the Holy Ghost. For the promise is unto you, and to your children, and to all that are afar off, even as many as the Lord our God shall call. (Acts 2:37–39)

You must not confine this to certain temperaments, certain types. If the gospel cannot make everybody happy, it is no gospel. But not only that, surely the nature of man demands that this joy should be universal. It is wrong, it is a false anthropology and a false psychology, to say that there are certain people who can never be happy. That is a libel. It is contrary to what is true of human nature. We all have these different aspects to our nature, and all are meant to be involved in this great salvation.

But there is also another argument. The nature of truth itself insists upon this being true of everybody. My argument is that the truth is so great, it is so glorious, so marvellous and transcendent, that it can almost move a stone. The teaching of the Scripture is that God will take away the stony heart, and give a heart of flesh (Ezekiel 11:19), and that is the final answer to the psychologists. It does not matter what you are by nature, what your temperament may be, you are given a new heart, and what makes this possible is the truth, the greatness and glory of the truth.

And as I have been showing you, the examples of history demonstrate this beyond any doubt whatsoever. I have given you some great contrasts. You cannot imagine two more different men than Martin Luther and John Calvin: Luther, a kind of volcano, bursting forth constantly; and the systematic order and discipline of Calvin. Yet both of them testified to the same truth, and both of them experienced it. Likewise George Whitefield and John Wesley: Whitefield, the orator, the emotional personality, as the psychologists put it; and the ascetic John Wesley, the intellectual, the calm, unemotional, phlegmatic, typical Englishman. Yet here they are, both of them, with hearts moved and warmed and released and showing forth the same joy in the Lord, and emphasizing it in their preaching and teaching.

So we must get rid of the notion that this deep joy is not for us, that it is only for certain people. That, of course, would be the case if we were dealing with a human teaching. People react differently to music, to films, to beauty in nature and so on. But here we start with the doctrine of a rebirth, a new nature, a being 'born of the Spirit', a 'heart of flesh'. Since this is common to all, the possibility of joy is open to all.

Now having said that, I must say this, lest I depress anybody. Our business is to give the truth concerning these matters, so I give this as my next point: though this is for all, there are variations in its manifestation. This is an important point, but it is also very subtle and difficult. Have you ever considered the place of temperament in the Christian life? Does it come in at all? The answer is that it does. It is bound to.

'Well, then, how do you reconcile that,' says somebody, 'with what you have just been saying about the new heart?'

There is no difficulty; we put it like this. The Christian faith, unlike the cults, never produces a uniform type. It gives a uniform, universal experience but it does not produce a standard type of person. Now the cults do. Psychological movements also do that. People look the same, they repeat the same clichés, the same phrases, all in the same way. But that is not true of Christianity because here is something that deals with the whole person. Christianity does not crucify the temperament. The temperament remains. But here is the difference: whereas people who are not regenerate are governed by their temperaments,

Christians can govern theirs. The unregenerate are slaves to their temperaments but Christians never are. They become aware of the temperament and of its danger, and therefore they apply the gospel to it. They master it, they control it; and as they do so, it becomes very wonderful.

Take the obvious illustration. Look at what God does in nature. All the animals or plants within a single species have the same characteristics. Yet no two flowers are identical. There is a variation in the intensity of the colour, perhaps, or in the shape. There is a sameness, and yet there is a difference. And it is the same with human beings.

Take another illustration. Look at the writers of the Scriptures. All these men, we believe, were moved and led, inspired and controlled by the Holy Spirit. Peter says about the Old Testament prophecy that none of this came 'of any private interpretation . . . but holy men of God spake as they were moved by the Holy Ghost' (2 Peter 1:20–21). 'All scripture is given by inspiration of God, and is profitable for doctrine, for reproof, for correction, for instruction in righteousness' (2 Timothy 3:16). But then go back and read the Old Testament prophets. Look at the different styles, for instance, of Jeremiah, Amos and Isaiah. They are all inspired by the same Spirit. There is this common element, which is most important of all and controls everything. But that being said, notice the individual characteristics of style and of emotion and reasoning.

Then come to the New Testament – it is exactly the same. Take the style of the apostle Paul, the style of Peter and the style of John. If somebody read out a portion to you and asked you, 'Now who wrote that?', if you were familiar with your Scriptures, you ought to be able to answer without any difficulty at all. If you cannot tell the difference between a passage taken at random out of Paul or

Peter or John, or James, too, then I say you are a very poor Bible student. The difference in style is obvious. In Paul's letters there is the profound reasoning, the rhythm of the argument, and then the breaks in the rules of grammar because he is suddenly caught up, as it were, and indulges in some ecstatic utterance. Then he may come back and complete his sentence, or he may not. That is typical of Paul. John's style is extraordinary – instead of leading up to a conclusion, he starts with it and then explains it: and he alone does that. And then we see Peter with his more ordinary style, more like ourselves.

Now here is the point: they were all of them controlled by the same Spirit, but the Spirit did not eliminate the temperament or personality. He used it, he controlled it, he disciplined it, he employed it in order that the one truth should be manifested to us in a variegated manner. And so the whole is a kind of spectrum manifesting the light of the glory of God in the face of Jesus Christ. Temperament, therefore, does come in and we must not exclude it.

Now I emphasize this because it is pathetic to find a man trying to be ebullient or demonstrative when that is not his nature or temperament. There is nothing that is more ridiculous. We should be natural in this matter. Each of us in our own way shows the same truth. We must not try to conform to a type, we must not try to imitate other people. Oh, it is very sad to see people repeat glib phrases, and I know more or less where they have got them! And then they think that this is being pious. How contradictory of the teaching of the Bible. No, no; be yourself, and under the influence of the Spirit, he will show you the joy that is in you.

Or let me put it still more clearly. There are variations even in the one individual. No one is always the same all the time. And I go further, no one is meant to be. Psalm 103 reminds us that 'he knoweth our frame; he remembereth that we are dust' (Psalm 103:14). While we are in the body in this life, in this world, we will experience variations and changes within ourselves. Do not be troubled by that. The body and the spirit, the mind and the heart, all react upon one another. There is nothing wrong in that, in and of itself, as long as we do not become victims of that. You will have moods, you will have states; do not be a victim of them, deal with them, but do not expect always to feel the same, always to be constant. We have to know ourselves. We have to treat ourselves, we have to go back to the Scriptures, where our hearts will be roused and moved.

And not only that, we can go a third step and say that in the same person this joy, this happiness and love do not always show themselves in exactly the same way. I am not talking about the degree, I am talking now about the expression of these feelings. Have we not all experienced this? Let me use a familiar quotation:

To me the meanest flower that grows can give
Thoughts that do often lie too deep for tears.
William Wordsworth

Sometimes the emotion is such that it is 'too deep for tears'. But you must not deduce from that that this man never sheds tears at other times or under other circumstances. No, no! Sometimes you are so moved that you are speechless; at other times you are so moved that you are tremendously eloquent. But they are both all right. You are not bound to be shouting, you are not bound to be singing, you are not bound to be weeping. Emotion expresses itself in a great variety of ways, and it is a great error to standardize feelings and to say that it is only when you are clapping your hands or have gone off into some ecstasy that you are really feeling a deep emotion. That is quite wrong. It is a misunderstanding of emotion.

So we must not put limits on how we experience our feelings. Be wary of putting a limit on ecstasy, or upon rapture. 'Quench not the Spirit,' says the apostle to the members of the church at Thessalonica. We always have this danger. 'Despise not prophesying.' That is said in the context of 'Rejoice evermore' and 'Pray without ceasing' (1 Thessalonians 5:19–20, 16–17). Problems had arisen in the churches. Some people were guilty of emotionalism and others, in their dislike of that, were quenching the Spirit. Both are wrong. We must not quench the Spirit and we must not try to work up an artificial emotion. We are to submit ourselves always to the truth as it is in Christ Jesus. It is he who gives us this 'living water' that thus moves the heart.

Now the next question – and I am only going to put the question to you now, because we will have to go on and consider it in great detail – is this: How does our Lord do this? How does he give complete satisfaction to our hearts, to our emotions? How is it possible for any one of us to conform to that statement of Peter: 'Whom having not seen, ye love; in whom, though now ye see him not, yet believing, ye rejoice with a joy unspeakable and full of glory'?

The secret is this: we are always told, you notice, 'Rejoice *in the Lord*' – 'Rejoice in the Lord alway: and again I say, Rejoice' (Philippians 4:4). How do you do this? How does he give this 'living water'? Here is the usual way: through the Scriptures. It is here we find him. We search for him, we look for him, like the woman in the Song of Solomon, and we find him, and our heart is moved and raptured. But it is not the only way. God willing, we shall go on to remind ourselves of the other great way next Sunday morning – Whitsunday morning – as we think again of the pouring of the Holy Spirit upon the waiting disciples.